UPS AND DOWNS

By the same author

Memories
Friends in Focus
Julia
A Pacifist's War
Everything to Lose
Hanging On
Other People
Good Company
Life Regained

UPS AND DOWNS

DIARIES
1972–1975

Frances Partridge

Weidenfeld & Nicolson
LONDON

First published in Great Britain in 2001
By Weidenfeld & Nicolson

© 2001 Frances Partridge

A CIP catalogue record for this book
is available from the British Library.

ISBN 0 297 60717 0

Typeset by Selwood Systems, Midsomer Norton

Printed in Great Britain by
Butler & Tanner Ltd, Frome and London

Weidenfeld & Nicolson

The Orion Publishing Group Ltd
Orion House
5 Upper Saint Martin's Lane
London, WC2H 9EA

TO GEORGIA TENNANT

DRAMATIS PERSONAE

BRENAN, GERALD, writer and hispanologist. He had been one of Ralph's greatest friends ever since they were together in the First War, despite rows caused by his making love to Ralph's first wife Dora Carrington and to disagreements over the Second War. He spent time between England and Churriana in southern Spain. He had been formerly married to Gamel Woolsey, American poetess, and had one daughter.

CAMPBELL, ROBIN and SUSAN. Cyril Connolly had introduced us to Robin in 1948, when he was living near us at Stokke with his second wife, Mary (now DUNN). He had lost a leg and won a DSO in the war. After his divorce from Mary he married Susan Benson, writer of cookery and garden books, and himself joined the Arts Council. Robin and Susan had two sons, William and Arthur.

CARRINGTON, NOEL and CATHARINE, Dora Carrington's youngest brother and his wife (née Alexander). Ralph had been at Oxford with Noel, who became a publisher and designer, and died in 1989. They had been country neighbours in easy reach of us at Ham Spray. Of their three children we saw most of Joanna.

CECIL, LORD DAVID and family. We had known David's wife Rachel, daughter of our old friends Desmond and Molly MacCarthy, since she was a schoolgirl, and travelled with her before and after her marriage. Their children were Jonathan (actor), Hugh and Laura. The whole family were very kind to me after Ralph's death and I often stayed with them. Sadly Rachel later died of cancer and David was to follow soon after.

COCHEMÉ, JOAN, painter, especially of children's portraits, and a faithful friend for many years. Her husband had been Jacques Cochemé, biologist, native of Mauritius, and a member of the Food and Agriculture Organization in Rome. Jacques had died suddenly of pneumonia and Joan was now a widow.

DUNN, LADY MARY. Our warm friendship began in 1948 when she was living (and actively farming the land) at Stokke with her second husband Robin Campbell. After their divorce she made an unhappy match with Charlie McCabe, columnist of a San Franciscan newspaper. She divided her time between Stokke and San Francisco but her first husband, Sir Philip Dunn ('the Tycoon'), lived not far away from the former in Wiltshire. They were eventually to remarry. Philip and Mary had two daughters, Serena and Nell, friends and contemporaries of my son Burgo's.

GARNETT, DAVID and family. Only son of Edward and Constance Garnett, the eminent translator from Russian, David was generally know as 'Bunny'. He married my sister Ray in 1921, the year that I was taken on as assistant in his bookshop, Birrell and Garnett. He was thus my boss, my brother-in-law and a great friend for life. When his first book, *Lady into Fox*, won the Hawthornden Prize he left the shop to write over twenty more. Ray died of cancer in 1940, and in 1942 Bunny married Angelica, daughter of Duncan Grant and Vanessa Bell. He had two sons by Ray (Richard and William) and four daughters by Angelica; Burgo married the second, Henrietta, in 1962; the others were Amaryllis, and the twins – Fanny and Nerissa.

GATHORNE-HARDY, JONATHAN (Jonny) and SABRINA. The popular nephew of Lady Anne Hill and Eddie Gathorne-Hardy was at the time married to Sabrina Tennant, daughter of Virginia, Marchioness of Bath, and David Tennant, creator of the Gargoyle Club, and was launching a career as a writer.

GOODMAN, CELIA, one of the well-known Paget twins, who used as girls to make glamorous appearances at concerts and

Glyndebourne. Her sister Mamaine married Arthur Koestler and died at only thirty-seven. Celia's husband was Arthur Goodman, who had spent a gruelling time in a Japanese prison in the war and was now working in Shell; they had two young children.

GOWING, LAWRENCE, painter of the Euston Road Group, had married in 1952 my 'best friend' Julia Strachey. She was eighteen years his senior, a gifted but very unproductive writer, an original, eccentric and at times difficult character. Her first husband had been Stephen Tomalin (Tommy). After Julia and Lawrence divorced he married Jenny.

HENDERSON, SIR NICHOLAS (Nicko) and LADY (MARY). Ralph and I had been friends of Nicko's parents, and he had come to swim in our pool as a boy. After he married Mary they had often come to Ham Spray. After he was refused by the RAF on medical grounds he joined the Foreign Service and had an important diplomatic career as an Ambassador. They had one daughter, Alexandra.

HILL, HEYWOOD and LADY ANNE (née Gathorne-Hardy). Our friendship began in about 1938, when they were both working in the famous bookshop in Curzon Street created by Heywood, and which still bears his name. When Heywood joined the army in the war, Anne kept the shop going with the help of Nancy Mitford. The Hills had a house in Richmond which they shared with their two grown-up daughters, Harriet and Lucy. Anne had four brothers, of whom the second, Eddie, had long been a friend of ours.

JACKSON, JANETTA (née Woolley, now Parladé). Ralph and I met her as a very attractive young girl of fourteen, in Spain at the start of the Civil War. Young enough to be our daughter, she instead became one of our closest friends, and figures prominently in all my diaries. Her marriages to Robert Kee and Derek Jackson both ended in divorce. In this diary she is married to Jaime Parladé and living in Spain. Her three daughters were Nicolette (Nicky) Sinclair-Loutit, Georgiana (Georgie) Kee and Rose Jackson.

JEBB, JULIAN, grandson of Hilaire Belloc, to whose small house in Sussex he sometimes invited his friends. Always interested in opera, theatre and cinema, he was a journalist and television film-maker. An excellent mimic and raconteur, and an affectionate friend.

KEE, ROBERT, Oxford friend of Nicko Henderson, who brought him to Ham Spray soon after his release from prison camp in Germany, where he spent three years after being shot down while a bomber pilot in the RAF. He very quickly became one of our greatest friends, and before long married another – Janetta. They both figure prominently in my earlier diaries, but the marriage became stormy, and by 1963 they had parted and Robert had married Cynthia Judah. He had one daughter, Georgie, by Janetta, and a son and daughter, Alexander and Sarah, by Cynthia. He is a writer of novels and history – in particular Irish history – and has also appeared in many television programmes.

KNOLLYS, EARDLEY, one of the three original owners of Long Crichel House. He had given up working for the National Trust in favour of painting. He lived in West Halkin Street and had found me my flat there. We would often meet for impromptu outings. He died of heart trouble.

MCCABE, LADY MARY see DUNN, LADY MARY

MORTIMER, RAYMOND, writer on art and literature, at one time literary editor of the *New Statesman*, then for many years top book reviewer on the *Sunday Times*. Our neighbour when Ralph and I lived in Bloomsbury, he became a close friend of us both, coming often to Ham Spray and travelling with us by car to France. He joined his three friends at Long Crichel House soon after the inauguration. Travel and reading were his great pleasures. He lived in North London with Paul Hyslop.

OLSON, STANLEY, writer. Stanley was much younger than me but became a real friend. He was American and rather like Henry James in character. He had a passion for collecting and was very witty. He wrote a Life of Sargeant which was published after he died of a stroke in his forties. He never married.

PARLADÉ, JAIME, eldest son of a prominent Andalusian family. Ralph and I met him in the Fifties in Marbella, where he owned an antiques shop, which afterwards developed into a decorating and architectural business. He is now married to Janetta.

PENROSE, LIONEL and MARGARET, and their extremely clever family. Lionel was an FRS and Galton Professor of Genetics; his wife Margaret had been my friend at Bedales School, Newnham College and ever since; Oliver and Roger are distinguished mathematicians; Jonathan was British Chess Champion for ten years; Shirley is a clinical geneticist. All addicted to music and chess.

PHILLIPS, 'MAGOUCHE' (now FIELDING). American by birth. Her first husband, the famous Armenian painter Arshile Gorky, gave her her unusual name. After his death she married Jack Phillips. Later she came to Europe and lived in France, Italy and London with her four daughters (Maro and Natasha Gorky, Antonia and Susannah Phillips), in all of which places she made a great many friends. I got to know her through Mary Dunn and Janetta.

PHIPPS, LADY (FRANCES), widow of the diplomat Sir Eric Phipps; she had been made Ambassadress at Berlin and Paris. She and I made friends late in our lives but had quickly become intimate, agreeing on such subjects as politics, war and peace, sharing many tastes in books, opera, and even for driving Minis. She was a talented amateur painter.

RYLANDS, DR GEORGE (DADIE), Professor of English at King's College, Cambridge. I'd known Dadie since Cambridge when our times overlapped (I was older). In later years we got into the travelling business and ended up taking many 'little' holidays together.

SHAWE-TAYLOR, DESMOND, one of the three original owners of Long Crichel House. Writer on music and other subjects, he was a music critic for the *Sunday Times* and one of my dearest friends.

STONE, REYNOLDS and his family. We first met them as country neighbours during the war, and acquaintance became friendship later when they lived at their romantic rectory at Litton Cheney, Dorset. Reynolds was a brilliant engraver on wood and stone, painter of trees and designer; Janet is a professional portrait photographer. They had four children: Edward, Humphrey, Phillida and Emma.

STRACHEY, ISOBEL, first wife of John (Lytton's nephew who had intervened in the Bussy inheritance), but long since divorced. Her only child Charlotte had been a great friend of Burgo's since childhood and was now married to Peter Jenkins. Isobel had published several novels and stories and was a dearly loved crony of mine.

STRACHEY, JAMES and ALIX (née Sargant Florence). James was Lytton's youngest brother. Both were practicising psychoanalysts of long standing and James had translated the entire works of Freud in twenty-three volumes, indexed by me. Ralph and I felt towards them as if they were blood family.

STRACHEY, JULIA *see* GOWING

TENNANT, GEORGIA, daughter of David Tennant, creator of the Gargoyle Club, and Virginia, Marchioness of Bath. I first met her staying with Janetta in Alpbach, Austria, in the summer of 1961, and took a great fancy to her, which built up into a firm friendship. A delightful and intelligent girl who is now living with Paul McNanney, a carpenter. They have one daughter, Ella.

WEST, KITTY, the painter Katharine Church. She had married Anthony West, son of Rebecca West and H.G. Wells, who had left her and made a life in America. She was living in a charming little Dorset cottage to which she had added a big studio, and had also opened a gallery and craft shop in Blandford. She had two children, a daughter, Caroline, and a son who is a doctor in America.

HOUSES

Crichel

(as Long Crichel House, near Wimborne, Dorset, is affectionately known to its intimates). At the end of the Second War
three bachelor friends decided to look for a country house
where they could gather for weekends and holidays, and invite
their friends to stay. There were two music critics, Edward
(Eddy) Sackville-West and Desmond Shawe-Taylor, and
Eardley Knollys, representative of the National Trust and later
painter. They soon found what they wanted – a charming
Georgian stone house, formerly a rectory, with three good-
sized living-rooms and a plentiful number of bedrooms. Great
thought and care were given to the decorations and furnishings;
the garden had a well-kept croquet lawn, several statues, and a
terrace sheltered from the wind by glass sides and with a floor
decorated by the owners with their initials in mosaic. Two sets
of what were then called 'radiograms' of the highest quality,
quantities of books, a series of resident staff and one or two dogs
completed a ménage where conversation, music and croquet
thrived. A few yers later Raymond joined the original three as a
resident 'Crichel boy'. In 1949 Ralph and I spent the first of
many greatly enjoyed visits there.

Hilton Hall

near Huntingdon, was acquired by my sister Ray from a legacy
and is still inhabited by her elder son Richard and his wife
Jane. She and Bunny fell in love with it from a photograph
in a newspaper. It is indeed a very beautiful, stately but not
large, Queen Anne house, and until Richard's day had been very
little modernized. It still has panelled walls, flagged stone
floors and a fine staircase of dark carved wood; in the sixties it
was one of the coldest houses I ever slept in. All Bunny's

children, by Ray and Angelica, were brought up there and loved it dearly.

Stokke

near Great Bedwyn, Wiltshire. Robin and Mary Campbell were living in this rambling, Virginia-creeper covered house when we first got to know them, along with Mary's daughters by her first marriage and Robin's two sons by his. Mary was farming the surrounding land. The large garden was somewhat unkempt, except for Robin's rockery. Indoors the atmosphere was lively and semi-bohemian: youthful feet might be heard echoing along the upstairs passages in a game of cocky-olly, while downstairs in the long L-shaped living-room their elders sat round the big stove talking and laughing with visiting writers and painters or an occasional philosopher or millionaire.

ILLUSTRATIONS

On the way to Salamanca
Janetta in Oca
Jaime at the monastery of San Lorenzo, near Santiago
Mary Dunn in Majorca
Bunny Garnett and Rose Jackson in the garden of Bunny's house
   in France, Le Verger de Charey
Desmond Shawe-Taylor and Frances having a picnic in the
   Pyrenees
Desmond and Julian Jebb
Eardley Knollys and Dadie Rylands on the lake in Zurich
Magouche with her daughter Maro and two grandchildren,
   Saskia (left) and Cosima (seated), at Arane in Italy
Jaime and Janetta on the terrace in Tramores
Cecil Beaton in his conservatory in Dorset
Henrietta at Charleston
Sophie in Frances's flat on West Halkin Street
Jaime near Oaxaca in Mexico
Frances and Jaime at the University Posada in Milta
Jaime and Janetta outside the Hotel Ranchso, with San Cristóbal
   in the distance
Eardley and David outside a café at Urk

FOREWORD

In my bedroom stands an old French wardrobe inherited from Lytton Strachey via my husband Ralph. It is an attractive object made of walnut and it is lined by stiff calendered cream-coloured linen decorated with a red crisscross pattern, and here he used to keep his suits. I decided to keep my archives in it (diaries, letters and photo albums) to which end I had shelves put in horizontally. It is now nearly full as the diaries were followed by copies made by my typist Topsy. When I go like Mother Hubbard to my cupboard I only find a few Diaries that have not been published and one is *Ups and Downs*. Old age was creeping on and I could not see any clearer and as I approached the age of 100, I said to my publisher, 'What's to be done? They need to be revised for the public.' Valiantly they said, 'We'll make a BIG COPY, and then you can revise it.' So this was what we did and I put on my spectacles. Here it is.

Frances Partridge, June 2001

I

2 JANUARY
TO
26 DECEMBER
1972

January 2nd: West Halkin Street

A few mornings ago poor Joan[1] again burst into tears over the telephone. It was partly from a feeling of anticlimax after trying to keep a face up by giving a drinks party. Yesterday, therefore, on my suggestion we spent an afternoon together – beginning at the Wallace Collection, on to a Buñuel film (*Tristana*) and then back here to supper and to listen to part of *Tosca*. All of this was first-rate and enjoyed by us both.

Joan is someone laying herself bare with an honest scalpel, yet the operation isn't all plain-sailing. Not only did I feel I enjoyed looking at the pictures more than she did, but also that I knew rather more about the painters – she seemed never to have heard of many of them, whisked past a stupendous Titian with hardly a glance and complained of the 'brownness' of Rembrandt and 'black and whiteness' of a fine Rubens portrait. I think I see a clue to her disapproval of other living painters: I believe she always sees paintings as if she had painted them herself.

We talked about the sad Penrose situation. On Friday I played trios at Golders Green, after lunch consisting of terrifying 'garbage' soup ('my own invention,' Margaret said, 'it's made of duck bones and apricot yogurt'). Lionel was present but went off to his office, saying 'I can't think why I'm so cold on such a warm day.' The reason was plain. First that the day was in fact freezing, second that there were no fires in the house, only one or two pitiful storage heaters. I deliberately stayed behind after our pianist Anne had gone and asked Margaret about her life with Lionel. It seems to be pretty awful. He's furiously angry all the time, never looks at her; they have

---

1 Cochemé.

I

no conversation except when driving, when he often hits her; he gnashes his teeth or contradicts her if she says anything.

An old botanist with a Chinese wife, who stayed with them recently, wrote her a note (which she showed me) saying that they were naturally distressed by 'the situation' and felt Margaret's rights should be protected by a judicial separation. Yet she had never mentioned the subject to them. 'Well, perhaps they should,' I volunteered. She finds the present state of things intolerable, yet 'I can't live alone.' Well, others do, I reflected. And Lionel is quite unable to fend for himself, she believes. It's pitiful. When he returned we had a drink, sitting all three round the fire, and some talk. I watched Lionel and noticed that he doesn't in fact ever look at her. They pressed me to spend the evening – go out 'for a club sandwich' – And then sit between them, as they fell asleep in front of the television! I couldn't face it.

January 4th
I've got myself into a pretty odd state by trying to organise Ralph's[1] letters to me. Many of them are only hypothetically dated, some are in faint pencil. Of course I sink in deeper, re-live it all, ask myself questions that remain unanswered, get tired of typing out the letters, leave it, and then come back to it obsessionally. I even got out my own letters to Ralph and tried to check some references. Now I'm on the bottom of the ocean, fit for nothing but my bed, yet it's barely ten o'clock. Joan asked me to join her and Eardley[2] at dinner, Magouche[3] stopped her car beside me in the dark as I went to the letter-box and asked me for a drink. I rejected both. Where am I going to? And how shall I get my life in hand again?

January 6th
Julian[4] came to dinner last night and stayed till one. Not a

---

1 Ralph and I were married for thirty years. He died in 1960.
2 Knollys.
3 Phillips, later Fielding.
4 Jebb.

moment too long and I can't say that of many companions. Even so there was *not enough time*, and lots of areas were left unexplored ... I had a good picture of Tramores[1] Christmas – very explicit and vivid. It certainly restored him to health and stability, and the only upsetting thing was that he was seized immediately on arrival by a passion for Ed,[2] which Ed wouldn't gratify. Julian was too sensitive to follow Janetta's[3] grave and gentle advice (marvellously reproduced by Julian), 'I think you'll have to RAPE your old friend!' I feel a great and grateful sense of my own experience having been enriched.

Yesterday Francis Nichols rang up to say Phyllis[4] had died. I more or less expected it, felt deep sadness but was glad for her. She died unconscious – oh what a blessing. My presentiment in the summer was that I shouldn't see her again, and I have a remembered vision of her blue eyes with tears in them, and her slightly tremulous farewell.

January 12th

A patch of hurry-skurry has prevented my writing. How did I ever manage to fit in work as well? Yet I try, I'm not quite sure why, to get more, so far without success. Meanwhile I have become increasingly involved in sorting my correspondence with Ralph. It's difficult because he wrote so frequently. I've become absorbed by this task and suffer less from shock than at first. And I'm staggered by his extraordinarily analytical approach to himself, to me, our relation, and everyone else, and by many other things, including moments of weakness in so strong a character. But heavens, what a lot I owe him! I was a dumb, inarticulate creature before he took me in hand and liberated me in more ways than one, partly from a lesser form of Ray's[5] mental paralysis, partly from every other sort of sexual and other inhibition, and made me – for good or ill – a realist.

---

1 The Parladés' house in Andalusia.
2 Friend and artist, employed by Jaime to illustrate architectural plans.
3 Parladé.
4 Lady Nichols.
5 My sister, who was married to Bunny Garnett and died of cancer.

As a realist, I reacted once again against the world of the very rich (Stowell) to which I went with Dadie,[1] a splendidly lively companion, for the weekend. Philip[2] was nice enough to his guests but contradicted every word that poor Mary said. She stood up to him bravely and declared it had been 'one of the nicest weekends.' A lovely long canal walk with Dadie, on a moist still afternoon, past a family of adolescent swans, their whiteness patched with grey. A pleasant lunch with the Hobsons,[3] who live a civilised life in charming surroundings, with nice children, dogs, library, and delicious food. On Saturday night the Darwins came to dinner. Robin[4] is rapidly smoking and drinking himself to death (he's had a heart attack already and breathes with obvious difficulty). He declared that he 'had never been so unhappy in his life since relinquishing the Royal College of Art'. But he holds his liquor well. After several whiskies and brandies he gave us an affectionate, admiring but critical and subtle exposé of Rodrigo Moynihan's character and work. Tempo too slow for some, including Ginette. 'You're *sew* slow, darling,' she hissed at him. I had more sympathy with her attempts to keep him off the whisky and brandy, but none with her constant references to 'if Robin dies' or 'when Robin dies', and to tombstones and graveyards. No wonder he's unhappy. In despair at finding myself blanched with fatigue at getting stuck with her, I began talking about Peter Luke[5] whom she knows, and was given a long lecture for minding the dreaded play. 'I should be *sew* proud if anyone wrote a play about Robin, only they wouldn't because he's *sew* boring.' There was lots more, repetitious and inane, on this subject. 'You ought to be proud to have the marvellous people you knew made into a play. After all – let's face it – no one's going to remember Lytton Strachey for his *books*.' And a good deal on the themes of 'History is all *lies*', and 'You see, I'm not *like* that – I'm *sew* loyal.' I suffered an

---

1 Dr George Rylands, Professor of English at King's College, Cambridge.
2 Sir Philip Dunn.
3 Anthony and Tanya.
4 Former head of the Royal College of Art, and his wife Ginette.
5 Playwright, author of *Bloomsbury* which was staged in July–August 1974.

agony of active boredom which kept me with difficulty from rushing from the room. Indeed I did disappear briefly once, hoping someone else would take my place beside Ginette, but no such luck.

The subject of rich and poor didn't mercifully 'come up' over the weekend. I can't be temperate about it, nor accept the smug confidence of the rich that riches are their right.

January 13th: London

Dinner-party last night with Billy Henderson,[1] Frank Tait and Rosamond[2] – a good combination. They obviously admired Ros and she preened like a charming swan in their admiration. I have another tonight 'to the young'. *Ay de mi!* I suppose I shall survive. This morning, I walked in the rain to have a back tooth out, walked back and dealt with mountainous washing-up. I think Joan was almost hurt by my firm refusal of her offer to come with me to the dentist – an extraordinary misconception, for I didn't mind an atom. Janetta writes about Gerald[3] going to Tramores and talking about Ralph as 'unintellectual, hearty, never reading a book... I could see how intensely irritating he must be to you when he goes on like that.' And today I have a letter from Gerald patting himself on the back because a young man who wants to marry Lynda[4] had been to stay and she had refused him. He writes that this shows 'how much love and devotion she can put into totally asexual relations... She likes my being in love with her and showing it and encourages me to show it – only one thing being necessarily barred.' There's something abnormal about Lynda, then, surely.

January 15th

At Kitty West's. Before I left London yesterday Joan came to lunch to eat up the remains of my 'young dinner-party'. When I said what a good thing it was she was going to Lanzarote she said

---

1 Doctor and painter.
2 Lehmann.
3 Brenan.
4 Price.

'I simply dread it', buried her face in her hands and burst into tears. I know no one who suits the action so completely to those words. It was a real burst and followed up by 'I *hate* my life'. I'm glad she's going and confident it will do her good, poor creature.

I'm here in the rain alone with Kitty and Caroline, who looks tremendously happy.

January 16th: Sunday a.m.

At Kitty West's. It pours and pours, blows and blows. Forced myself out for a brisk walk under an umbrella as far as the King's Evil Oak. Outside in the dripping garden I see fresh clumps of tiny cyclamens and big curling grey leaves.

Last night Raymond[1] and Desmond[2] came for a drink bringing two Americans – Munroe Wheeler (late head of the New York Museum of Modern Art) and toothily smiling Glenway Westcott.[3] Both were voluble, friendly, liking to talk about themselves and about money. They both treated me with a sort of deferential respect – as what? A dodo? On leaving, Munroe Wheeler took me aside and said, 'Raymond told me just now you were the woman of greatest intellect he knew. But don't tell him I told you,' and he squeezed my arm, and said he would like to come and see me in London, but of course he won't.

January 17th

I've now read two books by Rosseter and thought a lot about them. His visual descriptions are sometimes marvellous, but at times creativity and madness swop over disturbingly. I've always felt this power to express heightened consciousness is what matters most in art – or heaven knows if it matters *most*, but it surely must exist. Yet Rosseter has it to such an exceptional degree as to make it terrifying, a menace. He doesn't, like Francis Bacon, present his sensitivity in terms of ugly squalor; beauty and significance, symbolism and humour are all present.

---

1 Mortimer.
2 Shawe-Taylor.
3 Wheeler's partner, a writer.

Time to consider the subject of aesthetics again, I reflected, turning over the Bacon catalogue at the Sterns,[1] and thinking to myself: *'I don't like them.'* I *don't believe* he is a great artist whatever 'they' say. The view of life an artist presents must be important – in Goya's horror there is beauty, nobility, indignation, pity, satire. I can't see in Bacon any of these qualities except satire which revels in human squalor. I'm tired of being 'impressed' by him. As I sat in the Sterns' drawing-room, my dislike of what he does arose like heartburn within me.

January 19th

Strange new vulnerability – scar tissue perhaps dissolved by my researches into my past life: now it was about Burgo.[2] When looking at an atlas of England, the sight of the Somerset town where his school was and the places we took him to at half-terms suddenly stabbed me to the heart.

I have written to Janetta about a trip to Galicia next month, but haven't heard back from her and I feel a longing for a carrot to tempt me along my road.

January 20th

Magouche came to dinner last night, and she too 'burst into tears' – but tears that were bitterer and more painful than Joan's – as a result of reading old letters of Gorky's.[3] Perhaps all this return to the past is a bad idea. I can't face my old letters to Ralph. They seem to make nonsense of the most important emotion I ever experienced, feelings that were utterly real. And now today, I'm possessed with a restless misery so deep that I can't remember having been so low for years. After trying to persuade various people, Julian, Joan, or Magouche, that their lives are worth living – and even succeeding sometimes – I now feel profoundly convinced that *mine* is *not*. I don't at this moment, 3 p.m., want to do anything at all except become unconscious. This sudden drop, like an aeroplane's into an air pocket, has really frightened me.

---

1 James, writer, and wife, Tanya.
2 Our only son who died of a heart attack in 1963.
3 Arshile, her first husband.

8.15. I'm just off to dinner with Magouche, in a state of trauma — traumatised by the sight of my own sudden instability, the overwhelming feeling of losing heart and an inability to tackle anything at all. Now I believe I'm just beginning to haul a little courage up from the bottomless pit, hand over hand.

January 22nd

The remembrance of that traumatic drop into the abyss still haunts me, although I did pull myself out pretty quick. Where had my courage gone to? Or my normal ability to *stump* ahead, well aware of what 'ahead' means? The first warning I had was my 'strange new vulnerability' of last Wednesday. By the time I went to Magouche's it was no longer a question of putting a good face on it, so that the others (the Campbells and the Kees) wouldn't realise my gloom, but of an actual change of mood. There was a lot of laughter and talk of a gossipy non-ideological sort. Next evening I had the Kees and Lionel and Margaret for dinner. The Kees were delighted by Lionel, who, as Robert said, arrived pale and piano and blossomed like a rose, until he could hardly be induced to go home. He was wonderfully funny and charming, enjoyed his food and drink, and loved talking about his own subject and everything else. Margaret nearly fell asleep, but before that made her own contribution. She's now in Persia visiting Shirley,[1] though in answer to her telegram suggesting she should go, she got three back: 'doubts' was the first, then 'terrible weather' and lastly 'many commitments'. I don't know what quality in Margaret made her defy such a chilly welcome.

January 28th

Remaining steady in spite of no possibilities of work, and further excavations into my past. Some large questions arise from these. What did Ralph, who was so intensely analytical, suppose would result from our journey to Spain in 1925? We both knew, I think, that we should become real lovers on this holiday and surely he understood my character well enough to

1 Their daughter.

realise it was all or nothing with me? That I should want to live with him altogether? Was he surprised at the agitation of Lytton[1] and Carrington? Or should I have been the one to forecast the future? Looking back on those unhappy weeks between our return and our setting up at 41 Gordon Square, I marvel at the intense and long-lasting happiness that resulted. Of course as there are practically no letters between 1926 and Ralph's death – thirty-four years – the emphasis is curiously shifted by these early letters, because we were almost never apart. What I've always remembered since Ralph died was our long years of married life – this excavation of its prehistory is what has agitated me.

I had a lovely afternoon with Sophie,[2] who came back here with me to supper after tea with the Kees at Kew, and spent some time and emotion studying the books of photos of Burgo. Last night, Raymond, Eardley and Joan came to dinner – a successful quattuor. Raymond genial and amusing, but I'm surprised how he totally fails to remember what it was like to be young. He couldn't imagine youthful doubts about one's identity and had been shocked by them in Liz Spender.[3] Has he forgotten too the obsessional egotism of youth? I go to visit Alix[4] and spend the night with Clare Sheppard,[5] who is convalescing at Marlow, tomorrow.

January 30th

I enjoyed staying with Clare Sheppard in her borrowed riverside cottage, the earth iron-bound with frost and sparse flakes falling. Our talk ranged through all her children and grandchildren, the Cecil family, her health, politics – about which we were in agreement. She finds David's conservative and aristocratic side even more unsympathetic than I do, and is censorious about his children, who she thinks have been spoilt and compare unfavourably

---

1 Strachey.
2 My grand-daughter.
3 Daughter of Stephen and Natasha Spender.
4 Strachey.
5 Sculptor; first cousin of Rachel Cecil.

with her own (brought up the hard way). Even Dermod's[1] family came in for a good deal of criticism. I liked being with her, liked her whole-hearted laugh, her look of Molly[2] (stronger than ever), her solidity and sensibility, even the salty flavour of her censoriousness. The odd lacuna in our talk was Sydney.[3] She hardly mentioned him, and plans to go to a French spa with Gerald and Lynda to Greece, but with no mention of Sydney.

February 2nd: West Halkin Street

I went with Desmond to Albee's new play *All Over*, which takes place around the bedside of a dying man, and wherein variations were produced by the different characters — wife, mistress, son, daughter, doctor, nurse and best friend. We were both enthralled and appreciative; the critics are down on it. Very nice evening with Desmond afterwards and talk on the eternal subject, I saying that one was driven to think about death more as one approached it and friends are knocked off one by one, he that 'there was nothing to think about, if one was a non-believer.' I see he's right in one sense, but not in another. Death is as important and interesting as the last act of a play. I'm amused by the shadow-boxing that goes on between Desmond and Raymond, each pitching into the other in his absence. 'Raymond wouldn't like the play,' said Desmond. 'His boredom threshold is very low.'

Certainly I think of death many times each day. John Banting[4] is the latest recruit. I dreamed that M.A.M.,[5] after receiving complaints from Eleanor[6] and me about our unsatisfactory lives, went off and committed suicide. I don't know if that amounted to a statement that I wished I had never been born. I don't think it's true, but it might have been a good thing to succumb to that scorpion's bite.[7]

---

1 Younger of Desmond and Molly MacCarthy's two sons.

2 MacCarthy.

3 Sheppard, also a sculptor.

4 Surrealist painter.

5 My mother.

6 The youngest of my three elder sisters.

7 Suffered in Spain.

February 8th

Returning from the nicest possible weekend at Snape. Anne,[1] hobbling around on her stick, does seem to have aged rather, but was valiant and jolly. Chief topic of interest to them was that Bob Gathorne-Hardy has been left Old Master drawings worth a million pounds by an uncle. How does he intend disposing of them in his will? To the Ashmolean, to the indignation of the Gathorne-Hardy clan. Anne is up in arms on behalf of Rose and Jonny[2] and his children, Lucy and Harriet.[3]

Julian came with me to *The Makropulos Case* last night, a stirring occasion, and with a large enthusiastic audience filling the great place with youthful 'Bravos!'

I forgot to mention that the Hills showed a noticeable detachment from Lucy, who had told her parents 'in the nicest possible way' to keep off the grass, as they are utterly absorbed in their Muslim life. Geordie[4] has gone to Mecca and I was shown extracts from a letter of his to Lucy (or Rabia as she now has to be called) speaking of the agony and joy he was experiencing. 'You will understand.'

February 14th

We are back in the full grimness of crisis – there has been no settlement of the miners' strike, electricity cuts and their depressing or frightening (in the case of traffic signals) results. That the Conservatives are generally and rightly blamed for their futile ineptness is no consolation. I hope to fly to Madrid today week – that is much more of one. At Crichel, with wood fires, candles and people to talk to, I was sheltered from the storm. Now, back in my silent flat, I look nervously at the thread of electricity still glowing and feel restless. At Crichel I was alone with Paul Hyslop[5] and Raymond. Raymond has treated me with angelic sweetness ever since our Italian trip – I

---

1 Hill.

2 Her niece and nephew.

3 The Hills's children.

4 Lucy had married a very good-looking man, Geordie.

5 Architect and old friend of Raymond's.

don't know what to make of it. He said yesterday, 'You have a much more powerful intellect than I have.' And when I disclaimed this – 'Oh yes, much. I've always known it.' But what's more to the point, we get on so well; he has been enormously companionable, and looked well and happy also.

Grouchy old Paul, bent over his petit-point, emitting interrogative grunts, seems to take practically no interest in the public events that crowd the scene so ominously, and both he and Raymond were amazed at my desire to hear or see the news.

February 16th

Whence this restlessness? Two nights ago I drove to dinner with Stanley[1] in Golders Green. Setting off cheerfully, I suddenly plunged into primeval darkness, halfway up Park Lane; out again further north; *in* – out, *in* – out. Crossing the Marylebone Road without help from traffic lights was horrific. The streets further north were unrecognisable with their blackened faces, and I felt overawed and terrified by the tall anonymous silhouettes of houses. The feeling of lawlessness – for some drivers dash along recklessly, over-excited by the withdrawal of controls – and that the skeleton, the frame of reference of life has been withdrawn, is curiously upsetting. At Stanley's I found a coal fire, good food and plenty of wine. Michael Holroyd[2] arrived just as shaken as I was. Jolly and rather drunken conversation. Stanley was still spouting about the 'mysterious necessity of personal relationships' when I left them to it well after midnight. Michael is a different fellow with his contemporaries and much more at his ease.

February 18th

I went to see *Eugene Onegin* with Mary and Loelia (Duchess of Westminster). Found them having drinks by candlelight at Eaton Place plus Philip. Of course the comments of these rich people about the strike *would* have made my blood boil over,

---

1 Olson, American Ph.D. student and writer on Bloomsbury.

2 Biographer of Lytton Strachey.

had I not been totally prepared – I had inserted an invisible glass anti-boiler, as with milk. Loelia Westminster (dripping in mink and diamonds and saying that she was putting up a Fortuny umbrella with its handle made of a single amethyst for sale at Sotheby's) kept saying how 'bloody the miners had been'.

An even madder reaction to the strike: Lucy Norton,[1] when I said I was going abroad, said, 'Well, *I* don't feel I could go away. It's like the Blitz, I feel one ought to stay, because there are some people who want to and can't.' She has mentioned the Blitz nostalgically before and I dare say a lot of other old warhorses, male and female, are rubbing up their Sam Browne belts and going round turning off lights.

February 21st: Madrid (Hotel Victoria), 7 p.m.

In my funny, slightly stuffy bedroom looking out on the blank wall of a narrow well. Neither Janetta nor Raymond would stand it for a moment, but I believe it will be very quiet. I'm feeling quite pleased at how well I've managed so far and that I've enjoyed a lot of things. One advantage of age is that one is anonymous; age isn't queer, it's a great leveller. Magouche sweetly drove me to the terminal. In the bus a round-eyed lady asked if she could travel with me, as she had never travelled alone before. Of course I said yes, though I'd been shunning her because she was snuffling into innumerable paper hankies with which her bag was overflowing. I believe they were actually tears at parting from her 'hubby', not a heavy cold. I melted to her, heard about the boarding-house she kept at Skegness and made her drink some of my wine on the aeroplane.

I believe the secret of not feeling bewildered when alone is to wade boldly in with the help of a map. So I rejected the temptation to take a taxi straight from airport to hotel and began at once tipping porters, speaking Spanish and taking bus tickets. When I said this later to Janetta she couldn't help signifying her *moral* (because yes that's what it is) disapproval of taking buses.

This hotel is an Art Nouveau building among the real streets

---

1 Writer and translator.

of the old town, surrounded by cafés, antique and woodworkers shops.

I arrived at four-thirty, since when I've walked out, bought a guidebook, gloves (left mine behind) and chocolate, had two cups of excellent coffee in a café, and visited the Accademia on Raymond's recommendation – a dusty, dark, sad old place, where dozens of bored guardians were at the eager service of me and one other visitor. One room contained fine Goyas and Zurbaráns and a Velásquez.

I've ordered Solares, shall have a bath and drink whisky till dinner, in the hotel.

February 22nd

How odd, how intensely odd it was to find myself alone in a Madrid hotel looking at a dim television screen showing President Nixon and Chairman Mao grimacing together in China.

Jaime[1] telephoned last night, and said Janetta will arrive between one and two tomorrow, so I have another half-day to myself. Today has gone well. I wonder how long I could go on existing alone in a foreign hotel without losing my identity and most vividly remember my struggle for survival in the Hotel d'Angleterre at Menton. The Prado was my object for today. I walked there in the bright, almost springlike morning and spent about four hours looking and looking. Relations with pictures should be lifelong – I try therefore to grapple those I love to me with hoops of steel. But first one must decide which are worthy of it. I don't think I've seen the 'black' Goyas before. Poussin typifies my early taste, and still satisfies me as much as Bach does by the reliability of his formal relations. Looking at the particularly juicy Rubenses I wondered if they fitted with my theory that good art is based on a good view of life. Velásquez and Goya just as splendid as ever; I'm stunned by the sureness, the confidence of Velásquez: while Goya is satirical, tender, indignant, horrified. How Tintoretto glorifies the way light falls on rounded human limbs! Where I miss company is in having no

---

1 Parladé.

one to sit and exchange impressions with in cafés. I lunched in the Prado buffet. Later to the Plaza Mayor, which looks bigger and emptier in winter without its café tables. Splendid Spaniards, to allow no cars to park there, as the Italians certainly would. I enjoyed rambling in the streets, but how they gabble, and at what a rate.

February 23rd: Salamanca

Janetta arrived even earlier than she'd said. I had spent the morning in the Palacio Real, being shown round with about four Spanish tourists. The guide was amazed that I could understand Spanish and kept asking me if I was enjoying myself. I was, very much, particularly the rooms lined with porcelain, and one vast Tiepolo ceiling. Something made me feel I must cut short the long tour, and sure enough, when I got back outside the hotel stood the big white Mercedes; inside it a brown shape was very slowly moving, like a hermit crab in its shell, as Janetta crept out. Delightful meeting. Over glasses of manzanilla we discussed our plans. We werc at one in deciding to get outside the city before we lunched, and then go on via Avila to Salamanca.

Stopped at a wayside lorrymen's café, for eggs and wine and cheese, and then off again across the wide vastness of pinko-grey Castile dotted with small dark trees such as children draw. I've always wanted to see Avila and now at last I did. We drove through a gate in the portentous walls and went into the cathedral – tall, narrow, built of rich blotchy mauve granite, intensely cold. Then on to Salamanca, arriving fairly early and covering a lot of controversial ground, as one always does on first meeting Janetta. Walked round the glorious Plaza Mayor, circling the arcades amongst a cheerful crowd. Then back to our sympathetic hotel, ramshackle but very comfortable.

February 25th: Santiago, 10.15 a.m.

In bed in the huge beflunkeyed and expensive *parador* after breakfast. And oh, after all, Jaime never did arrive last night.

Yesterday, in bright weather under blue skies, we went into Salamanca University and the Escuelas Menores with its painted ceilings, and were shown the cathedrals Old and New by a dear old man with rheumy eyes and a voice whose loving phrases died away at the end, giving them an odd sort of tender emphasis. I fell in love once more with this golden town on this, my third and longest visit. We tore ourselves reluctantly away for the long drive to Santiago – north to Zamona, Janetta driving impeccably, through a series of passes between high mountains patched with snow. A little green, but no flowers at all; it looks more backward than England. Lunch at the Albergue at Puebla in a wild valley, of delicious little fish cakes and cauliflower. For the last hour we drove in darkness.

February 26th: Villagarcia, 8.15 p.m.
Well, Jaime *did* arrive all right, thank heavens, debonair and obviously unaware of any confusion.

Meanwhile, Janetta and I 'did' the enchanting town of Santiago pretty thoroughly in spite of heavy rain and umbrellas everywhere. It's much more real than most places of pilgrimage, with solid arcaded white and grey streets, whose shops (instead of religious frippery) sell sweets, cakes and breast-shaped Galician cheeses (actually called *tétillas*). (Galician women are short and immensely thick, without necks, like bootboxes on strong and fairly nippy legs.) Saw over the cathedral and its museums, lunched in the *mirador* of an excellent fish restaurant. Out again after a semi-snooze.

Today's journey was due south and not far. Nothing could be more different from the *parador* of the Reyes Católicos than this simple inn with a bar downstairs and a long flight of dark stairs leading to totally unheated bedrooms. Janetta is all douceness and docility. She and Jaime have a bathroom with the only hot water in the building. My room is freezing, but has two beds, so I shall pile the blankets of both on to mine and fill a hot-water bottle. It's been a day of menacing black clouds, heavy showers and lakes of blue sky. Cold as it is we have seen lots and lots of camellias and mimosa and some magnolias in flower, bright green meadows, and brooks flowing past clumps of large very pale primroses and violets. We visited three gardens. The most charming was the Oca Palace now being restored by its owners after years of neglect. Neglect and damp climate had given it a special bloom by covering trees and statues with moss and ferns. A long water-garden contained a stone boat with stone men in it, while a mossy stone lion gazed sardonically down on a perfectly green stone picnic table and seats, and large moss-covered balls. Nothing was harsh or exact in outline, all soft, crumbling, variegated.

February 28th: Vigo

I got up fairly early in my cold room at Villagarcia, dressed hastily, and after putting away a small cup of coffee, a roll and masses of butter brought me by an old black crone, I was tempted out by the pale blue sky, and walked to the edge of the *ria*. Women with strong brown bare legs and feet, shawls and full skirts were dredging up shellfish into buckets. I sat reading the paper and drinking more coffee till Janetta came down, when we set off to visit the Pazo and garden of friends of a friend of Jaime's nearby. The family came out to greet us – an attractive sexy young woman with a complacent-looking young husband and a flock of very Galician strong healthy children between four and two, 'and I am again expecting,' she said proudly. There were twin boys aged two in comic trousers, who trotted purposefully about with expressionless faces, bounced balls and rode shining bicycles to the brink of stone steps, were shouted at by their parents, bawled a little. The family atmosphere was thick, extrovert, materialistic and friendly, wife and husband fondled one another publicly; she kissed Janetta and me on parting.

February 29th: Túy

We ought to be in Portugal, but I'm quite glad that instead we're still in Spain in a quiet pleasant *parador*, looking at it across the wide river. When we got to the frontier, Jaime – covered in shame and confusion ('*que cabeza*') – admitted that he had forgotten his passport, and a temporary one couldn't be got until this morning. I'm quite thankful for this spell of quiet and I think Jaime has been cheered up by our obviously being pleased to stay.

Yesterday we saw another camellia garden near Vigo and a

desolate farmhouse in a Sleeping-Beauty wood, with huge clumps of primroses. Everywhere great trees had fallen across the path, and this wasn't the first sign we have seen of a violent tornado which struck this coast two weeks ago, destroyed roofs, uprooted huge strong trees and broke others clean in half. Worst of all was the havoc on the way up to a pilgrimage place called Santa Tecla, perched on a limestone hill, where I made my solitary botanical find – *Helichrysum foetidus*, smelling of goat's cheese. Then along a wild and beautiful coast, where the leaves – but no flowers – of spring bulbs were appearing and the grey sea hurled huge waves on the shore; and up by the Spanish bank of the river to this nice little old town.

Lunched and dined in a very cheap, popular restaurant (lunch for three plus wine came to fifteen shillings). The cooking and washing up were done in the dining-room behind a long counter of polished steel. Much jolly life and absence of tourists.

March 1st: Oporto

Now we *are* in Portugal, land of phlegm as one is instantly reminded. A man who sold me a newspaper could hardly wait to get outside his shop and discharge a great dollop with a deafening crash. Is it the climate, which is pretty rotten taken all in all?

Safely across the frontier and the river Minho, we drove on to Braga, a handsome town. A palace (*de los Biscainhos*) was in the workmen's hands, but they let us wander in and out, admiring *azulejos* and pretty painted and moulded ceilings. In the garden the camellias and azaleas had been mercilessly clipped to turn them into mushrooms or summerhouses. What a strange light this throws on the Portuguese character. It's as if they couldn't stand the slightest wildness or deviation, yet they have plenty of visual taste. Another sign of childishness or lack of seriousness is that the statues were all of buffoons and dwarfs, grinning crazily. After lunch, to the cathedral – everywhere we see beautiful tiles. A market was clearing itself away, and country-women in shawls were moving off carrying huge weights on their heads. Finally to the pilgrimage church of Bom Jesus, led up to by an enormously long flight of steps, flanked by camellia gardens, statues and grey and white pavilions.

On southwards to this huge town with its congested traffic. Found a hotel and at once walked out (the sun was shining) to the cathedral and down a long winding street of gold- and silversmiths shops almost to the edge of the river. Oporto is on many levels, and the lower orders live like Niebelungen below street or even river and flood level, but in pretty old houses decorated with balconies, tiles, birdcages and washing. Jaime rang up Miss Tait, an Englishwoman to whom we have an introduction, and we dined in a good restaurant recommended by her.

March 2nd

Well, here we are, at Buçaco in the most amazing fairy-story Palace Hotel, five star and de luxe, built in an extravagant 19th-century imitation of the Mañueline style — with curlicues, *azulejos* and everything as spacious and sumptuous and spurious as possible. We arrived in the dark, only glimpsing the tall straight trunks of the rare trees in the forest surrounding us. I have a vast two-bedded room with a vase of camellias, a bath-room almost as big. Only two other people are staying — an American and his pick-up. We had quite a day of it yesterday and have now seen enough camellias to last a lifetime. But first we went to two churches in which baroque gilt woodwork had run riot — in Santa Clara it produced a festive joyful effect and was seeded with flowers and cupids, in San Francisco a pompous overpowering one, reminding me of the last Spanish episode in Saint-Simon. Over one altar was a naïve but remarkable tableau of monks being decapitated by Saracens. The anguished head of one was held up by the hair, another was just falling from its neck, and three others stared in horrified expectancy of the blow.

To lunch with Miss Tait. She was the epitome of all old gardening Englishwomen, tall, with blue eyes looking out of a pink veined face, beaky nose and fluffy white hair. You could have popped her as she was into a general's uniform. She had had three teeth out the day before and was bearing up bravely in spite of 'trouble with her new plate'. She had been born and always lived in her charming *quinta*, which stood in a large walled garden — a happy blend of Portuguese and English — and looked more like a country house than a town one. We had dry port followed by a delicious lunch served by attentive maids. She's an ancestor-worshipper and name-dropper, often referring to 'second secretaries of the Embassy' or Malcolm Sargent and Suggia as 'sweeties' and 'pets'. Her views in fact were *antipático*, she adored God and the Queen, yet one had to admire her stalwart way of enjoying life, her indomitable acceptance of age, and her passion and genius for gardening. In her garden everything grew free, not in the Portuguese style, but rampaging happily, whether camellias, magnolias, tulip trees or the primroses and tiny daffodils which fringed a stream. We admired it greatly, and genuinely, and were then taken on to visit a lady of very high degree (so we were given to understand), descended from John of Gaunt – the Condesca de Campo Bello I think she was called. She was a round rubber ball of immense vitality and considerable humour and charm, spoke fluent English rather in the style of Boris.[1] Her garden had received the devastating Portuguese treatment; her house was more interesting, old and with a superb view over the town and river. The rooms had lovely domed wooden ceilings and fine if heavy furniture but nothing in the faintest degree modern. Even the photo of her married son represented him as a boy of six. She pressed us to stay on, sent for tea and gave us 1875 port – remarkable but rather sick-making. Drove Miss Tait home, and through the gathering darkness to the monstrous fairy-tale palace of Buçaco.

March 3rd: Obidos

The forest of Buçaco, though large and full of thriving, enormously tall trees, was rather too organised to be exciting. On down a most beautiful valley, peaceful and so alight with mimosa that it gave the illusion that the sun was shining rather than glimmering through the clouds. At Coimbra it was grey and later the heavens opened in torrential rain. We saw the marvellous library (second time for me) and the museum (the first). The magnificent bulks of Batalha and Alcobaça were

1 Anrep, Russian mosaicist.

reflected in the soaking wet paving-stones as if in a lake. Deciding it was too wet for Nazaré we came instead to this romantic little *posada* buried inside its castle, where Ralph and I stayed years ago. It still only had seven rooms, but they cost one third the price of those at Buçaco, have shining red-tiled floors, an earthenware jug of drinking water, charm and simplicity.

p.m.

This morning, in brilliant sun and wind, we drove to the self-consciously picturesque fishing village of Nazaré. There was a sparkling mist of foam from the great rollers breaking on the wide sandy beach, and against this background bright-coloured solid boats, turned up at the end like Turkish slippers, were drawn up (some even in the streets) and old men and women in national dress sat waiting to be photographed in their tartan shorts and bobble caps. It's rather shocking that after a life of toil and danger these distinguished-looking old gentlemen, weather-beaten and toothless, should pose as models for tourists' cameras. Lunch at Tôrres Vedras of various sorts of fishcakes. 'What are they made of?' we asked. '*Feix*,' the waiter said with the bleak uninformative expression I find so typically Portuguese. They reject one thus, as well as by their hawking and spitting, as the Spaniards do not. We only had time for the library at Mafra, but it took half an hour to walk there along endless corridors and through echoing rooms.

In Lisbon, our tempo pressurised – for me by departure, for Jaime by having to see business partners – and through the fearful traffic up to the Castello where we had been lent the same flat as once before. Janetta sweetly came with me to collect my air ticket to Madrid; we were appalled by the complete lack of taxis and cafés, but having walked from Pombal to Rocio we at last found both, and so got home. Janetta's favourite minus-word is 'worrying' and her plus-word 'calm'. One night in a noisy place she told me she couldn't sleep for 'worrying' whether I could, whereas I had earplugs in and slept like anything. Her sensitivity is exquisite and touches me deeply, but I do worry about her worrying. Perhaps she worries and trembles as a result of the conflict between her gentle, sensitive side, thinking imaginatively about other people's feelings, a side that is appreciative and adaptable, and the more demanding 'princess' who likes to reject rooms and dishes in restaurants – though I remember how she loathed it when clients of the Fonda[1] did the same.

March 5th: West Halkin Street

Jaime and Janetta angelically got up early (which I know they hate) to take me to the airport and nothing could have been gentler than the touch on my arm with which Janetta woke me. It took me a good deal of the day to get home, changing at Madrid, but was restful and uncrowded. London horrifyingly cold with a searing wind and today it rains steadily. Kind Joan had left me an enormous bunch of flowers.

I have managed to restart my Mini and gone in it to buy Sunday papers. On the cover of the *Observer* supplement is Bunny's[2] face enormous and lifelike. It was extraordinary to see the newspaper man take away a huge pile of other Bunnies.

March 8th

This is Bunny week. His *Sons of the Falcon* is out today; this morning a presentation copy came through my letter-box. It's his eightieth birthday and we celebrate it tonight with a party at Magouche's. Poor Magouche herself is stricken in some mysterious way and was persuaded to lie in bed yesterday and not go to Foyle's luncheon at which Bunny had to make a speech and read a poem about his own death. *The Times* writes a short paragraph of undiluted praise, the *Listener* has a disagreeable and rather mocking review. The *Guardian* a long, enthusiastic one.

March 11th

Bunny's birthday party was a delightful occasion and not so grey-bearded as I had feared. Susu, Antonia and Henrietta[3] (accompanied by Nicholas Gormaston), the Garnett twins, Richard's boys and Sophie, Nicky, Patrick and Noah (alight with

---

1 A very pretty hotel run for some time by the Parladés.
2 David Garnett.
3 My daughter-in-law.

family happiness) and Rose[1] looking especially pretty and radiant, though it wasn't until next day that she heard she had passed her interview for London University. Quentin's[2] three children, William Garnett beamingly happy because he now has a daughter as well as a son. Angelica,[3] with a fringe, not at her most beautiful, and Duncan[4] (looking at most sixty-five).

March 13th: Litton Cheney, with the Reynolds Stones

Today we had a lunchtime visit from Desmond, Julian and two of their guests, all, as Reynolds said, 'buzzing like happy bees'. In the evening another tonic – a visit to the Hubbards, a talk about painting with John, and Goya in particular. This sunny, sociable day was sandwiched between two bleak snowy ones. But now returning in a warm shut-in carriage I have just eaten the picnic Janet provided, including (so thoughtfully) a small bottle of red wine. It's not negligible at all to pay such attention to one's comfort and happiness, and I glow with gratitude and reflect that wine (especially red wine) has the marvellous quality of bringing out – not superimposing – a rich interesting glow, from all that impinges on one's senses – at this moment the striking composition made by the cranes outside Southampton harbour and the stumpy red and black funnels of some huge liner beyond.

Janet grows more companionable and has dropped off some of the nonsense resulting from social anxiety, which happens much later in people's lives than is generally supposed. She looked frail and rather round-shouldered. Reynolds looks like Napoleon when listening to records of Chopin with closed eyes, but his brand of nonsense – over-frantic love and respect for trees – increases. We sat in the sun discussing Roy Jenkins' admirable speech about what the Labour Party should aim at – dealing with poverty. 'Yes,' said Reynolds, 'but to me it's even more gratifying that he wants to preserve the environment.'

---

1 Jackson, Janetta's youngest daughter.
2 Bell.
3 Garnett.
4 Grant.

Hearing on the wireless that the gales had blown down a tree, killing a man who was teaching his son to drive a car, Reynolds was more sorry for the tree than for the father and son. 'I'm very shocked,' said Janet, and so was I, but Reynolds saw nothing absurd in it.

March 15th: London

The second of two days that are both warm and sunny have brought me out to sit on a seat in the square. There is a tentative twittering of birds, the noise of the gardener hacking at the flower-beds, and lots to watch: two little greyhounds, too tremulous to live, one or two very young toddlers with difficulty progressing on their hind legs, stopping to stare and stare at each other and the dogs.

I spent an evening being taken to an old-fashioned play by Lyn and Stanley[1] and eating queer fish in a Chinese restaurant afterwards. Stanley had spent the afternoon with Michael Holroyd's Philippa[2] – who was in despair and 'under sedation' because Michael has just decided to leave her after several flaming rows. I could hardly disguise my relief for I like Michael and find her maddening. Stanley blames Michael for his 'timing' and thinks him emotionally immature. Being with Stanley is like being hit by a quick fire of little choppy waves. I tend to abandon myself to them, but my own desire is always to follow things up, chew the cud, so that our conversation is sometimes incoherent. I spent another evening at the orchestra, enjoying myself rapturously; perhaps it's because it's one of my few remaining forms of activity – one that fits in with my philosophy of life.

March 19th

The drive to Kitty's was no strain, from which I derive modified consolation. She wasn't there when I arrived, but the country peace struck me almost like a blow and Emma the grey veteran cat came to greet me. Daffodils, birds singing, otherwise quiet.

---

1 Olson.
2 Pullan.

Yesterday again we had summer heat, and lunched out of doors. Desmond and Pat[1] to dinner. Good conversation, but how much of ordinary conversation is exhibitionist in one way or another? Kitty tends towards it, and got dangerously on to her own sex-life. But Pat's mental processes concern me most at the moment. At a very rapid speed he churned out what seemed to me often superficial and invalid statements. This rapidity, and the fact that he kept taking us up for 'misusing terms' (which he seemed to be doing himself), made me think that, if not exhibiting, he was competitively trying to crush. Not my idea of conversation, which is to illumine a subject from the disparate angles of the talkers. We talked of loyalty, my theory being that it's either a word for something else, such as friendship, sympathy, pity, or it's something disreputable like abnegating your critical sense or denying your deepest beliefs. You give all the support you can to someone out of friendship or sorrow for their unhappiness, but you don't, for instance, feel that you must take on as your own that friend's hostility to an unfaithful wife, or his beliefs, out of this strange concept of loyalty. Pat kept rattling away that friendship was a passive state, and loyalty an active form of behaviour. But every emotion or attitude has both an active and passive aspect, not least friendship. Much good it is if it hasn't. Kitty said afterwards that Pat was talking nonsense, and often did. It was certainly undigested material. People who think really deeply and constructively (Moore, Russell) don't rattle.

March 20th

The drive home partly crowded by cars taking advantage of a fine Sunday was a strain and I spent yesterday evening giving way to total exhaustion and drinking too much whisky. The bath of blissful country peace makes me wonder again whether I should go to live in the country. It would have to be Dorset where I seem to have most friends but could I subsist there alone? If not, who with? Joan? But even if I were, would she be willing?

---

1 Trevor-Roper.

March 23rd

The amazing summer weather, cloudless and hot, goes on heart-breakingly from day to day. Joan said last night that she found her matelessness agonising. I felt aware of the difference in our values last night, though, as ever, grateful for her loving friendship. For how can I care a fig about my appearance? Then she almost too frequently reminds me of my approaching death, as if I wasn't fully aware of it. She virtually said, 'I must make the most of you, because though I can't bear to think of it the time will come when you won't be here.' How does she know for certain who'll die first, eh? She questioned me closely about the age at which my parents had died. All this intensified the insistent vision of myself as walking the plank over the bottomless sea.

When I got home, and my gold necklace (which Ralph gave me, and which I always wear and feel links me to him) fell from my neck, its catch broken, it seemed yet one more nail in my coffin in a day given over to thoughts of death, partly because I went to the memorial service for Phyllis Nichols in the morning. It wasn't a moving ceremony. I sang the untuneful hymns and was terribly aware of the bogosity of Christianity. I thought of Phyllis affectionately, but rather enviously. On coming out, there was the usual confrontation, Anne[1], sympathetic and very youthful-looking, Dicky Chopping[2] in deep black, Jojo[3] in bright scarlet.

Joan rang this morning, and I think was aware how she had twanged on the string of my mortality, for she said 'We won't talk about it any more.' Which I second gladly.

March 24th

I've just been lunching with Dadie and Eardley with a view to fixing details of our Skye holiday. Dadie goes to our heads like champagne. Does he go to his own?

---

1 Phyllis's sister.
2 Richard Chopping, artist and illustrator. We had compiled *English Botany*, *Volume One* together during the war.
3 Phyllis's daughter.

March 25th

Easter coming up fast, and I plough my way through muddles and guilt feelings. Am I a 'worrier'? I think I do worry morbidly when I believe I have hurt someone's feelings. Not that this should *not* be a subject of guilt, but it's possible by brooding to get it out of proportion and make matters worse.

4.30 p.m.

Arrived at Crichel in a grey wind sprinkling a few raindrops on the grey-brown landscape lit up by yellow daffodils which I don't like as much as I used to. Des, Andrew Porter[1] and Raymond were on my crowded train, Pat and Richard come this evening. Raymond looks pale under his Egyptian tan, resulting in further daffodil colour which goes ill with his favourite bright red scarf. I've taken Moses out for a short blow, and now prepare for life in the community — but is it better to forget my sex (which comes easy to me) and hope they will, rather than be consciously a non-man along with a different sort of non-men? Four days of reading and talking and walks with dog Moses lie ahead.

March 31st

With Des, Raymond and Andrew (whom I began to like better) I was in no way, not for a second, aware of being an exception to the rule. The arrival of Pat[2] and Richard Sippe brought a change. Pat at times looks and talks to me challengingly and aggressively. At dinner he raised the question whether behind one's 'civilised' friends you would always find a possessive 'boorish' mum. It became at once clear that he was only speaking of men and their mums, and 'moreover' equating 'civilised' with homosexual. I asked if this was what he was doing and he admitted it. I'm on guard and didn't challenge the equation itself, though I think it as monstrous as saying friendship is always passive.

---

1 Critic and great friend of Desmond's.

2 Trevor-Roper.

April 3rd

About to return, a day earlier than planned because on a delightful outing yesterday to Badbury Rings I badly gashed my shin on barbed wire. This happened when, encouraged and helped over a gate by Pat and Andrew, and following (as I believe) their instructions, I jumped down into a loop of barbed wire on the far side. Though unpleasant, I was unaware how bad it was, and could do nothing about it, anyway, so I walked some miles to the Rings and back to the car, negotiating several other obstacles and crawling through holes in hedges. Arrived home I asked Pat for a bit of Elastoplast. He gave me the only one he had – much too small for the large messy crescent moon of bleeding, distorted flesh which was revealed. I had therefore to ask for more, and there were cries of horror and amazement and kind sympathy and exclamations at 'how stoical I had been'. (I hadn't really – there was nothing else to be done and it didn't hurt much, though it does more today.) Indeed I was slightly shaken myself by the sight of it and have made an appointment with Moynihan[1] to dress it tomorrow morning.

A comic sense over dressing my wound; no Elastoplast, dressings or antiseptic ointment in the house. 'We need some powder to prevent it sticking,' said Pat. I offered my talc powder, but he insisted on using a very old and rusty tin of Tinifax, a cure for athlete's foot! I must add that he offered to drive me straight to Westminster Hospital to have it properly dressed on arrival this morning, and Desmond had offered to take me to the doctor. But I prefer to go to Moynihan.

April 4th

Returned from Moynihan who threw up his arms in horror. 'It should have been stitched! And it's got some dirt in it and is already septic. Well, you may have trouble I'm afraid. It's a case for prayer.' He gave me antitetanus and antibiotic injections, as well as antibiotics to take by mouth. I couldn't help making a funny story out of Pat and the Tinifax. He was highly amused, knows Pat well, and I fear may tease him about it. 'Of course

---

1 My doctor.

28

he's absolutely brilliant at his own line but fairly hopeless about every other branch of medicine.' I now sit peacefully and resigned with my leg up.

Looking back on the incident I do rather wonder how much hostility against me as a female was involved, for after all, it was Pat who set this obstacle race hardly designed for a septuagenarian. He and I had a short, sharp but not fierce revival of the argument about the passivity of friendship and activity of loyalty, in which I only gather from what the others said that Pat thought he had been worsted. So do I. He hadn't a leg to stand on. God also came up but here Pat was set about much more by Desmond and Andrew than by me. On the other hand in the train to London Richard, with a meaning smile, showed both Pat and me a quotation from his book (Dr Johnson): 'And here a female atheist kills you dead.' I really like Pat and he was charming to me after my accident, but I resent what I can't help (my female sex) being held against me.

April 6th
Another visit to Moynihan who thinks I have been lucky and all is so far going well. I have tried to resolve my grudge against Pat – for I see I had one – by writing him a friendly letter. I've just had Faith[1] to lunch, so I have a feeling that I'm gradually cleaning my slate of guilt. The next fence to be taken is Thorington and its cold, dirt, inedible food and 'inharmonious' impact on the nerves.

April 7th
At Thorington alone with Margaret. She says she is 'happier without Lionel', who seems to be postponing his arrival till the evening. So am I without both of them, much as I enjoy Lionel's conversation. The day is cold, windy and intermittently wet, the house inconceivably icy, as it has been unoccupied all winter and has no form of central heating. Last night, wearing overcoats over winter clothes, we ate excellent fish and chips (bought *en route* at Sudbury) in the freezing kitchen, and then

---

1 Henderson, mother of Nick.

repaired to the television room which we made snug with a coal fire. The blankets are too narrow for the narrow beds and won't tuck in, the electric blankets are of a special kind that gives only minimal heat and must be switched off when the bedside lamp goes on. There are one or two 'electric heaters' so-called, which seem to contain a single light-bulb and give out no heat at all. The bathwater turns cold after a few moments. I noticed that my breath made a cloud of steam in the frigid air of the hall. However, all that said, Margaret and I get on perfectly well and I am enthralled and delighted with Quentin's Life of Virginia, Vol. I, which Julian sweetly lent me, and sit reading it crouched over the fire I have managed to concoct out of balls of paper and scrounged logs.

Being here is an odd sensation, like being at school, divorced from all creature comforts, though not from mental stimulation.

April 10th

On Saturday Lionel arrived with his face set in an averted mask of gloom. Shirley came in later in the evening, looking ravishingly pretty, but she ate no dinner and vanished upstairs to her bed. Lionel had got into an old gent's mood of inaccurate reminiscence about Adrian Stephen[1] (based on my talk about Quentin's book). The ghost of boredom even made an appearance.

On Sunday morning, quite another state of things. The sun came out and it was possible to sit out in it, rather than in the frigidaire of the house. Lionel and I sat alone (the others were out walking), and beginning again from Adrian, a fascinating conversation developed. Adrian had deviated from Bloomsbury's worship of G. E. Moore much to their disgust, going so far as to say he was 'a fraud'. I said I rather thought so too, even in Cambridge days. Lionel agreed. Thence to our feelings about philosophy. Lionel said that solipsism had always been a frightening thought to him because it couldn't be refuted. I said that though I agreed about this it was, to me, no more frightening than God. God *might* exist, no refuting that,

1 Brother of Virginia Woolf.

but since his non-existence was unprovable one could ignore him and shove him aside as it were, as I did with solipsism. Both hypotheses seemed to me almost infinitely unlikely. Apart from this we agreed about much – there being no such thing as certainty, but only degrees of probability; the possibility of describing values in terms of biological relevance; the beauty of nature (rather obviously); and, as Lionel pointed out, formal relationships and our power to comprehend them increases our power to grasp our surroundings and so help survival. Literature of course relates to communication – a vital human need. Lionel had some theory about music and I think human emotion or physical rhythms, which I forget; but to me the inclusion of the formal aspect is necessary to it. I said what chiefly worried me was that some people with more scientific knowledge than I have said that causality could no longer be accepted as a universal principle. (Julia[1] was in my mind.) To my delight Lionel said that that was 'absolute rubbish' and that scientists in every department accepted and acted on causality, so that I could relegate this fear, along with solipsism and God. Then back to Bloomsbury. He agreed with me (but perhaps he agrees too readily) that James[2] was a more admirable character than Lytton, because more considerate of other people's feelings, less prone to cause pain.

A different Lionel appeared in the afternoon when plans for our return were discussed, and indecision and delay gripped the whole family. I have had a feeling that Lionel's glooms may often be connected with physical symptoms. He suddenly mentioned nitro-glycerine in the car. And it's easy to forget how his disability[3] may haunt him.

April 13th
For sleeping purposes I've made a trial move away from barbiturics to a drug called Mogadon, which produces a different sort of sleep, shallower and full of dreams. Mary takes it and says the

---

1 Gowing (née Strachey).

2 Strachey.

3 Heart trouble.

same. One wakes and returns to sleep, and often to a dream which concerns ambiguity – two opposite but coinciding interpretations of a single state of affairs.

I also have dreams that are visual, coloured and beautiful. As, the other morning, that I was in the Arctic among brilliant and transparent icebergs which gave me acute pleasure: the inhabitants were simple, silly people wearing funny hats.

My young friends sometimes visit me to seek advice, as Georgia[1] did this morning. Should she or shouldn't she throw up her job? I try to pin my mind to the problem, but the fact that it doesn't seem immensely important made it more of an effort. Then Bunny rang up wanting to be asked to dinner, but I invented (as I did to Mary) an imaginary engagement, in order to have a quiet evening to myself. Not that I want to cut myself off completely from people, but occasional privacy is vital, I find. Stanley has just rung up wanting to complicate tomorrow by bringing me his rewritten piece about Ralph. I already have Julian coming with a photographer and Janetta to lunch and a journey to Lincoln in the afternoon.

April 18th: Doddington Hall, Lincolnshire

A walk in a marshy wood intersected with broad green rides, whose tall trees were full of herons' nests. The huge prehistoric birds perched with their crooked necks erect. We found broken eggshells of a curious matt blue. 'Poor Old' Ralph[2] looked terribly ill, gaunt and with indigo lips, but seemed all there mentally, and I liked his son Anthony, his clever little wife Vicky, and three attractive little girls. The house, though large and forbidding outside, has great elegance and a certain lightness within. We were done proud in food and drink, and had only one formal evening of velvet smoking jackets and withdrawal of females.

Last night came Janetta, looking fine and young and almost plump.

A book of memories of Virginia,[3] including one by me, has

---

1 Tennant.
2 Jarvis, owner of Doddington Hall.
3 Woolf.

come out and Cyril[1] gave it a long review on Sunday. I had quite forgotten what I wrote, but he said in his review that I had mentioned two instances of her rudeness, including one to Ros.[2] Oh Lord! Ros rang up, saying, 'Virginia was *never* rude to me.'

April 23rd: Cambridge (at Celia's[3])

Austere and flowery: a nun in garlands. Or else it's that I'm staying in a nunnery. I take Koestler's maddening book,[4] glorifying the principle of chance and 'seriality', off the shelf: it refuses to allow chance the status of causality. I enjoy reading and disagreeing, but put it back on the shelf between reads. I brought down Robert's book,[5] hoping to interest Celia and her visitors in it; but its bright green shiny cover must seem to her an outrage, for it was brought up to my bedroom whenever I left it lying on the sofa. Celia gave a dinner-party last night, and I know the effort nearly killed her. I've had the much-praised Dr Munby[6] and his handsome wife, and a pair of archaeologists of whom I very much liked the American wife. Lots of people love Munby and I think he's a good, kind, clever man, rollicking and boozing gently, and genial in a confident Common Room way. But I missed something – what? Astringency, critical bite. Such a lot of these academics are like that, and I suppose it means their life is a happy one. Celia seems happier than before, as compulsively neat; everything tidied and straightened. Her daughter Ariane is now an intelligent and conversible sixteen and a half. It seems a pity she should be excluded from dinner-parties.

April 25th

Since I got back from Cambridge I've been to two Art occasions. Yesterday to a cocktail party for Duncan's[7] private view,

---

1 Connolly.
2 Lehmann.
3 Goodman.
4 *The Ghost in the Machine.*
5 *The Green Flag.*
6 Librarian of King's College, Cambridge.
7 Grant.

given by the Dufferins. Duncan was lying back, relaxed, on a sofa, being 'eaten up' by a young woman with a dark blown-up fuzz of hair. There were a great many strikingly beautiful and elegant young people. Two young men were thumping out duets compulsively on the piano with the smug expression common to players of duets. Fairly soon I longed to leave, and did, driving Sonia[1] home. She asked me in to supper, but I couldn't face it. How dreadfully pointless parties are when one is seventy and doesn't find old friends there. Now I've just been to Mary Potter's private view – very delicate, some really lovely paintings, in a limited range of muted colours – yellow, grey, dull orange and forget-me-not blue. I met a figure from the past, Sophie Shone, ex-Ambassadress and mother of Burgo's friend Michael. 'I have a little house within shouting distance of the North Pole,' she announced loudly, standing stiffly erect and schoolmistressy with specs and pulled-back hair. Her voice was like a foghorn and later I heard her still saying, downstairs, 'within *shouting* distance of the North Pole'.

Margaret is in the Royal Free Hospital having the cause of her womb trouble investigated. I rang Lionel who was full of solicitude for her, such as she won't credit him with. He was glad the surgeon said she 'would do the minimum'. I think Margaret believes he wishes her dead. Oh what a pathetic air of playing the solo part in the Festival Hall is displayed by a poor patient preparing for the surgeon's knife. 'Theatre' is an apt name for it.

Anthony West and Desmond have just been to lunch with me, Anthony, brown, bulging and genial, with his dark hair hanging grizzled on his shoulders. They talked so much, I need hardly have put a word in, but felt I must keep my end up, just.

April 28th

Bonjour tristesse. There are moments, and this morning was one, when one sees the crescendo of age in all its horrid fury, realises the erosion of the few years remaining, and feels with bitter sorrow the loss of physical vigour. Somehow the sight of Bunny wandering rather forlornly among the young and beautiful

---

1 Orwell.

34

people at the Dufferins' party struck me to the heart. He took Janetta and me out to lunch earlier, stuck his fork into a chicken kiev and covered his new suit with great dark stains of butter. Janetta kindly rushed to Temple and Crook and returned with cleaning materials which only made matters worse. So there he was among the frilled glittering young men, having changed into his thick tweed suit.

I was thinking of Koestler's absurd credulity about portents, precognition and psychokinesis as I drove from my orchestra in the dark the other night. A huge black van came lumbering round a corner, bearing on its front what I read as 'Cancer' (I saw later that it was 'Langer'). Koestler would have taken that as an omen, and it had a dire quality. So I write it down here — to see if it is one.

May 3rd

Such radiant weather really does drive away *tristesse*, and I begin to look forward to going to Skye. I'm lying on my face on an overcoat on the grass of Belgrave Square, the ping of tennis balls agreeably accompanied by the hum of traffic. Ever since I woke I have felt serene for no reason. Yesterday I fought my way through a surging nursery-garden and brought back some boxes of plants. I spent nearly all this morning digging them into my window-boxes, and now their neat flourish gives me great satisfaction.

On Monday Robert[1] gave a party for the appearance of his book, *The Green Flag*, at Brooks's Club. I enjoyed it as much as I *dis*enjoyed the Dufferins'. It was bound together as a good party should be by the love and admiration of the guests for Robert. My feeling was that the company wasn't merely beautiful (as at the Dufferins') but also interesting and distinguished. So many friends that there was hardly time to get a sentence out before being whisked away. Georgie, Henrietta, Nicky, Georgia, all represent youth and beauty. Freddie Ayer, Noel Annan, Ran Antrim, Faith, Raymond, Maude Russell, Nicko and Mary,[2] and

---

1 Kee.

2 Henderson.

dozens of others, intelligence and being in the prime of life. At one moment I was rather purposefully dragged before Karl Miller, I can't remember by whom. I told him I was an ardent admirer and constant reader of the *Listener* (which he edits). He looked at me sombrely and said, 'You wrote me the toughest letter I've ever had in my life.' From total oblivion emerged the recollection of writing to the editor about his wretched choice of Bridget Brophy to trounce Virginia as a writer (it must have been ten years ago). What happened next, I don't remember. On clouds of champagne someone whisked me away. Julia was there with Margaret in attendance. Robert told me she presented him with a small paper package saying, 'I've brought you something appropriate to your book.' He opened it and it was quite empty! Later someone found what looked like 'a little salad' lying on the floor! Again I greeted Julia, and I'm toying with the idea of writing to her to suggest 'having another try'.[1] As we left I saw Nicky, Patrick and Noah, and Anthony Blond with his arm round Henrietta. He was dishevelled, his face dark and furrowed. 'Why are you looking so worried?' I asked him. 'Because you don't like me.' I couldn't make myself say, 'Yes, I do,' but only, 'Oh, well,' and as I turned away I heard him mutter, 'Clever woman.'

May 6th

I've thought and written so much about death, but yesterday morning in the small hours it came close quite suddenly and clutched me by the throat. The night before I had dined with Tristram and Virginia[2] at Stockwell – a large merry party of young people, including two Jonathans – Miller and Cecil. Miller, drinking nothing but Cokes, voluble, Jewish in the fair style, extremely clever, excitable and amusing. Another actor came in with his silent girl afterwards and there was theatrical talk, imitations and laughter. At first I thought it was too much 'in-talk', but I was soon laughing delightedly – they were so funny. I was a bit scared of Jonathan Miller, who is also

---

1 We had fallen out sometime previously.

2 Son of Anthony Powell, and his wife.

passionately interested in spiritualism and hypnotism and philosophy; but we got going about Cambridge, philosophy, spiritualists. He was an Apostle, he told me; I liked him. I started home at twelve-thirty or so and got, as usual, humiliatingly lost among the dark railway yards of Stockwell, drove for miles, agitated and puzzled but determined, and saying to myself, 'I *will* get home.' And I did an hour later and to sleep.

Then the experience. I woke about five, took half a sleeping-pill and some time later came out of a dream where I was wearing a corselet of pain. It wasn't very acute, it started under my breastbone and radiated insistently outwards, gripping me, and going gradually upwards and outwards till it reached my left jaw. Something between toothache and cramp, something I'd never felt the like of before. I massaged myself gently; gradually the pain went, and I lay wide awake, considering. I wasn't panicky, oddly enough. I felt perfectly calm and detached. But I realised it was *something*, a presence, a portent. By now, six-thirty, or so, my pulse was very fast but strong, my concentration on my book poor. I tried to think sensibly, and made up my mind I'd ring Moynihan just before nine and tell him. 'Could you come and see me at nine-thirty?' he said. I got there, feeling a bit shaken. After I'd described exactly what I'd been through he said, 'It's a classical experience of anginal pain. It obviously wasn't a bad attack, but we must get a cardiogram made.' As I left he muttered more to himself, 'Don't want you having cardiac failure.' What I was writing the day before about Margaret applied now to me – the theatrical element, the poor patient who isn't quite sure whether she's the leading lady or the subject of an experiment. Radiologist clad all in black, with apparatus, was followed by cardiologist ditto. Margaret arrived in the middle and when they'd gone we ate boiled eggs on a tray on the floor. I felt tired and didn't really want to talk to her. She made it clear she was worried at leaving me alone in my flat, but couldn't think what to say to me, nor I to her, so it was a relief when she went. I spent the afternoon dozing, interrupted by a telephone call from Moynihan, saying he was 'happy to say the tests showed that I had *not* had a coronary', but I am to have the regular heart pills by me.

Later Frances Phipps[1] came, whose beauty and sweetness dazzled me, though her talk exhausted me. I couldn't face asking her to stay to dinner and thought it best to say I just wanted to topple into bed, where I slept long and well.

This morning Mary telephoned and very sweetly sent her maid round to make my breakfast, clear up and wash up for me. She collected my pills and I have felt pampered, relaxed, and calm. I think as I woke to that pain I realised how little I valued my life. If death could only be just a peaceful unflurried infiltration, I wouldn't fear it at all. And in fact a part of me desires it.

May 8th

Gradual restoration to normality. On Saturday Bunny visited me and his slow tempo exactly suited me. Yesterday I felt equal to Stanley for lunch, and discussion of a more taxing sort: vanity, whether it always signified lack of security. Stanley has a different vocabulary from mine and sometimes we stare at each other in confusion while his face pinkens and he talks of 'polarity' or 'acceptance', and then looks puzzled. I said I thought vanity couldn't always be diagnosed in the same way as physical symptoms but it sometimes signified genuine over-estimation and sometimes under.

After Stanley, who was a bit tiring, came Sophie and Henrietta, and later on dear Magouche, whom I love more and more. She told me something which has indirectly comforted me more than anything: when she was only forty she woke with a go of angina obviously far worse than mine and lying in a pool of sweat. She felt, as I did, 'this is death' and could think of nothing to do but sit up and write feverish letters to her loved ones. It went off as mine did, she never alerted a doctor and it has never recurred in eight years. Bunny said his mother had an attack, and one only, and lived ten more years. Well, I don't want to do that. These two instinctively said what has given me confidence. I rather fear Joan's fussification when she returns and I tell her. My one wish is to push the whole thing into the background and think of it as little as possible.

---

1 Widow of Sir Eric Phipps (Ambassador).

Dr Moynihan on the telephone has just explained that 'since there was no muscular lesion' the attack was a sort of cramp and that I should by now be back where I was before. 'Can I walk as much as I want in Skye?' I asked. 'Oh yes, but take your white pills with you.'

May 11th

Plans for Skye are chaotic because the railway go-slow is on again. Eardley has masterfully taken over, I'm glad to say, and suggests that if need be we drive. I would rather fly to Inverness, but we shall see.

Last night to a private view of Reynolds Stone's paintings, followed by dinner for fifteen or so at the Ritz. I sat between John Sparrow,[1] not my favourite man but we got on all right, and a young man called Hussey, a philosopher and supposed to be supremely clever. Well, maybe, but I had the greatest difficulty in getting him to commit himself to any opinion, except that he couldn't tackle Ethics because it was 'such a frightfully difficult subject'. Why? I asked, was it because its terms ('right', 'good', 'ought', etc.) were so tainted by their use in ordinary conversation? To all my questions he gave a slow pensive 'Ye–es'.

May 14th: Kyleakin

Two days of doubt and confusion about our journey here and whether the trains would run or not and our sleeper bookings be valid. Eardley went twice to King's Cross and was told yes the first day and no the second. Telephone calls to and from the Mackenzies. Colin said if we flew to Inverness he would arrange for a car, so we bought air tickets and I spent the evening we should have taken the train dining with my fellow-travellers, Eardley and Dadie. I had spent the day for the most part in flat suspension. The exception was a call from Janetta because she had heard from Ed that I hadn't been well.

Saturday morning – 6 o'clock telephone call and off to the terminal. Comfortable flight in half-empty plane. The air at

---

1 Historian.

Inverness cool but transparent. We were met by the Mackenzie gardener, Gordon, smiling, young and charming. I'd forgotten about 'aye' and 'wee'. ('Aye, I'll just have to stop a wee while in Inverness.') A beautiful drive across the entire breadth of Scotland, all along Loch Ness, past Monster-observation-posts and across the Kyle ferry in bright sunlight. We are pampered and spoiled by Colin and Pin, who produce comfort and luxury as efficiently as three maids and a butler, and both look rosy and well. They are really great dears and everyone is getting on well, though Eardley is perhaps a little shy, but was reassured to find pictures by Duncan, Vanessa and Frances Hodgkins and a splendid library and garden. Dadie keeps up our level of high spirits and fun. I'm only worried lest he makes me pound along too fast. Woke in the night to brood over this a little, and decided if necessary to alert Eardley, who I know will kindly support me. This morning I went flower-hunting by myself but not much is out.

May 15th

The Mackenzies' hospitality is overwhelming. The sun was hot enough for us to drink after-lunch coffee out of doors against a bank of flowers. Later Pin and I and 'the boys', as she calls them, took the two comic Pekineses for a walk in the valley, where the youthful Serena dashed off at a rocking-horse gallop, flouncing her cream-coloured skirts and leaping into the air regardless of pools of sea water among the thrift-spangled turf, after seagulls and indifferent pompously stalking herons.

May 16th: Ord House Hotel

Here we are and it's a magic place. We arrived on a day of crystal beauty and clear blue sky, and sat down in the tiny lounge to a delicious tea of home-made scones. The little main building of the inn is perched like a begging dog at the top of a grassy slope going down to the edge of the sea loch. Smooth grey stones, sheep and lambs. We three have rooms in the annexe, a bungalow reached by a flagged path; it seems to be made of cardboard lined with flowered papers, like a doll's house, but all rooms have basins and running water. Every cough, rustle and snore is heard through the thin partitions. Margaret, the maid, is supposed to be seventy but looks fifty, with dark curly hair and a sweet smile full of false teeth. She waits efficiently on the half-dozen tables, and brought us hot-water bottles, benevolently beaming, as we played Scrabble in Eardley's room. Four-course dinner, including pâté and a kirsch soufflé. Colin has with almost embarrassing generosity sent us a whole case of wine. Fellow guests are mostly elderly: two white-haired ladies (one called Miss Mess), a professional-looking figure with tufted whiskers. Dadie rallies Eardley and me a good deal.

May 17th

I'm feeling proud because I've weathered a longish day's walk, about nine miles with picnic lunch, and some steep hills. All spring flowers are out at once – a profusion of primroses, violets, anemones, young ferns of a tender green. The Ord, a brown burn, flows between gnarled oaks, whose sprawling arms are covered in dark velvet moss. Yesterday morning we walked up it, and in the afternoon along the shore to a beach of broken white coral and shells. Margaret was keen for us to take a picnic today, so we made off south along the coast, to the scattered village of Tarskavaig where we ate our sandwiches on the flowery shore. There were a great many very white sheep and plump lambs with black faces and knees, sheepdog puppies, a harem of speckled hens clustered round a rooster, wading birds with orange bills. I detected a church marked on the map at the end of our track and led my incredulous friends to it. There it stood lonely, simple but romantic, hidden in a green basin, above a beach with two or three boats pulled up on it. Slogged home on tired legs to a brilliant and perfectly still evening.

May 19th

An awful shock prevented my writing anything here yesterday. The evening post brought a letter from Joan telling me that Lionel was dead, indeed must have died the day before we left London. I dread that it may have happened in such a way as to embitter Margaret against Dunyusha[1] and so add to her

---

1 A young Polish woman who was a close friend of Lionel's.

unhappiness. Of course it hammers the nail into my own situation a bit further – the rope has swung its deadly weight and carried off another victim who leaves a gaping hole, whose face and voice I so vividly remember, an irreplaceable friend. I can't stop thinking and wondering, and fearing that Margaret may at this moment be lashing herself into a frenzy reading Dunyusha's letters. Now I can't help looking round for the next. Duncan? Raymond? Bunny? Me?

Before this dreadful news came we'd spent a lazy day, taking our lunch only a little way along the shore beyond the coral beach, reading, picnicking, watching seals. Today, more energetic again, a woman taxi-driver with a schoolmistressy, informative style, took us through Broadford to the nearest point to the Cuillins. We walked up the lower slopes of Mount Blaven, a blue morning turned to a slate-grey afternoon, suiting the grimmish scene. After our picnic Dadie and I went on and up to a waterfall dropping past a cliff covered in ferns and primroses into a silent pool. In the middle of the stream I gathered a clump of mountain sorrel, never found before. We saw grouse, and on the way home a golden eagle high above us with two young ones following.

May 20th: 8 a.m.

When I wake each morning I feel a certain surprise that I'm alive. Eardley laid before us a favourite theme about time, as we plodded uphill. He likes to think there is no reason why we shouldn't see the future as well as the past, because of the fact that we are now seeing stars that ceased to exist millions of years ago – a curious inversion. Dadie, with surprising modesty, credits himself only with knowledge of literature, absolutely denies possessing the sort of intellect possessed by most Apostles, the capacity for thinking about abstract ideas, and described his wondering admiration of those of his fellow Apostles who possess it.

We have been having amazing weather – so still and variously beautiful.

May 21st

Yesterday, the hottest yet, we took our taxi-driveress Boadicea to Portree for the first day of Skye Week: this took place on what's called 'the Lump', a green hill hollowed in the middle and going sheer down to the sea on three sides. This perfect arena was crowded with cheerful people watching little girls in kilts dancing Highland flings on neat legs, strong men tossing the caber, strong young women doing tugs of war and innumerable pipers and drummers in full rig. Among the crowd were tiny purple-faced boys (the day was *really* hot) in kilts and sporrans, and many military bandsmen in Highland dress whose noble bearing and swinging stride contrasted with the bad posture of a small collection of the Scottish aristocracy, grouped against a wall, with their bent shoulders and extraordinary poking faces like prehistoric fish, and crooked gaping mouths. An old gentleman near ninety (a Macdonald we heard later) had dignity and charm, but the younger men had stupid greedy grinning faces and stood about awkwardly not knowing what to do with their hands (whereas the men of the lower orders knew exactly what to do with every bit of their bodies), and their tweedy female companions took up ungainly positions on shooting-sticks. A fascinating spectacle to all three of us.

There are three little mongrel dogs in the hotel, offspring of a now dead cairn and a poodle 'who came to tea'. One dear little curly creature called Honey has taken us in tow and comes on all our walks. She has beady eyes looking out from silky creamy-gold curls, and we all love her dearly. This morning we took her on a scrambling walk up hill and down dale, through bog and burn. She likes one to throw a stone for her and then brings it back and lies gazing pleadingly with her nose close beside it till it's thrown again.

So far I've been equal to all our walks and am losing my nervousness except about forgetting my pills.

Scrabble each evening. A conversation about what we thought about when walking. Dadie admitted to deep gloom which could only be dispelled by three cups of strong tea.

May 22nd

Woke on this our last day in Skye to the sound of gently falling rain and clouds hanging on the mountains. In bed I finished the last volume of Edel's biography of Henry James and saw the poor old fellow into his grave after several weeks of depression, fear and resignation by turns, and to me very pitiful mental confusion. So thoughts about death crowd in again.

The Mackenzies came to dinner last night, very successfully. I'm glad that both my companions responded to their niceness. We gathered in my room before and after dinner.

Later today the clouds suddenly rolled back and left such a serene blue sky, such colours everywhere enriched by the rain that we gasped. Dadie and I walked along the shore to the coral beach and beyond, and watched two seals frolicking round islands in the glassy water.

May 25th: West Halkin Street

Back to a life of stress and commotion, if more mentally active. In Skye, we led a life of pure absorption in the visual scene. Margaret was obviously the first person I must make contact with. She came to dinner last night. I hadn't envisaged how it would be. Though as honest in her way as Joan, her reaction was very different. No tears, and emotion only shown in an accentuation of her usual wound-up state. She admitted that she felt 'numb – and almost *less* pain than before Lionel died'. His removal, to live – that's to say sleep – in a flat with Dunyusha had been a cruel blow, she now says, though at the time she told me it had made him nicer to her and so was an advantage. I suggested the number of stairs had been bad for him; she agreed and said he seemed to have helped take his harpsichord up them and was playing it when he got his fatal heart attack. (How soon afterwards?) Dunyusha 'tried artificial respiration' and rang for an ambulance. He was taken to hospital, unconscious I rather think, and the first Margaret knew was being woken by a call from Roger telling her to come to the hospital. She didn't know he was dead until she saw him lying on his bed with his mouth open, still warm. Was Dunyusha there too? Yes, she must have been, because Margaret said she drove her home and threw at her the yellow counterpane in which his body was wrapped.

I wished, but couldn't (yet, anyway), suggest to Margaret that she behave as Queen Alexandra did to Mrs Keppel.

44

Margaret has been giving a number of strange cocktail parties, at which Roger explains and displays Lionel's puzzles. A colleague of Lionel's, Barry, who has been or still is an admirer of Dunyusha's, rang up to ask Margaret to be kind to her because she too was really unhappy. Knowing her good nature, I think she eventually will.

This afternoon I go to Glyndebourne, stay with Duncan at Charleston and we are both to be driven to Crichel for the Bank Holiday weekend.

May 31st

Monteverdi's *Return of Ulysses* was superbly put on and sung, specially by Janet Baker, whose 'Torna, Ulysse!', repeated very softly, rings in my head and brought tears to my eyes. They played the whole opera with all possible passion and even sensuality – none of the prim austerity sometimes given to baroque *opera seria*. The Venetian clothes were dashing and emphasised the masculine pressure urgently converging on Penelope. Monteverdi is the Masaccio, I think, among composers.

I loved being at Charleston again, with beauty everywhere, some of it crumbling; mortality staring from every wall. The essentials are there – hot water, excellent coffee, even if the bathroom pipes are for some reason wrapped in newspapers twenty years old, and when one pulls the plug much of the water cascades down outside. Duncan is amazing in his mental alertness and fresh response. Merely the physical frame is failing. He still has his characteristic style of paradoxically witty reply, but his voice is softer and gentler. He doesn't seem deaf at all. He is looked after by an attractive family, a young painter and sculptress with two small children. The little girl trailed into the garden in bright fancy dress in true Charleston tradition, to show us the donkey and goats; she put her soft arms round my neck to kiss me goodbye.

Our journey to Crichel was very long and tiring, held up for hours at Salisbury by holidaymakers driving their boats and caravans through the blustery rain. Poor Desmond had sat up most of the night writing his review and spent an hour telephoning it to London. He took an exhausted nap before setting out.

Raymond greeted us in a somewhat guvvy manner, saying that Kitty was coming to dinner and that we were late. Of course he was put out by Kitty's having more or less invited herself, and she should have known better than to do so, I fear.

On the way through Salisbury Duncan suddenly remarked from the back, 'I know this is rather a change of subject, but do you know that if you put a baby under a laburnum tree it dies – instantly?'

The characteristics of this long weekend? Appalling weather, hurricane winds and rain, croquet in the rain. Not much music but a lot of talk. I exploded (I'm sorry to say) at being constantly taken up over pronunciation which has now ousted fact and grammar. They pay no attention to what one says, or how, only to how it is pronounced. There was some goading at poor Pat's belief in God on Desmond's part and talk about the solipsism of aristocrats, who don't believe lesser beings 'exist' in the same sense of the word. Instances: Eddy saying, 'I think it's getting rather cold, I shall go to bed,' and switching off the fire before leaving the others. And my story about Rachel[1] asking David to get more butter from the kitchen (for me), and his '*I* don't want any more.' Andrew Murray-Thripland[2] arrived, all charm and smiles and attentiveness to everyone. Raymond has quite ceased to criticise him as he used, and at times the open over-excitement of these four elderly males over this sweet young man was almost embarrassing. But Duncan was more interested in getting visits from David Papes, a tall conventionally handsome but somehow unattractive Canadian staying nearby, who was pronounced 'a crasher' by all the others. Desmond, Duncan and I were left alone with him on Monday night, and I was shocked by his insensitive refusal to take the hint to go at eleven-thirty, and by feeling that he was unfit to take the tender care of Duncan he deserves.

Next morning Desmond exhibited his well-known frenzy to such a degree that we actually missed our train and had to wait

---

1 Cecil.

2 Of the Welsh family, wealthy friend of Pat Trevor-Roper and Julian Jebb, later married.

an hour at Salisbury station. He talks now so compulsively and excitably that he ends by being almost as bad a listener as Raymond. Also the vein of aggression came out when lunching with Kitty 'to say goodbye to Caroline before she went to Ghana'. He launched a violent attack on Angela David and Black Power, and continued his frenzied shadow-boxing, though no one took him up. When I taxed him with this on the way home he actually said he'd 'hoped to sow a seed of doubt'.

June 2nd

A nice evening with Joan, going to *Twelfth Night*, in which Jonathan[1] was a very funny Andrew Aguecheek. Her warmth towards me is very comforting and I make her my first confidante of troubles that are too boring to set down here. I find she told Eardley about my 'attack', so I probably caused him more anxiety rather than less in Skye by not mentioning it to him. Bungling on my part.

June 6th

I bumble along in a state of semi-conciousness, deliberately holding up a hand (as Georgie used to when a little girl) to fend off what I don't want to see. Yet these last days have included moments of 'allrightness'. On Sunday I drove poor thin little Rose to the Kees for lunch, on the eve of her exams. She and Robert had both rung me up to discharge their anxiety, and I had felt feebly inadequate to hold the platter. But the Kee afternoon in its strange way went rather well, in spite of Robert's shaggy harassed look. The children seemed healthy and happy and I introduced a parlour game which was a great success (rain pouring outside). But I wish Cynthia wouldn't wear bellbottom trousers with a heart embroidered on each knee.

Last night flowed by in an effortless stream of talk and laughter with Julian and the Campbells. I wish everything was as easy and enjoyable.

Joan, who drops words of great sense at times, has borne in on me that where 'what one doesn't want to see' is concerned

1 Cecil.

one must *just look at it steadily in the face* and where there's no hope for it, accept it.

At times I rather wish I had got a translation to do. Lifebelts have their uses.

June 10th: Snape

I've been here for two nights for the Aldeburgh Festival. Weather dreadful: cold, grey and wet. Hills relaxed and calming. Other guests: Bob,[1] who came when I did, and Des yesterday. Bob's continuous talking is rather more than a joke and Heywood says to him openly: 'Bob, do stop talking and *listen*,' which he receives with great good nature. He has a snapping motion of the mouth which makes him extra-unintelligible, and takes snuff incessantly with a snuffling sound, leaving an ugly brown stain on his upper lip. There's something dry about his remarks, something snobbish, intellectually or otherwise, but beneath this one observes heart and kindness as well as the desire to impart information. Des comments on Bob's compulsive talking and does just the same himself. Neither listen, so Anne, Heywood and I tend to fall silent. On a walk yesterday during a dry spell we were discussing people's bad habits (such as Bob's over-talking). Desmond said one ought to tell people about them, and I longed to mention Crichel's mania about correcting one's pronunciation, but thought better of it. He said 'they' had cured Raymond of his 'I mean I mean I mean' and 'heavy sighing'. This was given as an example of how it *was* possible to improve after fifty.

Concerts – Fischer-Dieskau singing superbly (Schubert and Britten) the first night, and last night a mixed programme including some Danish works and a setting of Ronsard songs by Lennox Berkeley. Bob and I both loved this. Desmond was curiously down on it. Formerly he has crabbed Lennox for being too flimsy, now it was because he was trying too hard to be strong. I get the impression he doesn't much *want* to like his music, but can't imagine why. Luckily Bob and I had both overflowed with enthusiasm to Freda,[2] and I think that pleased her.

---

1 Gathorne-Hardy.

2 Berkeley.

June 13th

Well, I took the bull by the horns, and Desmond round the garden, in a bright spell, and discussed the situation caused by my health problem. I've had one or two uneasy moments since the original attack and my whole attitude to life – and death – has shifted in its bed. I told Desmond that I had no desire to conceal the facts, but that I felt it was impossible at this stage to know whether I might or might not feel up to being his sole prop on a motoring holiday. I gather Jack[1] might still come, in which case I dare say we shall set forth. In any case it has given me a loophole.

June 17th

Solitude of summer begins; mighty few friends remain in London. I see a lot of Joan. She said to me yesterday that she believed she – and perhaps Janetta – were the only ones among my friends who realised 'what went on inside'. Everyone thinks of me as 'a great enjoyer'. *Tant mieux*, and anyway so I am in a way. Certainly I'm enjoying reading Quentin on Virginia[2] for the second (and first proper) time. Also the rather querulous reviews. There are so many things I want to read, or re-read, like Swift. But as to Virginia, what the reviewers (except Raymond) fail to see is how *moving* the story is, perhaps because of Quentin's admirable and amused detachment. I do find the characters alive and don't think it's wholly because I knew them. And dashing ahead to the end of his next volume, I wonder what thoughts and feelings led up to her suicide, and how (or if) she prevented someone as close as Leonard from observing them. What intense pain she must have suffered! And what courage and also what intense cruelty to inflict what she did on Leonard.

June 19th

Yesterday was a very wet Sunday and I was kept in London (as I shall be next weekend) by concerts. Tremendous rehearsal, over three hours long, on Saturday afternoon, doing the

---

1 Lambert.

2 Quentin Bell: *Virginia Woolf: A Biography.*

glorious Beethoven Mass with choir and soloists. I took Sunday at a steady tempo. With Joan to the National Portrait Gallery in the afternoon, to sup with her at night. That strange whispering ghost, Justin Vulliamy,[1] to tea to talk about book-binding. Joan and I advance in intimacy and there's almost nothing we can't say to each other.

June 20th

Very very nice visit from Eardley last night, who contrived to convey affection and support in a way that deeply touched me. I really do love him. He says Jack is definitely not coming on the projected French trip, and from what he told me about his character it's perhaps just as well. But he gives me comfort about Desmond as a travelling companion.

Stanley has just paid me a visit and we had a jolly talk chiefly about his problems, and 'boredom'. Is boredom a special state? I'm not at all sure. Its chief symptom in his case seems to be lack of concentration. He very kindly brought me flowers. I know I didn't give such thought to elderly friends when I was young, and I find it very appealing, petrol to feed the failing engine.

June 21st

Waking in the small hours I read *Jacob's Room* for about an hour. There is so much colour in Virginia's writing – actual colour: pink, yellow, green. Also of course sound, and even smell. I opened novels by Morgan,[2] Bunny[3] and Gerald[4] at random, and found practically none of these directly sensory adjectives.

Last night my orchestra[5] gave a concert in the church of St Bartholomew the Great, where David and Rachel[6] were married and I've not been there since. The church was icy and had no lavatories. I was glad of my little bottle of whisky and

---

1 Assistant mosaicist to Boris Anrep.
2 E. M. Forster.
3 David Garnett.
4 Brenan.
5 I played second violin in the London Medical Orchestra.
6 Cecil.

slice of cherry cake. The freemasonry of a concert is always enjoyable.

June 22nd

I took Rose out to dinner last night and tried to cheer her up in preparation for today's exams, her last. How do people manage to eat so often in restaurants? Dinner for two cost £7. Joan, who rings me daily with a mixture of affection, grotesque flattery and tactlessness, thought that I had had a good effect on Rose. I said I wished I had some work. 'Well, you've turned every stone,' she remarked briskly, and a little later, '*I* should go mad if I had nothing to do but read books and see people.' I should go mad if I had nothing to do but buy clothes and go to osteopaths! But I didn't say so.

June 28th

Pecking round, like a hen, for grains of comfort or pleasure. Given the right mood, of course, a great deal can be extracted. Rose made me very happy indeed with a postcard showing that she had been aware of how I had tried to support her through her exams and that it had been a help. It is such a pleasure if a friend understands what one is trying to say, exactly as it is meant.

A telephone call from Julian, just back from Spain, was another pleasure, and I hope to see him tomorrow. Yesterday Frances Phipps came to lunch and delighted me with her sensitivity to visual things, also her appreciation of such people as Eardley. She said of Joan, 'I don't think we speak the same language. Am I right?' This is an awkwardness about Joan.

June 30th: Kitty West's

Where I came by Mini yesterday. A good deal has happened, in purely psychological terms, to give me food for thought and two bad nights. On Thursday I dined at Eardley's alone with him and Raymond. I had looked forward to this meeting with old friends, and rather expected some solicitude from Raymond. But no, he entered in a rebarbative and slightly petulant mood, greeted us perfunctorily, and very soon said to me rather aggressively: 'I hope you're not going to throw Desmond over. I'm scared stiff that he'll try and join our party.' More in the same strain, which quite took me aback, and prevented my asking (or thinking of it even) why on earth, if he was so scared, had he chosen a date and a route almost identical with Desmond's which he had known about long ago, as it was discussed with him. Silently simmering for some time, I finally said, 'I'm really rather shocked by your egocentricity. I'd expected some sympathy for having to take Desmond on single-handed, now that Jack's backed out.' 'Oh,' said Raymond, 'it never occurred to me you wouldn't want to.' F: 'Well, I think that's rather unimaginative. I love Desmond dearly, but I know his reputation as a fellow-traveller and naturally dread three weeks alone with him, and hope still to find a third. But I don't want to let him down, and I can't bear people feeling rejected and unwanted.'

I got a strong impression of Raymond's self-centredness, but my responses to it filled me with such guilt later on that I lay awake for hours, and was much mollified when Eardley rang up and said I had been splendid, having himself received an impression of Raymond's unfriendliness to him personally. He said he had practically not spoken to him (E.), though they hadn't met for ages, and 'not for want of trying on his part'. (I remember Raymond saying he thought Eardley was 'lonely and short of friends'. But I think it's quite untrue.)

Anyway I resolved to be more amiable, told them about a visit from an extraordinary pair of Bloomsbury-addict hippies, and asked about Finland, etc. There was much talk of how the pleasure of travel had quite gone because 'so many people do it, moving about the whole time. Why do they do it?' Why does *he*? It was typical talk of the privileged resenting the encroachments of the masses. We sat as the light faded, throwing only a pale oblong on to a picture by the door, and the enveloping dusk softened the disquiet in the room. Talk of books. Mary, who can swallow a good deal of trash, found Cecil Beaton's Memoirs 'too trashy', and no one I've met believes his story of his amour with Greta Garbo. But Raymond believes it all: 'There was some bad spelling and grammar, but I found it immensely readable; it was about a lot of people I knew.'

Next morning I telephoned and tried to make amends.

July 5th

The Desmond holiday is beginning to take on a pleasant aspect.

On Saturday last I was bidden to lunch at Crichel; Kitty was arranging an exhibition. So there I was as usual, sitting down among five homosexuals. Julian, praise be, was one. Raymond was obviously depressed, and I got the feeling (as Julian says he did too) that he was finding Desmond virtually unliveable with. Poor Des is aware of this, Julian thinks, and said to Julian that Raymond never listened to anything he said or laughed at any of his jokes. I've asked Raymond to a tête-à-tête dinner next week. As for Des, he really is a caution. He said he had a lot to talk to me about, but after lunch he suddenly began worrying about Moses's paw, hurt months ago, and saying he must take him in to the vet. He hurried off to telephone and came back later, when I suggested he combine it with a visit to Kitty's show. 'Oh no-o-o-o. I couldn't leave Moses in the car. But if I go now, will you promise to be here when I get back, Fanny?' I said I would if I could be left quietly reading while the others (all constitutional nappers) napped.

Julian talked to me for a while and then I sat happily reading. Des flew in later (the vet had done nothing to Moses except say 'Come back in six months'). 'I've got something *terrible* to ask you, Fanny, *really* terrible.' This was that I should convey one of his huge loudspeakers to London in my Mini. F: 'But do you think it'll go in?' D: 'Let's try and see.' So, puffing and scarlet, he hauled and pushed, and tried the object in all eight different positions it was capable of. Finally, after infinite struggling, it was jammed in (though my heart sank as I felt sure it would rattle and bump all the way to London), whereupon Desmond at once said: 'Oh! I've just realised it's quite unnecessary. There'll by much more room in Paul's car and he can leave it at my door.' So out it came again. This is what Raymond aptly describes as 'heavy weather'. But all is not well between Des and Raymond, I'm afraid.

Another Des story from Bill Pollock. At a concert of Bruno Walter he fiercely 'shushed' two ladies in front of him. Then

53

one made matters worse by taking some paper and writing on it, with accompanying noise. More shushing. One lady turned round and said, 'I am Mrs Bruno Walter, Signora Toscanini was just writing you an apology.'

July 10th

Mary[1] has written saying she has booked me a ticket to Majorca in a month's time, so after a long spell of yes-no, yes-no, I guess I shall go, and try to exercise my willpower by leading my own sort of life there, not theirs. Mary says sweetly I need never go in the boat unless I want to.

Angelica came to see me one cold dank day (as many have been) with plump beautiful arms bare to the shoulder. Sweet Sophie played to me really charmingly on her recorder with long confident fingers, and obviously enjoying it.

July 13th

Yesterday summer suddenly began. I drove north to collect Sophie from school and take her to her music lesson, where with a small mushroom hat on her pretty curls she played again very sweetly with her young teacher, and later was joined by an attractive dark girl called Fabia. After three and a half hours of the darling girl's company I went round to pick up Raymond and brought him back to dinner.

Raymond (like Des but in a different way) is a *caution*. After my own and Julian's observations and his own confession of despondency, after his apparent eagerness for a tête-à-tête dinner, I thought we might have *some* sort of human conversation, about our lives. But no; he showed not the slightest interest in mine and didn't ask a single question about it. Nor any desire to talk about himself. Just books, books, books. I almost begin to hate the subject and his adjective of high praise: 'bookish'. Our talk was chiefly of Henry James; and there were the usual comments about the stupidity of most people and the appalling badness of all modern art. So of course I gave in. I do believe he enjoyed our evening, which I must say I found

---

1 Dunn.

54

inhuman. He is quite unaware of other people. Of Julian, who worried so about him and is so tortured at times, he simply said how marvellously high-spirited and entertaining he had been at the weekend and how he hoped he had enjoyed himself. He cannot *accept*. Perhaps Morgan's famous saying[1] should be altered to 'only accept'.

July 20th

Raymond asked me to re-read 'The Beast in the Jungle' and I did so, beginning with a sensation of floundering through feathers, but finally gripped. The Beast as revealed by confrontation with true grief is the hero's recognition that he had never been able to love wholeheartedly and it was now too late. Perhaps he had unconsciously known all along about himself – this dreadful incapacity. It made sense all of a sudden, and I felt this story was a *cri de coeur* from H.J. himself, who (according to Edel) only became aware of physical passion at a late age, and then for men, and was probably unable to give way to it. I was moved by this, and also felt it might give me an insight into the spook element in H.J.'s work as a whole – perhaps it often represents his unconscious self-knowledge.

I wrote all this off to Raymond on the spur of the moment and this morning he rang up to thank me 'for my most interesting letter'. H.J., he thought, was absolutely content with his dedication to his art. He had not recognised his homosexuality until late in life but it was evident early on in his descriptions of handsome young men. He repeatedly dismissed the story and my views of it.

More 'bookishness' – I devoted yesterday almost entirely to reading Quentin's second volume, lent me by Stanley, who has just lunched here to discuss it.[2] He has many criticisms, which I'm trying to dent. I think it first-rate; I'm dazzled and carried away by the blazing truth of it all. Reading it was a tremendous experience. I started the evening before, and read steadily all day, except for a satisfactory check-up with Dr Moynihan, and

---

1 'Only connect.'
2 Of Virginia Woolf biography.

55

then read on till bed-time, when Stanley rang up to hear my reactions. He boggles at my word 'truth', and wades into philosophical waters, turning a pale pink. All this has made my life far from dull lately, and I have not written about other events. Many delightful and communicative meetings with Julian; evenings at *Hedda Gabler* and hearing Caballé in *Traviata*, a starry occasion for all its small defects.

A thought about Virginia and Henry James: *she* couldn't accept sex, but she could and did love Leonard thoroughly and with abandon, so that that Beast was not in her jungle. I'm pleased that Quentin got Ralph so right, including the Tidmarsh trio and his attitude to saving Carrington's life. Judgement as well as truth.

July 21st

To a Handel opera with Des in Goldsmiths' Hall. In the entr'acte he suddenly remarked (apropos of I forget what): 'Joan says you don't want to live, and I must say if that's true you keep up a very good face.' I felt faintly annoyed with Joan, and as if she was trying to encourage the death-wish in me. In any case I don't want her spreading abroad what I say to her in gloomy moments, and we have agreed that what we tell each other is totally confidential. I am conscious of both life- and death-wish. At the moment the life-wish is uppermost.

July 25th

Joan comes to dinner tonight. How strange — and is it purely fortuitous? — that I woke at five-thirty gloomy this morning, all my recent cheerfulness sunk. Is it pure imagination that she in some way *expects* me to despair, 'not to want to live', is in truth my 'little angel of death'? I can't imagine what she would say, good kind little friend that she is, if she read these words.

A weekend with Judy[1] did not depress me, it never does. Her wits bright, and her energy stupendous, she wields a heavy fork and digs her garden at eighty-one. A heavy hot still mist covered the landscape and shrouded the shorn sheep on Romney Marsh very dismally.

---

1 Rendel, my eldest sister.

Appalling political crisis again, squaring up of industry and capital to one another. I think everyone now realises that the 'workers' hold all the cards. We have had no newspapers for several days, and piles of smelly rubbish begin to collect on the pavements. It seems idle to assume one will ever get out of England; BEA is already having a one-day strike.

July 31st: Snape

Heywood lent me Morgan's *Maurice* to read. I didn't find it so much 'bad', as lacking in goodness' in any shape or form. There's a certain sogginess about young men and homosexual love – and oddly about 'gentlemen' and gamekeepers. Also about the Greeks. Is it just because they were so candidly homosexual? Virginia pined to be allowed into the sanctum of Greek language and literature. In fact they were pretty bloodthirsty and fascist and beastly to women. The thing I most shrank from in *Maurice* was its way of conveying that women are monsters and rather disgusting. A battalion of 'queers' came for a drink at Snape, after the ballet, and one who talked to me was both handsome and charming, but Harriet said she resented the feeling that as a group they thought all us females 'disgusting'. Harriet and Lucy, both with husbands and children, looked anything but 'disgusting' – happy and pretty. Amazing contrast between the two sons-in-law: Tim,[1] almost gracefully gawky, endearing, beaming, tumbling over his words in his eagerness; and lower-class Scotch Geordie,[2] splendidly handsome, with jet-black hair and eyes, flashing white teeth; gentle in the special manner of large strong men, with a low, very seductive, very Scotch voice. He is extremely articulate and intelligent so it seems when one talks to him, ready always for discussion, yet somewhere within is whatever has swallowed the supreme mumbo-jumbo of Mohammedanism. With golden-haired Fanny and Algy[3] (talking exquisite Italian to each other) and little Abdullah (as Justin now has to be called – Geordie is Aziz and

---

1 Behrens, married to Harriet.
2 Married to Lucy.
3 Children of Harriet and Tim.

57

Lucy Rabbia), the house and garden were like a Victorian story-tale, burgeoning with life and happy mess.

Heywood and I took two long walks. I feel peculiarly at my ease with him. When I thought of this today (back at home) I felt a sort of shock at having assumed intimacy, having seemed to intrude – but perhaps fictitiously – into someone else's mind and feelings. How well do I really know my friends? I think I know Joan, Janetta, Julian, Eardley. Then suddenly one steps back with a feeling of strangeness and uncertainty.

August 3rd

The 'richest' evening ever of talk with Julian, we both agreed. He arrived overflowing with it – all sorts of topics public and private. It was a gloriously communicative stretch of time – Ulster, industrial problems, strikers, the rich, Janetta, Peter Eyre, what I'm to do about Desmond, work, what he's to do about the Commune.

Desmond comes tonight after the Prom so I suppose something will be settled. Julian advises me to hold out; Heywood thinks I must give in. Knowing my weaknesses I shall probably do the latter. Talk, talk, it's pretty well all I do these days. I feel like a thin-skinned haggis bursting with things to say.

I went to the Prom the other night with Peter Eyre.[1] The Mad Hatter in person with his large questing nose, shock of perfectly straight light hair, yet there's a certain gentle appeal in his expression. We sat in a box high above the vast auditorium of the Albert Hall – the orchestra seemed a very long way away and the cellos no bigger than violas – Peter had a pair of very Mad Hatterish opera-glasses, long and black, with which he raked the audience missing nothing – either in Tippett's new symphony or in the audience. He came back to eat with me, and sat down like a child expecting instant food. Easy talk about music, acting (nervousness and learning parts), family life (they are RCs). I like what I know of him, but a core of reserve remains hidden.

Then last night another Prom, with Desmond. I must practise

---

1 The actor.

taking him more calmly; as it is, even when all goes smoothly, I am left quivering slightly.

August 8th

Desmond has just been here to a most successful 'working lunch', at his sweetest and most adaptable. We have made a rough scheme of our movements in France to both our satisfaction – and I am scarcely quivering at all.

Weekend at Cranborne, where were Hugh and Mirabel[1] celebrating their engagement with a to me slightly distressing brouhaha. They have a right to fuss and flummery, if that's what they want, and her brother Sebastian wants to give them a jolly party for young friends in the evening, but that's not enough – there must be a reception for two hundred or so at the Ritz or even the House of Lords (she suggested, but they aren't entitled to that), and lists of presents at shops. She arrived clutching a copy of *Bride's*, and wearing a long flowered skirt to the ground. They are, I think, very keen on each other and smacking kisses resounded through the house. On Friday night I became aware through deep sleep of someone moving cautiously in my room. Then the bedside light was switched on and I rolled over to see Hugh, stark naked, modestly dipping below bed-level. 'Oh my God! I'm so sorry I woke you up. You won't say anything will you?' I said of course I wouldn't, and slipped back into oblivion. Rather comic though. And does he really suppose David and Rachel don't know they go to bed together, when Rachel even got them EQ's[2] cottage to pass their last holiday in alone together.

Walks with Rachel and with David, a sopping Sunday. Lunch at the big house at Crichel with the Martins. I sat next to a young Lord Binning from whom with a slow and careful corkscrew I extracted that he believed in Flying Saucers ('had seen them' even), was a friend of John Michel, and subscribed to his unorthodox theories about stone circles and 'lines of power' down which the Saucers moved. He gazed at me sideways like a horse about to shy.

---

1 Walker.
2 Elsie Queen, daughter of novelist Leo Myers.

A visit to the Trees – Anne Tree[1] has great charm, like Andrew's,[2] and I like her. She told us about interviewing girls in prison. Remorse was unknown, only annoyance at 'being caught'. She believes in hard sentences for first offenders as a way of frightening them off crime – her sister Elizabeth in giving them a chance, before they have been toughened up by contact with old offenders. I'm sure Elizabeth is right. The Crichels came to drinks. I have a feeling David becomes slightly less rigid in his views and religious beliefs as he grows older. He told me he didn't think Hugh was a Christian, but was glad he wanted to be married in church, recognising that it might be to please him and Rachel. On Sunday night he read aloud a new chapter of his book on the Cecil family; once more I greatly enjoyed it; once more Rachel's dear little shining brown head nodded asleep.

Got home to a visit from Stanley. Spent the evening finishing reading Stuart Hampshire – I don't think I've got much out of him except revived interest in Spinoza. In bed I read Bertie Russell's summary of Spinoza's views, which doesn't tally at all with Hampshire's. Interested by Hampshire throwing off casually (unlike himself, for he often labours his points) a view about sentimentality which overlaps mine, but doesn't I think cover the whole subject. With a supposedly painful emotion, such as regret, remorse or sympathetic pain, he thinks that enjoying the *idea* that you are feeling it constitutes sentimentality. I worked this out myself long ago – but I think there's also room for sentimentality with emotions that are not painful. Perhaps Mirabel is sentimental about her engagement, for example. Though there's no mistake about enjoying the emotion, you are enjoying a different aspect of it, or for a different reason. I like philosophers to think about such subjects instead of their endless emphasis on propositions, and epistemology, and I remember how much time Ralph and I used to spend talking about subjects like sentimentality or jealousy. No one does it much now – is it because we're all too old? I must try them on Stanley.

Margaret rang up, and harped somewhat hysterically on

1 David Cecil's cousin.

2 Devonshire.

money and property. I couldn't help feeling that she was in some way enjoying her new power and financial independence rather than regretting Lionel.

August 11th

Tomorrow I'm off to Majorca. Yesterday on the spur of the moment I drove down to lunch with Alix,[1] and found her leading her self-contained life though it's becoming somewhat 'cribbed and confined' by her increasingly poor sight. But at once we got on to conversation that was all far more absorbing than anything said at Raymond's last night, when the four of us – Paul,[2] Honey Harris,[3] Raymond and I – got involved in a sort of petit-point chit-chat, about the difficulty of getting one's comforts these days and lack of sympathy for everything modern. A withered dry, lavender-bag exchange which left me bored and even a little sickened, not so much because of its lack of stimulation, as because of the condescension and smugness and total lack of humility or humanity in it.

August 13th: Alcanada, Majorca

The switchover has become so familiar that it has perhaps lost some of its magic. As for the place, I had forgotten its beauty and the real, solid charm and good taste of the house. The view across the bay, the island with its lighthouse straight in front, and the wooded promontory to the left. The high barn-like sitting-room painted Ricketts blue to dado height, furnished with comfortable chairs covered in local stuff with white fringes. I even have the same bedroom as before, in which I've just slept away an hour or more of the afternoon. The heat is moist and heavy rather than fierce, with a hint of storm in the air. This morning it was the routine I remember so well. Juan the boatman, who looks more like a German than a Spaniard, rowed us out in the boat to bathe, lie on blue cushions and drink

---

1 Strachey.
2 Levy.
3 An elderly spinster who lived in Chelsea.

white wine. The Briggses[1] come in two days, and Mary doesn't 'put on dog' as she would say, and wears a touching chauffeur's cap of hard shiny straw on her scanty locks. I have had quantities of books pressed on me. The countryside is burnt biscuit colour, but relieved by plenty of olives and holm-oaks, with only a few oleanders and geraniums in flower. I feel relaxed, calm and unstimulated; ready for what may come.

August 14th

Expanding slowly, like a Japanese flower in water, I've begun to enjoy myself in a simple physical way I would hardly have thought still possible. I love getting into the sea and swimming about, and it gave me a certain pleasure to find that my effortless backstroke kept me abreast of Mary's snorting crawl. I enjoy meals on the wide terrace, wearing very few clothes. Yesterday afternoon I pegged out an individual course by walking across the burnt fields to a farm where enormous black and white pigs lay smiling under the shade of a carob, among some tame pigeons and a few hens, but almost no flowers.

I must admit to an awareness of alien values, which makes me want to go off alone sometimes. Last evening I walked up the sloping valley behind the house, towards the hills. Instant peace, tinkling sheepbells and a farm dog barking in the distance. I picked my way between thistles and stones, and came back with a handful of flowers.

The Briggses, Asa and Susan, were due on the last plane, and though Mary wanted to 'get some sleep in' before they arrived and then come down to meet them we started playing patience and in the end stayed awake till they arrived about one. First impressions: he is very square, with thick curly brown hair, jutting jaw and subfusc North Country accent. She is more disconcerting – tallish, with an oval medieval face that should be wearing a wimple, as she seems to realise by having her hair dyed an unnatural yellow and lifeless as flax, and drawing it over an obvious pad on the top of her head, with a dark purplish line where it meets her forehead. The effect is distressing. They

---

1 Professor Asa Briggs and his wife Susan.

were both talkative and friendly and wolfed down several whiskies; I think she's shy.

August 17th

Briggses are really very easy. Great readers, intelligent, talkative, drinkers – what I'm not sure about is whether or no they have social ambitions. Today being judged suitable by Juan we took the boat round the headland to bathe, returning for lunch on the terrace. As well as white wine, the dreaded cocktails made of rum, lemon juice and honey were dispensed, and made everyone both jolly and boring. The Briggses hold their drinks well; Mary is reduced to 'er – and – er' and 'so on and so forth'. I stuck to white wine and the bathe was delicious in a clean peacock-blue sea.

After tea Philip drove me to look at a little very old and not particularly interesting church in Alcudia and then to the Protestant cemetery to look for the tombs of a couple who had both committed suicide because she was dying anyway. We were taken there by a ghoulish old man who pointed to a bare piece of unmarked earth, where lay, he said, '*un hombre y una mujer*'. Only this morning he had seen a corpse in the water of the Puerto. Had he been drowned when swimming? I asked. '*No se sabe*', and he did his best to imitate by macabre attitudes what the corpse looked like.

Bridge for the other four after dinner. I happily read and play patience.

August 18th

Visitors in the evening – a curious trio from the mountains, said to be 'rich'. One was a fruit farmer, a youngish trendily dressed American ex-banker called Ben, with a glamorous Eurasian-French mistress Yannick, and a friend, also American with a flashing smile full of marvellous teeth, a slow very deep voice, and dark hair in a long tail behind like a matador, a man of considerable charm. I sat next to him at dinner and he told me his ideas about bringing up 'my two children' and that he was a painter. Asa was quite interesting about his problems as Vice-Chancellor of Sussex University. He makes no bones about having humble origins, and Susan seems to be a farmer's daughter who got herself to Oxford.

For the dinner-party we ate one of Philip's active Roman-nosed sheep, as tough as boot leather. For the most part the food is good and simple – vegetable soups, eggs, salads, mashed potatoes and Minorcan cheese. Drink abounds and is sloshed down in quantities.

August 19th

A battle with a mosquito last night kept me awake, and this morning a high wind is blowing and there are grey skies. Yesterday was hot, blue, settled. We took the boat to a further bay and lunched there. I feel gratifyingly strong, and enjoyed diving into the deep blue-green water and swimming to shore, where I sat on a seaweed-covered ledge. The others' idea of swimming is to circle the boat once or twice, then scramble up the ladder and drink. Today Philip got on to politics and history with Asa. Mary said to me suddenly that 'eighty per cent of people in England had plenty to live on, everything they needed, and a car. Right?' I *had* to contradict her. In fact she doesn't usually like to talk about such unpleasant subjects.

August 20th

Grey, cool morning. Philip, Mary and I walked down to the tree-clad point, where quite rough seas were beating. I'm beginning to feel I've had enough of living among alien values; even the Briggses revolve in a kaleidoscope taking different shapes and colours. Asa is a fat, greedy fellow, a voracious reader and card-player; clever of course and a kind good man. Susan's endlessly level tones begin to *donner sur mes nerfs* a little. She has what she calls 'tummy trouble' and she has been talking coyly about 'Tum', personalising it as it were. ('Tum thinks a campari would be just the thing.') But she's not stupid, or malicious.

August 26th: England

Bewildering change after only two nights in my own nest, during which Gerald and Lynda and Julian came to dinner. Gerald was in good form and looked well and young; Lynda on the other hand too thin, large-eyed and overwrought. I was able to agree with Gerald about almost everything – the horrible selfishness of the rich, and what was wrong with our present money-based civilisation. They are staying with the Pritchetts, and praised their kindness and happy marriage. V.S.P.[1] says that 'there's no conversation in London.' What on earth does he mean? Where else will he find better? Also that 'there are no meetings between literary people.'

On Thursday I drove down to Thorington, a journey of horrifying noise and ugliness, clatter, heat. I found Shirley (pregnant) here alone with Margaret, and the house in the hands of myriads of jolly workmen, stripping the plaster and practically putting their heads through walls. I have brought a large pie and bottle of whisky, hoping to get at least one good meal. As the house was full of small black flies I persuaded Margaret to get a spray, and attack them; she said, '*I'm* not fussy.' She was looking in the dirty clothes basket for a sheet to use as a table-cloth when Dicky[2] and Denis[3] came to supper before taking us to a Donizetti concert at a large house bought by Robert Carrier and newly done up in vulgar primary colours. This was a jolly evening and we had a decent meal. She is reluctant to give me any of my own whisky ('Would you like some *sherry?*'), though tippling away at it herself all day long. Poor thing, I'm sure she's unhappy.

We had some delightful trio-playing, and this she enjoys so much that she developed a stubborn desire to play 'just one last trio' before the others left last night. After some still warm days, when one could get out of the cold house and lie in the sunny garden and read, it turned grey and icy yesterday and we huddled in coats. A walk through rich warm golden fields of cut corn – extraordinarily beautiful with the now dark green hedges and trees, and lowering grey sky.

But oh how sad this house is. I make a sort of camp in my dusty room, wash out the dirty basin, pull the tattered, looped,

---

1 V.S. Pritchett, novelist, writer of short stories and literary critic.

2 Chopping.

3 Dicky's partner.

thin white curtains and creep into bed, egotistically concerned with my own comfort.

I'm writing in bed, the morning of our last day. I'm driving Margaret back in my Mini tomorrow. It is Bank Holiday today and we have of course run out of bread and cheese, our mainstay. One cauliflower is all that remains.

August 30th

The weather recovered, the others all left, and Margaret and I were alone for a warm sunny Bank Holiday Monday. We took a long walk through ripe cornfields to the broken bridge over the Stour. Margaret walked so slowly that, drag my feet as I would, I had to sit and wait for her quite often. But she relaxed, and this made all the difference in the world. She was so nice, so companionable, that I could forgive her her extraordinary habit of using her hand instead of a knife and fork to eat risotto and cauliflower. I drove her back to Golders Green yesterday and was touched when she showed me charming recent photos of Lionel. I said, 'I hope you'll be able to forget these last painful years and remember the rest.' She said, 'I'm trying to but of course it does soften the blow.' In her own way she faces facts as much as Joan does.

Little Rose has got into University College, with distinction in French. Hurrah! I had a sweet letter from Mary, flattering in a way that made me feel guilty about my acidulated jottings. 'We all miss you and you know P. and I love you.' She speaks affectionately too about Philip, worrying whether he isn't well. I hide my guilty critical head.

Stanley has been here this morning. He really is a dear fellow.

September 1st

Somewhat piqued by Gerald's saying he thought I had seemed 'tired or ill' when he came to dinner last week, I made every effort to be lively when I dined at the Pritchetts to meet him and Lynda, and we did in fact have a very jolly evening. The Pritchetts delighted me by seeming so flourishing and at the same time warmly welcoming. I do hope we can keep the dialogue going. V.S.P. was in high spirits and brilliance, Gerald very much under the weather of a heavy cold.

September 5th

Henrietta came, without Sophie, whom she had left at school. She explained her attitude to the new arrangement[1] and I found it comprehensible and realistic. She looked lovely, sweet and gay, told of wildly successful holidays, and after going over all the possibilities, the most hopeful seemed to board Sophie during the week with Sarah Montagu, mother of two children, one a friend of Sophie's who goes to the same school.

Stanley came to dinner and we listened to *Aida* from Munich, marvellously sung, but the thread broke in the final scene in the tomb and we were fobbed off by a record of the detestable Callas singing through a saucepan-scraper. Stanley talked a good deal about being rich. I see that his parents are immensely so, which I hadn't realised, so that my attacks on 'the rich' put him on the defensive. He is half-boastful, about 'my shirt-maker' (after which there is a noticeable pause for reaction) and the expensive restaurant his father took him to, half-guilty.

My attitude to life changes all the time as I feel myself coming to the end of it, and I think about it and try to analyse these changes. I think I *float* more, in that the earth seems further below, less important; on the other hand I cling desperately to mental activity.

September 7th

This nightmare world of gangsters, guerillas, political murder, in which nine wretched Israeli athletes were held up by masked gunmen for long hours during the Olympic Games, only to be shot in the end – the police of the world unable to save them – sickens the heart and makes one restless.

September 9th

In preparation for going to France next week – including Nohant – I've been re-reading Maurois on George Sand with delight. With all her extravagances and absurdities I love her

---

1 For school.

independence, *bonté*, love of life (skeletons, flowers, fossils, dressing-up, grandchildren, marionettes), and am moved by relationships such as that between her and Flaubert. When she got him at last to leave Croisset and come to Nohant, he dressed in Spanish female attire and danced a fandango. I've not read French for pleasure for some time and am revelling in it. I read much more these days than I used to, having more time, and often the need for information possesses me, so that, reading in the night, I creep next door in my nightgown and look up genealogical trees or meanings of words.

It is grey, wet, cold. There is small comfort to be got from looking in any direction. Happy babies, like Nicky's Noah, pierce one's heart because they don't know what they are in for. I've thought at odd moments how difficult things have been for Gerald and Lynda.

September 10th

Why do I hurry out and buy the Sunday papers, only to have my heart go pitter-pat with agitation, even fear? They call up a view of human beings all glossily dressing in trendy clothes and fitting our families into horrible carefully planned passage-like slits, while all around as far as the eye can see across the world and beyond, stretches nightmare, endless nightmare? The possibility that the next lot of guerillas will get hold of an atom bomb and use it for blackmail was thrown out by some writer in the press.

September 14th

In the train from Waterloo. First lap of the French journey. Georgia definitely comes part time. Julian to lunch off the last eggs and bacon, the last human interchange under pressure of time. Now I sit in a grubby train heading for Salisbury and Desmond. I wouldn't take any bet at all as to how I shall feel about this enterprise in seventeen days' time, but at the moment I'm determined to make a success of it if it's humanly possible.

Later: Crichel

Desmond was at the station looking anxiously up the platform. Frenzy began almost at once: in the narrowest thoroughfare of Salisbury he drew up on a yellow line and dashed off to buy tissues and a notebook, causing a bottleneck and two visits from a traffic warden. First efforts on my part towards detachment, dissociation; *calme*, *luxe* and *volupté* can bide their time. There were of course great piles of letters, parcels, bills to be paid, suitcases to unpack from Edinburgh and re-pack for France. I wonder if we shall catch the boat? To leave Des in peace I took Moses for a walk through the woods. We went to Kitty's for supper, but I'm sure he'll be up till two packing. Found Chopin's letters to George Sand and read them in bed.

September 16th: Pont-Audemer (Auberge des Vieux Puits)

Waiting for breakfast in a small clean room nearly filled by a large bed. Glorious morning yesterday and also today though it's fast fading. Des came down to breakfast yesterday five minutes before starting time, and the drive to Southampton was beautiful. Mercifully the sea was calm, as the crossing seemed endless and the slow hours passed in a daze, partly sitting in hot sun on deck. Then horror slowly dawned on Desmond's face – 'O – o – o – OH!' He was almost sure he had left all his traveller's cheques behind. Dozens of plans were made, rejected, re-made. Should he telephone Jack and ask him to get a locksmith? Have them posted to Bunny? Send them out with Georgia? Telephone his bank for more? I don't yet know which he'll do.

We had a delicious dinner last night, yet not heavy, and I slept like a baby. This beamy old hotel is built round a courtyard, old wells and tanks full of trout; looking out I see a figure in a shiny red dressing-gown, somehow monk-like with its fringe of hair round the central baldness, stooping apologetically as he goes in search of breakfast. He looks out of his window later (I by now sitting under the green drapery of a weeping ash surrounded by flower-beds, mill-wheels and white chairs and tables) to say that he is writing a letter to his bank. One good job is that as he has made such a howler himself I hope my sins will be forgiven me. Maids stump in and out, carrying huge piles of dirty bed-linen.

Last night we bowled out of the belly of our big boat between 6 and 7 p.m. and got here very quickly.

September 17th: Chartres

The blue morning sky at Pont-Audemer vanished while I sat waiting for Desmond under my willow tree, and the picnic we just had time to buy before the shops shut at twelve had to be eaten in the car, and without any forks, knives etc., jellied egg flying about. Stopped at Conches to look at a church with fine stained glass and then at Maintenon to see the château. In front of it stretched under a cold grey sky, an ornamental water spanned by a ruined aqueduct built by Louis XIV. It's a quiet place, making one feel sympathetically drawn to Madame de M. Her bedroom is lined in pale blue silk. As we approached Chartres the twin spires of the cathedral looked gigantic and out of scale, seen through the pale afternoon mist. Rush-hour traffic appalling, Desmond good and calm. I don't see why we shouldn't get on well, he's so spontaneous and easy. Chose the Hôtel de France in the big square (Ralph, Janetta and I lunched here a good many years ago). Walked out to see the cathedral and found the statues blacker and less marvellous than I remembered; the glass the same – splendid as nature is splendid. I want time alone each day; it may I think be the hardest thing to get, but I shall try for it. And I had a short space this evening and the blessed swig of whisky, before we set out in search of dinner and a cinema – *Chère Louise* with Jeanne Moreau. Back at midnight – but oh, in this fearful cold I have only one blanket and a papery cotton quilt. It's a sort of servant's room. But I dread making demands, and got my hot-water bottle from the car and slept in my winter dressing-gown.

September 18th: Montoire-sur-le-Loir (Hotel Cheval Rouge)

I was woken at about six-thirty by gurgling pipes, stamping feet and noisy throat-clearing. Cold grey weather still, walked back to the cathedral, where being Sunday we had the added stimulus of organ music, incense, candles and singing. Would it add even more intensely to the experience if all this 'meant' something to one? I doubt it. Desmond not prepared to think so either, or perhaps not interested in my speculations.

Then south to Illiers, where faint sunlight peeped through; we lunched and made enquiries about Proust. We were directed to the house of Monsieur le Maire, and thence sent off on a Circuit Proustien, to the river, the hawthorn hedge and the Pré Catalan – all this was humble, on a miniature scale and charming. The Pré Catalan was well tended and stocked with petunias, dahlias and sprinkled with various little ornamental summer-houses like pepper-pots. But our most moving experience at Illiers was a speech made to a group of about twelve Proustiens by an enchanting old gentleman of ninety-two, who rose up and addressed us fluently and eloquently, his face rippling with interest and emotion, poetry and humour, while he emphasised his remarks by lifting up and plumping down his soft black hat on a little table in front of him. I quite fell for him and he infused the old-fashioned, bourgeois and humble little house of Tante Léonie and its contents with a species of magic.

This hotel has two stars and gave us a star meal, but a not very *bon accueil*. Mousseline de turbot, followed by fonds d'artichauts, and chocolate ice contained in an outsize 'jumble'. We meant to stay two nights but they can't have us and on the whole I'm not sorry.

I think Des and I are doing rather well. He's not produced a full explosion once, there's plenty to talk about and his enjoyment is unflagging. After our good dinner, the idea was to read our books in the bar, but I soon noticed he wasn't turning the pages and had gone off into the quietest possible sleep. Also 'they' practically insist on our retiring to bed at ten or soon after. Which suits me, as I like reading in bed and solitude.

September 20th: Le Pin-sur-Creuse

On the brim of a narrow, quiet valley, this sympathetic little hotel has provided a refuge for two nights, it being impossible to see Nohant on a Tuesday. The weather has been a sore trial, cold and wet. The hotel is full of ancient *pensionnaires* – the rain has driven four English to play whist. A baby has just been carried in and is being greeted by general clucks.

Desmond has gone in to Argenton to get a paper. The only thing I've been taxed with is 'a shocking tendency to self-sacrifice, a very bad characteristic'. Little does he know that but for my 'self-sacrifice' I shouldn't be here! Raymond crops up often in the conversation, and often I fear critically. His spirit hovers over us. 'What would Raymond think of this place? Raymond wouldn't like this' and so on.

I have a rather delightful room across the garden which gives me a sense of privacy, vital to my happiness.

Desmond is kind, considerate and enthusiastic. His famous fussing is directed towards the minutiae of life. For instance, what happened to the franc I handed to him from the common purse to tip the hotel boy with? (It turned up later in the boot of the car where he had dropped it.)

On the way here we saw the château of Valençay, which at the last moment Des remembered having seen before, and I had twice, the last time under snow with Ralph. He is surprisingly prone to praise the prettiness of girls, and at dinner last night confided that he had once been to bed with Nancy Cunard, 'not a great success but she was very kind'.

The baby has begun bawling intolerably while everyone coos 'Pauvre petit – il crève de faim' and only I am glowering, sitting at bay in this stuffed and stuffy sitting-room.

Later

Before lunch it suddenly stopped raining and we walked down into the valley and ate our lunch by a log fire in our hotel. Visited the painted church and George Sand's cottage – both interesting. Desmond is a very thorough sightseer; and often follows the score more conscientiously even than the music. Next to the church, sunk in the leafy valley was the sad romantic shut château. Walked to the head of the valley and back in warm sun, dahlias shaking off their raindrops, leaves only just turning, apple trees laden with fruit.

The pensionnaires dash in to dinner when the bell rings at seven-fifteen, probably so as to get the best seats in the telly room afterwards. Des and I sat on wooden chairs whose design enraged him, in the bar, and laid plans for the future. When we joined the viewers he quickly fell asleep. His French isn't very good and he hears little and understands less.

September 21st: Tulle (Tocque Blanche)

Yesterday was long and tiring. I do no driving but all the map-reading and current guidebook consultation, and I distribute the common purse. Our conversations grow less restrained, sometimes Desmond's voice grows so loud that people look round. Such was an argument about pacifism at Le Pin. 'Do you mind – perhaps I oughtn't to ask ...' it began. F: 'Good heavens, of course not.' But it ended with an impasse: the first war produced the second, I said, but whether the second would produce a third must of necessity be a matter for speculation.

At last the weather has blossomed into full September beauty. We drove through country as peaceful and rustic as the Auvergne and far more beautiful. Early in the morning we were shown round the Donjon of Saussac, a remarkable old object with four cylindrical towers, by a gnarled old man with his stout bandy legs encased in long black stockings. He carried a crook with green ivy leaves carved on it.

Arrived at Nohant in time to join a small highbrow party conducted by a thin intelligent birdlike guide. One of our group was a white-haired lady in trousers, so deeply involved with George Sand that she couldn't keep silent. At last the guide said it was '*bien logique*' and '*bien normal*' that we too wanted to talk, but it made it hard for him. He softened the blow by saying it was pleasant to guide people who knew what he was talking about and that some were so ignorant that they asked what George Sand's wife was like. House and garden are charming: the blue bedroom with matching curtains and paper: her tiny workroom, the music-room (with a piano that isn't Chopin's, which she sent away during the pain of the break), pictures of lovers and friends, Maurice and Solange '*la petite peste*', the dining-room set with *placements* by her granddaughter (who died not long ago, at over ninety) for an imaginary dinner of habitués – Chopin, Flaubert, Liszt and Madame d'Augoult, Turgenev, Pauline Viardot, Balzac, Heine; close by were Delacroix's studio and the theatre and puppets all dressed by G.S. herself.

We sat down content with our morning, outside a café opposite in hot sun, and lunched off crusty rolls filled with pâté, and white wine. A few kilometres to the north the small church of Vicq was lined with remarkable, early and stylised frescoes.

Soon to this long town stringing along the two quays of a river, joined by many bridges. Desmond had been craving another star meal and his mouth began watering when I read out the specialities of the Tocque Blanche, restaurant *avec chambres*. Only one room was left so he had to go elsewhere for a lodging.

More observations on my travelling companion – he is deaf but won't recognise or admit it, so that, though I speak loud and clear in his ear, he repeats on a questioning note something laughably different. He also forgets one's answers to his questions at rare speed and asks them again. And although I always read him the guidebook account of what we are to see before we get there, he has to read it all over again *in situ*. To my tastes there's too much going into *what is happening* in a sculpture or painting, à la Raymond. This, and his need to make and re-make the tiniest decisions ad nauseam lead to considerable delays.

September 22nd: At Bunny's Verger

It's lovely to be here, even more so because Rose stepped out of the darkness to greet us. She's only here for one night. Desmond is disarmingly enthusiastic. As we approached I told him I had a great favour to ask him – would he leave it to me to choose whether I slept in the studio or the spare room. Suspicions and explanations. Was I being self-sacrificing again – with the usual purpose of that activity – to inflate my self-esteem? 'In a way I'm tougher than you,' I said. But of course he didn't agree. It's true, however. I can make myself comfortable in situations he would find intolerable. How to explain that one can genuinely be made more uneasy by thinking someone else is unhappy than by arranging one's own comforts? And I'm not upset by things like lack of curtains and the reading-light being on the wrong side, which often drive him to frenzy. Perhaps I meant 'more adaptable' rather than 'tougher'. Anyway my precautions were unnecessary as of course Rose and I shared the two-bedded studio. The Verger's spare room has a new bed and as Desmond says 'all the world's best books'. Good little Rose was busying herself fixing up reading lamps and changing fuses.

We drove here from Tulle through brilliant sunshine. By tiny white roads to charming Carennac, which again I found ravishing. Fénélon's château where Ralph and I stayed is no longer a hotel, as both proprietor and his wife have recently died, so a sweet-faced knitting lady told me. Then Desmond had the idea of following a '*circuit touristique*' which savoured to me a little of packaged tour, and wound to and fro across the Dordogne, so that by the time we crept down the funnel to the Verger our headlights were on. Before we went to bed Des said to me enthusiastically and touchingly, 'What a marvellous evening! What a splendid man Bunny is! Thank you so much for bringing me here.' Bunny told me afterwards that he had taken against Desmond at first, thought him too affected and modish. When they got to talking about George Moore and so on he grew to like him.

September 23rd

Fine warm breathlessly still weather goes on. Blue sky; trees green but picked out, a leaf or two at a time, with bright yellow, except for the maples which are vermilion. I love being here at Charry[1] and am full of admiration for Bunny's determination, philosophy and appetite for life – at the opposite pole to that petit-point evening with Raymond, Paul and Honey talking about their tiny comforts. In all essentials Bunny, as he says, 'lives like a king'. Delicious food, plenty of wine, natural beauty, and as a companion a young and stertorously purring tabby tomcat!

Philosophy in the lay sense of the word he has any amount of; Raymond none; Desmond more than Raymond. *His* trouble is that he feels the physical universe is conspiring against him and he must be always battling against it and is generally defeated. When corkscrews and clothes-pegs get the better of him it doesn't occur to him that *they* are all right, the deficiency is his. In fact, I don't think he likes to admit anything is his fault,

---

1 A charming little cottage he rented in France.

though he complains of this very feature in Raymond! Yet he makes up for it by relish, appreciation and vitality.

Yesterday morning, Rose, Desmond and I walked down the lane to the valley. The tunnel of box trees has grown so close that it was quite alarming to meet in it a scarlet tractor driven by a grinning black-bearded Italian. Rose is still thin, but bright-eyed and talkative, and even tries to raise her voice for Desmond's deafness. He thinks her 'adorable'. Later in the afternoon she and I took a walk up into the château woods and found autumn squills. She left us, alas, by the night train to Paris. Desmond and I sat over the fire reading and talking desultorily. I got worried because Bunny was so late back from Cahors, and with reason, as he had run into a pile of logs and had to stop for repairs at a garage.

September 24th

Divinely beautiful and hot. I love our dressing-gown breakfasts of croissants and honey and excellent coffee. Drove to Cahors in time for the market, shopped for food and espadrilles and sat drinking Pernod. We meant to give Bunny a good lunch in the restaurant at Cabernets, but received a frigid welcome, and a bleak, '*il faut attendre*'. Desmond, egged on by me, had a swim in their pool in his underpants and we then went crossly off to Marcilhac, where Bunny said the restaurateurs were his friends. So they turned out to be. 1.45 is late for France, but with great amiability and no delay at all they brought us melon, a huge pâté, tender cutlets and tarte au pommes. The sting in the tail of this outing was that I lost my camera, and for all my belief in not crying over spilt milk I grieve for it. Left an address and drove sadly home.

It was a long day and perhaps tiring, anyway I woke this morning with a touch of migraine. When Bunny called me I asked his advice, which he kindly gave, saying he would tell Desmond I couldn't go on to Toulouse with him today to pick up Georgia.

September 25th

Desmond was sympathy itself but OH the fussification. He was pink-faced with it, and though Bunny firmly said he wasn't to worry me with plans but just telegraph later where they were and if possible I would join them, it was *plus fort que lui*, he constructed a thousand elaborations, which fell down like card-castles, and it was true enough that I couldn't bring my mind to bear on them and my brain reeled. Bunny went off to make a bonfire in slight protest; I took a rest on my bed and poor Desmond, wearing his fuss like a visible halo, got off at long last – I have said I'll try and join them after two nights more here.

Now, writing next day, after going to bed at nine and sleeping well, I feel quite restored. When I said I hoped to join them on Wednesday I silently reserved the right to return quietly and earlier to England. But I'm beginning to feel equal to the last lap.

I'm happy here alone with Bunny and Puss, and an extra delight is that Bunny has just come waving a telegram from Marcilhac saying '*appareil retrouvé*'. So we go and fetch it tomorrow.

What I mind most is a sense of failure – I had determined to make this trip a success.

September 27th
We take each golden day followed by a clear night and huge moon, absolutely for granted.

No news from Desmond and Georgia, and I still worry about them rather. Bunny has just come out to where I'm sitting, chuckling to himself and saying what a good Henry James story could be made of the situation – nothing more would be heard of them until their engagement was announced in *The Times*.

We drove to Cahors to shop and change money, and thence to Marcilhac for my dear old camera. It had been found in the middle of the road (fallen from the top of the boot of Desmond's car) by a lady whom I thanked as well as I could with words of gratitude and money. It's better to have lost and found than never to have lost at all.

How beautiful the countryside looks now that the sun has soaked up the last vestiges of mist and the air is crystal clear. We lunched at Marcilhac again and Bunny, having swallowed a good deal of red wine, drove back at alarming speed, testing my imperturbability which survived – just. We talked about civilisation and what we considered the basis of morality. Bunny says 'responsibility'. I add kindness and respect for other people's happiness – perhaps the same thing. Sitting over the log fire later, up came Turgenev and Shelley. He brought me *Julian and Maddalo* to read (a great delight) and *Knock, Knock*, the last stories of Turgenev's his mother translated, which were not up to standard.

September 28th: Breliquet (Hotel de l'Étape du Château) at the head of the Gorges d'Aveyron

Desmond's telegram came announcing their arrival here and we set off – too eagerly as it turned out – soon after lunch, obsessed with the desire to rescue Georgia as soon as possible. We needn't have worried – they didn't arrive until dinner time and apparently in tearing spirits and delighted with each other. Bunny's Henry James story not too far from the mark! Desmond had got so confused over our discussion of plans that he wasn't expecting me until today. And as there was no more room at their rather squalid little hotel I booked myself in at this much more sympathetic one with a wide sunny terrace overlooking the valley. Bunny and I had arrived mid-afternoon and explored this very picturesque little place and then sat drinking Ricards and giggling over the postcards we were writing until the sun slowly sank behind the hill.

Bunny was quite unjustifiably indignant on my account at my friends not being in more of a hurry to rejoin me, as they had come from so close a place as Castres. Georgia arrived wearing a blazing-red linen jacket with USA written across it, which Desmond had persuaded her to buy for £11 and in which she looked splendid. I'm delighted they seem to have hit it off so well, and Georgia has introduced a youthful, non-Crichelish note. We all had a simple dinner at Des and Georgia's hotel and then Bunny left us. He had felt touchingly 'responsible' for me, and said he would never have left me before their arrival.

We now plan to spend three or even four nights in the Pyrenees; then they drop me at Toulouse airport, stay another night with Bunny and wend their way home.

September 29th: St-Bertrand-de-Comminges – again

It's my third visit though I've never stayed before in its charming hotel. The weather is superb, and everything perfect. We had a marvellous picnic. Georgia wanted to drive, and drove well, but signs of nervous exhaustion appearing I persuaded her to let Desmond drive and read the map herself.

When at last we saw the great silhouette of the Pyrenees shining mistily pink in the fading light she was wild with excitement, and her pleasure in our charming hotel was apparent even to the waitress, who said, '*Elle est contente!*' Her French is almost perfect and spoken with a very pretty accent; she's so thoughtful and well read, in fact a delightful fellow-traveller.

Desmond fussed a lot at dinner; there was a draught in his back, he didn't like our table. He will never learn to suffer physical imperfections, nor believe that other people aren't as deeply distressed by them as he is. After dinner we were shown to a tiny sitting-room with a wood fire. We are to be *pensionnaires* here for four nights.

September 30th

The morning sun outside the hotel is very hot. After breakfast (in bed of course) we sat outside at firm slate-topped tables, writing and reading. Then into the church, whose extraordinary charm and beauty bowled me over yet again. It's good to know we all have time to investigate it thoroughly. The small low cloister, with one side open to a green and peaceful view of the mountains and the flat-bottomed valley far below; the astonishing wood-carvings, many so 'secular' as Georgia expressed it, with the heads of men and women craning out from the rood screen, and every sort of vision, religious, poetic, or sturdily peasant is expressed on the stalls. I hunted round for the head of a girl, pensive and rather sad, with flying hair, because I remembered Janetta catching her breath at it, and at last I found it. Desmond gave these portents little of his attention, but preferred a seat outside where he could close his eyes to the sun. The waitress is a pungent character and doesn't altogether approve of us. Desmond announcing that we 'were different families and two sexes', she replied, '*J'ai remarqué ça.*' Like all the locals she speaks the hideous '*champagnang*'.

At lunch the conversation turned on Bunny's way of life and his passion for looking after himself and whether writers would do better to employ someone else to do that. Later we took a walk up the green valley below the village, sprinkled with autumn crocuses and with the shadows of the surrounding trees lying clear on the grass as if reflected in water. On the way home we were amused by the sight of the battered chassis of an ancient Mini into which two fat pigs had snugly tucked themselves.

October 1st

This is my last day in France and yesterday seemed at moments like my last on earth. We decided on a picnic in the mountains – pâté, ham, fromage, pain, vin, fruits. Desmond wanted an ambitious excursion involving two passes. We drove to the first up a *route forestière*, where incredibly tall and straight beeches and other trees towered over our rough track, or lay where the foresters had felled them, shorn of their branches like giant pencils. We ate our lunch on a beautiful lofty green plateau, with bracken to screen us from the trees and a population of shy cream and mouse-grey cows jingling their bells. Pure air, sun, food and wine, drowsy happiness.

After lunch we turned east over another pass. Higher and higher we climbed through villages which (like their inhabitants) grew more gnarled and Niebelung-like. Egged on by a village woman we took a strictly forbidden *route forestière* to what seemed a huge height – perhaps 6,000 feet or so, and then began to plunge downwards. On this bleak northern slope were growing tall purple-blue or yellow spikes of monkshood. The valley seemed hundreds of miles below and thick trees and rising afternoon mists clothed the slopes, but we glided slowly down an appallingly bad road till we came to a fork with no indication. 'To the left,' said Georgia. Desmond and I fatally decided 'to the right', which we took, and after a kilometre or so it was completely blocked by foresters' trucks between which we couldn't possibly squeeze. There was nothing for it but somehow to turn the car between the precipice on one side and the cliff on the other – to which crisis both Desmond and

Georgia rose magnificently, she planning exactly how the operation could be done, he keeping his head and showing complete trust in us both. My heart was in my boots when I thought we should have to go right back up the pass in the fading light. It almost stops beating now when I think how easily we might have let Desmond back over the cliff. But there is a strange emergency tank in most people which produces courage and quells imagination during a crisis. He showed it.

The operation was done at last, and going back to the parting of the ways we found Georgia was right and her road did descend. I've never been so glad to get down a mountain before, nor to drink my swig of whisky on return. Desmond was really splendid in this crisis.

October 2nd

Yesterday devoted to further complete absorption in the church; Desmond had his head well in the score of artefacts and Georgia and I, standing in the cloisters, looking down at the dear green valley, talked about religion, and beliefs about the nature of the universe. I wish I could remember what I said because she told me afterwards in her emphatic way that our conversation had settled the question for her 'for good and for all'.

Then we drove to the prehistoric cave of Gargas and with a small group of French tourists penetrated its vast echoing depths. It is never narrow and claustrophobic like the Font de Gaume, but the very width and lack of height of its further chambers was somehow terrifying, making one aware of the great mountain above. An intelligent young student showed us round and pointed out the few animal paintings and the famous imprints of mutilated hands. Georgia and I heard, understood and were moved. Desmond, either from deafness or inadequate French, couldn't understand a single word. He couldn't accept the reason, however, for this, but complained bitterly and repeatedly that the guide 'talked indistinctly', 'didn't bring his lips together' and 'it was really too bad of him'. This refusal to take the blame is curious. What does it come from, I wonder? Modesty or the reverse? At dinner he stretched hastily for the wine and spilt most of a bottle over me and the cloth. Why not just say he's sorry? No: it was somehow the fault of the bottle, the waitress, the table, perhaps Georgia and me.

Today they drive me to catch my aeroplane at Toulouse.

I do think the holiday has been a success and that my relation with Desmond has expanded and deepened.

October 6th: West Halkin Street

I've been back four days, and I feel as though buckets had been emptied over me, electric currents sent through my body and some vital substance drained off it.

But first: when I got back from France I heard that Sophie was going the very next day to a cranky boarding-school in Sussex. It was a shock, and I'm still anxious but beginning to think it may all be for the best. I talked to her on the telephone and she sounded very grown up. It's a co-ed school, and the most important thing is that her friends Bella and Esther Freud go there as day girls.

Angelica and Henrietta to lunch. Angelica seemed to have been carried away by Nerissa's strong personality, so as to become a sort of fanatical follower both of her mysterious philosophy and the technique of family analysis. Her line was that it 'had been awful but was now really rather marvellous'.

October 9th

Came back from a weekend at Crichel and have been in a defeatist sinking state all day. In the train I was reading *Le Rouge et le Noir* which has been steadily gaining a grip on me. Julien Sorel shot Madame de Reynal just as we pulled in to Waterloo. I've been able to do nothing since I arrived but lie on my bed and go with him to the guillotine, also wait for a telephone call from Janetta. And delightfully enough she comes here to eat tonight.

Georgia and Desmond arrived back from France on Friday night, excited and beaming, and received an awkward greeting from Raymond, who said, 'You're late' and then could hardly talk to or look at Georgia, though he didn't mean to be rude I'm sure. I was forced to turn away my head and look into the fire so that he should sometimes address her rather than me. Later he thawed and was charming to her, and she liked him and said he was 'so playful'. Of Raymond's own French holiday I heard – 'Dadie lost his temper violently with me twice,' and that they spent a fearful lot of money, being driven about in a hired Mercedes and going to grand hotels, and staying three nights with the Rothschilds.

Desmond came up to my room one night and delighted me by saying how much he had enjoyed the holiday: 'in some ways it was the best I've had in my life.'

October 11th

I've just spent a morning with Stanley, who has dwindled in size so much that I can't call him Wombat any more. He talked and talked and talked about Virginia; I'm impressed by his intelligence and thoughtfulness, also by the dedicated concentration which made him think so obsessionally when writing about her that he couldn't sleep and lost a stone in weight.

Months ago Julian signified that he would like to be taken to *Les Troyens* and it must be when both Baker and Veasey were singing. I got seats for tonight, and yesterday, if you please, he rang up and said he didn't want to come. 'Thank you for being so understanding.' I'm not; I'm angry but accepting. I can't (and have no desire to) railroad him there against his will. But I spent hours on the telephone trying to find a substitute at this short notice – everyone 'dying to come but engaged'. Well, Margaret will come, and doubtless fall fast asleep.

The other night Janetta described the agitation she was thrown into by 'cities'. I begin to feel the same, and for the first time wonder seriously whether I shouldn't withdraw to the country. I myself seem to lead more of a country life here in London than I used to – that is I devote more of each day, and gladly, to solitude and reading. Went to the London Library yesterday and stocked up with Stendhaliana. *Le Rouge et le Noir* has quite converted me, as the *Chartreuse de Palme* did not. I'm absorbed by him.

October 15th

I now find a London weekend if led like a country weekend

positively restful. Several things that were actually *nice* have happened. Darling Sophie sent me a good, steady, characteristic letter saying she likes her school. I had a simultaneous visit from Robert and Janetta, and though they talked a lot about their worry about Georgie, they didn't seem 'got down' by life. Robert, who has just taken on a new telly job, has in fact not appeared to me so handsome, confident and resilient for a long time. Janetta came bringing me lovely flowers and her usual sweetness. Today I've had a visit from Stanley, bringing some more of his book to correct and a Wagner record for us to listen to together.

I continue to turn over ideas for living. Return to work; could I find some? Or retreat into my burrow with books and music. Or to the country. Joan says she would come with me, but I'm afraid that wouldn't do. Though I value her affection and am really fond of her, we haven't a great deal in common, either in interests or values. I become irritated by her endless repetitions about Rose's being so untidy. It's not her affair anyway. I'm afraid I upset her by saying I thought *she* was 'obsessionally tidy'. And her tidiness does grate on me in a way she can't I think imagine.

October 17th

Julian arrived to dinner on Sunday in Russian blouse and boots, looking charming and seeming 'all right' until, after being a perfect listener to my travel tales, he opened the door on to his own deep unhappiness. He feels the 'front' he puts up to the world is false, and I understand that but do not think it entirely true. The tragic eyes with which he talked of his dreadful longing to love, and fear that he was incapable of it, pressed a dagger into my heart; I suppose it does in some sense corre- spond to the truth – but so I feel does the gaiety and sympathy of his response to friends. Alas for anyone whose jungle is haunted by Henry James's Beast, I am all too aware of the desperateness of their plight, but I can't feel it is inevitable in Julian's case, innate in his character. It is so much a matter of circumstances, like the element of chance in a game of patience. Of course under the blast of his unhappiness any residue of indignation about *Les Troyens* melted instantly. Indeed, such petty annoyance should always be swept under the carpet immediately. As he talked about his inability to love, I wondered how much of a 'normal' (in the French sense) person's life is spent in loving. From my advanced position on the ladder, different forms of loving do seem to merge together, but my difficulty in consoling Julian, or trying to, is that I do really feel the stalkings of that particular Beast are the worst fate anyone can suffer. *He* shouldn't. I'm convinced he has the capacity to love in him somewhere.

October 18th

More cries of pain. Last night, as I was dropping off, Stanley rang to say it had been 'the worst day of his life' — a sense of total futility, wasted years, pain caused to others to no purpose, tears on the way from the British Museum, the humiliation of reading Goethe. And so on. I did my best, but fear 'my best was bad'. He has been absorbing most of my morning going through his chapter on the Wolves, and the rest of the day I have spent reading Quentin's Vol. 2.

October 19th

Last night Magouche and Janetta came to dinner; they are both infinitely sympathetic to me.

4 p.m.

Resting oh so deliciously on my bed, after a completely meaningless smart lunch at Boodle's club given by Loelia (Westminster) Lindsey. Noel Parker, Raymond and Philip Dunn, and all to meet a horrible rich noisy American, who told me he was hurrying back to America to vote for Nixon. 'Do you have great confidence in him?' I asked. 'No, but he's better than McGovern. *He's* a real Bolshie, wants to slash incomes and give everyone 1,000 dollars.' I silently resented his assumption that everyone must agree with him.

Coming back, London looked brilliantly pretty under a bright blue sky, a cold wind. And then I was brought to earth by the sight of toadlike, old women, clutching bags in their reddened claws, with great thick blubbery reddened lips, and a fortune spent on their bodies. Pestiferous rich!

October 23rd

Hugh Cecil married his Mirabel the other day in a large secular-looking church in Bryanston Square. The clergyman conducted the service in the tones of the chairman of a board meeting. Hugh wore a magnificent black velvet suit, Mirabel a pale apricot one, Rachel a brown one, and there were lots of fur hats. Afterwards to the Reform Club where an enormous flunkey dressed in a red suit bawled our names at the waiting row of hosts. I went in after Jonathan and Laura and on hearing Jonathan's name the flunkey was so excited that he virtually dropped his duties. 'Mr *Jonathan* Cecil? Are you on tonight, sir?' I talked to the Stones, Pansy Lamb, Frances Phipps and found my old wrinkled face being kissed by the equally old wrinkled face of Roy Harrod,[1] who sat beside me discussing Maynard's[2] sex-life. 'They say he had *ejaculation praecox*. Is that true?' I said I hadn't ever been in a position to know, but had always heard so.

There has been considerable discussion between me and Stanley over Quentin's book; he rings me up for hours at a time. I was really shocked, and said so, at Michael's[3] dull and crabbing review in *The Times*, and now that he's done it twice, it's impossible not to think envy is a motive and even if subconscious, the world says, or anyway all those connected with the Bloomsbury world say that Quentin's is a far better book. At first Stanley ran down Quentin in the identical term Michael used ('too much chronology, not enough interpretation' etc.) out of loyalty to Michael; then he enjoyed the book out of loyalty to me. So he doesn't know if he's on his head or his heels. He gave a superbly cooked dinner (not by himself) to me, Lyn, a very intelligent and charming young German art historian and someone called Robert. The standard of talk is as high at Stanley's as anywhere, oddly enough.

---

1 Economist.
2 Keynes.
3 Holroyd.

October 24th

Dadie's seventieth birthday party last night, given by the Annans. 'What are you going to give him?' I asked Eardley. E: 'Nothing at all.' In the event the present opening after dinner was a star performance, and I was very glad that I'd taken him my nice Napoleon brandy glass (almost the only un-chipped glass I possess). I took an immense fancy to Peggy Ashcroft, with her intelligent, sweet-natured, altogether charming face and manner. Hester[1] wore an extraordinary wool dress trimmed with fur, and festooned at the hem, her figure topped with a great busby of white hair. 'She looks as though she were off to Leningrad,' said Raymond. Her eyes are splendid however, and we had a talk, sitting side by side, wherein she told me, 'I thought you might like to know – I've always meant to tell you – that I was *madly* in love with Ralph between my two marriages, but *madly* ...'

The rest of the company didn't mean a great deal to me – Steven Runciman, John Sparrow and a dull legal fellow to whom I talked about prison reform. Noel Annan was very friendly; to be so constantly beaming is bound to take effect on one.

October 25th

A pale sweet light picks out the chimney-pots behind my flat, and the wireless chimes in with arias from *Zaüberflöte*. I await a visit from Stanley – not really wanted, but I don't like to say No. I have been trying to weigh up his character – brains excellent, character very good (by which I mean kindness); his habit of repeating himself (i.e. whenever a performance of Wagner is mentioned 'Oh it was so ex*qui*site – is was so be*au*tiful') rather endears him than otherwise. I think perhaps people should have their leitmotifs, so long as they don't overdo them.

October 31st

Back from what I devoutly hope will be my last trip 'abroad' this year – to the Wexford Festival. But while I say that and mean it,

---

1 Chapman, Dadie's cousin and a writer.

I'm well aware also of the featureless greyness of the winter months ahead, perhaps with a power cut, and with what feels like a steadily sinking morale and frequent intimations of mortality.

I met Desmond and Raymond at the Cromwell Road terminus, where a bus-load of brave souls was just setting off for the battle front in Belfast. What a world!

Arrived in Dublin in greyness and rain, collected the car Desmond had hired, and almost at once saw the soft grey felt roof folding back to leave a watery forget-me-not sky, stillness and peace. Both Desmond and I responded (perhaps because of our Irish origins) to this quiet beauty, as Raymond, I think, did not. 'I'm hoping to feel I'm abroad, he said. 'I don't yet.' He mismanaged the seat at the back, which was a curiously collapsed affair leaving its inmate very low; his lips were often white, I noticed, with pill-taking ('I think I need a little anti-sugar') and he was obviously tired. I soon got him to sit in front.

Arrived at White's Hotel, Wexford, an urgent need for whisky took me out into the street where I ran into Bryan Moyne and attendant females. He invited me to the Guinness supper-party that night, to which we all went. Raymond murmurs a list of Irish inefficiencies: 'The light over the basin is too dim to *shave* by. The paper doesn't un*roll*.' Also: 'I didn't have enough time for my *rest*.' On the aeroplane and at White's we ran into Jack Lambert and his handsome wife. I remembered the beastliness of his letter to Desmond, and also most of what was said years ago. In any case their ebullient jollity would have jarred, reminding me of a less talented Jack Hulbert and Cicely Courtneidge. Bellini's *Il Pirata* was very well done, with two really fine singers. The seats are acutely uncomfortable, as Raymond was all too aware. Desmond's enthusiasm for everything glows like stained glass lit by patriotic feeling for his native land. (He quoted Moore at the Meeting of the Waters, now a morass of quarrying and mud.)

Everyone is friendly, informal, and does not await introductions. At the Moynes' party an Irishman asked my name and when I told him said: 'Lady, Mrs or Miss?' which was somehow a very un-English reaction.

Saturday morning was brilliant, with immaculately clear light showing up the curious combinations of colours on small houses and the worn patina of riverside warehouses. We were booked into a lunch-party on a boat upriver from New Ross. I first took Raymond for a stroll down to the quay. He had 'slept *well*, had good *sausages*, but breakfast-room *cold*'. In getting started in our hired car for the river outing Desmond had one of his prize burst-balloon explosions. He got stuck, couldn't get into reverse, and when approached by a lady asking for a lift because her hired car wouldn't start, he shouted, 'Oh I *can't* reverse. *Bloody* woman!' She turned out to be someone he knew from the BBC, and was on Christian name terms with. The odd thing is that he forgets his own moments of hysteria almost instantly. She got in and Raymond and I were crushed into the back seats, more uncomfortably than need have been and when Raymond asked how long the journey would take, Desmond yelled, 'Oh Raymond, don't *fuss*! You've done nothing but *fuss* ever since we started.' R: 'Fuss! from you, Desmond. Really!' (This was the worst moment of the Irish outing.) The boat had a full cargo, mostly of English who seemed to be assuming an Irish riotousness not entirely natural to them – Norwiches, Beits, Antonia Fraser. The start of our journey up the river in the sun on deck, sipping our drinks as the banks of the wide river rolled by, was extremely pleasant. Then we descended to the cabin and ate a quite good lunch in a London cocktail-party hubbub.

In spite of Desmond's blow-out at the start of the outing, he and Raymond are trying to be nice to each other, and there's no great tug between them. However, renewed frenzy in the evening when poor Des, red-faced in his white evening jacket, appeared bawling (the only word): 'ALL the opera tickets have vanished!' by which he managed to convey that the tickets, not he, were to blame, and the physical universe had played him false again. But the kind and casual Irish made light of this – 'everyone always loses their tickets at Wexford' – and our seats were allotted us.

Katya Kabanova was a notable experience, a marvellous work, moving, extremely well produced and sung. Desmond was in tears, and clutched my arm saying brokenly: 'It's a masterpiece *isn't* it?' We came out into pouring rain, and all repaired to my room for nightcaps of 'Paddy'.

Next day, Sunday, was what the Irish called 'dishperate' weather – heavy rain and violent wind until tea-time. Des and I drove off none the less to look at Jerpoint Abbey in a gothic storm, and lost our way home, as one always seems to with him. Weber's *Oberon* that night was, to my mind, a complete failure. A fairy play, its text rewritten with coy passages, amateurish to look at, and the principals an ill-assorted couple – an enormously tall Finn and a hideous negress – both with huge voices and no volume control.

So back next day, yesterday, to Dublin. I wouldn't have missed *Katya Kabanova* for anything, but I feel rather doubtful whether I shall go to Wexford again.

This morning I awoke to 'dishperate' gloom; the world is a horrific confusion of savagery and stupidity. The radio announcers tell one in dispassionate tones of deaths and disasters, hijacked aeroplanes, terrorism, the raping of small girls. I fully and frankly wish I were dead – and there's little more to say about it.

November 1st

So on we go from month to month. Time fills up all too easily with the chores connected with keeping one's wretched self going. I resent this and wish futilely I had some work. Also a gruelling orchestra rehearsal last night shook my confidence and made me feel hopelessly bad at everything.

November 2nd

Feeble efforts to fight back at life, but it's a tough adversary. Yesterday's afternoon spent playing trios with Angelica and Margaret span itself out into five solid and exhausting hours, two of them spent sitting in traffic jams, caused by an almost comic protest of taxi-drivers who drove their cabs in a solid stream round Eros, hooting and with headlights on. They must have enjoyed themselves thoroughly – and I wish I had seen it instead of feeling the interminable after-effects.

Pleasures: listening to Brahms' First Piano Concerto; reading, remembering suddenly very vividly the extraordinary feeling of a door opening on to a fresh landscape full of spreading paths when one discovers a new author.

This morning I have walked and walked. It is much more refreshing than driving is – I must do it more.

November 3rd

Pleasures – another to record. Going to Prokofiev's masterly *War and Peace* last night. I took Stanley, who was the perfect companion, as he sat silently absorbed and enjoying, though he arrived 'exhausted' and burst into floods of undigested thinking in the interval. He does a lot of that, and I'm very ready to put up with its occasional divagations or, as he would say, 'extrapolations'. I have asked Joan to come to lunch, must get over the shrinking I feel from forcing my ghastly wrinkles etc. on her, also from a certain banality and repetitiveness which is 'coming out' again as it were, after being temporarily dislodged by her acute pain over the loss of Cochemé.

The Prokofiev, and particularly Norman Bailey as Kutusov, made me long for Ralph to have been there – he so acutely understood and was moved by the qualities of *War and Peace*, which this opera faithfully expressed. Anyway I woke this morning feeling refreshed and stimulated by it and more able to face life.

November 6th: Weekend at Stowell

I begin to long for quiet 'country weekends in London' and feel that unless it is to be with dear old congenial friends like the Hills a weekend is very expensive hard work.

And this one was no exception, though there were some pleasures – chiefly my walk down through the still damp woods to the canal, three swans frozen motionless on the dark green water, like a dream floating on sleep that invites but is unattainable. Fustiness of meadowsweet and other November smells. I met Frances Phipps hobbling towards me along the lane; embracing her, the pale light showed up her age, and the fact that she was wearing a wig. Yet she often looks really pretty. Inside her cottage we sat down opposite each other to talk, she in her wig, like characters in a Russian play. Her fifteen-year-old grandson was playing the piano next door but eagerly joined us. I asked him what he was playing. 'My own composition.' Did he like concerts? 'I've never been to one.' A strange, rather mad, and very self-centred boy. He wanted to talk about an 'evil' boy at his school. Frances grew restive and tried to get him to go for a walk – he said he would come with us. I was uneasy at the thought of 'rejecting' him but Frances (obviously irritated by his continued and hampering presence) took me up to her studio to look at her Fantin-Latour-like paintings. As we left the studio, he was hovering in a room nearby.

Walked home alone and found lunch visitors (Allan and Jill Hare – *Financial Times*, well off, musical, friendly) and weekend guests – Geraint Jones, conductor and harpsichordist and his violinist wife and little dog. I liked honest soft-voiced Winnie Jones. Why do the right-wingers so often assume one is of their kidney? I find it irritating. Geraint held forth about the horrors of Communism and Mr Wilson; otherwise I thought his conversation masturbatory and mostly aimed at establishing his own status. Mary said afterwards she thought he was scared.

Philip has been dismissing servants and limiting Mary's nest-making, so that her energies have no outlet. She naturally loses heart and becomes a bad housewife. My room had no fire, heating went off at night and when I asked for a hot-water bottle there was none in the house. She went off to her own electric blanket with some remarks suggesting that I find out what time the Joneses were going on Sunday, as it would be fatal if they wanted to stay till Monday.

November 13th

Stanley rings me up almost daily; I enjoy our conversations and am surprised that he feels the need for them. One day he'll say, 'I've been thinking that a face is like a map.' And the next day – 'it's not a map to show where you're going but where you've been.'

I saw Alix on Saturday. As usual our conversation was a delight, but it began thus:

F: 'How are you, Alix?'

A: '*Well*, I'm getting a little *deafer* all the time. Then my *sight* is deteriorating, so that I *read* more slowly.'

F: 'Oh what a horrible nuisance!'

A: (holding up her hand for silence – I was still on the doorstep): 'Wait – that's not all. As a result of my operation on my nose, I can't *smell* anything, and that makes me very uneasy in case there's a horrible smell I'm unaware of.'

After which during two hours she proved that her mind had deteriorated no whit at all.

Pigeons – two have made me think of death. Going out to post a letter I found one in an attitude of despair with its head pressed down against the front doorstep. 'Oh God, ought I to kill it?' I thought – I but when I came back from the letter-box it was gone. Perhaps it had been stunned by a car and was sensibly getting over it.

Another was flopping feebly with outstretched wings against the Carringtons'[1] garage wall, when I arrived Saturday tea-time.

A copy of my last translation was awaiting me here, and made me feel more like a 'translator' than I have for some time. Also an amusing letter from Bunny, after a visit from a couple, the wife of which he is I gather on bedding terms with. 'Marriage is a dreadful institution and I have been a witness of its awful features,' he writes.

November 14th

Looking at my translation has cheered me up. I nerved myself to compare the book with my MSS, and have been gratified to find so few, and such trivial alterations, particularly in the case of Borges, because I remember when I went to hear him lecture, and how his official translator, di Giovanni, said almost pityingly that my position was an awkward one, as Borges speaks perfect English and my translation would have to be gone through by him and Borges together, and nothing left 'as Borges would not have expressed it himself'. Finding so few changes has set me up no end.

Cold winter has struck suddenly.

---

1 Noel and Catharine.

November 16th

I realise that I had invested a lot of libido in Julian's promise to bring his whizz-agent Diana Crawford to lunch today. Or perhaps it's more accurate to say that the idea roused the moribund desire in me to be at a translation again and, nice beautiful girl though she is, I'm not sure if she can help. She doesn't really deal with translators or know how to. I also went to a translators' party at the French Embassy, and this had the same effect. I'm plunged in gloom and frustration as a result. I dare say I shall 'come to terms' with the situation and maybe make one more effort with the Translators' Association before I sink beneath the waves.

People ring up and ask me for weekends and I haven't one free till after Christmas. The evenings too get just as full as I could wish. Yet how many *real friends* have I in London? I fear that Joan and I are both realising our lack of compatibility and our relationship is dwindling to telephone conversations, which end monotonously with her saying, 'Well, it's a lovely day,' or 'Well, it's not very cheerful weather.' So I'm sorry to say I find her gramophone record has a certain monotony, and also – to speak truth – her incessant preoccupation with clothes and neatness bores me. She goes for three months to South Africa and has been fussing about her trousseau for weeks. 'I've got so much to do.' 'Madge Garland says one must take four silk dresses ... and *hats*.' Really, in the plural!

I think what has moved me most lately has been hearing Norman Bailey singing Kutusov in *War and Peace*, twice.

November 21st

The loosening of buried desires and emotions from the depths, bringing them to the surface yet not allowing discharge – this has more than once been disturbing me, as it has with my translation problem, activated by three things: the translators' meeting, arrival of my *Seven Voices* from America, and talking (I now think to no purpose) to Diana Crawford. *Eh bien*, I mean to shelve it for a day or two and then take action.

Snape for the weekend, blustery without, warm and companionable within. Bob was there, talking non-stop and telling stories which (having been heard at least fifty times before) cause Heywood and Anne to droop their heads. Heywood begins, I think, to feel that even Anne talks 'too much and too fast' like the rest of her family and she begins to know he thinks this, and say so, and apologise. All in a friendly way, without breach of their admirable relation and only resulting in their taking me aside to talk to separately. Heywood and I talked on two walks, Anne and I one evening in the kitchen. Apart from the unacceptable Muslim life led by Lucy, I don't think they have many family worries. Anne had, long after the event, got wind of the rumour of Tim's[1] affair with Amaryllis,[2] only to dismiss it and say Jonny says there's nothing in it. Anne's tiger-woman loyalty to her family is fierce, irrational and touching. Irrational beliefs, she said defensively, are passionately held by a lot of young people 'like Tim', as if their presence in Tim made them valid. Bob and I agreed in saying the young *ought* to try to learn to be rational. It certainly isn't the mode at present. A young man from Sotheby's called Julian Stock, a self-made art expert, friendly and with quite dazzling expertise about Italian drawings and engravings, was staying there. We had lots of in- and out-going sallies for drinks and Bob stood us lunch at the fish restaurant at Orford.

Poor Kitty West, who came last night, has heard nothing at all from Caroline[3] in Ghana for two whole months, after a regular to and fro correspondence when she first got there. Real cause for worry.

I compare my friendship with her and with Joan. Kitty said – but without a trace of cattiness – that she didn't like Joan's visual taste, found her too conventional and that she never said anything interesting. When she went to stay she poured out her grief for Cochemé with floods of tears. Kitty, who is a more stoical character, hadn't wanted this and felt it was time (after more than a year) for Joan to control such outbursts. I know she did likewise to Mary, and I think perhaps it's true. And that

---

1 Behrens, married to the Hills' daughter, Harriet.
2 Garnett, Bunny's eldest daughter.
3 Her daughter, married to a Ghanaian.

greater outward fortitude (like Judy's[1]) does *not* mean less grief.

November 22nd

Joan, at her very best yesterday, came and spent the morning with me at Whitechapel Gallery, lunching here afterwards. She has been attacked by various friends for going to South Africa, country of apartheid, and though I told her (as is true) that I was positively in favour of going to any country, however much one disapproved of its regime, she was too full of her response to these attacks to staunch the tide, which imperceptibly overflowed into anti-black feelings. Talking of 'separate lavatories' for blacks and whites she said defiantly (as we whizzed east in a taxi) that she would much rather go to white lavatories. 'Why?' 'Because the blacks are much dirtier.' 'Do you mean they pee and shit on the floor?' '*Yes*.' Well, she's lived in black countries but I can't help wondering if she shared their lavatories. Then, she whirled on to 'equal money for everyone'. Again a certain personal, defiant note; that if one believed one had no right to unearned money one should give it all away (this was aimed at me presumably). She herself felt that Cochemé had worked hard and for the general good, partly so that she should have enough to live on comfortably. I much prefer Joan in this thoughtful, if bellicose mood, and there was absolutely no heat in our discussion. What's more, I feel the relevance of her attitude about money. I do think, with her, that if one believes people should have equal money one should do something about it. 'Besides talking,' she said, but in fact I think talking is action and in some ways the only effective form of it.

Last night after three hours' violin playing I went to dine with the Wests. Lily[2] peered out of a mass of hair, a nervous rather awkward hostess. The drawing-room was horribly cold, a pile of unlighted logs lay in the grate. Anthony suddenly entered the room, large and grim-looking: 'Disaster. There are no potatoes.' Convinced that none was wanted, he then sat down and

---

1 My eldest sister.
2 Second wife of Anthony; American.

said: 'Since you're such a very old friend I can tell you there's some very bad news. Very bad indeed. Caroline has had a very bad nervous breakdown.'

Kitty must have found a letter from Osei[1] on her return, telling her this news. Caroline had been for a month in 'the Swiss Clinic' and has now returned but was in 'a state of apathy, and wouldn't speak or show interest in anything'. Gloomily (and no wonder) Anthony 'supposed someone would have to go and fetch her home'. But would that be a good thing? he went on. She was anyway supposed to be returning for Christmas.

Other dinner guests, sitting rather awkwardly in pairs on sofas ranged round the cold drawing-room, which contrived to glide wildly about on very smooth castors, were two couples. One had just adopted a Pakistani child. I liked them both. The female of the other pair sat opposite me at dinner, and I took an instant dislike to her ferrety face looking out of a wiry mane of reddish hair, as she obviously did to mine, for whatever I said she said, 'I completely disagree with you.'

November 28th

I saw Kitty at the Sterns[2] at the weekend, and she showed us the letter from Osei – a good kind letter, containing no mention of actual nervous breakdown, but merely of Caroline 'not being very well,' and 'not sleeping'. He took her to the Swiss Clinic for a month, but she 'wouldn't co-operate with nurses and doctors; he had to do everything for her, bath her and even brush her teeth.' (What a sad picture that conjures up.) She was home now, but apathetic, answering only 'Yes', 'No' or 'I don't know'. I think in a way both Tanya and I were as much distressed and imaginatively stretched as Kitty herself – yet in the end how much can one empathise with other people's troubles? And those of poor Caroline, unable to cope with this new world and surrounded by perhaps hostile black faces and strange voices, are too unknown to comprehend. Suicide of course occurs to one. Kitty says she has written to them to come back

---

1 Caroline's husband.

2 Jimmy and Tanya.

as soon as possible and she'll pay their fare, but says she feels Caroline is more Osei's wife than her daughter. She said this composedly, yet her irritable rather aggressive attitude to Jimmy, Tanya and me in turn showed that she's suffering from angst acutely.

I like both Sterns. Jimmy is nicer to be with and talk to, because more relaxed. Tanya, intelligent and quick-witted, is tiringly over-excited, waves her hands, fixes one with her boot-button eyes; and like surgical instruments they drain the life out of one. They can't talk without irritating each other (not that they don't love each other – they do). I had therefore to do double-time talking; and talking, that strange and simultaneous combination of responding and thinking, can be very hard work.

When I got into my train on Sunday evening and sat down in a dirty buffet car with a beaker of whisky, I felt peace and relaxation – in spite of the squalor of a sloppy baby opposite, half-chewed pieces of bread, ash, and screws of paper. 'Alone at last' was my feeling and it often is. I'm not alone as much as I want to be.

How pretty the Wilts–Dorset border was with its erratic lanes and valleys, stone houses, the velvet bloom brought by the onset of winter, leaves reduced to one or two on bare boughs. I walked twice with Jimmy – once we went to look at Swallowcliff, Julia and Tommy's[1] first abode. Windless, frosty, a streaky blue winter sky and faint mist.

December 5th

Yet again (after an evening with Julian this time) I'm left astonished at the contrast between the animated optimistic 'face' and an inner wish that one was dead. Aware that this dichotomy is present in many people, one is reluctant to load any surplus misery on them. I wonder if that was partly the reason that Kitty hardly spoke of Caroline's predicament until Sunday evening during my weekend with her. Of course I referred to it, but as she said that it was still too early to have heard from them and that there was nothing to do but be patient and try not to fuss, I

---

1 Stephen Tomlin, sculptor, always so-called.

took that as my cue. She has naturally had difficulty in not fussing and taken to sleeping-pills for the first time in twenty years.

On Sunday night she suddenly brought me a very nice letter from Mary Trevelyan,[1] saying that through Julian's relations she had discovered the woman at the Foreign Office responsible for Ghana, got in touch with her and found her understanding and sympathetic. 'How splendid,' I said, 'and how kind. This really seems a practical move.' And I was amazed when it turned out that Kitty had neither answered nor acted on this letter. Having hesitated to give advice and perhaps thrust surgical implements into a raw wound, I now did say I thought if I was her I would at once get in touch with the Ghanaian specialist at the F.O. and also that Mary Trevelyan should be thanked. We went on to discuss the financial side – would they have money available for their tickets? Ought someone to go out? The last idea she shrinks from, probably rightly, but slightly shocked me by saying, 'It would be too expensive.' I told her I could and gladly would raise the money. She can't – as I do – envisage the suicide possibility, but in any case saving sanity is as important as saving life or more so. I've since talked to Anthony, who says he has got in touch with the lady at the F.O. who is contacting the British Consul at Accra.

December 8th

Stanley and his interesting German friend Rüdiger came to dinner on Wednesday. Stanley brought his will for us to sign and then exclaimed that we couldn't because we 'benefited' – a transparent manoeuvre but also rather touching. How absurd to put *me* in – to receive a Japanese scroll which I don't even remember, alas.

Rüdiger, a tall tawny-haired extremely intelligent German art historian, was struck on entry by Carrington's portrait of Lytton, gave it in his quiet voice high praise, and then sitting at dinner pondered her Spanish landscape. I therefore brought out Carrington's painting of Tidmarsh Mill House after dinner and

---

1 A painter.

placed it opposite him. He gazed at it sunk in thought for a very long time, while Stanley and I prattled. 'What do you think of it?' asked Stanley. Rüdiger knew nothing about Carrington but he came out with the most astonishing analysis of her character and work, which seemed to me as I listened what I had always known, but never formulated. 'You were her friend, so perhaps I shouldn't say this – there's something stiff, stuck, naïve, yet the naïveté isn't genuine, it's a mask, false. You see the charming natural things in the foreground – the grasses, water, swans? They are deliberate distractions from the house in the background which is somehow *rigid*. I can't get over the holes' (by which I think he meant the windows as well as the very Freudian hole for the mill stream) – 'they seem to be *gulping*.'

Both Stanley and I were amazed. I don't think I had ever consciously or thoroughly believed that Carrington's naïveté (childish clothes, turned-in toes, little white socks, and rather mincing voice) was a sort of disguise, but Rüdiger's diagnosis might explain why she gave over painting anything except as 'distractions' – flowers, glass-pictures – unable to face her own hard rigid 'gulping' core. Where then can one fit in her genuine imagination, creativity, originality?

Yesterday two returning wanderers – Magouche and Mary, delightfully free, easy and rollicking. In the evening Isobel:[1] 'Oh I met an American writer the other day who had just brought out a book on Corvo. He was called *Higgs*. He was clever. I suppose I ought to have arranged to see him again but he was *so* little and unattractive and had *very* long finger-nails.' She goes to stay with Blond in Corfu for Christmas.

After she left the bell rang again and up she came. 'I've left behind *both* my pairs of spectacles. I shall *never* get to Corfu!'

December 12th

I enjoyed Cambridge (Tom and Nadine[2]), spent a happy afternoon at the Fitzwilliam by myself and met and talked to a lot of

---

1 Strachey.
2 Marshall. My brother and his wife.

stimulating people: Tom Faber (a physicist) and his wife (who had been at Oxford with Burgo), the Postans, Godleys, and the delightfully intelligent new head of Newnham, Jean Flood by name. These people with their academic bent produce conversation that I liked more than I did with those with whom I dined last night. Why? What was wrong? There's a flavour of competitive political *gossip* rather than of general ideas, political or otherwise. Typical was a large man, big-headed both physically and psychologically, whose self-preoccupied left-wingedness somehow infected the atmosphere, and also his sharp-featured, aggressive mistress (who got into a rough and tumble argument with Robert).

Kitty has just rung up saying she's had a cable from Osei: 'Caroline recovering rapidly', and that they return in a few days. Relief!

People are charging away for Christmas. Stanley rang me from the airport on his way to America. On the night he brought Rüdiger here he announced that 'Susan Loppart had taken Lyn's place and he thought he might marry her.' I can't really take it seriously. It would be madness for him to marry yet, I vaguely feel.

December 13th

An American professoress Doctor Virginia Mitchell came to see my Bloomsbury pictures not long ago. Dressed as a Russian officer in *War and Peace* (blue military coat with brass buttons, cavalry twill trousers and top boots, and with short grey hair), she sat herself down and opened fire about 'Art – for art's sake.' What the hell does it mean? After coffee and whisky she opened up and became genial if scatty. She has now sent me Roger Fry's letters and writes to ask my opinion of Denys Sutton's introduction. From obsessional conscientiousness I have gone back – after reading the letters – to Roger's other works, particularly on the theory of aesthetics,[1] and been fascinated and impressed. They are more modern than I had remembered, more pragmatical, attaching the artistic impulse to man's physical needs and

---

1 I was reading his writing on Indian art in *Last Lectures*.

suggesting all sorts of lines of thought. I'm bent on going into his aesthetics and re-organising my own. The subject seems susceptible to experiment, unlike metaphysics. But what an effort consecutive thinking is! Getting older necessitates keeping one's body as elastic as is pitifully possible. But even more one's mind. In the light of an incredibly sweet kind letter from Janetta, laced (because she sensed that I was depressed) with outrageously flattering remarks, I believe that the quality I have more of and am less credited with than some others is a sort of obstinate perseverance – I'm a natural swot. And my swotting is made harder by the normal failure of memory that comes with ageing. I often have what seem at the moment illuminating thoughts which I long to remember, but don't; I may turn on the light in the night to jot them down, and then lose the envelope they are written on. The subject of aesthetics, which I mean to explore, looms like the great wide prehistoric cave of Gargas, but I wonder if I shall ever go as far as I would like to into its depths.

December 15th

Musical evening last night with Angelica and Tam.[1] This after a day that was full to the brim, not altogether meaninglessly. The door was opened by Tam who said when I asked where she lived now, 'Here.' I had the curious impression (or perhaps it wasn't curious) that there was a love affair between them of some description. Caressing voice and looks (but these Tam always dispenses freely), and a community of attitudes – for instance in their wild dedication to music. Wild in the sense that there's a touch of the maenad in both. But it was lovely playing string trios with two such enthusiastic musicians. They told me how they had played to Julian and his two blackamoors when they came to dinner. The blackies were quite pleased and stroked the instruments saying, 'Nice,' but Julian had looked (and admitted to being) horrified. On the telephone he told me that he was shocked by their 'intensity' and had 'never been in a small room with people playing on instruments before'. Angelica does I

---

1 Later married to Andrew Murray-Thripland.

think like to play to people, which modesty forbids my doing except in an orchestra. I fear she has plans for me to take part in a performance of some kind at a Twelfth Night Party she's giving. Ralph and I used to deplore the fact that the performances at old Bloomsbury parties had ceased, but they were I think more light-hearted. Now that everyone can hear the best on records, why watch their friends seriously sawing away?

Another student of Bloomsbury, Miss Gottlieb, has been to see me; she seems to want to extract a poet and mystic from Leonard's[1] ashes. Everyone she has been to see, including Angelica, has told her she is on the wrong tack. So did I. Then she tried to equate mysticism with beliefs that are not purely material.

A marvellous day with pale blue sky and a pink light on the white stucco has tempted me to walk about the Christmassy streets.

December 17th

Drove to the Slade[2] with Eardley and Mattei and back very early, tonight Sunday. I get the feeling that Eardley has a private and secret life of his own. Where does he disappear to in the car 'to telephone and do one or two things'? Arriving home here about six-thirty the least I could do was ask him to join my scrambled eggs. He excused himself politely, again because of 'things to do'.

Very quiet mild days with mist morning and night, no breath of wind. I read and read – not what I'd meant to tackle (Roger's aesthetics), but books on Delacroix and then his journal. Then I walked along the lanes letting the hedges and banks go by like gentle music, picking harts-tongue fern and late-flowering weeds. After plunging along in mist, it suddenly cleared and all at once birds began singing, clear spring water was running in the gutters and a cottage came smouldering into view. There were low cliffs beside the road of ancient whitish stones with ivy streaming down them.

---

1 Woolf.

2 Eardley Knollys' small country house in Hampshire.

Mattei was indignant with Eardley for saying that he was good-looking when young and that that was the only reason he got to know any Bloomsburys. 'I would *never* think I had been good-looking and *never* say so,' he said almost irritably. He was equally but more rationally annoyed by Eardley saying that his own educated voice made him feel ill at ease with the lower classes like Mattei's workmen. But I don't want to imply that there was friction. On the contrary many delightful talks *à trois*, about the difference between cleverness and intelligence for instance.

A complete snub from Penguins. *Fortunata y Jacinta*[1] is in process of being translated, and will I keep in touch? and 'perhaps in a year or two'. I have a new philosophy – to accept that this is the end of my working life, in an active, positive way, and try to enjoy the end of commitments which I half realise would (if I had them) prove over-exhausting. Where I used to lug translation and dictionaries away for the weekend I now take letters to write and don't write them, filling my time all too easily with reading and walking and talking as I did at the Slade.

December 19th

I think a good deal about re-orientation towards a sort of fatalism, or at least acceptance. The work I did was not, I must face it, of any particular use to mankind, even if I'm right in thinking I can do it well. There is Desmond, five years younger than me and much better at his job, craving retirement passionately. The important thing is to construct my new life not apathetically, but putting everything I can into it. One decision I've tentatively taken is to write to Julia, and say that if she cares to have another try at meeting I would be delighted. If she says no, at least my conscience is cleared – as a pacifist I hope she will say yes and that we can have at least a shadow relationship.

I'm reading with increasing interest Walter Scott's Journal, a present from Julian. He writes: 'If the question was eternal company without the power of retiring within yourself, or solitary confinement for life, I should say "Turnkey, Lock the cell."' I wouldn't, but it's a ghastly alternative.

---

1 By Perez Galdós, a Spanish masterpiece I hoped to translate.

Well, I've popped the following into the letter-box to Julia: 'This is merely to say that if with the passing of time you should ever feel like giving our meetings another trial, I should be only too delighted. I miss your company very much, and the word you so vividly apply to the Universe – "eerie" – seems to me applicable to such an end to a lifelong friendship. However, if you would rather not, of course I will drop the suggestion and the subject instanter.'

True, but I think the odds are about 50-50 whether she says yes or no, and the strange thing is that, though true, I really feel indifferent to the outcome. The advantages or disadvantages are so evenly balanced. I wrote a very long letter to Joan in South Africa today, but didn't confess to this demarche, which she would certainly disapprove. I have discussed it before and she begged me not to.

December 20th

Last night's dinner-party – Campbells, Rose and Peter Eyre – lingered on till nearly two, when after about six hours' talking I sank exhausted into bed, and woke at a quarter to ten this morning. A success one must therefore say. Peter, now more at ease with me, develops (or releases should I say) more of his essence. At the end of the evening he began talking about the drug 'scene', as experienced at a wedding and dance in Wales. Georgia had just rung me up about it, full of elation, and the pleasures of dancing and dressing-up and wearing the necklace I once gave her. But Peter's account was a grim one and very different, though he had enjoyed it.

A great many rich junkies were there, weaving about and 'making no sense' on heroin and cocaine. He reinforced this by far worse accounts of drug-taking in America. It is mainly the rich and the poor – the middle classes are less affected. Impotent, tired feelings of dismay assailed me at the thought of all this wasteful misery. Sophie will soon be in sight of the drug belt. Rose (the Campbells had left) was anxious that the drug-takers should not be blamed but helped. Heavens yes, but how? Peter Eyre, a nervous fellow, tumbling over sentences sprinkled with 'sort-of's, has I notice abjured spirits and smoking. I think he was appalled — he said he felt like Mrs Whitehouse — yet there was a 'sort of' excitement in his voice as he described it all, including a girl who had taken cocaine to brace herself to meet her ex-lover, and yet wept for eight hours.

December 22nd

Sophie — affectionate, pretty, sweet and apparently happy — came with me to *Treasure Island* yesterday afternoon. I was a bit anxious whether it would turn out to be too violent and terrifying, but it wasn't really. Blind Pew's false white eyes caused the nearest to alarm, and a dagger sticking all too visibly and bloodily into one of the pirate's backs. We sat in the front row and when white smoke-foam came seething over the edge of the stage and enveloped us she dived under it and vanished from view; several boys copied her, and in this and other ways she showed herself as given to leading the rest. But my violin was her great excitement. She longs to play, and music and the Bible (for which she clamoured) are her obsession at the moment. 'Religion' was one of her classes at school. Henrietta joined us at supper and said to her firmly, 'I don't believe in God.'

December 23rd

Cosi fan tutte last night with Desmond, and back here to supper. Celestial music though it is, I find it impossible not to be bored by the tra-la-la of the action, and would really rather hear without seeing it. Desmond very gay at dinner, and I felt it was quite like old times being with him.

Now I tremble on the verge of tomorrow's departure to Cranborne when I am supposed to drive Laura and Paul Levy down for Christmas. No reply from Julia yet. From Anthony I hear that Caroline and Osei are back. Caroline adores Osei, who is loving and patient with her but she can't take life in Ghana and this has led to her 'very bad breakdown', something which Osei says happens to 80% of white girls who marry Ghanaians. He appears to be much grander than anyone realised — his family owns a vast area and has numbers of people working on it — and he can't leave.

December 26th: Boxing Day at the Cecils

Quiet weather, fairly cold; soft light on motionless trees, a very pale blue sky.

Jonathan appeared on Christmas Eve – on the morning of which we went to a crowded pointless jabber-session at 'Duchess' Ashley-Cooper's, squeezing from room to room, talking about nothing – mere sounds issued from our mouths, chit-chat concerning dogs, walks, plants.

On Christmas Day an orgy of present-giving, too many, too much, and today (with the arrival of Hugh and Mirabel) the excitement and materialistic self-indulgence began all over again – bottles of wine, bottles of scent, soap and bath salts, scarves gramophone records, covered in gift wrappings and red bows – and all to cries of 'Marvellous! Just what I wanted!' 'How did you know? It's just what I like!' till I felt a positive craving to hear critical and astringent talk, and for someone to burst out, 'It's beastly! I *hate* it!' For Julia, perhaps? But I do except Jonathan's generous and touching present to his parents of a colour television set, 'because I may never be earning so well again and have the chance to give you a really nice present'.

David read us the last chapter of his history of the Cecil family, about his uncles. Very good, and he described the eccentric set of brothers, and two ugly sisters (known as the 'Salisbury Plains') admirably. Hearing about their belief in reform and individualism, support of Conscientious Objectors and of course Lord Robert's invention of the League of Nations, Paul and I exclaimed: 'But your uncles have had a profound effect on ideas.' (David had said that they didn't.) 'They were the precursors of liberal views. There was nothing egalitarian about them. They believed firmly in the hierarchy.'

The hierarchy certainly dominated our Christmas evening and a visit to 't'Manor', as the Dorsetshire lady who brought up my breakfast called it. Later, ushered in by the butler, we stood round the dark panelled walls singing 'The Holly and the Ivy', benignly observed by Lord Burleigh and other portraits on the walls. Then Robert Cranborne[1] dressed as Father Christmas

---

1 The Viscount.

descended the stairs and started giving us bags of sweets, little purses and boxes of nuts out of his sack, while several small children screamed in terror and had to be carried out. We were summoned upstairs for drinks afterwards, where I sat somewhat uneasily making conversation (about dogs, horses and plants) to the two Lady Salisburys, one on each side of me, though Betty[1] (who has almost refused to leave Hatfield) hadn't been on speaking terms with Mollie[2] for two days, because of differences over Robert's choice of a Catholic bride.[3]

Well, and what of the members of our house-party?

David I think sinks a little further into traditionalism and family feeling, as Ralph always predicted he would. Blood will out. Rachel was like an active fairy, kind and thoughtful for everyone, so anxious to spare Olive the cook any trouble so that we never had any form of potatoes except warmed-up crisps, nor pudding except tinned fruit. A possible edition of Desmond's letters[4] has been mentioned again, as though David might at last read them and write a preface. Out of a sort of compulsion I encouraged this project but I'm not really sure I should have. And I greatly doubt if he even will read them.

When I first met Paul Levy at the Cecils' I was struck by his bright-wittedness. That's still in evidence, and so are other qualities like kindness and good nature, and maybe a little snobbery. On the whole I warmed to him more than I've done for some time. He *is* clever and kind, he's *not* at all malicious or spiteful.

Tomorrow back we go into our lives, and I'm as usual quite ready, pleasant and easy though these days have been, wherein I have slept deeply, relaxed completely and read a good deal.

---

1 Wife of 'Bobbety', 5th Marquess of Salisbury.

2 Wife of 6th Marquess of Salisbury.

3 Later Hannah, Lady Cranborne.

4 I had been invited to edit these, but the offer was withdrawn out of fear of publicity. I did considerable work on them which was later included in an excellent book on Desmond and Molly MacCarthy.

December 31st: West Halkin Street

This afternoon Georgie[1] brought her two little ones to see me, along with Jean-Pierre later, and their restful prattling and gurgling was quite soothing.

The night before I had had Stanley here from eight till midnight when I told him I was tired. I rather fear I hurt his feelings a little – I do hope not. Less than nothing remains of our conversation in my mind except an excellent phrase of his: 'a shepherd's pie of words'.

I've heard from Julia and she has accepted my olive branch and to dinner next week. I tremble a little, but it was a joy to get a letter in her familiarly comic style. She writes from Lawrence's at Leeds: 'I expect you have heard that Lawrence and Jenny have adopted two tiny little jet-black baboons, aged one and a half and two and a half respectively. These have built-in megaphones in their speaking apparatus – and the house echoes momently with either deep bass tiger jungle roars, or else to high treble shrills resembling the deafening sounds reminiscent of the old engines on the railways we used to know – as they were about to enter some tunnel.' Which seems to show that her literary style has become if anything even more involved along its old familiar lines, I'm glad to say.

---

1 Martel, née Kee.

II

2 JANUARY

TO

30 DECEMBER

1973

January 2nd

Gerald has written that he wants to publish the last volume of his autobiography, and, 'it's the most intimate book that any English writer has ever published.' *Ay de mi!* – that means just a distorted picture of Ralph all over again.

January 3rd

In half an hour Julia comes to dinner. Heaven preserve me! How long is it since our last meeting? Goodness knows. The problem will be to steer between speaking well of everyone, which she hates, and ill of them which she'll repeat and use to make mischief.

January 5th

She came and left with no blows exchanged, nor even a hint of tension. She was wearing the same several overlapping layers of familiar trousers and jackets I remember from our last meeting of two years ago, giving her a somewhat tramp-like appearance. She refused all alcohol and drank nothing but water – 'You know how it is, one has a glass of whisky at one's elbow all day and takes sips from time to time, and I don't want any more. I was trying to write about Aunty Loo.'[1] I can't say she made the faintest impression of intoxication. I had deliberately given very little thought ahead as to how we would manage, but as soon as she was here, it was obvious: I must confine myself to questioning her, and her supreme egotism would take over. Then, of course, never disagree and never (above all) contradict on a matter of fact. Following this recipe there was no awkwardness and no dangerous corners to negotiate.

---

1 The first Mrs Bertrand Russell, who brought her up from an early age.

She started on Christmas at Leeds – a pretty violent blast, funny (particularly when describing the little black children[1]) but venomous also. It had been ghastly; an appalling journey to get to a horrible little town villa. Jenny[2] rushed about with a haggard face 'looking like Aunty Loo', never smiled or relaxed at Julia's jokes, was horribly unkind to Lawrence who was frightfully unhappy, and not very nice to Laura who was driven into a corner by the two black babies. 'Then Laura and I used to have rather a tender relation but Jenny has turned Laura against me and she doesn't like me now.' Several times she had suggested taking the next train home but Lawrence talked her out of it.

Then came a stream of the old old complaints emerging quite unchanged from their hidden source. No servant would stay with her, the terrible business of shopping took up most of her day, and her 'business correspondence' the rest, so that she 'couldn't get on with her writing'. What can her 'business correspondence' possibly be? And though it was the same farcical old egocentric story, she does manage to spread it with the jam of her own original flavour.

She stayed until eleven, and on the whole I think it was a success. She doesn't look ill but has hunched and shrunk a little. She told me she had quarrelled with Ben Nicholson, because he said 'she didn't like children' and that when he asked her to his usual Christmas dinner she said, 'I don't want to come, since you think that about me,' and I think she was rather piqued because he accepted her refusal.

The chief impression made by our renewed relations is that they had never broken. Nothing seemed new or strange or the slightest bit awkward. My reaction at least is almost boringly nil.

January 8th

At Angelica's Twelfth Night party I talked to Olivier[3] Bell and heard to my amazement something which if possible underlines

---

1 Adopted by the Gowings as company for their daughter Laura.
2 Lawrence Gowing's second wife.
3 Wife of Quentin.

Julia's egotism. Talking of the Gowings, she mentioned 'this appalling thing that has happened'. It seems that only a month or so ago, Lawrence, Jenny and Laura had had a serious motor accident in France – Lawrence had forgotten the rule of the road – and Jenny had been badly injured and rushed by ambulance to hospital in Chartres where she had been operated on and a kidney removed. She had to stay *six* weeks, and the French family with whom they had collided had angelically taken in Lawrence ('distracted with anxiety') and Laura all that time. No wonder she looked (as Julia said) 'haggard'. But how incredible that Julia never mentioned it.

I've spoken to Ben Nicholson, who told me about his quarrel with Julia, said she had taken umbrage at a joking remark of his, that her quarrels were getting too fantastic for words, and that he proposed to 'wait a year, say, to cool down, because it would be absurd to apologise when he didn't feel he had anything to apologise for'. So she wounds another devoted friend to the quick, as she did me, and time must pass before the bleeding stops, something undoubtedly being lost in the process.

The party was as Julian said, '*echt* Bloomsbury'. Delicious food, a great deal of assorted wine but no hard liquor, curiously empty unfinished rooms lacking furniture, even chairs to sit on. My delight and joy was darling Sophie, looking as pretty as a picture in a long dress with a bustle, and dispensing drink and food with loving care.

The young Bells and young Roches clustered together, and there were not, I felt, enough other young people to admire the beauty of Quentin's daughters and the Garnett girls; Henrietta wore a slinky twentyish evening dress and acted (rather amateurishly) a short play with Richard Shone; Fanny looked rosy, practical and happy in a fur hat, and Amaryllis was telling everyone 'I'm so *vague*', which threatens to become rather a bore. Julian arrived extremely late followed by his 'two blackamoors': Egyptian Osáma is a tall, noble-looking, handsome fellow, Hassani more ordinary, smaller and blacker.

January 9th

Ever since the New Year began, and I think before, I have been chewing over a new practical philosophy, and today walking back from buying 'lingerie' in the sales I gazed up at the even pale sky through the black lace lingerie of the plane trees and their bobbles, and wondered whether it would 'hold'.

Roughly it is that I have decided to be realistic about having no translation and no prospect of getting one. I see it now as a life-belt which I couldn't possibly have done without in the first dreadful years of my loneliness; but, like a child suspended by its swimming-teacher from a fishing-rod which she silently withdraws, I find I can now swim without its support. At least I think I can, and *if* I can that is all to the good; so much gained in realism. As for my social conscience about helping my fellow humans, there must be better ways of doing that.

January 11th

Last night Anne and Heywood came to have a drink, and this morning I met Heywood again in the Harvane Gallery, looking at an exhibition of Boris's work, the centrepiece of which was the fireplace he gave Ralph and me for a wedding present. It gave me a sharp pang to see it there in alien and public surroundings when it had been so closely bound up with our life. I remembered how exciting it had been to see Boris put it in place on the half-solidified cement and then work like a fiend in Hell rubbing off the brown paper that covered it, to reveal the pattern of shells and their formal border, 'like your books, which are always crooked in the shelves'. (I don't think they were.) Heywood went sadly off to visit Nancy Mitford, who is dying of bone cancer, poor creature, after years of frightful pain. They tell her they can control it, whatever this means, and she has to put up with being pummelled by someone she calls 'Stout Cortez', joking to the last like Mercutie.

Stanley has passed his oral examination and therefore gained his Ph.D. He came here to lunch with his girlfriend, Susan Loppert, reeling with relief and pleasure.

January 15th

Yesterday morning Stanley rang up in masterful mood to say he would 'require two days of my time to help him put the alterations into his thesis'. Today he arrived before I was out of my bath and we sat at corrections, hammer and tongs, until a quarter to four. I marvel that someone so intelligent should make so many spelling and even grammar mistakes – it shows something about modern education – but the time wasn't wasted, and it seemed a much more real and congenial way of spending it than my days at Stowell the weekend before.

Philip was still in Majorca, and Mary had invited a party of youngish jet-set. Mary MacDougall, slim and attractive and a compulsive bridge-player, had a maddening way of talking in a pseudo-baby lisp, as did her friend the pregnant wife of the Knight of Glin. 'Brookie', Lord Brooke, son of Mary's recently dead friend Rose and Lord Warwick, was handsome, confident and clever in his way, or perhaps sharp is a better word. He told me he never looked at television, listened to music, or read anything except *Paris Match* and (I think it was) the *Daily Express*. What then does he do? So far as I could see nothing at all except shake up cocktails and play cards. One wouldn't trust him an inch, but now and again I felt a twinge of pity as I noticed a scared little boy peering out from the hard man-of-the-world's face. I liked best Mark Amory, a tall young man with a black beard, an indrawn laugh, and a slight look of the young Lytton.

Mary was in her element. It's not mine, and I retreated often to my room. 'The Knight', as they called him, and Amory are both probably quite intelligent, and work in museums or publishers. I can't imagine why they have to fill every sentence with witless laughter and sit down to drinks and cards at every spare moment. It was a relief to walk down the canal and visit Frances Phipps, and spend an hour talking to her – laughing, oh yes, but not cackling at nothing. We talked about Roger Casement, about why people painted pictures, how to deal with what she calls 'the last lap' and our feelings about nature.

January 16th

I awoke gloomily, thinking of last night's pointless dinner given by Dr Virginia Mitchell to me and my old Newnham pal, Heather Harvey, whom I remembered as a good-looking girl with large hips and a sense of humour. Luckily she evidently took to me as little as I did to her. I rather liked Virginia Mitchell, and would have chosen to talk to her about aesthetics, which I've been thinking about a lot thanks to her magnificent present of Roger's letters.[1] I've also been re-reading Clive,[2] and am amazed by his absurdly simple theory: he constates that what arouses the aesthetic emotion is significant form, but doesn't attempt to define significance. On the other hand I was delighted by his definition of sentimental art much like my own long-held view: he thinks it calls for a response which isn't direct, but is second-hand or disguised, for which he has found the excellent word 'complacency'. Someone looking at a sentimental picture of a doctor and patient may *think* he is feeling pity and admiration, when really it is only complacency at being so pitiful and admiring. It's ironical that by their concentration on Pure Form both Roger and Clive have been midwives to abstractionism whereas the Bloomsbury painters very soon abandoned it.

Thoughts on Julia's egotism: she's a practising solipsist where other people's troubles are concerned. They simply don't enter her field of vision – Gamel's[3] death, Cynthia's lost baby, Jenny's accident all are brushed impatiently aside. The darts of misfortune fall on her and her alone. So that her persecution mania 'stems' (as Stanley would say) from her solipsism.

January 18th

Dinner last night to the Kees, Annans and Raymond. Preparations were such a fearful sweat all day that by the time they arrived I was in no condition to enjoy it. I *hope* the guests did, but I found Noel Annan a little too rumbustiously bonhomous, and preferred the attractive Gabby, who disconcertingly turned out to know Rose's Robert and believes him to be 'Hell on wheels'.

Janet Stone to lunch yesterday. Dressed like a modern Ottoline, she has changed her hair from orange to yellow.

---

1 Fry, edited in two volumes by Denys Sutton.
2 Bell.
3 Wife of Gerald Brenan.

Eardley says she wants to give the impression she is having an affair with Kenneth Clark, without actually saying so. Well – perhaps she is.

January 23rd: Crichel

Alone with the three inmates, their music, books and information. Desmond played me more than half of *Tristan*. Hooked at first, I was overtaken by a feeling of surfeit – not that it was too long, but too uncontrolled and self-indulgent, harped too much on the same emotional key. Raymond was amassing information about genetics from a popular book suitable for school-children, and interrupted whatever we were saying or doing to communicate a new fact. He is a gourmand for them. Kitty came to dinner, and met with great sympathy about Caroline's troubles, but also fairly harsh criticism from everyone except loyal Desmond. She described how Anthony had tried to get Caroline to talk about her state of mind – 'Wasn't it wrong of him?' ('No,' said Pat) – while she herself had taken her some wool and told her to 'knit a teddy-bear's scarf or a doll's blanket', pathetically but misguidedly casting her in the role of eternal child, and retailing her remarks larded with 'Mummy's', a word Caroline never uses. (This is almost too painful to be recorded.) After she had left, Pat commented that she had said a good many very stupid things. Poor Kitty, how wrong she often puts her feet. She is enduring a horrific time and I felt very guilty for taking her up sharply once or twice. The trouble is that profound sympathy and even understanding do not quell all criticism.

A breakfast conversation about how much one could love oneself. Desmond murmured, 'But supposing one can't like what one knows?' It seems to me one should treat oneself as one does one's friends – critically, but with affection.

A long frosty walk with Desmond, starting among fields white as a Christmas cake, and with motionless trees swathed with chiffon scarves, standing under a sky of palest blue. When we got home it had all vanished.

London

Janetta is here: she had talked to Gerald about his autobiography and suggested that he suppressed what would hurt me. He came out with the same old view of Ralph to her, repeating that he knew him long before I had. He has written to me asking me to find out if the Dobrées[1] are still alive 'as he doesn't want to hurt their feelings'. I've written back saying 'how about not hurting the feelings of your very old friend Frances?' and suggesting that he allows me to vet his remarks about Ralph. What, I wonder, will he reply?

January 26th

Janetta came again, with Julian, and we ate two delicious red-legged partridges brought from Spain. Both admitted to feeling 'queasy', but ate and drank and talked bravely. I'm left with a residue of guilt – the English disease – about having talked too much and self-indulgently. Julian reminded me of a characteristic Isobelism[2] which delighted me: 'I'm beginning to come round to the idea of *public* executions, because when they take place inside the prison apparently all the other prisoners *batter* on the doors.'

Now I'm sitting in a state of agreeable confusion and daze, as if I had just passed through a maze of mirrors, as a result of finishing Goethe's *Elective Affinities*, given me by Stanley. It moves along at a stately pace like a Bach fugue and (like Bach also) contrives to impress profoundly by purely abstract qualities; but also by others of a very different kind – such as the contrast between the detailed, coloured, variegated background of streams, formal gardens, 'moss houses' and pavilions, and the characters progressing through it, whom I saw as silhouettes, mere outlines filled with whiteness against the coloured scene. I was obsessionally gripped, and yet I'm not sure what Goethe was trying to say, except that it was something very dear to his heart. He sets an ambivalent scene of conflict, and I was left with the feeling that he had resolved it. Stanley comes to dinner on Sunday 'to discuss it'.

---

1 Valentine and Bonamy.
2 Strachey.

January 29th

Yesterday, after tossing during several of the small hours, as is my present habit, I woke late and scarcely had time to get to Golders Green for Margaret's birthday lunch, followed by three or four Haydn trios and a Mozart quartet. I had just got home and stretched out on my bed when there was a ring on the telephone. Rose said she and Robert were in a state of Sunday gloom and would like to come and see me. Yes? Then they would start at once. Before they arrived another ring. Robert Kee. What were my evening plans? He arranged to come between Rose and her Robert, and Stanley. Robert Kee came before they had left. My instinct that he had something special to say was right, and he lost no time in getting down to it: 'Things have been very bad.' I poured whiskies. I felt he was summoning all his excellent faculties to give a fair picture and make an accurate decision about Cynthia, but that the decision was virtually made. He went off, declaring that he 'wanted to have everything out tonight', and was so closely followed by Stanley (with whom I talked about Goethe, pacifism, Wagner, and who gave me an account of his short trip to Germany and his reflections there) that I dropped into bed and sleep before I had digested the implications of Robert's decision.

And today all has been silence. Not a soul have I spoken to except Mrs Murphy, and I have pondered and raked among the coals of the Kees' crisis and of Janetta's meeting with Robert Urquhart.[1] I'm a little worried because she had promised to ring me and tell me about it. Nothing could be stranger than the contrast between the clotted consistency of yesterday and empty today.

January 30th

I remember walking along the highroad at Hindhead as an adolescent, when a moment occurred like Proust's madeleine to him; what flooded me there was the realisation that I was an independent human being, that I alone was responsible for my own thoughts and my own life which stretched ahead like an

1 The boyfriend of Janetta's daughter Rose.

exciting adventurous journey, even though symbolised by the straight macadamised Surrey road I was walking along. It was my thoughts in particular, I reflected, that no one could take away from me or forcibly alter. But I didn't for a moment think of them as influencing other people.

This morning, however, it is other people I am worrying about, and whom I do feel it might be in my power to help. Growing old is a withering away, the stem that remains is my responsibility for my friends. I think of the crises in their lives as wounds waiting to be dealt with, and myself as a clumsy nurse preparing bandages and disinfectants. And I feel real guilt about long-term patients in the background – like Julia.

February 2nd

Another perfect visit from Janetta. She seems to have liked Rose's Robert. At dinner last night Julia warmed to Henrietta's admiration and magic. With Eardley on the sidelines, it was a really pleasant evening. Henrietta told me that Sophie had been up to London for a weekend, and was 'suddenly changing, getting darker, had grown several inches and is not like me any more, but suddenly so like Burgo in gestures and movements and sidelong flirtatious glances that it gave me quite a turn.'

Professoress Virginia Mitchell to lunch yesterday. Talk about Roger's[1] effect on painters. She had been to see Richard Carline, who believed he had been destructive and stultifying except to the chosen few, and had manifested the persecution mania caused by Bloomsbury exclusiveness. But was that any-thing more than having high standards? Carline is a nice friendly, tail-wagging dog, but I don't think anyone rates him high as a painter. It's still probable that Roger's searchlight shone too narrow a beam.

February 6th

When there are blue skies overhead the deluge suddenly descends. The lease of my flat comes to an end this year. I got Mungo to sound my landlord about a continuation, and they

---

1 Fry.

replied that the lease would not be renewed – they 'require vacant possession'. I went down to the basement and talked to that crafty little Alberich or Mime, Mr Sultana, our Maltese caretaker, who says the house is structurally in a bad way and they are rebuilding it. 'So does no one have a lease beyond this year?' I asked. He said not. They obviously want to make more smaller flats and exploit them. And I don't want to move; I don't really want to go on existing anywhere else. At the same time comes a long tiresome screed from Gerald raising various points about Ralph, twanging away at that old compulsive string till I could scream. And yet another chord is painfully thrummed by the news that Sophie and another little girl ran away from school two days ago and took a train to London where they found no one but Olivier Garnett.

The old ghost of Angst raises its head, and I don't feel equal to it, but long to sink down and quietly disappear. Arrangements, responsibilities – oh how I dread them, how painfully unequal I feel to them.

Bob Gathorne-Hardy is thought to be dying of a disease of the liver. Anne appeared on Monday night at a dinner-party of Patrick Kinross's[1] – hunched and peering through small blue spectacles. I felt terribly sorry for her and she brought with her a waft from the hospital.

February 7th

I sent Janetta Gerald's dossier and told her to show it to Anne, who has always furiously defended R. against Gerald. They have both taken up the cudgels manfully on my behalf, and say they will write to Gerald. I told Janetta I should be extremely grateful if they would.

I saw poor old Sir Walter Scott into his grave this morning (in his diary) and heartily wished I could follow him, being at the moment supremely conscious of having *had enough*. Scott killed himself with working, and I'm haunted by his last futile attempt to hold the pen, with the tears streaming down his face. What shall I read, now that his life is done?

---

1 Writer.

Janetta says she can't help feeling shocked at the amount Anne talks about money. It is in the Gathorne-Hardy genes; she has less of it than most of them. Also the stress of Bob's expected demise has knocked her off balance. He has inherited drawings by Mantegna, Michelangelo etc. worth over a million and has not signed a will, nor is it thought that he is capable of doing so.

February 10th

Two operas two nights running, *Tristan* and *Don Pasquale*. To *Tristan* in a box, with Mary and her brother David. It was badly conducted by Colin Davies, who received a round of booing painful to witness even if deserved. The more I think about Wagner and his extraordinary music the more I am perforce increasingly baffled by the problem of its emergence from so unpleasant a character. Meanwhile even if Stanley suppresses some of the swooning adoration he used to display at the mere mention of his name, he certainly still feels it. To *Don Pasquale* with Janetta, and afterwards back here for the best sort of communicative conversation. I cannot get over her great sweetness to me.

Bob Gathorne-Hardy is unconscious but still alive.

As for my other main source of Angst, Gerald, he rankles within me like an ulcer. At lunch yesterday Julian advised me earnestly to return him soft answers, and merely step up the pathos – '*please please* don't, it makes me *so* unhappy.' I don't believe I'm capable of it. I think Gerald is wrong and I must give a rational explanation if I am to make any response at all. Janetta was furious when I read out some extracts from his letters (to Stanley for instance), and is all for my writing exactly what I feel – reasoned fury. 'I'll go and see that *beast* as soon as I get back,' she said. But anger is a horrible feeling; it erodes my peace of mind. I wake in the night and write letters to Gerald in my head. It's a disease, and I only survive by taking too many sleeping-pills every night.

February 15th

I spent most of yesterday (bitter cold it was too) writing Gerald a five-page letter, in defiance of Julian's advice but in accord with Janetta's. I didn't disguise the pain and upset he had caused me, but also went into what I believed to be the reasons for them. I don't feel at all sure it was in any valid sense the 'best' thing to do, or even in key with my ethical views, and I don't suppose it will have the same effect, but in some indefinable way I feel it would have been a betrayal of my love for Ralph and my knowledge of his character *not* to have written something of the sort, and as a result I slept more soundly than I have for weeks.

More music: to *Siegfried* last night, marvellously conducted and sung – a major experience. Stanley sat beside me, motionless with attention, a perfect companion for it.

February 21st

I took Rose and her Robert, and also Stanley to see a Verdi curiosity – *Stiffelio*, and they came back to supper. Stanley and Robert talked enthusiastically and highly technically about music, chiefly Wagner, and seemed to get on well. Robert then gradually climbed on to his Marxist horse and became rather a noisy bore. It started from his criticisms of Gerald's Civil War letters which I had lent him. Gerald hadn't taken sides sufficiently – and if one didn't take sides absolutely in such a contingency one was automatically supporting the Right. Lorca had done so – true he was shot by the Right, but he had in fact withdrawn from the conflict and gone on writing plays and poems. I put in a word for Individualism and said I respected those who went on doing what they were good at, and that Mozart had done more for humanity than most politicians. Robert said he would swop Mozart for Lenin any day and that outstanding men, whether good or bad, were just products of the environment. 'Aren't you forgetting the genes?' I cried. Heat was beginning to be generated. Robert said heredity and environment were all one (he was talking more and louder than anyone, with Rose setting up a quiet echo, and Stanley putting in a few very pointful remarks), and went on to instance the effect on the unborn child of what happened to it in its mother's womb. Perhaps like many Marxists he believes with Lysenko that acquired characteristics can be inherited. At half past one I felt tired and rather irritated by Robert's fanatical pursuit of the party line, and said 'Let's go to bed', perhaps too abruptly.

February 23rd

I wrote Robert U. an amicable letter and have just received a long and amicable reply, which may or may not bridge the gulf between our views. I've not yet managed to read it all. Days are full: Tam came to lunch and stayed talking (partly about Marxism) until Stanley arrived with a review of his for me to read. Afterwards he confided that he was suffering from shock at discovering that his 'girlfriend' was in fact, and had been for years, a lesbian. I feel very warmly to Stanley and am discovering that he is not only intelligent and kind but extremely sensitive, so that I shared his distress.

March 3rd

Gerald has written me a frenzied ten-page letter, going into my points at length, telling a number of whopping lies, and saying that as a result of my letter he had become 'vague and senile', 'fallen into the *cañada* and been unable to get out', 'nearly got run over' and 'thought he might have had a small stroke'. What a very unexpected development! Declaring his love and admiration for me, the old humbug, he begs me not to answer: he cannot bear the sight of my writing and will tear up any letter unread. Now, however, he is 'quite restored to vigour'. Lynda, that model of intelligence and detachment, believes it 'to be a storm in a tea-cup', me presumably the tea-cup! I want to stop thinking about the whole affair. I've no desire to give Gerald a stroke, but don't regret giving him a few unhappy hours.

March 6th

I have a somewhat modified view of what Frances Phipps calls 'the last lap'. I want to get through it as quickly and painlessly as possible; I want to burn up *the stump of my candle*.

At the Carringtons' I saw Joanna and Christopher Mason.[1] Gerald has accepted Joanna's cuts in his manuscript, which

---

1 Painters; Joanna is Carrington's niece.

Christopher obviously dislikes more than she does. He has described her as being 'obsessed by Carrington', 'very neurotic' and 'having thick negroid lips'. She says she wasn't obsessed by Carrington at all. Everyone is agreed on at least one of Gerald's characteristics – his fantastic egocentricity. But how trivial in a way all this seems if one takes a scared look at the world scene: strikes in the French airlines have led to a collision of two planes in midair with sixty-eight dead and others in hospital. Only one operating theatre remains open at Bart's; patients are being sent home before their time, only 'emergency cases' dealt with. It's a sorry spectacle and I find it hard to orientate myself. Many of my friends, like Faith yesterday, think me wildly tolerant of the strikers. To a few, like Rose and Robert, I probably don't go far enough in their support. When I think of the plight of modern man I remember a frog I saw on a walk at Kitty's – a beautifully pressed frog with arms and legs outspread (run over by a car I suppose) on the road.

I visited Alix on the way to Lambourn. She is increasingly deaf, and so it seems at long last as if her bright wits were slightly tarnished. Her obsessional approach to the details of life, while considering the major issues with rational detachment, delights me. The upstairs cat came to the window to be let in. An elaborate ritual of signals had to be gone through before this was possible, and then she said to me, 'Will you hold her while I shut the door into the hall? She likes to go up the *main* staircase because it has a carpet and is softer for her paws, but I'm afraid of her bringing in mud so I make her go up the *back* stairs, which she doesn't like at all.' Sure enough poor Pussy baulked at the back stairs which were slippery and steep, but finally took them. I never saw a cat with such snowy paws however.

Stanley has been to lunch and stayed talking till nearly four. Now I'm lying on my bed listening to comments on the budget.

March 9th

Which shall I put first – the surprising public events or more encouraging private ones?

I'll start outside – a number of presumably Irish bombs went off in London yesterday, one injuring more than two hundred people. Descriptions of screaming people with blood pouring from them, the inevitable 'just like the Blitz'. Other bombs were found in cars and made safe. After the first news I heard a bang in the early afternoon and thought apathetically 'a bomb I suppose'. For all the hysteria in the press and on radio my main feelings are disbelief and detachment. Perhaps a slight dislike of the idea of going into large buildings. The rush of patients needing treatment to hospitals brought some hospital workers back from their strikes to look after them. The railways and traffic in general are still in dear old 'chaos'.

But my word, venturing into the unknown bits of London in the dark is something I *do* find really terrifying and I got absolutely lost at Camden Town and thereafter, trying to find the Anreps at Highgate Village last night. Near comic situations – a striped barrier across the road saying 'Local Traffic Only'. Was I local or not? How could I say? I threaded my way stubbornly through it and had the greatest difficulty in ever getting out again.

Private news: Janetta, that knight-errant, that unequalled diplomat, has bearded Gerald in his den and actually tamed him. I sent part of his explosive ten-page letter out with Julian enclosing a note saying, 'Don't talk to Gerald on my account. He might have a stroke!' She writes that she had already been and is glad she had because she thinks she has done some good to him as well as to me. At first he became frenzied and incoherent and shouted, 'I won't talk about it. It's killing me! I don't know why, but it is!' With her marvellous gentleness Janetta said – 'But why *not*, Gerald, why *don't* you want to talk? You're very good at saying what you mean.' In the end he did. From a long letter I will extract: that Lynda does *not* agree with Gerald and was 'very *very* good', that finally he began saying 'such nice things about Ralph', and when she asked 'Why don't you say that?' he suddenly began saying, 'I will, I will.' That he told her she had helped him enormously, and she was so pleased she could have wept. And that he is going to alter a lot and show it to her for her to let me know. It exceeds my wildest hopes.

March 13th

I try to diagnose my strong feeling of restlessness and conclude that it is largely the sense of impending political crisis. My rage rises in my gorge like heartburn at the smug obstinacy of the Government refusing to budge an inch to give the underpaid hospital workers a penny more, to the grave danger of us all. Doctors have petitioned them, have said that people are bound to suffer and die. Heath has merely retired to his tent like Achilles and maintains a stubborn silence. Barber took tax off those piffling articles that produce fat white children with bad teeth – sweets, potato chips, soft drinks; but it is clear that it is the rich who benefit from his budget, for all his murmurings about 'pensioners and lower paid workers'. It is sickening and I find it hard to concentrate on other things. Then what salary do they propose for the members of the Prices and Incomes Board? – £16,000 each! One glimpses from the wireless the ill-feeling that is festering in places like Bermuda and South Africa among the poor and black at the squandermania of the rich and white.

I took Julia to a cinema the other night, which luckily she chose and we both enjoyed. On the whole I thought her 'low', but pretty sane. We had a meal in an Italian restaurant afterwards and she blew her top at the wretched waiter for bringing the wrong sort of potatoes: 'I asked for sauté potatoes and you've brought *fried*! Didn't you hear what I *said*? I can't eat these – they're just warmed-up packet potatoes. Take them away.' I sat sheepishly by while my guest thus made a spectacle of herself. Yet 'Lawrence always hates it when I do this,' she said. Of Leeds she said she loathed going there, it was a long, tiring journey and no pleasure when she was there. 'Then is it really worth going?' I asked. 'I only do it for Lawrence's sake.' I do get pleasure from her wry humour – otherwise how can one contemplate her existence without profound sadness; it is a drawn-out tragedy.

A very nice interlude: On Sunday Stanley and I went to hear three string quartets on the South Bank (Haydn, Beethoven and Schubert) very well played. The Beethoven – his last – was to me the most thrilling by far, in fact I can't remember experiencing such a sustained physical thrill for a long time. Beethoven is not Stanley's favourite musical country, but I'm trying to indoctrinate him. We came home to tea here. It seems odd in view of the huge difference in our ages, but I now feel he is one of my great friends. He loves thinking, and that is everything. On this occasion he came out as a complete pacifist and asked, 'Didn't you realise I was one?' I realise that pacifism means so much to me, and so few of my friends share my belief (Stanley and Julia are almost the *only* ones) that I hesitate to express my views, especially when they appear to enrage people so, as they did at Robin and Susan's fatal dinner-party.

March 18th: With the Cecils at Cranborne

I drove down with the Sheppards. Clare is something of a dictator; I'm not sure whether Sydney resents or enjoys this – he's certainly well aware of it. She relegated him and me to the back seat 'as I like to drive in grim silence when I'm speeding'. So she did, and drove well and carefully but with never a smile and hardly a word, making stylised pecks towards her driving-mirror. She is censorious, suddenly funny, determined. Her health has become a preoccupation, and she carries about a squalid packet of cold ham, which is all she feels she can safely eat. Sydney's tempo is so exceedingly slow – and I feel this means slow thinking as well as slow speaking – that it's difficult for him to get a hearing in this fast-talking family. When he does it's worth waiting for. Discussing the new pornographic film, *Last Tango in Paris*, he came out very slowly with 'I like to – do – my – own – sex.'

David was specially benign, appreciative, happy and plump. Food has sunk to a new low – there was a pudding of hot puffed wheat dowsed in chocolate sauce and cream. Weather divine; we had two wonder-walks, the Sunday one (to be long remembered) was to a deserted farmhouse standing alone in a hollow under a wooded hill – we climbed it and walked through these woods, sparkling underfoot with dog's mercury, and looking out on the cream-coloured fields (no rain for weeks, no mud, all dry as a bone) picked out with dark yews.

Conversation literary or about people, not much about the political situation which David tends to sweep aside with 'all is for the best'. I neither wanted to say what I really feel nor what I don't, and in fact did both or neither.

March 21st

I sit in the square, in summer heat and beauty. This morning the better to enjoy the fine weather which shows no signs of stopping, I walked across the park to the public library – the beauty of the day, children happily skipping, a fat little dog cantering after its elderly master, crocuses, daffodils and forsythia, fresh green grass and birds, all this made me feel sad, as if it were somehow too much.

A party last week for the presentation of the Duff Cooper Prize to Quentin Bell. John Julius Norwich made a very ordinary speech. Quentin's own was refreshingly short, funny and unconventional. We swigged champagne and I talked to Angelica, Henrietta and Amaryllis, Norah Smallwood (who broached my 'helping them' with some book or other),[1] Jock Murray, etc, and round and round went that deaf Walter who Juanita[2] was once engaged to. I couldn't remember his surname and nearly introduced him as 'Walter Mitty'.

My mind hops like a cricket in this hot weather, and responds to little jabs of emotion. The extraordinary implications of the words 'my children'; class – how much is it dead or dying, what would its temperature-chart look like. Yesterday I went round to see Mary just back from Arizona; she was full of the delights of first-class travel. She told me that in some aeroplane emergency the 'first-class passengers silently gripped their seats, while screams and yells came from the second class'. So now we must think that the possession of money makes one braver!

March 27th

'No' springs more easily to my lips than it used to – and so it did when Janet[3] suggested coming to lunch at the last moment last Thursday. Then I went quickly into reverse and she came, hatted and veiled as usual, and over lunch (very naturally and quietly) came out with the confidence that for the last fifteen (?) years or so Kenneth Clark had been 'madly in love with her',

---

1 She ran the publisher Chatto & Windus.
2 Japp.
3 Stone.

and she – it was implied – with him, only 'of course Reynolds always had and always would come first.' She had come up to London to see him. I felt no surprise, because it came out so easily and Eardley had hinted at something of the sort, except perhaps that she had kept the secret so long. He would, it seems, have been glad to divorce Jane his wife and marry her, but she wasn't willing. I don't in the least suspect exaggeration. A letter followed begging me to keep her secret.

On Friday Raymond, Des and I took a morning train to Crichel, arriving in summer heat which continued all afternoon through a walk with the dogs, tea actually on the lawn. Thenceforth cold showers broke up the extraordinary beauty of spring. Julian came in the evening. An outburst from Desmond about the 'squalor, filth and hideousness of most young men's clothes', and indignant questions as to 'why they obviously *wanted* to look so revolting?' It was mere shadow-boxing, as we none of us stuck up for filth and squalor, but he failed to notice this and thundered deafeningly and excitably on.

Reflections of the weekend in general – Raymond comes near boring-point with his informativeness at times. He really loves Julian and his clever amusing company, but complains endlessly of his literary style. Frequently referring to himself as a 'dodo', he trots out a number of prejudices – e.g. against the Japanese and the Germans. I defended the latter, and he said – like an old colonel, 'Well, they involved *me* in two world wars.' As Julian said, it was 'a regular Headlong Hall'. When Desmond and I entered the drawing-room shaken up by violinist Weiss's brilliance, Pat was holding forth about 'meditation' such as he told us he had voluntarily carried out many years ago for an hour a day after an operation in hospital. 'You make your mind a complete blank) – and then wait to see what comes seeping in – *You* and Fanny would of course think it was the unconscious,' he added to Raymond.

Desmond turned on his heel and left the room saying, 'Oh I can't take that,' only to return later and apologise. I murmured, '*Ni moi non plus*,' and buried myself in my book. Julian was justifiably indignant with us both, and later on with Raymond, for 'interrupting' with unimportant questions. I knew we were being intolerant, but sometimes it's hard not to be, and surely when anyone really makes their mind a blank they just go to sleep? What interested me most in this incident was Julian's reaction – he became much agitated and at the same time quite uncharacteristically incoherent, yet longing to get Raymond (and even more me) to give 'meditation' a chance. He 'wished Georgia was there, because she has such a lot to say about it' (she has never made much sense of it to me, and at Saint-Bertrand what ninepins she did set up went down with a bang before my very first tap). It was no doubt arrogant to avert my mind from what Pat had to say, and I feel somewhat ashamed, though my view of 'meditation' remains stubbornly unchanged. But the fact is that for the *first time* I felt there might be some truth in what – Tam perhaps? – said: that Julian would one day return to the faith and the fold.

Other subjects – racial prejudice, as a result of a harrowing telly programme on anti-black feelings. The faces of little black children saying they 'wished they were white because then people wouldn't say things at you'. The pretty faces of little upper-class boys from Summer Fields describing 'poor children dressed in rags with their toes coming through their shoes' with startling ignorance and lack of feeling; the silly inarticulate would-be charming smirk of their headmaster; the sound blazing sense of a Central European female professor from Sussex University, who declared that these 'privileged boys were the biggest evidence for Comprehensive education she had ever heard'; the condescension of an idiotic white female with a beehive hair-do, towards a really beautiful Indian woman (*'now she knows* what I think of her and that pleases me', and the Indian: 'I feel merely sad – there are some things better left unsaid'); and, worst of all, the hatred or stupidity of a batch of policemen towards a far more civilised and kindly batch of blacks. All this gave food for thought, sadness and indignation. Julian was much affected; so much so that he had to leave the room; Raymond perhaps least – he even thought the invariable white complaint about the 'smell of curry' might be justified, instead of just a symbol. We had had curry for lunch as it happened!

All through the weekend I thought about privilege and prejudice and the need to redistribute wealth, and bored Julian with my outbursts – though he seems to agree. It is my obsession of the moment. I have a new idea for first-class travel – it should be available without extra charge to everyone over seventy, or with a medical certificate, or delicate and important work to do at the end of a long journey, like Cabinet Ministers.

March 30th

My difficulty in making plans hinges on the future. To go on to Italy from Switzerland? To go to Spain in July, when Mrs M. is away? Mexico in the autumn with the Parladés?

Dadie and Eardley came to lunch yesterday to plan for Switzerland. From behind the mask of a wound-up whirring exterior I looked with a sinking heart at brochures of hills cloaked with pines sweeping down to chalets, tennis courts, piscines and golf-links where people leapt and ran. Oh! How little appetite I feel for it all!

April 1st

Weekend in London, cold, drizzling, grey. Yesterday I drove out to Chinnor to lunch with Paul Wilkinson (the doctor I got to know in Cyprus) and his wife, who had been ill. Tommy's youngest sister Helen and her husband were there – she looked remarkably like him and also like her fiendish old mother Lady Tomlin. We were treated to delicious food and drink, but it was an odd interlude, a sideways step out of my ordinary life.

After I got back Georgia rang up asking if I would 'like a little visit'. We talked for hours, mainly about Julian's unhappy predicament. She is convinced there's no happiness for Julian until Egyptian Osáma leaves, and was in her most dynamic mood, almost prepared to get rid of him herself.

The evening before I spent with Rüdiger and Stanley, and I have brought away Rüdiger's catalogue for an exhibition at Kenwood, to correct his English. They both spoil and flatter me outrageously, and I can't pretend to dislike it, though I very much doubt if it's good for me. One of the flattering things Stanley said was that he was amazed by my 'open-mindedness

and interest in everything'. The trouble I find about being interested in things at my age — and on the whole I accept the charge
— is that it is almost too much for me, in the sense that intense
pleasures, such as listening to music or having an absorbing conversation, reduces me to quivering over-agitation. If that gets
worse, where shall I be? As a form of second childhood I try and
learn things, and fill up the yawning patches of ignorance —
lately the odd trio Wagner, Marx and Trotsky have been my
concern.

Isobel came to dinner, wearing a long kaftan, her hair in a
fluffy aureole, pink-cheeked and indignant. 'No fury like a
woman scorned!' she cried as she sat down — the scorner had
been the horrid young man with an eye-shade, James Graham by
name, friend of Elisabeth Cochemé — and of Isobel too it seems,
though of late he has roused her passions and refused to satisfy
them, saying horrible things to her, until yesterday she 'flew at
him and hit him'. She said, 'I *always* remember Ralph saying that
Jan *couldn't* face the fact that she was no longer a sexual object.'
Isobel's indignation and flushed face became her so well that she
almost looked like one. But I do thank heaven that my life isn't
complicated by that problem at least.

April 3rd

Last night I dined with Magouche and the Sterns. Jimmy was
limping, looking rather ill, and tried in weak plaintive tones to
get a word in edgeways against Tanya's spate of talk.

How charming is German Rüdiger, who came to receive his
corrected manuscript with a two days' growth of stubble on his
chin. I like him very much indeed.

So fine, if iced, a day was it that I walked into Hyde Park and
as far as *Physical Energy* and back by the Albert Memorial.
Willows faintly touched with yellow-green reminding me of
Cambridge; bursting buds and pink blossom in marvellous
scarcity; very grand babies in smart prams with stupidly croon-
ing nannies; children madly bicycling — a great deal of happiness
and beauty in fact, and London's face wearing a curiously
unchanged and old-fashioned expression. I think perhaps the
parks are the best that's left of the old place.

April 6th

Just off to Stowell for the weekend, though with a slightly sinking heart. The gap between Mary's values and mine has widened a great deal in the last year – or perhaps it's true to say between our interests. I took her to a play about Edward VIII's abdication, where we met Francis Watson,[1] and I was almost nauseated by the competitive boasting between the two of them about their knowledge of and intimacy with all the members of the Royal Family. At supper beforehand Mary said to me in a pleading voice, 'You're not *against royalty*, Frances, are you?' And when I said laughing, 'Why, you know I am!' she said quite seriously: 'Oh, *no?*' The days when she and Robin[2] voted Labour have been long forgotten.

The play had a bearing for me on the fact that Dadie has sent me a copy of Peter Luke's play, now called *Bloomsbury*, about which Luke and I had some correspondence eighteen months ago. Lytton, Carrington and Ralph are the chief figures. A character at the end seems to be a composite of me and Henrietta Bingham. I'm really too fed up with the whole business to go on putting up much of a struggle. And as in *Crown Matrimonial* we saw the present Queen Mother as a young woman, exploding with indignation over Edward VIII's selfish behaviour towards her husband, I can't really think that anyone is going to bother about my feelings.

Now death is striking in most unexpected quarters – Michael MacCarthy is the last to fall.

April 11th

Read Peter Luke's play throughout the weekend, making critical notes. It is silly, but I suppose it might be worse. Mary also read it, spectacles on nose, and noted down her reactions. Since then I have been fully occupied, writing to Dadie and Luke's agent, telephoning here and there (Michael Holroyd, Paul, Dadie, Alix). I don't think there's the smallest chance of stopping the play, but possibly any infringement of copyright might

---

1 Director of the Wallace Collection.

2 Campbell.

allow us to bargain for some changes. This is my present hope. It has been worrying and agitating but does not disturb me as much as the Christopher Hampton project did.[1] Perhaps I'm getting hardened. Luke has (as he said) become fond of Lytton and Carrington and is not antipathetic to pacifism. He likes Ralph too but it suits his plot to make him a hearty soldier saying 'bally well' and 'tophole' and that 'Shirkers should be put up against a wall and shot.' There is a scene showing L., C. and R. all in bed together, and another when Lytton is dying and Carrington says 'Lytton believes in God' twice, then producing from her pocket some verses which she reads aloud. The comments of Ralph and others add up to the conclusion that Lytton died a Christian. When I told Alix this on the telephone she exclaimed, 'Good God!'

It was an easy weekend at Stowell, mostly alone with Mary and Philip. Mary was looking fine and radiant, and now enjoys walks, which contributes to my pleasure. We took a splendid one over the downs with the ex-wife and children of 'Brookie' (Lord Brooke of my last visit). There are strange lapses into meanness, which I don't actually mind at all, when I'm not introduced to anyone, or even offered a drink, like the governess. I'm quite sure they both mean to be very kind to me, and I quietly enjoyed my stay, reading (*Madame Solario* among other things) and breathing in the glorious air. Serena came to dinner. Francis Watson to lunch next day, perfectly pleasant.

Magouche has been to lunch and was lovely and lovable. She has asked me to Avane after Switzerland and I really think I might go.

And two nights ago I invited Angelica, Nicky and Patrick to dinner. The girls were both splendid, but I rather took against Patrick alas – he seems to be a bit soft in the head, though argumentative. He and Nicky utterly exhausted me by staying till after one o'clock, while Patrick tried, so far as I could make out, to discredit medicine, particularly for the mad, and most particularly electric shock or drug treatment. Why? I asked, and he said, 'I'm not any good at dialectic' and that if he did support

---

1 The film, *Carrington*.

medical treatment it would probably be Brahmin or some such
sort. But discussion with him was like fencing with swords made
of cotton-wool.

April 14th

Saturday morning in London and mostly in bed. I revelled in it
and spent much of it writing a long letter to Janetta.

The plot of Luke's play thickens, and after the darkness has
come a faint dawn. I went to see Mungo who was marvellously
in command of the situation. The contentious issues, by making
a whole scene out of Carrington's letter and quoting a poem of
Lytton's, are clear he says, and I could insist on them cutting
these out, but this is not what I want. He and I are therefore
pitting our wits to use them to get the alterations I do want. I
hear that I am to meet Unna, Luke's agent, in Mungo's office on
Tuesday.

I wish I didn't find it all so damned disturbing, and wake in
the night making speeches, or tormented by scenes from *Tosca* –
always those to do with Mario's execution.

The same evening as my visit to Mungo I had Julian first, then
Julia to dinner, and I persuaded Julian to stay on. He looked
much better and told me he was going to a lay analyst – a
delightful old man in his seventies. Bryan Walsh's blackamoor,
Hassani, has been had up as a pusher of drugs, and his story
(which I can well believe) is that the police made him empty his
pockets and then planted the stuff on him. He was to be tried
next day, Richard King[1] but probably not Julian giving evidence. He was telling me that he had not yet been able to bring
himself to tell his analyst about his sex-life when Julia walked in.
Good evening with her. When I mentioned Luke's play she was
inclined to hector me a bit and say, 'It must be stopped!' or
'Yes, but does it give a fair picture of Lytton?' but when I told
her I was worn out with trying to fight it and could hardly bear
to speak about it any more (I had done so at length to the much
more realistic Julian) she said, 'Poor Frances' and dropped it.

After Julian left at about ten, she and I had the most

---

1 Cambridge friend of Julian's.

138

sympathetic conversation for ages. She spoke of her horror of growing old, of feeling herself no longer sexually attractive (how long ago I faced that), yet how young men still attracted her and she longed for them to kiss her or write her love letters, how she was 'always in love'. Anthony d'Offay[1] is her love of the moment, that's very plain, but she mentioned two young queers who greatly admired her writing. 'I've made some new friends,' she said. On the minus side, she had actually sent two pieces of memoirs to the *New Yorker* and had them returned. Also her last visit to Leeds had been the worst yet. I asked for an illustrative incident and got one. The children adore Lawrence – 'it's "Daddy! Daddy" all the time.' Lawrence was cutting up the meat for one of the tiny negresses, when Jenny bustled forwards and said, 'Let me do it.' Julia said, 'Can't you see Lawrence wants to do it?' (I can imagine in what tone of voice) and Lawrence responded by giving Julia 'a hefty kick on the shin with his fourteen-inch foot. It jolly well hurt, I can tell you.' Some correspondence had followed. Much can be read between the lines but none of it very cheerful.

I said, which was true, that I had lately come to think of death as a close reality, and that the main horror to me of getting old was how one's friends died one by one. F: 'I do miss Lionel.' J: 'Yes I do too' (but not with great enthusiasm I thought) and with much more she said: 'And I miss *Ralph*.' This touched me very much, and I said, 'I'm glad.'

I had set aside yesterday, Friday, as a day of total calm and vacancy, but of course it didn't turn out exactly that way. Stanley rang me in the morning and arrived bearing white lilac and a really excellent and witty piece about Gerhardie which makes me see a bright future for him as a writer. After going over it we cooked and ate some sausages. I fell deeply asleep in the afternoon; woke up and went to the bookstall at the Carlton Towers, where I was surprised to hear a voice saying, 'Hullo Frances.' It was Tristram,[2] who said he had just popped into the Gents there. He came back with me for a drink, and when I

---

1 Owner of art gallery.
2 Powell.

inevitably unloaded my worries about Peter Luke's play he was extremely encouraging, in that he said so many plays are taken up and dropped, altered, tried out in the provinces, and never get as far as London. In any case years often pass between the alpha and the omega. I felt as if my fur had been stroked the right way, and was considerably reassured – but woke this morning between three and five to a state of renewed worry, accompanied by tunes from *Tosca*. The most loved tunes become horrible when they accompany anxious thoughts.

April 18th

Yesterday I was visited by two representatives of Peter Luke's agents, one male with gold teeth, one female with gold hair, both of them distasteful. I started by being fairly tough about not having been sent the script of the play, and then got down to telling them what I should want altered in order to grant copyright. They scribbled away (I feeling like some absurd kind of schoolmistress dishing out a *dictée*), and then I said that if these changes were made I would be satisfied, and might even be able to help the director with photos etc. Of course I may be wrong but I *think* they might get Luke to make the changes I want.

While I was trying to compose myself for their visit, and feeling as if I were going to take a viva in my tripos, Julia rang up; could I take a taxi at her expense at once, and try and bring my mind to bear on her problems. I told her I couldn't until this morning, and this morning I did go. The problems are as before – suicidal gloom, desire to be unconscious, which drives her to amphetamines and 'swigs of whisky all day long', the impossibility of eating: and then – an inconsistency which she was intelligent enough to accept when I pointed it out to her – on one side, 'she must have something to do to keep her mind off her troubles', on the other 'she had so much to do (teaching her 'helps' to cook) that she couldn't get on with her writing'. It is a measure of our new good relations and the friendly way she took my advice that she did absolutely nothing but thank me for my trouble. And poor creature – damn little did I do. My heart most truly goes out to her for her misery; it is really awful to be aware of it.

Robert to dinner alone was a great treat for me. We discussed Peter Luke's play – but now that Tennants have accepted it I doubt if anything but my legal rights (if those) will carry any weight.

April 24th

Easter – past and gone. I spent it at Snape in the always sympathetic company of Anne and Heywood and that old reprobate Eddie,[1] looking as Heywood says like a 'very old seagull', debauched at that, limping to and from the drinks table and plumping with a deafening thud into his old armchair. A cold north wind blew strongly amid spatters of rain, but there was some sun.

Eddie erupted like a volcano with violent and disgusting coughing and noseblowing. 'I think I'm starting a cold, my dear, so I won't kiss you.' Thank heavens for that! Also with sodomitical jokes. Otherwise he was genial, on the spot, and spoke affectionately and in triplicate about various old friends. 'I must say, my dear, I *adore* Billa, I adore Billa, I adore Billa, my dear.'

He got his chance to be an *enfant terrible*, however, and my! how he took it, when an extremely nice and eminent American surgeon called John Reynolds came down for the night. He isn't used to such talk 'before ladies'; they don't do it in America, Anne said. So there was a certain silence from his corner, and next morning he said to Heywood, 'Your brother-in-law's extremely frank isn't he?' I liked him very much; he was friendly and charming, and knowledgeable about music.

Other company – a visit from John Saumerez-Smith of Heywood Hill and Co. Ros for lunch on Easter Sunday. She had tried to get Eddie and me over there without Anne and H., which we thought rude. It's a measure of the isolation of East Anglia, lack of interest in the outside world and dependence on gossip, that this exciting piece of news whirled by telephone via Sheila Hill to Ruth G-H, to Ros's best friend, a lame lady, who had to be rung up by Anne so that she wouldn't repeat it back to Ros. Ros looked splendid and blooming in forget-me-not-blue,

---

1 Gathorne-Hardy.

and black glasses. Eddie was noticeably restrained in her company and said afterwards: 'I love her, my dear, I love her, I love her. But I must say, my dear, I thought she was pregnant, my dear, I thought she was pregnant.'

Anne is adorable to Eddie, as is Heywood (and he appreciates it); she is quite well again and has recovered her sweetness of expression. Heywood a little rosy barrel, fast going bald. Their little world is incredibly cut off and I miss general conversation – it is all about people, money, books. Eddie's reading and memory are very wide, but he won't have any truck with foreign writers, such as Turgenev or Flaubert. Hard to fault him on English literature and his memory is wonderful. He talks cheerfully about his plans for being eighty, but with dark bags under his eyes, he looks a 'bad life' to me.

The two great subjects were Bob's will and Peter Luke's play. Poor Anne gets stinkers from her brother Jock almost every day and even Fidelity says he's 'mad on the subject of money'.

Luke's play was read by all three. Eddie pronounced it, 'Tripe, my dear, absolute tripe; tripe.' Neither Anne nor Heywood said anything very constructive. And of course I'm pursued by doubts. Should I have tried to marshal more violent opposition, so that Tennants think it will be a flop? A letter from Janetta this morning says that he wrote several untaken plays before *Hadrian VII*, but producers are sheep and one success attracts them fatally.

Music – I nearly forgot. There were three occasions. A dull concert of much too early music including a 'very early' perhaps 'the earliest' of Passions of St Matthew. I was actively bored and disliked Peter Pears' way of singing. The *Messiah* with Heather Harper and Shirley-Quirk and a young strong-voiced tenor was fine, and on my last evening an enjoyable concert of romantic music, with Harper and Janet Baker, Quirk and Pears (who stands on tip-toe, elbows raised, music advanced, in a quite ludicrous way). There were many religious murmurs among the audience, of 'Have you heard how Ben is?' (he's had a heart attack) and 'Peter seems in rude health today' (he was 'indisposed' yesterday).

On the way to Salamanca

Above Janetta in Oca

Left Jaime at the monastery of San Lorenzo, near Santiago

Opposite page above Mary Dunn in Majorca

Opposite page below Bunny Garnett and Rose Jackson in the garden of Bunny's house in France, Le Verger de Charey

Desmond Shawe-Taylor
and Frances having a picnic
in the Pyrenees

Desmond and
Julian Jebb

Eardley Knollys
and Dadie
Rylands on the
lake in Zurich

Magouche with
her daughter Maro
and two grand
children, Saskia
(left) and Cosima
(seated), Arane
in Italy

Jaime and Janetta
on the terrace in
Tramores

Opposite page above Cecil
Beaton in his conservatory
in Dorset

Opposite page below Sophie
in Frances's flat on West
Halkin Street

Above Henrietta at
Charleston

Right Jaime near Oaxaca
in Mexico

Frances and Jaime
at the University
Posada in Milta

Jaime and Janetta
outside the Hotel
Rancho, with
San Cristobál in
the distance

Eardley and
David outside
a café at Urk

I suddenly spotted Stanley in the front row, and talked to him and a very plain girl in the interval. He comes tonight to supper.

April 26th

A marvellous blue day and I have just burst into tears for the first time in years. Henrietta's very quiet voice rang up saying 'I've got some very bad news.' My heart stood still — Sophie? 'Amaryllis is dead. She seems to have drowned herself several days ago. They've just found her.' The agonising pity of it! Stanley was arguing last night that pity was merely a debased form of sympathy, a theory that has a lot in it. But how else to describe one's feelings about such misery on her part, such desperate courage, and Bunny and Angelica's grief.

April 27th

Robin and Susan came pleasantly and alone to dinner and temporarily the Garnett horror faded. It returned as soon as I got into bed, but I slept a doped and fairly sound sleep. This morning I've talked to Henrietta and she and Sophie are coming to lunch. Angelica is flying out to see Bunny, taking Ali,[1] which I can't but think a great mistake. Bunny will bitterly resent him — he could I suppose support Angelica on the journey, but I shall know more later. I have steadied up — yesterday I couldn't have supported a fly I believe, but I do feel guilty for not offering to go round to Henrietta at once. I shall take my cue from her when she comes.

April 28th

Henrietta arrived with darling Sophie and I just persuaded her to swallow a steak before going off to see Amaryllis's last (?) boyfriend, Gordon, who would be 'in a terrible state'. She looked dreadfully white, stricken and tired. Sophie seemed to have managed to escape the horror. I can't resist spoiling her hopelessly — but perhaps it doesn't matter. We shopped widely and wildly at Harrods for clothes and books; she was admirably decided about what she wanted. Then back for tea, music,

---

1 Her youthful French friend.

143

games, gramophone, singing. She has a perfect ear and a delightful way of trying to put part to what we are singing, or
improvising on the piano. Because I see her so seldom I feel
the need to expend all the emotion I contain of that special
family sort on her; it's as if a magnet were pulling out all my
stuffing and I end up feeling drained. Henrietta was to return at
seven-thirty. Then she rang and said she was 'terribly exhausted' and would I mind keeping Sophie till eight-thirty? We
had supper and card tricks and then she was so tired that we
lay on my bed and I turned out the light and she slept for
a while. I had been made very anxious by a call from
Richard Garnett who wanted to know if he could help in any
way by staying in London. As I stood in my kitchen staring out
into the dark at the cars flying down West Halkin Street my
imagination flew too, and I could hardly bear to think of the
dangers of life for sweet Sophie lying asleep in the bedroom
behind.

I'm still no wiser about this ghastly affair and it's not merely
morbid to want to know. It is horrible to fumble in the dark of
emotions. Henrietta arrived in a hired car with a young man I
had never seen just before eleven. I gave them a drink, they left
with Sophie and I dropped into bed and slept for ten hours. The
young man's Christian name was Michel but his accent was
American. He was smartly dressed, long-haired, thin, pleasant
but not handsome, intelligent and nice to Sophie, who seemed
to like him.

Today, Saturday, has been very odd. An immense and extraordinary call from Julia when my voice was still hoarse from
sleep and a slight cold – I had to shout everything twice, as she
couldn't hear. She had heard about Amaryllis, wanted to know
more, but finding that I didn't know anything began putting
forward her own theories. Over two years ago she had seen
Amaryllis with her friend Tim Behrens 'and he's such a remarkably fascinating and attractive young man, you know.' I mentioned Tim's friendships. 'Oh yes, I know Heywood said of
course Harriet didn't in the least mind Tim's little flirtations
and escapades.' I said I thought she did mind but had done her
best to accept them, as they were so frequent; also that

Amaryllis herself had had at least one steady boyfriend, including Gordon, since. 'Oh yes,' said Julia (who has included Amaryllis among the girls she admires). 'I'm sure the young men must have been all over her. Such a lovely girl, but rather passive somehow; I wonder what sort of childhood she had.' I said that they had seemed a remarkably happy little nest of singing birds. 'Oh really? Yes but what really matters is, did they have *love* and *hugs* – before they were six, that's the time that really matters.' We got near an argument and my being accused of not accepting every tenet in the Freudian calendar. But I think I got away unscathed and have promised to let her know if and when I hear more – but I must be careful what I say because she's a dangerous and unbridled gossip.

I breakfasted so late that I've missed lunch. Went later to the London Library, when I ran into Giana Blakiston, Rosamond's daughter-in-law, and Pansy,[1] who kept me standing outside ready to get into my Mini for about half an hour with a quite incredible lecture, first about the 'book she was weading, about the Meditewwanean as a centre of culture and history', and then about 'St Patwick'. I gazed in astonishment and real pleasure at her sweet face and lovely grey eyes as she bored on and on, hardly drawing a 'bweath' until at last I managed to get in a word: 'Speaking of long journeys, has Frances Phipps[2] got safely back from Buenos Aires?' and, hardly waiting for her to say 'Yes, she's back,' I jumped into my car and drove away.

April 30th

I'm reeling from a further shock – Alix[3] is dead. So the tumbrils roll us one after the other to the guillotine. A week ago I telephoned her and she said she wasn't feeling well. 'I've had some sort of bug and the doctor gave me antibiotics and I feel as if I was dying.' She said it in such a tone that it flashed through my head: 'I wonder if she is, and knows it.' Then Paul Levy came to

---

1 Née Pakenham, wife of Henry Lamb RA.
2 Whose son was married to Pansy's daughter.
3 Strachey.

see me and said he had seen her since this, and she was up and about. It seems that Philip, her brother, had been down to visit her, she was better and he went back north and then her heart suddenly gave out.

The news seemed as logical as her own superb mind, and I thought I had assimilated it, but all evening I felt shaken to the core by a sense of loss. Tonight I'm expecting Henrietta, to talk about Amaryllis I suppose. And indeed I need to know.

May 1st

Henrietta and I talked for hours about Amaryllis, covered a lot of emotional ground and shed tears – yet I feel it is all still something of a mystery. What then emerged? – the various family reactions to the event; the horrific arrival of the policemen, Henrietta's shock and horror at having to tell Angelica. Sophie burst into tears. She doesn't know it was suicide and that is just as well I think. She went back gaily to school, accompanied by Fanny and Nerissa. Henrietta is 'worried' about Nerissa, thinks she needs treatment badly and that she showed (frighteningly) *no* response to the news. I think Henrietta has been living in a haze of misery but has obviously propped up the rest of the family, and went with Angelica to the mortuary for the grisly 'identification', which mercifully was only of clothes. Otherwise they do it by fingerprints. Poor Bunny, who only received a telegram saying Angelica was arriving, went through hours of agony. His grief was appalling, but he is saner than most of the family, and Magouche was marvellously kind. Angelica is now home again.

Henrietta spoke of her extreme closeness to Amaryllis since babyhood, of their great intimacy and love; yet she seemed unable to account for the desperate act, except to say that she had never been able to abandon herself to a relation with another person. She had turned against the stage and talked about the possibility of 'architecture' as a career – a crazy notion as it is the longest of trainings. She had then got mixed up in a Gurdjieff community in Gloucestershire.

None of this, to my mind, adds up to a reason. She was 'lonely', Henrietta thought.

Henrietta's young man, Michel, came again to fetch her. She is full of him and said he had 'been marvellously helpful'. I get the feeling that he's registering all sorts of impressions like a cine camera. I liked the way he looked at my books and pictures.

I have been struggling to write something about Alix for *The Times*, and was rather pleased with some of it. Now Paul – who urged me to do it – says that Philip wants to.

I feel terribly restless and can only think of walking somewhere – but where?

As for Henrietta – she has been warm and articulate, and I think we understood each other. She talked quite a bit about Burgo's death, how much she had loved him, but how different it made it that he had been swept away by fate. A young suicide is a terrible thing to everyone. I rang Nicky to tell her, and she burst into tears of genuine horror and grief and 'I suppose all her friends must feel it', guilt.

Amid all this sadness I detect another small element, which is something to do with the *cleanness* of death, away from the tortuous muckiness of life.

However, death isn't always clean, as has just been revealed by Margaret Penrose, for half an hour over the telephone – money, property, 'mine', 'my houses'.

I hear from Nicky that Janetta is arriving tonight. Perhaps I won't go to these funerals – Alix's on Friday I may have to, but the Garnetts have, with characteristic incompetence, failed to get theirs announced in the newspaper. It may or may not be tomorrow.

Julia in her own way is just as egocentric as Margaret, and expects everyone at this juncture of catastrophes to see Tommy's[1] exhibition as the most interesting forthcoming event. I don't think she has been to see Alix for literally years, yet she says 'I was very fond of Alix, you know' and I think it's true. She has had a letter from Angelica saying that she didn't believe Amaryllis had committed suicide, her state of mind didn't justify it.[2]

---

1 Stephen Tomlin, Julia's first husband.
2 The alternate view was that she slipped on the board outside the waterside dwellings, and fell in.

May 3rd

I awoke to horror about the two funerals, and a cowardly feeling that I couldn't face them, which I bolstered up with all the usual fumbling arguments: 'They are totally irrelevant. If you have them they should be private. I never expected anyone to go to Ralph's or Burgo's, nor had a ceremony of any sort. Why then should I go to these?' But then there's the confusion resulting from it's being other people's feelings that are concerned, not one's own; how to sort out selfishness from cowardice?

I rang up Janetta, and without the smallest pressure she gently persuaded me to go with her to Amaryllis' ceremony today. I drove to Warwick Avenue in ghastly deluges of rain and horrible traffic jams, and found Janetta deftly organising her belongings in her room. Through the dreadful rain and soused glistening streets we drove to the great red palace of death. We were shown into a very small chapel, where we were joined by Richard and Jane[1] (looking curiously stern), Nicky, some young friends of Amaryllis and then at last Angelica, Henrietta and Fanny. Angelica's face was pale and swollen with grief, we hugged each other and shook with suppressed sobs. When we had sat ourselves down, men carried in a long purple coffin covered in flowers and placed it on a slab. Another man stood silently facing us while amid Fanny's loud hysterical sobs and the quieter weeping of a little girl with woolly hair like a sheep's, the object and its unthinkable contents slid through a hatch like that leading from dining-room to kitchen. Nothing more. No catharsis, no detente, but out again among the steel rods of pelting rain, like the décor now sometimes adopted for opera – heartless and impersonally grim. Is it any good? *Muss es sein?* I think not. The whole procedure was unbearably painful and didn't even add the balm of beautiful music.

Back here to my flat where I lie weak as water on my bed listening without pleasure to the horribly grating voice of Callas singing *Rigoletto*.

---

1 Garnett.

148

May 5th

On the same evening as the funeral I had already invited Stanley to dinner to meet the Powells, and to fill up, also asked Henrietta and Michel. Henrietta's courage was extraordinary. She rang up at about quarter to nine to say she had been asleep and only just woken up, but wanted to come. Come she did, looking stunning, and kept us all going with her stimulating and amusing talk. Stanley was a very great asset, and got on well with the Powells. Then just as the Powells were leaving, Henrietta pitched forward out of her armchair in a faint on the floor. Michel was extremely kind, calm and efficient. She soon came round and they went off in a taxi. Everyone was moved by her brilliance and her collapse. Stanley said, 'Henrietta's really a marvellous girl' and Tristram has rung up to ask after 'that brave Henrietta'. Earlier I had been appalled because Fanny rang up to invite herself to dinner which was both impossible and undesirable, so instead I asked her to lunch next day (yesterday). Was I subconsciously making it impossible to go to Alix's funeral? Anyway Nicky and Patrick very kindly carried Fanny off to Wales, so I *did* go to Alix's cremation after all.

Well, it was a very different 'go' to the last – a humanist service, in a more cheerful green and flowery setting at Putney. Once again, I saw it gives pleasure to the mourners if a lot of people go, and so I am glad I went. But I took the plunge after pathological wavering. There was a smallish gathering. The chapel was light and cheerful, and we entered it to live strains of 'Jesu joy of man's desiring'. The coffin was already in place (somehow it had been horrible having Amaryllis's *carried* in) and an intelligent grey-haired man rose and gave a short oration, including inevitable remarks about life and death, and a brief account of what sort of person Alix was. Then more music and out we came. If one must have a ceremony, this was the best I have ever been to.

I returned and slept, but woke still feeling terribly tired, hesitant, bungling, and crashed my car's light into the one in front when driving poor Janetta to *Fidelio* to which she took me. I saw she thought I wasn't fit to drive, and almost took my arm to support my reeling steps, and she was right. But lovely music soothed me.

I'm now hesitating whether to drive down to Judy[1] in a grim downpour or to take a train. It has been a week of exceptional emotional tension. The agonies of poor Angelica and her daughters show up other people's worries as tawdry.

May 8th

Lucy rang up to ask me to write a short piece about Alix which was printed by *The Times* yesterday. It wasn't bad, but I wish it had been better. Anne and Heywood and Janetta and Eddie all seem to have liked it; Paul and Michael both kindly wrote to say it was 'perfect', which has comforted me. Stanley is the one person who has shown marked reserves.

In the end I took the soothing, cowardly, expensive train to Judy's and taxied up from the station. I found her remarkably well, and completely on the spot. It is rather a relief to find my family doesn't tend either to senility or deafness in old age.

A letter from Magouche, long and spontaneous and moving. She says Bunny has been 'absolutely magnificent' and 'you see how he will deal with it, struggle with it naked as it were.' Magouche repeats that she firmly holds the view that it was not suicide. She also says that Amaryllis was 'on LSD' – so I see the possibility of it being something between suicide and accident. Magouche worries about Bunny being alone too long at Charry. There is obviously the suggestion that either I or Henrietta should go out. Yet she 'expects me on June 7'. Well, I could go to him then perhaps. Oh the 'oughts'. Ought I to throw up Eardley and Dadie? Magouche writes almost poetically: 'But that glowing dreamy beautiful creature, what broke her? If you take drugs in despair the suicide is already there, or do they take them out of curiosity, with-it-ness, even on the pleasure principle and then, like foolish sailors ill-equipped far out to sea, sink in the first storm?' And again, of Bunny: 'he *must* have felt how loved he was in this house

---

1 Rendel, my eldest sister.

and how much he taught us all about sorrow, the dear grand fellow.'

May 14th

I've had such a tough mum letter from the 'dear grand fellow' that it has quite dashed and puzzled me. No question of wanting me to go out, or of wanting anyone, or making any human reference whatsoever to Amaryllis, Angelica, Henrietta, Magouche or even Ali. I see a shut, expressionless face and hear a voice talking of kilometres, of hoopoes and orchids, and whether France is prettier than Italy; but I can't diagnose what lies behind, and don't know how worried to be. It is a form of cicatrice – scar tissue.

I've returned from a cool changeable weekend at Kitty West's; the sweet look of the country doused in occasional showers and sun also; but the delicious eternal springtime tweedling of the birds is in its way a heartbreaking sound. For me, too much social life, but they were all nice people – Billy Henderson and Frank Tait, and Carol and John Hubbard one night, Gilbert and Molly Debenham another. Kitty cooked lovely food, and was looking very handsome.

On the way back I drove to Cranborne Garden Centre and bought a few plants for my balcony from a coy woman in a plastic pixie hat. I complained of the difficulty of getting someone to cut off dead heads while I was away, and plants getting straggly. She replied, 'Yes, but they don't care about *us*, you must remember. They just want to make babies.'

May 16th

A much better letter from Bunny, through which I hear his recognisable voice.

Yesterday brought two bits of news: One bad, Henrietta had been carried to hospital and had her appendix whizzed out. The other good: Tennants are *not* going to do Peter Luke's play.

Today we have wonderful weather and a sudden resurge of energy – goodness how welcome, and how lacking of late. I walked springily to Mungo's office and back and left the play in his hands. Later to see Henrietta, lying in her hospital bed, banked up with flowers.

Her friend Michel came in just before I left and I was suddenly moved by the great sweetness of his smile. He brings ther-
moses of food he's made himself, and nightdresses. He looks
after her, as no one has for years. Another thing that made me
think well of him was a masterly photo of Duncan and Henrietta
taken at Charleston and several charming ones of Sophie.
There's an artist hidden in him somewhere.

May 18th

Yet another celebration of death – a memorial service for Ralph
Jarvis at St James Piccadilly. I saw a familiar tonsure and
squeezed in between Heywood and a bearded greying man who
greeted me like an old friend and reeked of spirits. The service
was unimaginative and unfeeling. We droned out 'Oh God our
help', and the clergyman described Ralph's character in slow
pompous self-indulgent tones, told us that works of art (which
Ralph had loved) were acts of worship to God and that he knew
for a fact that Ralph had gone to a better world where he
had every 'satisfaction'. He proclaimed his strikingly happy
marriage; meanwhile one of his mistresses, behaving as such and
dressed in black satin and a large black hat, wept into her bare
hands.

What balderdash it all was, and people as intelligent as Robin
Fedden made up the captive audience.

Everything was taken back to God with such regularity that as
I hurried home past the Ritz I read a newspaper placard as 'God
War', which I saw later was 'Cod War'.

Angelica came to dinner the night before. We floated easily
from subject to subject. Bunny had rung up, anxious for
Henrietta to go and convalesce at Charry; this seemed to irritate
Angelica a little and I couldn't see why, but I do now. It was the
implication that she couldn't take care of her children.

Oh, dear, dear Janetta has gone, and Joan is away, and I shall
soon be flitting with Dadie and Eardley to Switzerland.

Henrietta is back at Ellington Street – a great relief – and
Angelica says she is much better. She wrote me a very good
letter.

P.S. Coleridge thought that the mind wasn't a barrel-organ

containing millions of possible tunes, but more like a violin, with only a few strings but a vast compass.

May 20th

A quiet pleasant day yesterday, with real contacts with the Young. Georgia to lunch – she gave a marvellous description of fireworks in Florence, and after having given me a splendid tutorial on Transcendental Meditation, with closed eyes, folded hands and feet, she asked my advice about organising her life.

The same sort of communication on the best level I had too with Stanley. In between their visits I practised Georgia's relaxation technique on my new mattress for an hour and went straight off into a few minutes' refreshing sleep. But if you empty your mind, what comes in? Nothing but freely associated images from the unconscious. If you had an abstract thought or a general idea, you would at once tense up again.

I am truly fond of dear Stanley, but he left a poisoned dart in me, which didn't take effect till nearly bed-time and woke me to uneasy thoughts about Luke's play. There have been rumours of a film on the subject, with Peter Finch as Lytton. Tristram Powell said he had heard of it from Jonathan Miller. But I pushed it aside. Now Stanley says that he swore every oath known to man that he would *not* tell me that this film has been brewing for four years! And it is now definitely 'on'. Who made him swear? Also according to Stanley, Quentin has sold the film rights of his biography of Virginia for a huge sum. I didn't realise there was a copyright in biography.

Slowly a bruise, a submerged soreness came out in me (especially when I woke in the night) because Michael Holroyd had never mentioned this film, while writing sympathetically, and offering to help fight Peter Luke's play. Well, of *course* if he stands to make a fortune he doesn't want me interfering. I see that part of me enjoys a battle, such as those with Ken Russell, Luke, or even Gerald. But another part is made unhappy, feels bullied, badgered and anxious. I wonder if I'm quite unique in minding the idea of these misrepresentations. I would like to ask this question of some perfectly detached observer.

And in the night I had a bad go of the death instinct, a desire to get away from this endless struggle and badgering. (Unless I can somehow manage to detach myself from whatever inaccurate portrait of Ralph is spread abroad.) A desire to go away and not come back. To live abroad. Yet I know my friends are my life.

I shall see Stanley on Tuesday, but I don't want to engage him in intrigue of a sort I think he rather enjoys. Michael is my friend too and I only approve of all-out measures and intrigue against the faceless ones, Ken Russell and Peter Luke.

May 22nd

Bags packed, I sit in my quiet flat reading about Abelard (who has suddenly captured my interest) in a book that must be left behind. Car in garage, loose ends I hope tied up. Stanley came to lunch. He has enormous common sense. It's no good trying to be what one is not, he says, so I can't pretend not to mind the misrepresentation of the past. I told him I had no desire to deprive Michael of the rewards of his book in film form, and from what I gather he has already been paid a large sum for the *option*. Stanley thinks it doubtful if he would get any more if it were put on.

May 23rd

10.20 p.m. *Zurich*. Miracle! I lie in my comfortable hotel bed, Eardley splashing in my bathroom next door. We had a worry-free journey, and since our arrival have been on a monster walk round the town – or the Old Town rather – savouring its Swissness, prosperity and sanity. As usual I start at once franti-cally trying to generalise; there seems to be a lack of imagination in the air, no mood of subtlety, and too much concentration on material objects. But the air is pure, and in front of us lies a huge rippling lake with some standoffish swans. Faces are a trifle unresponsive, and don't took as if they found it easy to smile, but would always behave correctly, obey the rules. German is spoken.

May 25th

We have had two whopping days of looking at pictures – too many to have time to wonder what painting is all about, except that it must be one of the noblest of human activities. Yesterday we were at the Kunsthaus here, and later at the Oskar Reinhart Collection at Winterthur (a short journey by train). My *hat* — what a lot of masterpieces, presumably used as investments by successful Swiss businessmen. Postcards are few and get posted off to friends, leaving a frustrating desire to devour, digest and absorb unsatisfied.

This afternoon Dadie made us walk all the way to the Bührle Collection, an immense walk it was too, though the splendid Courbets, succulent Chardins, the Daumiers, Picassos and Cézannes revived us. Rembrandts and Tintorettos were relegated to the staircase. Into this crowded day we also managed to squeeze a lazy sunny lunch on the deck of a boat making a *rundfart* of the Lake.

And tonight we go to the opera!

May 26th

Our seats for *Katya Kabanova* were close beneath the embossed and curlicued ceiling. A good production, not unlike Wexford. Before moving on to a spell of country life on the Lac de Joux, we went back to the Kunsthaus for another look at our favourites. I think mine is a Van Gogh of an underpass beneath a railway (my companions prefer a head of a boy next door), and I also love a Bonnard of Vollard looking tenderly down at a fat selfish cat on his lap, a cat that looked out at the world and not at him and took everything for granted, a cat of great character.

May 27th: Le Roseray, Lac de Joux

By afternoon light our train entered low hills — you couldn't call them mountains — and deposited us at the head of the Joux valley, where a little whistling one-track train bore us on our last lap. The hotel stands on the edge of a calm lake surrounded by pine-clad slopes. We are among French-speakers now and our dinner was excellent. Two much more human letters from Bunny awaited me.

May 28th

The blue sky is slightly veiled; there are a few white sails on the lake and rather too many doll's-house chalets stare at us across it. Dadie bewails the lack of snowy peaks. It might have been a little humdrum, but when we walked to the village we saw the short turf on either side of our path blue with spring gentians and pink with *Primula farinosa*. We have three identical rooms, each with showers, looking out on the hillside behind. Dadie and Eardley tease one another flirtatiously; Dadie has become very right-wing (or perhaps he always was); he says Eardley is too 'independent' and I am too 'rational'. We had a long, dull, uphill walk through conifers – I fear the lack of magic of the Swiss landscape is beginning to depress me.

June 1st

Yesterday we surmounted the largest local object, the Dent de Vaillon (5,000 feet), whence chains of snow mountains and the Lake of Geneva could be seen. Started by the little train to the far end of the lake, then the climb began. It was a relief when the armies of pines parted, leaving a broad stretch of flower-sprinkled grass with a river of marsh marigolds down the middle and martagon lilies bursting into bud, and further up still beautiful white pulsatilla anemones.

June 4th: Basel

Arrived here last night. My first impression is *horrid*: it's like a too rich person, ostentatious, and materialistic. German faces are deadpan. Loud plumbing noises and deafening hammering woke me early; I sent for my breakfast at seven. How one longs for it! What a buttery crunchy image it calls up, and the reality is never quite up to it – crumbs in the bed, one's body twisted on its axis.

June 5th

The part of the town round the cathedral has a sort of cuckoo-clock charm, but I don't like this country – there's something silly about it. Except for the Rhine, which is very far from silly, dementedly tearing through the town, grey-green and power-ful, carrying enormously long barges under its bridges with ter-rifying swiftness. Students were lying eating their sandwiches on its concrete verges. Morning in the Kunsthaus, again confronting marvels. Today I go alone to Italy and quite different preoccupations.

June 10th: Avane[1]

I said I would never again change at Milan after my last experience of it. I have and again I say it. There was cold, pelting rain and hellish chaos. Needless to say the transit luggage belt wasn't working, and two men were idly fishing up a suitcase by hand every ten minutes. I and two other people bound for Pisa missed the bus, and even the hostess in charge became anxious, but she rushed out and found us another, and we safely reached our half-empty aeroplane.

And there at Pisa was dear Magouche, brown as a berry, only back from Corfu one day. How awful if I had missed the plane. We drove in the dusk to eat under the arbour of a Pisan trattoria, where insects devoured my legs, and then to Florence, to the splendid studio Magouche's friend CloClo Peploe where we tumbled into bed.

Next day we helped hang pictures by Matthew[2] in a gallery in the Strozzi Palace, where he is to have an exhibition – a great honour apparently, sponsored by the Professor of Fine Art at the University. We gave Matthew and Maro lunch and drove back to Avane for the night. The beauty of the Italian landscape and the nobility of the Florentine houses, even of the villages, made me forcibly realise how very 'plain' Switzerland is in both particulars. If I go there again it will be just to look at pictures.

After one night at Avane we returned bearing bunches of broom from the roadside to deck the gallery, for the exhibition itself, an extraordinarily un-English affair, with speeches and the company listening attentively seated on gilt chairs or going round peering at the pictures with genuine interest instead of drinking and gossiping. After the show we had a somewhat uneasy dinner for eleven unmixable people talking different

---

1 Magouche's house in Italy.
2 Spender, son of Stephen and Natasha, married to Magouche's daughter, Maro.

languages. My bewildered head whirled with French, German and even Spanish. My bitten legs have blown up like two balloons.

Early yesterday while the morning was still fresh Magouche and I drove back to San Sano, and *how* I slept that afternoon.

June 11th

Avane has blossomed and flowered and become less dark inside. Matthew and Maro have covered it with pictures and frescoes and the outside with flowers and fast-growing trees. Two dear little blonde girls, Saskia and Cosima, complete the picture of fertility.¹ Saskia talks Italian and English indifferently, Cosima is a crawling rather plain baby, with limbs 'as solid as pasta', as Pia says. I like them and admire the life they have created here, and their indefatigable energy. I love my quiet rather empty room; outside it are the dovecotes where eggs are being hatched, and as well as a permanent *roucoulement* they give out their own dawn chorus. Two charming little tabby kittens frisk about and a pregnant Tibetan goat is tied to a tree, and eats the rubbish.

Magouche's sister Esther came to lunch with her husband and daughter. We ate out at a massive white marble table and drank a lot of wine. I strolled off to look for flowers, almost at once finding for the first time in my life a group of lizard orchids.

I read books about the painters whose work I saw in Switzerland and think a lot about painting.

Magouche, Matthew and I drove over to dine with Harriet and Tim and had a very nice evening. I got a sweet welcome from Frances and Algy.² We talked about how much the ability to draw was necessary to a painter and whether Francis Bacon could draw. Matthew answered 'yes', then 'no'. But Tim thought Bacon drew 'fantastically well, better than any living painter', but didn't much care for his work. Outside the fireflies danced magically in the darkness. Tim brought two in and set them on the dining-table and read about them aloud from his encyclopaedia. There was some talk about 'a fart in a

---

1 Children of Matthew and Maro.
2 Their children.

cullender', a sort of Russian scandal reported remark, and then (inevitably) the conversation turned to the death of Amaryllis. Magouche and I had agreed that we couldn't believe in suicide – it was an unthinkable way to kill oneself. Tim now said the same – he knew she was unhappy but he said she was a very feeble swimmer; that she drank a good deal and also took LSD, and could have slipped off the gangplank and not been able to get out. Surely accident is a less unbearable hypothesis.

June 12th

The evening of a day perfect in itself, but not entirely so to me. Surrounded by this beauty I felt unenterprising, and my bite-swelled legs prevented me getting into my shoes. Magouche wonders if I have phlebitis. I therefore didn't go with Magouche, Maro and Saskia to swim in the river but was left in charge of a teething Cosima and felt dreadfully anxious about her. Then we dined out with myriads of fireflies flashing, and my brief panic was over.

June 13th

Yesterday and today both began with fizzing crushing heat. Magouche and I drove off to Siena, and like all Magouche's outings it expanded in all directions like Japanese flowers. She looked a splendid figure in a trim sleeveless white linen dress and mushroom hat. After shopping in Siena we drove up to the walled village of Monteriggioni for a delicious lunch. In Castillano the first heavy drops fell and soon the sky cracked and split till a curtain of rain fell. We got home to find Bruno the gardener too scared to go out, and rugs, dolls and chairs lying soaked by the rain.

June 14th

The same pattern as the day before. Blazing hot morning, crash-ing storm and heavy rain in the afternoon. We breakfasted under the tree on the lawn – Magouche looking delightful in a blue silk shawl over her white Empire nightdress. The young couple have gone to Luca, and we are alone. When the rain began we sat on the landing cushions talking about abstract art. I said how my Swiss galleries had made me question it – and realised too late that Kandinsky and Klee were heroes to Gorky.[1] Magouche brought me Kandinsky's Credo to read and I thought it pretty good rubbish, inconsequential and mystical. I tried to analyse my objection, since I don't mind music being abstract. But why should the visual arts take over the function of music or mathematics, when they don't have to, when they can be so rich with their reference to human emotions. Is this logical though? For I don't like music that tries too hard to call up moods or visions of drowned cathedrals. Magouche thought I was being obstinate and put some heat into her defence, which I liked. I studied Kandinsky's pictures in his book, but was bored and couldn't go on looking.

Late, about ten-thirty, after we had give up on him, Tim Behrens came to dinner. (Harriet and the children have gone to England.) We talked about money. He is fast adopting his father's attitude and said in answer to a question of mine that when his children finished school they would be turned out into the world to fend for themselves. 'Without any money?' 'Oh, well – it goes without saying that one gives money to whoever needs it.' Magouche was about to tell him we were going to bed when in came Matthew and Maro with sleepy rosy children, having found no one to receive them at Luca where Sebastian Walker[2] and his boyfriend had invited them.

June 19th: London

The dazzling weather I arrived in has suddenly broken and with it has evaporated a sort of euphoria that has possessed me for the three days since my return. Now, what and who is real? I've been flattered by the warm welcome of friends and have seen quite a few; many telephone calls (Raymond, Eardley, Julian), and some parcels of other people's writings to deal with give a false semblance of industry to my days, which have been in fact very full. One of these packages was from David Gadd, the General who has had his book accepted by Chatto, on the old,

1 Magouche's first husband.
2 Brother of Mirabel Cecil.

old Bloomsbury theme again. I took the occasion to write out my criticism of what I called the Brenan–Holroyd distortion of Ralph's character and have sent it to him; I very much wonder what he'll make of it.

Now, in fear and no confidence, I'm going off to the orchestra. I half want to 'give up', half want to struggle on.

Mary took me in her box to *Wozzeck* last night. Robert rang up for nearly an hour to tell me that Cynthia has taken 'a week's shore leave' and he finds that she has gone to Tunis with a rather ugly French doctor she brought years ago to Ham Spray. He is terribly sexually jealous, very critical of her personally, but unable to abandon the marriage, bad though it is, and heaven knows whether he should or not.

June 20th

Henrietta has been to lunch, poised on absurd pink wooden sandals four inches high, a curious fashion that produces an ungainly walk as if on stilts. She is off with Michel to stay with Bunny, rather fearing whether they will get on. If they don't I think it's Bunny that will suffer.

June 21st

Julian to dinner last night has left me very worried. The more unhappy and suicidal he becomes the more frenzied the front he keeps up. Not to me, but to one or two other confidants – but it must be a strain on poor Pagliacci, and I feel his curious analyst (whom he speaks well of) has stirred up the depths without releasing the imprisoned desperation.

June 27th

Crushing grey sky, thunderous heat, finally orgiastic rain kept me floored all yesterday with migraine. 'Splitting headache', Nan and mother used to say. Mine seldom does, but this time it did. Rose came to see me and I peered at her owlishly through black glasses.

'Like a worm on a bent pin of unbearable thoughts,' I reflected, trying in vain to compose myself to rest this afternoon. Julian has just rung up, and to my 'How are you?' he answered,

'Mysterious.' But implied that his state was more nice than nasty. He made me a little more anxious about Rose than I had been when she came to see me yesterday. The remarkable thing – the most remarkable thing – about Julian is his great power of appreciating and entering sympathetically into the feelings of such a vast range of different sorts of people – from Germaine Greer to Anne Talbot, to name but two.

July 2nd

The demands or otherwise made on me by friends make the main strand in my life. Arriving back from a hot, serene, idle weekend at Crichel it was a bracing tonic to be rung up by Robert, who said he had tried to get hold of me through the weekend and could I come out to lunch at a pub. We talked there at length and freely, and more perfectly at ease than sometimes about his present position with Cynthia.

July 6th

I am a clump of mistletoe, drawing its sustenance from other lives, and when (as now) the branch I'm on is in need of support, I feel more as if my life was worth living than I often do. Robert has telephoned once or twice and just been to lunch. Two or three days ago he moved out of Kew. With good Magouche's help he got into the house in Chapel Street (the Peploes' – 'thoroughly Bohemian; the central heating can't be turned off in this stifling weather and the fridge can't be turned on.'). He is now telling everyone there is a temporary separation – the result: he gets showers of kindness and hospitality from friends. He has got thinner, handsomer and less fierce looking. I don't, curiously enough, feel so worried about him as I did when the marriage first went wrong.

I've been visited by David Gadd, the 'Major-General' to whom I sent my Ralph note. He was a tall grizzled, quite ordinary man, but obviously intelligent, and seems to possess both sense and sensibility. Also to have become really fond of his 'subjects', whom he treats with surprising understanding and lack of prejudice against homosexuality, aestheticism or pacifism. But what he really wanted was to talk about himself – and I learned:

that he gets up 'with the birds every morning and works three hours before breakfast', that he has written books under another name (I didn't ask it), one for the War Office I think, and one about Bath, and that he composes several *Times* crosswords a week! Perhaps I was a little disillusioned in my hope that I had found a champion for Ralph, but I think he'll accept my view.

July 7th

I'm in constant slight pain over my breach with Gerald and pleased that I have got on a friendly footing with Julia again. I took her to the Chinese Jugglers last night – she was funny and original and absolutely non-provocative. Discussing Robert and Cynthia's breach, as we did over dinner (Robert has told her himself), I noticed she was rather down on Cynthia and very solicitous for Robert. Cynthia was 'cruel' because she had been unsympathetic about Julia's bad back years ago, she was also 'stupid'. 'I know you said so long ago, and I was wrong. I thought her so beautiful that I didn't notice it, but she is.' We watched a comical display of little doll-faced black-haired girls and young men, bouncing, whirling plates or eggs on sticks. Far the best was the famous lion dance – two men to each lion with a face like Johnny Rothenstein,[1] marvellously agile and funny. Unfortunately this came first and nothing else came up to it. The acrobats were often supported by very visible wires which made their feats seem tame, but the audience were inspired by desire for friendship between the nations and clapped everything wildly. I'm left keen as ever on friendship between the nations but disappointed by tasteless clothes and décor and lack of imagination on the whole.

July 9th

There's a lot to be said for a weekend in London, and this last one was lit up for me by an extremely lively evening here with Rose and her Robert, Robert Kee and Stanley, talking so much that several voices often claimed the floor at once. He has just

---

1 Art critic, widely thought to look like a lion.

dropped a note in at my door saying it was 'a lovely evening' and he 'thought Stanley was quite special'. So he is, but Robert's confirmation delighted me. What is it about Stanley? He's so funny, kind, spontaneous *and* intelligent, and I love the way he does his own back-seat talking. Rose was in fine form, clear-headed, confident, smooth and round-faced. Her Robert on the other hand seemed rather quiet and down in the mouth, and really only came alive to any remark bearing on Russia or China. But it was Rose who seemed to have the upper hand.

I think constantly, anxiously and affectionately about Robert Kee. Robert's note ends, 'Feelings mainly now of horror at the appalling wasted opportunity of the last fifteen years come in waves like seasickness.'

July 10th

In a week I go to Tramores. As I wrote this the telephone rang, and it was Janetta on the line from Paris. She arrives in England tonight, mainly to see Rose. What with Gerald and Lynda and Julian and Peter Luke and her daughters, Janetta is – as I seem to be – a sort of lay analyst.

Robert on the telephone this morning sounded a little harder and tougher. Does that mean unhappier? I hope to call on him this evening so I may find out.

Another patient of mine was Julia, desperate on the telephone, but completely, touchingly unaggressive. She 'can't eat' and wondered if she could be taught some diet, as she 'can't boil an egg'; yesterday Ian Angus[1] had taken her out to dinner and she 'couldn't touch a mouthful of the veal and spinach set before her'. I noticed that she left the greater part of her plate of smoked salmon when I took her out. So it's not a question of inability to take trouble. She can nibble biscuits, that's all, and take sips of whisky all day, 'but it's not only that, it's my total inability to get up or make myself do anything.' I talked to her for some time without getting in any way under her skin, even asked if she was still taking purple hearts, as they were destroyers of appetite. She says she can't live without them, had

---

1 Friend of Sonia Orwell.

entirely forgotten about the destruction of appetite and admitted that by midday she had got into such a state of excitement that she needed tranquillisers. Then: 'the extraordinary thing is that the only time I feel all right is when I'm with Lawrence. I ran into him unexpectedly in Charlotte Street the other day and he was so affectionate and hugged and kissed me and told me how beautiful I was looking.' I rather fear another collapse into 'senile dementia' may be imminent.

July 11th

London in summer – at an open window in Chapel Street Robert was sitting, and I spent half an hour talking to him. I think he is accepting his situation, but whether he thinks of an eventual return to Cynthia or of finding someone else I don't know. He very easily could, exceptionally attractive as he is. The Campbells (whom I dined with) told me how the French ambassadress, Madame de Beaumarchais, took an immense shine to him at her party, pursued him all over the garden asking him to light her cigarette and when he wrote a polite note of thanks afterwards, sent him a cigarette lighter and a poem in French – to her *'beau allumeur'*. What I feel he fails to remember is that before her Tunisian escapade he was telling me that he thought the relationship between himself and Cynthia was ignoble, that there was nothing left but hatred and irritation, and that except for children both wanted to cut adrift and ought to. Robin also mentioned his curious streak of puritanism.

Before seeing Robert I had a visit from Stanley and then one from a really ghastly fellow who wants to write a telly script about Carrington and Gertler, merely because (as he told me three times) he had been twice in Gertler's position – i.e. obsessed with the fact that he was Jewish, and wanted to go to bed with a girl who was reluctant. I'm not surprised. He was tall, unclean, smelly, with greasy curly hair and blobby features. He seemed to know very little about anything ('I'm reading *Hole*royd, but really I'm getting fed up with that chap Strachey'), but like all these people he wanted to talk about himself, and I got rid of him as quickly as possible.

London in summer once again – after the Campbells' dinner I

came out coatless into the warm darkness. Even the new tower blocks seen from their terrace looked pretty, outlined in lights.

July 12th

A few days ago I was rung up by Catharine[1] saying that a rumour was going about that Gerald was dead. I was only shaken for a moment – then realised I would certainly have heard from Janetta. (She is here for two nights and invaded my flat with her sweetness yesterday.) This morning I get a letter from him. I had asked Janetta if she thought we could get our correspondence going again. 'Janetta has told me you would like me to write to you,' he rather gracelessly begins, or so it seems to me as it was he who broke off our communication. He goes on that he can't possibly go into all that has been happening, and then proceeds to do so at twelve pages' length. A more egotistic self-buttering-up, humourless production I never read. Though he tells me about Lynda's love affair with the Swede Lars, he (Gerald) has 'never been so much loved by anyone as by her'. Of Lars, 'I have never got a word out of him or heard him show a spark of animation with others ... He lived for years with a Dutchwoman so vulgar and overdressed that no one could face her ... He told Lynda he had a taste for vulgarity in women.' Then he describes opening a drawer and reading poems of wild abandoned passion 'such as I had never read before' to Lars, and how he decided to jump over the cliff at Ronda. He urged her to go away on a jaunt with Lars; 'the heat was insufferable, they both had diarrhoea and vomiting and lay sweating in their two beds all day without going out, and Lynda was enchanted to get back to her real life as she expressed it.'

Lynda says all this had drawn her closer to Gerald than before, yet she is coming to England to see her ex-fiancé John Gage in August.

Of himself, 'Jonathan Cape and two other publishers think my autobiog. may be a best seller – the best autobiography of this century in English ... it's quite possible that Lynda will rake in £18,000 on it ... I have done everything for Lynda, saved her

---

1 Noel Carrington's wife.

from sickness and despair, given her the period she needed for study and work, given her her house and books and car and she is I think, now that her infatuation with Lars is over, more solidly attached to me than ever. She has managed her life well.'

Well, well.

July 18th: Tramores

I'm here I'm here, I'm here. And the amazing thing was that as I drove out to dinner the night before I left, with Stanley and his girl, and Michael and his, I was fully aware of how it would look and feel, and myself in it. From the moment of my telephone call yesterday I didn't have a second's anxiety or fuss; I just imagined it vividly and then there it was.

Driving along the coast I didn't look at the changes – all for the worse – but unloaded my news to Janetta. Now I'm up here in the mid-afternoon, in the warm but not too warm air, with the constant sound of trickling fountain, scent of jasmine, roses. It is three years since I was last here and a lot has changed, burgeoned and expanded.

The pool was transparent and blue. I remembered my 'ten lengths a day' of last time and thought I'd be blowed if I didn't swim them again, so I did. Afterwards I sank effortlessly into a sound sleep in the monastic peace of my room, on the brass bed with lace and curtains. Jasmines, dahlias and zinnias are in three vases. *Immense* talk about Gerald and reading of his letters. Janetta, having seen his misery, is naturally more sympathetic whereas I'm not really sure I like him very much any more. Also his letters to Janetta provided a monster dose of rather humourless and pedantic egotism. I answered his letter to me just before I left, in what I hope was an innocuous and amiable way, and I'm glad I did so before having my stomach turned by the lack of humility and obsessional egotism of what I read last night. I woke in the night and thought about him and them. In one letter he said, 'I will perhaps write to Frances, but not yet I think, later on – perhaps in August.' I'm not keen to see him, though I feel the childishness of keeping apart on what might be our last chance of meeting. But I don't want to be treated like a naughty child, graciously taken back into favour.

Jaime arrived back about ten and we ate in the courtyard by candlelight, delicious little soles and fresh vegetables from the garden. Hard drinking isn't in favour at the moment.

My sleep in the afternoon was a life-saver. I tried out the 'air-hostess position' described by Michael's girlfriend, lying on one's face with arms curved. She said they were to do it to relax between flights. In the night I was set on by some little blood-suckers; I tried to read the Gerhardie book Stanley lent me but don't like it – I find the humour too forced and *voulu*. There are lots of books I want to read in the house, Popper for tough reading, and letters to write, and I am looking forward happily to the days to come, and glad to be here, here, here.

July 19th

The paradisal décor is set, the sky royal blue from horizon to horizon, the two fountains flow in their basins of Spanish tiles, cicadas whirr, frogs break into dramatic croaking, and every plant in the garden gives off its own peculiar scent. My day begins whenever I choose to press my bell, my breakfast tray is brought me by Toni the maid, a sweet young woman with a mellifluous voice. With her comes the beautiful Burmese cat, who is the colour of a bronze dancing-shoe with subfusc tiger stripes. 'What is his name?' I asked Toni. '*Púsi. Púsi es muy cariñoso.*' And Púsi certainly was; he flung himself into my arms purring loudly after peering at the contents of my tray. Leisurely bath, and then wearing the minimum of clothes I strolled round the garden to do dead-heading. Miguel told me the roses I was attacking '*no valen la pena*'. Janetta says they do. The different terraces and little plots in odd corners, lovingly planted, have yet to be learned. Over the pool are bowers of hibiscus, red, pink and yellow, which drop their flowers into it daily so that one must swim about and pick them out; also a yellow datura, and plumbago. Elsewhere roses, dahlias, gerani-um, jasmine. The water is naturally warm and blue and my ten lengths no effort. I'm so glad still to be able to do what I can do – I feel euphoric.

After our baths yesterday J. and I lay sunning and drinking iced vermouth. It was a holiday, so Jaime returned for lunch of mussels in a subtle herb sauce, eaten on the top terrace. I have read the life part of Gerald's book on St John of the Cross, well written of course and with some Geraldian images, but I'm disgusted by the competitive masochism and violent hostility between those monks who wore shoes and those who didn't and I find the doctrinal niceties rather boring. Gerald's analysis of the poems is very good and I quite like Lynda's translations.

After my siesta I walked up the hill to the left of the house as far as the col, finding a few wild flowers. I've never got these before, and the light was fading and Rosemary Strachey drinking tea on the terrace when I got back. Her twitching nervous face under a thick mop of dark brown hair isn't unattractive in its way, and now that she's given up sex and taken mainly to botany she's calmer and more conversable. She stayed to dinner, drinks and the night. She said she was 'in Gerald's bad books' because she knew about the Lynda–Lars affair. I asked what Lars was like – 'rather shy, but a very sweet person'.

July 21st

Wrote nothing yesterday because of half an hour's notice to get up and drive to Málaga with Janetta. I see that she must have long solitary days when Jaime is working. Yet their relation seems very affectionate and happy and mutually appreciative. I gather it's often nearer eleven than ten when he gets back, and immediately after supper – bed. There has been considerable talk (Janetta to me) about house buying, and I keep hearing of new flats, houses in Benahavis or farms at Ronda that Jaime has snapped up. 'He can't resist', 'he's always so optimistic about re-selling'. But I notice he often doesn't succeed. In fact he's doing what in theory I so much disapprove of, buying to profiteer out of people's desire for somewhere to live.

Another very wild letter for Janetta from Gerald, tacking and veering like a ship in a storm, sometimes he 'hates Lynda' sometimes he 'loves her more than he ever has anyone'. And then 'how badly she is behaving to John Gage' (whom she was at one time going to marry). Then he's touching: 'It's I, I, I, who am to blame.' At other times horrifying, rehearsing feeble but cruel remarks with which he tries to hurt Lynda, harping on 'how he's done everything for her', and 'what a lot of money she'll get when he dies', in an obscene way. On the upper terrace, roofed by bunches of grapes which are rapidly turning purple, there's a long cushioned seat covered in blue and white striped stuff. Here Janetta and I lay – it is delicious in the cool of the evening with the sun setting behind the mountains, frogs and crickets at it for all they're worth. We discussed what she should write to Gerald, for at present she's the only person able to influence him.

I think the final solution was mine, though I didn't have the job of writing the letter. Gerald is in grave danger, and must be warned that if he gives way to his hate, and his desire to hurt this sweet and patient girl her position will become untenable and she'll break away. I'm amazed she hasn't already. Janetta says she looks terribly thin and strained, though he boasts about making her well and strong.

I shied at Popper at first, but now I've got my teeth in, and am enjoying chewing away.

Janetta wrote an excellent reply to Gerald which she read me, more sympathetic than mine would have been. As usual we dined outside the kitchen by candlelight and I felt my way cautiously down the stone steps to my bedroom beside the gentle thunder of the fountain. Sky thickly sprinkled with stars and the Milky Way. Perfect stillness, scented darkness.

July 24th

As I sat down and began cudgelling my brains over Popper it occurred to me that doing this and swimming my ten lengths and walking up hills in Switzerland were just as much attempts to keep old age at bay as having face-lifts or spending hours at a beautician. One thing, however, I must restrain myself from is getting into twelve-year-old adventure situations which must surely arise from the death instinct. Yesterday evening, in the 'cool', which was still fizzingly hot, I walked down the bank to the valley, finding myself as usual trapped by the bend in the river. Starting to scramble up the steep high bank again, I realised how mad I was being when my scrabbling fingers caught at loose earth and stones, and retreated in time, with no worse than scraped shins.

Another letter from Gerald to Janetta apologising for the savagery of the last, looking forward euphorically to his trip to Sicily in September with Lynda.

July 25th

Jaime suggested that Miguel and his children should be urged to bathe in the pool. Janetta said quickly: 'Oh, no. I should simply hate to come and find them here.' And I remembered how shocked long ago R. and I were because Lady Hambledon refused access to her pool to the lower orders. With Janetta very elegant in a white cotton suit with blue stripes, I drove to dinner at Rosemary's little house much more in the country than I realised, bumping up a track under the velvety hills, and getting out of Janetta's huge Range Rover to the whirring of cicadas. Rosemary lives alone with a big soppy black dog and nine unfriendly cats, who leap on the table or stove every moment, grab food and lick frying-pans, a restless hostile population. While we were eating our dinner an orange kitten landed on the table and, without stopping talking for a moment, she seized it and threw it to the ground, all its paws spreadeagling from her hand. Rosemary works hard at her painting and also her botany, and showed me a lot of flowers she has found and pressed on various excursions, and a rare iris from Cazorla, which she is fostering in a pot.

July 26th

Very hot indeed. The thermometer has been moved into the shade on the terrace above my bedroom and it went up to 98°. Two candles in my bedroom have melted into a pathetic and obscene dangling position. Dead-heading even at 7 p.m. brought me out in a sweat – no question of being able to take a walk. A light haze like mosquito-netting veiled the sky. Janetta asked if I would like to drive up to Jaime's brother Paco's with a message – he lives at the Lodge to Cuscus. Feeling a need to get out and breathe the air in at the car window I went, though it was a pointless episode. Paco's pregnant English wife, a tall loud-voiced young woman, Rosemary and two females in long swirling skirts were sitting drinking indoors, while children watched a Mickey Mouse film outside. I talked to Rosemary, the only person who had anything to say to me. Stopped at San Pedro in the dark and picked up Ed,[1] who was in his 'good boy' mood, eager and tail-wagging, waiting to be patted. I was pleased to see him – he had been delighted by his London visit. I brought up my melted candles for the dinner-table to be greeted by ribald laughter.

July 31st

Magouche has arrived, and I have now practically decided to stay a full week more; and the idea delights me. Wonderfully enough I think they want me to, and my dread of outstaying is quieted. We all go to *Aida* in the bullring on Thursday, before Magouche flies off to Avane.

We have spent two nights in Ronda; and I have quite lost my heart to it and its surroundings. Before it had seemed a hand-some Andalusian town approached by a long grim winding ascent, but now I find there is behind it a rich area of old Spain, of spectacular pink mountains, streams, valleys, and untouched or sometimes crumbling farms, which the greedy hand of the speculator is already reaching out to grasp. Magouche for some extraordinary reason (having already her Tuscan house) has been carried away in the gold-rush, and this I find is why she has come out, recklessly extravagant as ever. But as it now stands, and before the inevitable defilement by the rich and non-rich from the coast – Maria Foxa, Jaime's father, Rosemary Strachey, Tommasito and *tutti quanti* – it is a place to fall in love with, and I did. We did no sightseeing, but when not visiting 'properties' I walked through the white streets with their grilled bow-windows and handsome doorways, enjoyed the life of the *paseo*, the charming little girls in their frilled dresses, the spot-less whitewash and the Irish sense of there being always time. On Saturday Jaime and Janetta had to attend their private view of hideous pictures, so Magouche and I drove up together in the fading light and shared a room in the old Reina Victoria with a superb view over the Sierra de Ronda, shining pink in next morning's light. We had wandered out and eaten our supper the previous night of bacon and eggs and wine in the middle of the

---

1 Jaime's illustrator.

street, with two old women and some frisky little girls for company.

Next morning Jaime telephoned from their hotel where they had arrived between one and two in the morning. They were eager to be off. I can't disentangle all the houses we saw, though I remember toiling up a steep shadeless track to number one in a lonely pink valley, all its vegetation burnt to dry biscuit colour except for a few slender delphiniums. It was a *cortijo* with handsome crumbling tower and its patio deep in thistles and weeds though it had only been empty a year, and some Victorian pictures, beds and chairs still forlornly occupied some of the rooms. While we were prowling, the late owners arrived in a body, friendly and garrulous, at least one of them grinning halfwittedly, and pointed out the attractions of the house, the chief being a huge stable and massive oil press. But how Magouche could for a moment consider the necessary operations to make this lonely dwelling habitable, including constructing a mile or so of car-drivable road, I really don't know.

Jaime's father has already purchased a huge tract of land including a house where his son Toti and four children are spending the summer, with a Scottish au pair girl who spends her time gallivanting with the local lads and sleeping it off after. We bathed in their green and shallow water tank and then picnicked beside it under a large tree, where we were joined by Jaime's father, portly but rather dashing, and Toti and his family. A marvellous performance was then laid on for our benefit. An aged goatherd appeared from nowhere bringing 700 goats of all colours and sizes to water at the trough, and stood leaning on his long stick and holding forth to the assembled gentry. I admired the splendidly dashing angle of his hat (like that on Jaime senior) and the style of his stance, his complete lack of servility. And after talking to us he turned to his goats and gave them orders in a high penetrating screech in what was apparently goat language, which has real words of its own. Then Toti's children and some cousins appeared, riding handsome horses with swishing tails, also to drink. They rode without rising from their Sevillian-style saddles with a support at the back. Andrès, the only boy in the family, about ten years old, dashed down in his tall soft boots, kissed all three ladies, leapt on his horse and made it cavort and prance like an expert rider at the Feria at Seville. 'Those children shouldn't be taught to ride their horses so cruelly, on the snaffle,' growled out Jaime's father. Then they galloped off wildly into the sierra, all except the littlest girl, Paloma, who bit her lip because she wasn't allowed to join them on her pony. I can't help finding Jaime's father rather charming. Janetta seems quite accepted by the family and especially the children, who call her Netta.

August 1st
Janetta has just looked in to say I'm only on the waiting list for Monday or Tuesday, and if I can't get on would I stay till Wednesday? Otherwise I would have to go tomorrow 'and that would be unbearable'. I said with feeling that I couldn't bear it either, and so it rests.

A quiet day to myself yesterday, just what I liked after the Ronda adventure. The others were lunching at La Cónsula and going to a bullfight in the afternoon. So I happily followed my routine – getting up at leisure, *embrassades* with Púsi, dead-heading, swim, lunch of two eggs, fruit and wine on a tray, siesta. Afterwards I picked and arranged flowers, they only last two days in this heat. I'm now reading a life of the Huxleys, and am full of admiration for T.H. I sipped my whisky and stroked the dog and cat. At quarter to eleven Toni cooked me some delicious little fishcakes and went off to bed. Not long after-wards Magouche and Janetta returned. Though in theory she was doing to me what she so hates from Jaime – keeping me waiting – I had expected it and it wasn't an infliction. Indeed my day of solitude, well cared for and surrounded by beauty, was a treat, as well as showing me what her life is like in Spain.

August 2nd
Janetta returned with my ticket for Wednesday so I linger on with some compunction and great delight. She has never in our long friendship shown me more sweetness. Magouche was in Ronda again all day reviewing the house situation, Jaime off at work. What a great man T. H. Huxley was with his firm

rejection of all irrational beliefs including of course religion, yet kind to his religious wife, and with his lack of jealousy to other scientific giants – Darwin, Hooker, etc.

Magouche returned fluttered and undecided. Janetta says someone has died and left her £20,000, so she can afford it. Ed to dinner, I drank too much and reeled into bed.

August 3rd

Crawled out of it, rather dim and met Magouche dim also, faced with departure, decisions and a cold in the head. She and Janetta went down to sign a power of attorney and I was left to greet the lunch guests, Mark Culme-Seymour[1] and his newly married wife Darrell, a neat ex-pretty American with whom nothing is wrong but a 'little-me' voice. At lunch Mark suddenly announced that he 'loved his life' and 'was very happy'. Before Janetta came he talked about Derek[2] – saying he was getting richer and richer and that Rose would not merely be 'a very rich girl' but 'the richest girl in England' with perhaps seven millions. Does he know? If so, what a fearful fate! Mark's views were surprisingly and to me sympathetically left-wing.

In the evening to *Aida* in the vast new building of Nueva Andalucia, the performance sponsored by the millionaire impresario of that synthetic creation, a playground for other millionaires. We sat on uncomfortable stone backless seats on little cushions, but being in front had a rail to lean on – others must have been in torture. They behaved as though at a *corrida*, walking in and out, talking, humming when they recognised a tune. A wind from the sea got up and heartily tore the orchestra's music from their stands, quite whirling away the sound they were making. The voices came across better, but Amneris' muslin cloak lashed around her. We heard afterwards that the hideous scenery had been torn to ribbons and the specially imported camels shat on the stage and had to be scrapped. All the same, even with the orchestra of mice from Barcelona, it was enjoyable to sit under the dark blue sky, moon and stars.

---

1 Janetta's half-brother.
2 Jackson.

Long intervals, late start. It wasn't over till nearly two, when we went off and ate tortillas and melon in a little restaurant and dropped Magouche to snatch a few hours' sleep before her aeroplane to Italy.

A horticulturist with an Austrian wife came up to tea; he has been responsible for the garden at Andalucia la Nueva for seven years and is heartily sick of being the employee of the immensely rich Banus, whose project it is, and who has two ladies both covered in jewels, enormous – his wife a blonde and his mistress a brunette, otherwise '*igual, igual*'. A letter from Joan saying that having commissioned portraits of both Jem and Reuben, Philip Dunn boggles at her price of £250 each and has written saying he will give her £150 for one of them, 'he can't afford them both, and doesn't want to go to the poorhouse.' She's written 'politely' to say he'd better return them both and no bones broke. Ach, the rich!

Jaime disappeared to a party and Ed, Janetta and I settled to Scrabble. Janetta says there are parties every night and she hates them.

August 7th

The last full day and I have awoken for an hour in the night contemplating the future. Hot, fly-ridden morning, the sky flecked all over with wispy clouds. Jaime went off to his Málaga flat for Monday night and according to Janetta was very cross when she tried to plan for the opera tonight (Caballé in *Traviata*).

I feel so intimately concerned with every corner of the garden, every bush and plant that I can scarcely bear to go and valet them now I'm leaving. Lunch off cold *pez de espada*. In the cool of the evening we braved the ghastly coast road and went through Marbella in a queue of cars and then took some plants to Rosemary, who showed us a beautiful painting she has done of the rare iris from Cazorla. It had flowered and been pressed and sent to Kew since we saw it, and this is really a triumph for Rosemary. Back to late supper and reading the horrors in the papers we had bought in Marbella – Arab terrorists shooting wildly among harmless holiday-makers at Athens airport.

August 8th (in the BEA aeroplane)

Traviata was a monster – due to begin at nine, it certainly lasted till two. Being a gala performance Janetta gave a lot of thought to her appearance and succeeded in looking like Greta Garbo and quite outstandingly distinguished, with her smoothed back silky hair, a long skirt of stiff black silk and a frilly blouse, among an audience of piled up dyed hair-dos, brassy grimacing faces, lacquered brown bodies and vulgar emerald green *décolletages*, all shouting and waving. Jaime was immensely elegant in a striped jacket, and we had little Vicente,[1] who touches me strangely.

The audience was more respectful and quiet than at *Aida*, recognising that Caballé was a great star if they most of them knew very little else about music, or so Jaime said. Rubinstein and his wife were, however, in the audience, also Banus and his bejewelled wife and his mistress, Jaime's parents and all the local and visiting millionaires, showing themselves off in intervals that stretched and stretched until the last (when they were arranging Violetta's death chamber) became almost a joke, chairs moved here and there, men coming in with one candlestick, discussions about where the bed should go, like a scene from a play by Beckett. Finally it was too much for the exhausted and hungry audience, and they burst into stamping and clapping. In spite of the nearly inaudible orchestra, and the vast open expanse in which she had to sing, Caballé never seemed to press at all, but gently floated her voice, most movingly, towards the black starry sky. Her tenor wasn't bad at all and looked the part. The décor was crude and hideous in supermarket colours.

Janetta had brought sandwiches and a flask of neat whisky which kept us going, though Tommasito and his girlfriends next door made brazen demands for a share, which Janetta rather grudgingly gave them. Their horticultural friend had decorated the scene with real camellias, oleanders and rose-bushes, though they might just as well have been paper ones.

I don't think Janetta has ever been able to see the point of Vicente. She told me she thought he had always loved Jaime (he's quite a lot older), and sometimes refers to him as 'Jaime's

---

[1] An elderly painter friend.

wife'. I like him, he paints sensitive pictures, and his gaze is full of feeling. I found him easy to talk to, and when I asked him which Verdi he liked the best he said, 'The Requiem.' I think his heart is seriously affected. Janetta said afterwards, 'Vicente and you seemed to have lots to talk about. He never talks to me.'

I've had the most restful, the happiest time for many years, and I've adored being with Janetta and Jaime.

Ah we're off the ground at last.

August 10th: West Halkin Street

So, once again, here I am. The smile still lingers, the feeling of a bee that has been at the nectar. After the lateness of *Traviata* I got up only in time for a last swim with Janetta, and a *despedida* lunch to which Jaime and Ed came up from the coast. We were to pick up the mysterious Mario who was also booked to London on my plane. He's a smooth customer and beyond that I know little about him. Most gallantly he took charge of my passport – not anywhere, after completely turning out all bags and pockets. So he vanished in a frenzy, to drive back to look for it, or telephone – anyway he was not on the plane and I saw him no more.

Freshness and relaxation on arrival about ten, I determine not to fuss, but that may lead to forgetting something vital. A pile of letters, two from Bunny, two notes from Robert, Colin, Catharine, bills, etc.

Next day, Thursday, I had Robert to lunch and Stanley to dinner. Both interesting, slightly taxing. Robert said he thought he was 'over the worst' of his parting with Cynthia. Meanwhile he's accepting every invitation that offers, had spent a weekend with Georgie in Paris and another in Ulster with the Dufferins. Lindy¹ might have been offering him solid consolation, and I'm sure others have too. Next week he goes to Avane for a week. He hopes there will be a lot happening, as he can't take things being too quiet and thence to Majorca with Mary.

August 15th

An English heatwave; almost hotter than Spain. To *Valkyrie* at

---

1 Guinness.

the Coliseum last night with Stanley. Every seat in the house taken, the heat was terrific. Rita Hunter and Norman Bailey both sang splendidly – I loved the first act and was carried away by the last. I must admit that the second failed to grip me, and my mind wandered off, a thing it never does during Verdi, say. I had the sense I'd had at *Tristan* – of wondering whether a lot of it was a huge confidence trick, of feeling that these endless repetitive waves of sound were nearly intolerable or in any case alien to me, that he ought to know when enough is enough. I wished he had more control or classicism, or heaven knows what. Rather to my surprise Stanley said his mind wandered too during the second act, though he claimed to tears during the third, which (after my patch of rejection and, it must be admitted, *boredom*) completely absorbed me.

The heat makes an outlandish backdrop to London, and walking into the blazing streets is like going into an oven.

August 16th

A high-powered dinner at the Pritchetts' last night – the widow of Vaughan-Williams, the composer (what's known as 'a nice woman' in the Elspeth style, but speaking in a most extraordinary voice, like a dog talking). A writer called Francis King, rather nipped in pince-nez, turned out to be friends with Angus Davidson and Barbara Bagenal. Far the most high-powered was Philip Hope-Wallace, tall, hostile to women I would say, and very funny, I think I'll have to say witty. There was a delicious dinner, a lot of laughter, and much euphoria on the Pritchetts' part. It was the sort of dinner-party where ghost stories are told. I talked mostly to V.S.P. and drove the two male guests home. Woke in the night realising I'd drunk too much. Woke this morning feeling sad and remembering how happy I was with Janetta.

August 17th

Crushing heat still – yesterday was worse than ever, and only by opening wide all windows and doors could I keep some semblance of freshness in the flat.

August 18th

Travelling down by train (oh how much I prefer it to driving) I re-read Freddie Ayer on the non-existence of God, a dustily dry analysis going carefully into the various assumptions of believers and destroying them one by one.

I arrived at Cranborne to find that advance copies of David's coffee-table history of the Cecil family had arrived, and were being proudly handed round. I looked to the end and found his credo set forth: 'They [the Cecils] saw their lives in the light of their faith in a Divine Reality, whose creatures they were; and in relation to whose being – timeless, changeless, all-powerful, benignant – all that happened in this dimension of fleeting time was, when all was said and done, insignificant.'

It's a bit of a facer to get this from so otherwise intelligent a mind.

August 19th

Chloe MacCarthy is my fellow-guest, and her grief over Michael's death (only a few months ago) exudes from her like a grey mist, and changes the expression of her face to a sort of grimace. There's something almost indecent in looking on at such misery. David admitted to me on a short walk that he couldn't find anything to say to her, and Rachel's great sympathy sweeps her away, so that I've had little chance to talk alone to anyone but David. And that I always enjoy.

Rachel is at long last becoming more of a conformist, and perhaps her amusing and original side is dwindling. She's a palimpsest, which I read by the light of past knowledge. She is also gaining confidence socially, and her deafness makes her talk loudly and sometimes drown David. Last night after dinner, looking at the telly, we saw the tail end of the Bywaters-Thompson case dramatised, in which Mrs Thompson was taken to be hanged by stern women warders, and (suddenly coming aware out of dazed doped stupor) fought and screamed and had to be dragged to her death. I was astounded by the total lack of sympathy of the Christians. 'She *ought* to have controlled herself and made a better death. One would have liked and respected her more,' said Rachel. Surely, I said, physical courage didn't always come from admirable characteristics but sometimes from stupidity, lack of imagination, vanity, all sorts of things. This was whisked aside. 'Oh but one would think *better* of her.' It was the repetition of a talk some years ago about 'dying bravely on the scaffold' when I had the Bayleys on my side.[1] I believe I have an average amount of physical courage, but I didn't always, and I profoundly sympathise with cowards. And who can possibly say if they would 'make a good death' in a sinking ship or a burning house? David backed his obviously strong feelings by saying irrelevantly that he was a physical coward himself. One might think it pragmatically better to get over the fear of flying most people start with, but surely there's no need to feel no sympathy for the Anne Hills. It's this cursed religion – the approach of death makes it tighten its grip. I wonder whether Chloe feels it a consolation or has none.

August 21st

I had an opportunity to talk to Rachel on one of our walks and on Sunday was left alone for a while with Chloe, who poured out her guilt and misery – the first quite unjustified – about Michael's[2] death. Rachel is joining the ranks of those who 'have no time for anything', like gardening. The Cecils' garden is a flowerless waste. 'All these servants take up so much time,' she said quite ingenuously (there are three on and off and a jobbing gardener). Their life is a curious mixture of the ramshackle and the safe. Their car is a battered wreck, which has obviously taken many severe beatings off gate-posts; the standard of garden and food are pitiful. Yet Church, Sandringham and the Establishment are absorbing more and more of their values now that the influence of academic Oxford has been withdrawn. Laura's arrival on Sunday night livened things up – they do at least accept her liaison with Angelo. Indeed David was anxious she should know how much he liked Angelo, and I saw signs that they would now welcome the respectability of marriage even with him.

---

1 John Bayley and Iris Murdoch.

2 MacCarthy.

Long sad hours of wakeful futility during the night, have left me convinced I've had enough of this life: yet Tramores *was* pure pleasure, and I suppose there could be more.

August 23rd

Starting from Wagner's not knowing when to stop, I've been thinking about that self-indulgence in art which often goes with great virtuosity. Then what is the opposite – not austerity I hope? Classicism, form, control. I can't find the word, but I do miss it in him. Reading Gerhardie, who is also in a very different way carried away by his own virtuosity, I see it can be a snare. Picasso also. Yet it is one of the very qualities that arouses most admiration.

Rose came last night and talked steadily from eight-thirty for nearly four hours. New light on her Robert, as someone unconfident, suspecting people don't like him, far from arrogant (though arrogance and cleverness is I think the first impression he makes). He got his BA three years ago and has done virtually nothing since – this seems to be his problem. She didn't say very much about their mutual relationship. She told me Magouche's niece was not well. 'Did you advise her to go to Hévesi; didn't he help you a lot?' 'Oh *yes*, but I think she likes her analyst. I did advise her to see less of her mother who's very dominating.' 'So her relation with Janetta *was* the source of Rose's trouble' was the thought that flashed through my mind – but she made no demur when I said Janetta was one of the most sensitive and sympathetic people I knew (she had just put me and Julian in that role) but that I thought she might have been, as a mother, elusive, though really always caring deeply about her children. Later when I showed her my Spanish photos of Janetta, she charmingly gave one of them a quick kiss.

She's all right I think.

August 24th

Margaret Penrose is contemplating marrying again. It comes as no surprise, I had twigged that there has for some while been 'something' between her and Max Newman. He, a very clever and musical mathematician of knots (if there is such a thing) of seventy-six, wants to marry this jolly, clever, good-humoured, noisy tub on legs aged seventy-two. She is hesitating whether actual marriage is a good idea, or 'living in sin', for they seem to prefer to keep their two houses going, one in Cambridge, one in London. She looked buoyantly happy and I dare say they have ten years or so joint happiness ahead. The pleasure of a focus to her life, instead of 'rejection', that dreaded state, has transformed her and also quieted her. She doesn't bang about so. It seems a truly excellent thing, and when I met Max Newman the other day for a second time I liked him. What reservations then do I feel? None. Much as I loved and admired Lionel I realise she had a rough time with him, for the last few years. Envy? Well, of course, I envy having someone to live for, a purpose in life.

August 29th

Gotterdämmerung was a stupendous endurance test, lasting under Goodall's skilled but slow baton from 4.30 to 11.15 when the audience as one man bawled Bravo and clapped and yelled, and I left them still at it. How much were they applauding themselves? I have been reading a book Julian lent me, which among other things goes into 'Wagnerolatry' and the violent antagonism it arouses. I'm certainly not an idolator, but nor am I in the opposite camp. I *think* I dislike religious attitude to any artist, even Shakespeare and Mozart. There were glorious moments in *G-g*, in particular those broaching the human emotions about love and death. There were others when I felt doubtful if I wanted ever to hear the work again, indeed began to think I wanted a long rest from Wagner or I should begin to feel I didn't love music. And I do. However, I go to *Tristan* with Stanley tonight. To me much of Wagner is formless and self-indulgent; I can't capitulate completely. Magee (the author of the book) is splendidly balanced in his views, but attributes Wagner's immense emotional power to his deliberately tapping the unconscious and so psychoanalysing his audience, says he was aware like Freud that civilisation was the result of the suppression of instincts. Why particularly do we have so much incest in the *Ring*? Was that important to him? It seems as if it were almost accidental. In the presence of idolators (like Robert

Urquhart) I'm impelled to say that I find its plot (with its magic potions, dragons and gnomes) childish and its lack of humans a defect.

Letters from Gerald and Robert. Robert's letter is full of brave fighting back at life and appreciation of kindness and is marvellously funny.

Gerald's is extraordinary. He's back at Alhaurín after three weeks staying with Miranda's[1] family in France. Lynda is still in England but expected soon. His tone is frighteningly cool. He seems to be assuming that her barren life was the normal one for the poor girl.

Of himself he says: 'I have managed to detach myself a good deal from her. I haven't missed her for a moment since I came back. She wants to go on living here indefinitely because it is only here that she can work and I need a girl who can cook and do the shopping in the car and occasionally talk to (!!). I'm working very happily ... we go out to dinner almost every night. So I am getting things on to a good material basis and hope to keep the love stuff and kissing out ... For her as for me work is the important thing ... and for that reason I shall have her here for five days in the week.'

As if she was a charwoman! And what is her work?

August 30th

The time has come for me to bring the curtain down on Wagner for a while. Not that I suffered at *Tristan* last night. I admired Helga Dernesch's Isolde. My mind never wandered, except to take stock that Stanley was weeping copiously into a large white handkerchief, and pale with emotion and over-excitement in the interval, which made him what he himself describes as 'silly'. There we ran into charming, soft-voiced Rüdiger (he had telephoned me earlier, saying 'Here is Rüdiger') who had never been to *Tristan* before and couldn't stand it. Unfortunately for him, being German, he 'understood all the words and was appalled'. I am tired of thinking about the old monster and being awash with his motifs – my chief conclusion last night was

---

1 Gerald Brenan's daughter.

that he achieves his notable effect (plus or minus) by violently assaulting one's senses and sensibilities so that personally I end up curiously unmoved but battered and shattered. I long now to be seduced rather than raped, and convinced of the rightness of what I'm hearing, the formal felicity coupled with inspiration and sweetness, rather than beaten down by reckless self-indulgence – for, yes, I must come back to that word. So now, a rest.

When Rüdiger expressed his quiet criticisms in the second interval poor Stanley grew painfully upset. White with emotion and his cheeks still wet and his nose pink with weeping, he cried, 'It's not! You're wrong! It's sublime! You're misinformed!' I found myself torn between my natural desire to criticise, and gratitude to Stanley for giving me this expensive treat and continuing his efforts to proselytise, which have been only partly successful. I rang him up this evening to thank him again and correct any impression of having been too critical. I needn't have worried – he was much too absorbed in his own highly emotional Wagnerolatous reaction.

August 31st

In the middle of dinner here last night with Julia, Heywood rang up to say that Anne (who broke her wrist a few weeks ago) had fallen down again and broken the ankle of the same leg that she broke so badly a year or two ago, so they would have to put me off for next weekend. Returning to the dinner table I found Julia looking blue and downcast – she had taken in the news, but been unaware of previous disasters. 'Out of touch I suppose. Anyway I don't feel sorry for people to whom those sorts of things happen ... Unless they are in pain of course.' I never saw such reluctance to feel sympathy in my life. Why? Because she is the only sufferer in the world I suppose. We talked about her last visit to Lawrence and Jenny in Dorset. Before she had said the holiday house they had rented was 'sweetly pretty'. Now nothing was too bad for it and for them. 'Fancy taking a house at *Studland Bay*! I ask you! All for the children of course – dreadful picnics on the beach. And only one sitting room where Lawrence was trying to write about Cézanne, while these ghastly children were shouting and careering on a strip of grass outside and every few minutes dashing in to ask someone to get down on all fours and be a horse or something. I asked Lawrence why on earth he did it and he said, "Because just for a moment it gives me the feeling I really exist." Oh I *hate* children. Ben was quite right – only he was wrong to say I was cruel to them – that I never am.' (I'm quite sure he never said so either; it was a 'distortion' as with me and my fatal remark about Jenny not enjoying music, which was turned into my saying she wasn't musical.) 'And really,' she went on with mounting indignation, 'everything's done for the children, nothing for the *guest* at all. I'm sure I used to treat my guests better than that.' I was interested that she thinks of herself as a guest of Lawrence and Jenny's. Also, of course she never had any children.' She continues to go there every other weekend, in spite of some fierce-ish rows, and Lawrence helps her with her fares. 'Then the food's so awful. Jenny's such a bad house-keeper. Jenny's idea of a picnic, my dear, is just a great big bun with a slice of meat in the middle. But Lawrence keeps on saying how wonderful everything she cooks is, and of course, the truth is they both come from the same sort of background – quite without feeling for food such as you and I like.'

She ate a hearty supper – two helpings of soup, chicken fricassee with potatoes and peas, cheese and biscuits, banana – complaining as she did so that she found it impossible to eat a thing. She is in fact quite plump around the middle, and apart from a certain hoarseness, seemed remarkably spry and very amiable.

September 4th

The ghost of a possible tiny job, but I think it's unlikely anything will come of it. Lucy Norton ringing up to say she wanted to get Lord's Wood and its contents photographed for *Country Life*, and if they agreed would I write something for it. I said Yes, as I said Yes when invited by Nicko and Mary for a weekend in Berlin – again with a feeling that the invitation wasn't serious. I believe I have an obsession about this, as I have about

---

1 She in fact had one daughter, Laura, and two adopted black daughters.

undertaking any activity that could possibly be called creative, started from my own impulse. I'm hardly interested to know the reason why.

Robert is back, lean and handsome and brown from Italy and Majorca. He came here for a drink, before we both dined with Nicko and Mary at Brooks's Club. He hasn't I think changed his line about his problem, and told me it never ceased to obsess him though he didn't feel he wanted to talk about it much either to Magouche or Mary. Very appreciative of both M.'s as people, but he said there was barely enough to eat at Alcañada, though the wine was good. He spent a few last days with Whitney and Daphne Straight, but showed detached amusement rather than the allergic rash which the company of the rich causes to break out all over me. But he thought Mary and Philip's relationship, with its unreal 'Darlings', rather degraded. He moved scattily from subject to subject and though he started many books he thought he didn't get far with any of them. At dinner Nicko said he was afraid he was in Janetta's bad books – she hadn't answered his letters or suggestions of driving her new car back via Bonn. I said I was sure he wasn't but have since remembered he is.

September 5th

Hendersons have not followed up their invitation to Bonn and Berlin, and I'm feeling less and less inclined to accept it seriously even if they do.

The fierce heat has returned; we swelter and pad about bare-legged, in extraordinary other-worldliness. Last night I went round to sup with Mary, who had sent Philip out to dinner with Nell, as she wanted to have a duo with me – 'agenda a mile long'. Most of this consisted in going over the Majorca relationship and the irritating behaviour of Mrs Peter Quennell. I listened and compared it with Robert's account. It tallied well. She says Robert is being fantastically sought after, and hardly has a free date till Christmas. I believe this too and wonder how it will affect him. He told me that Cynthia was annoyed at his 'telling all their friends', but how otherwise could he account for not being with her? She particularly minds the Annans knowing. She must be back in a few days.

Kitty has just been to lunch, very nice and friendly and bringing a huge bunch of flowers. She again said that she and Caroline had little to say to each other, and that when dining with the Debenhams, everyone had been discussing their characters and Kitty had said, 'Well, I'm very kind', Caroline had intervened, 'No – you're not *kind*.' I think this was because she deliberately, and as I gather on some weird sort of principle, tramples on Caroline's feelings by her remarks about madness and admitted that she got furious if Caroline didn't help in the house, but refused to let her when she offered! Honest at least.

September 6th

Can Stanley and I bridge the gulf of years, not to mention that created by alien origins and cultures, with the help of friendship and understanding and a good many tastes in common? I hope and think so, but just occasionally I feel uncertain whether I'm taking the right line about something or other. Yesterday he rang up several times, asking me to do various things – some unreasonable, such as write to his Council complaining of *his* landlords, others quite the reverse (which I have tried to comply with) like getting him tickets for Aldeburgh and a chance to stay in Bunny's house while he's away. One evening last week he rang in a state of 'nameless depression'. Today he said he wanted to consult me about a detective story he's writing, and fetch his umbrella and book; he would come along this afternoon about drink time. F: 'Yes, do. I *could* give you some supper if you'd like, but I'm afraid I've only got eggs.' S: 'I love eggs, that would be fine. I'd like that. Oh, good Lord, I've just remembered I've had no lunch.' F: 'Well, I'd better get you some steak.' S: 'No don't do that, I don't want you to go out.' All seemed to me at the time natural and considerate. I didn't buy any steak, but went round the corner and bought parsley to make my new parsley soup.

6 p.m. Stanley in a call box, sounding rather dim: 'Do you mind if I don't come? I feel I want to be alone. It's so hot.' I nearly said, 'Quite all right, Greta Garbo,' but (with a vague feeling that there was more in it all than met the ear) said instead: 'Since you're halfway here why don't you just come for a drink and fetch your brolly?' So he came, with news of various

disasters and his notes for his detective story. We mulled over these, and then we hotted up my soup and I made *oeufs à la tripe*, after which he stayed till eleven. Talk largely about drugs. He had been mixing with young trendy neighbours, whom he calls the Moderns, taking hashish, sitting up late, not sleeping. They are rich, uneducated young, who never read a book and think only of Jaguars and making money; they 'turn on' every evening to the accompaniment of pop music.

September 8th: Thorington Hall

Drove down here yesterday afternoon in Max Newman's car. He's a delightful man with a face, voice and laugh that are charming and eloquent of intelligence. Sitting in the back of the car I had a view of the lazy sprawl of his right arm on the open window, also the long fringe of mouse-coloured hair round his bald patch. At Chelmsford we stopped at a tiny villa occupied by gentle tentative Indians – the Mukerjee family – great admirers of Lionel, who gave Margaret some slides of him. The little girls all spoke pure East Anglian, but his beautiful wife descended the narrow stairs in a bright blue sari and pressed us, gently but insistently, to cake and tea while they all watched with dog-like brown eyes. Indians never eat with their guests it seems. The midget room was decorated in bright orange and dominated by a television set that was never turned off. A large vase of plastic flowers stood in the corner, but we were taken to admire a superb display of real ones (parsimoniously left unpicked another Indian superstition?) in the slit of back garden.

At breakfast Max showed himself a fairly pernickety man (he has lived a bachelor life for some time) who liked butter, salt, etc. to be in their proper containers, and I couldn't help wondering how he would support Margaret's noisy insensitive clatter. He set up his scream when she showed signs at lunch today of wanting to fish the chicken bones out of her filthy dustbin to make soup, described her kitchen *sotto voce* to me as 'terrible'. There has been no mention of marriage or joint life, though he talks of his cottage near Cambridge and Lyn's[1] (his

---

1 His first wife (deceased).

189

wife) disastrous will. I do hope it's not an illusion of Margaret's; I do think he's very fond of her and appreciates her fun and intelligence, and stalwart qualities; he is solicitous for her in all sorts of ways.

September 10th: In the train

Margaret drove me to the station and remarked that I 'seemed to get on very well with Max'. I said everything nice that I think about him – clever, kind, humorous, sane. 'Oh he has another side to his character,' she said. 'He's almost a dual personality. He can be terribly excitable,' and I remembered with a slightly sinking heart hearing something like a shouting-match as I dropped off to sleep last night. She also mentioned his 'pernicketyness'. She'll have to mend her ways – if she can. But she is I think very attached to him and was proposing to throw over a female friend with whom she had booked a tour to Sicily, on grounds of cholera in Naples, and go off somewhere with Max.

We had a visit from pretty Shirley,[1] her husband and engaging baby (to whom Max proved an assiduous and conscientious babysitter); I took a few walks, but the drought has left the countryside flowerless and powdered with white dust, and my favourite stream-side path is choked with nettles. It was a little depressing.

September 11th

People, people. Rose to lunch – charming and looking well. She made her problem about her Robert a little clearer. He is unable to get going on his book, has been for three years since he took his degree. She had a talk about this with him, it's something he shuns, and was able to suggest he would be more likely to get on with it if he took some other job. Had I any suggestions? He may go to America, for research into the book, and she thinks 'this may be a good thing, as she may perhaps make too many demands on him.' This was so touchingly said, with tears near the surface, that my own nearly spilt in sympathy. She has been to see Cynthia, liked her, thought she couldn't envisage going

---

1 Lionel and Margaret's daughter.

back to life with Robert – it 'had been *so* awful for *so* long' – but couldn't quite imagine what it would be like without him. With considerable percipience Rose said how she preferred being with Cynthia and Robert separately, and had felt there was something false that made one uneasy in their joint company. As I did. 'You once said you thought Cynthia stupid and I think you were right,' she said, 'but she's a nice person and I was happy with her on Sunday.'

Robert himself in the evening. I was delighted he came, and that I persuaded him to eat a scratch meal here rather than take me out. Conversation extremely easy, interesting and flowing. I had been prepared to back out of his life when other people took over. (Mary told me he was engaged up to the hilt, but this he said was an excuse partly to get out of going to Stowell. He made me feel I was still his friend and confidante.) He has seen Cynthia, still finds it upsetting and notices her bewilderment.

September 12th

Wake in a curious mood of detachment to the now inevitable blue sky, a blank day ahead of me. I have begun re-organisation of papers and contents of cupboards, clearing my decks. For what?

The rats are leaving the sinking ship. The jolly Belgian family on the ground floor left yesterday, so I'm rather relieved to hear the Alderman's heavy tread above me in token of his return from holiday. The Belgian *père de famille*, who came to borrow my ladder, made dark references to Haskins the landlord, and impossibility of dealing with him.

Curiously combined with this detachment is a calm but definite death wish.

Later: Belgian *p. de f.* back again, asking to use my telephone. A really nice man; according to him Haskins asked him £17,000 for a three-year-lease! and Sultana is 'a horrible man – and addressed him as "a bloody bastard"'.

Gabby Annan telephoned to ask me to *Tannhäuser* in the Royal Box; Julian to invite himself to lunch, Stanley wants to bring me his detective story (which I don't help with in the least) and Joan is back and comes to dinner tonight – so I don't feel rejected by my friends.

September 13th

Another letter from Gerald this morning, enclosing one from Lynda, saying she had tried to see me and wished she had. I wish so too. They must be off to Sicily by now, and Gerald feels he has calmed down after a period of insanity, which he attributes to a sort of infection from her 'hysteria'. When they get back in mid-November Lynda will spend her mid-weeks with Gerald and weekends with Lars. He now says she 'never, never wants to get married', she loves him (Gerald) more than ever, and their house and her work come first. He adds, 'I find it natural that she should not want to live with Lars as I could never have lived with Carrington ... it seems to me that there can be all sorts of reasons for separating home life from sexual life with a lover.'

I pondered this. When I fell in love with Ralph I wanted above all else to share my life with him, sleep in the same bed every night, hear and tell all thoughts and separate experiences, discuss the books we were reading, other people, what was in the newspapers, and this I wanted sufficiently strongly to fight for it with Lytton and Carrington. Our thirty-three years together, more than came up to what I had hoped and longed for. But it's rather old-fashioned to believe in love these days. I do, I do, I *do*, and I also believe in sex, and passionately in friendship. 'So therio!' as Gerald wrote to R. once.

September 17th

I have rather wildly now let myself in for this German jaunt next weekend, wonder what I'm at and feel agitated in a nebulous way by the prospect.

I picked my way, however, through the weekend with a certain amount of organisation, including a showery walk all round St James's Park, on Sunday morning, pelicans, gaudy ducks, dahlias, hundreds of orientals and Americans swinging their powerfully lensed cameras like machine-guns. Julian to lunch on Saturday was by a long chalk the high spot. Exhausted and black-spectacled from his crash-directorship-telly-course, he revived enough to be the best company, describing it all vividly, brilliantly mimicking Cyril at his birthday celebrations,[1] and generally making the time whizz.

I dropped a note in on Eardley and he came for a drink yesterday, but there's something odd there. I found him much less enthusiastically cordial than usual, rather wooden in fact and wondered why. Either he's depressed about his painting and Mattei (whom he never mentioned once), or his jaunt with Joan had made him anti-female. He had been to dinner with Duncan, Angelica, Ali and Fanny Garnett, and described being 'very rude to Fanny. I said to her, "One can never argue with a woman."' 'I hope she slapped your face,' I said. Really, to out with such a cracker motto to me, when he well knows that I love arguing above all things! I think in his caginess he was afraid of my repeating to Joan anything he said and this put a brake on our conversation. He had cut his hair too short, wore a shiny grey suit and couldn't relax. Poor fellow, something's up with him and I don't think he's happy.

Julia arrived to dinner in a highly tricky mood and I had to weigh every word, as everything I said was spikily and instantly taken up. Perhaps too much whisky and amphetamines. Her get-up was quite extraordinary. The dyed hair begins to look wrong. She is plump and pear-shaped, her waist being the widest part and this was emphasized by a very short dress to well above the knee and long woollen socks over her stockings. In silhouette the effect was amazing. 'I can't eat a thing,' she said, 'I know I shall get ill, at this rate,' and tucked in with a hearty appetite to my veal stew, coming back for a second helping. So I don't know whether to believe it when she said she hadn't slept a wink for several nights.

I heard the story of her latest quarrel with Lawrence. Robert had made her understand that doing his income-tax return might upset Lawrence, but only as a chore. She couldn't take in that he might have money worries and have to face that his expenditure (of which she is responsible for a large item) outruns his income.

---

1 Cyril Connolly was seventy.

September 19th

Very low yesterday, a 'had enough' feeling predominant, and the dark grey and sometimes watery skies underlined my depression. Agitated also by what now seems my absurd trip to Germany – and the complication of not getting on to my aeroplane. Having lain awake brooding over this last night I went down to BEA, and after first being told I was still wait-listed, the magic words 'British Embassy' (which I reluctantly let drop), I think did the trick. How Mary would have enjoyed it, and how ashamed I felt – but anyway he pressed the button of the computer again, said there was *one* seat now for me. My whole history was revealed on the machine by the wonders of modern science. Wonders that go too far at times. I heard a scientist on the wireless describing how by application of an electric lie detector he had proved that living things – plants, insects, eggs – responded to his killing others of their kind, and that eggs 'even faint', as he put it, when other eggs are put into hot water. Lawks!

The possession of a ticket to Bonn has, however, greatly cheered me, though I feel I may well be out of my depths in that milieu.

Another thing that also cheered me was taking Robert to *Katya Kabanova* last night and realising for the third time that it's a masterpiece. Back here to supper – a really delicious bottle of Meursault brought by Robert, and good talk on various subjects.

September 20th

A solitary Thursday, preparing for Germany. How very strange that I've not been there since I was twenty and then so briefly. The rain drips from a sky of grey felt.

Tea with Stanley at his nicest; brown bread (my make), honey and butter, eaten on our knees; complaints about his brother who has been staying with him and is obsessed by money and himself. It was a cosy tea-party, merging into dinner with Eardley and Roger.[1] I really don't know what to make of

---

1 Friend and picture framer.

Eardley's present state – he's defiant, a wilful little boy with a rather red face. We had a very nice evening and Roger was charming, describing a near disaster on his flight from Bulgaria most vividly and terrifyingly.

September 24th

A mint of experience, packed into two days, lies between this and my last entry. I also, so it happens, lie in bed with a slightly injured leg – the taxi bringing me and Robert from Cromwell Road having been involved in a telescopic near-collision which threw me violently forward off my seat. I believed myself quite uninjured but on getting home found blood on my shin, and fairly fast a purple egg' began to arise, horribly reminiscent of what befell Cynthia's mother in Portugal. Hers had burst in a flood of gore, so rather than have the same happen to me I telephoned Moynihan. Robert also came round (after he had rung up to see if I was suffering from 'delayed shock') and was kind and supporting, as only he can be.

Reflections on Robert: he is a marvellous companion, both for travel and sightseeing. He seemed to fling himself into enjoying all that offered, although ready to criticise as well as appreciate. But he is getting really almost too thin, and I worry about the fact that he probably doesn't eat enough, also about the uncertainty of his future and lack of a house.

Extremely good-looking as he still is, his face has a haggard, unhappy look at times. What will become of him, and how could one help him? Perhaps by looking for a house – he has so little time.

Germany: Absurd to reach any conclusions on such a brief dash, yet one inevitably does. Bonn is a peaceful town delightfully situated on the Rhine, and my room had a view over wooded hills on the further side. Though it got very little bombing, while of course Berlin is almost totally new, I think nothing of the older German architecture any more than the Swiss, and not much of what I saw of the landscape. The surprise was the German passion for trees – the great green forest

---

1 A blood blister.

that must have been in the very centre of Berlin, the trees everywhere along wide main streets and in residential areas, and the
smooth-flowing traffic. The Germans we met (and my word the
Ambassadorial social life is intense) were extremely civilised
and articulate, friendly, clever and lively. I couldn't help com-
paring their interest and appreciation for England (particularly
London) and the English, and their perfect command of the language is entirely written off by some of our intellectuals like
Raymond, or Eardley, who put on their stubborn faces and talk
about 'Huns' or 'Krauts'.

Just as in Warsaw, it was impossible not to enjoy the theatrical glamour and smoothness of Embassy life, being carried
everywhere in a huge Daimler with a fluttering Union Jack on
the bonnet, driving in right up to the aeroplane, relishing all
those privileges that I so often disapprove of in theory. Perhaps
it's just that I'm in favour of fostering interest, warmth and
human and cultural relations between the countries, and this
Nicko is particularly good at. Robert was told that he was enormously popular among the Germans and they loved his lack of
pomposity and relaxed behaviour. The few tight-packed days
spun out so that they seemed like a week. It would have been
fatal to have arrived at Düsseldorf, because a dinner-party in a
restaurant was arranged for that night, and as it was we barely
had time to bath, change and have a drink. The social secretary,
kindly asking if she could get anything ironed and what I would
like for my breakfast and when, replied to my question were
there many guests: 'Oh no, only about ten or twelve.' All spoke
perfect English, all seemed clever, interesting and charming.
My favourite was Willy Brandt's private secretary sitting on my
right (whose wife was also charming), quite a young man, his
face alight with animation and one of the easiest people to talk
about ideas – we ranged through education, Keats, music, psychology and a lot about Korea where he had spent the last two
and a half years. He was mad about the Koreans, their brilliant
level of musicianship, the charm of the children and he had
made many friends there. A really enjoyable conversation.
Opposite me sat the maker of Brandt's speeches, an amused-
looking version of Dr Moynihan, to my left the Minister of

Economics, a tall extremely attractive youngish man whose ditto wife was a judge.

Our other social occasion, in Berlin, was a lunch, where I sat between the Director of the Berlin Philharmonic and the Editor of *Die Welt*. There was also an academic economist, with a strong outward squint so that one didn't know which eye to look at.

As Robert said afterwards, lunch was really rather bad – a delicious mousse followed by tough, over-cooked inedibly stringy 'baby chickens', and an overpowering quantity of puddings dumped on one's plate by clumsy soldiers acting as butlers. Robert thought Nicko 'didn't take much trouble' with the Philharmonic Director's wife. But my goodness! the Ambassadorial life – with its cocktail parties, dinners, flying hither and thither, it can't be any joke. The Berlin Residence is only occupied for about four days in the month and all the rest of the time the Czechoslovak cook flies into rages, so Miss Taylor the housekeeper told me. What a world! Today Nicko goes to Munich, tomorrow to Chequers. Mary has covered every room in both Residences with Morris wallpapers, rather too much of a good thing. After our Berlin lunch the ladies were taken round to admire them. The short plain clever wife of the economist said to me: 'That I do not like. You cannot hang pictures on them. They *are* pictures themselves.'

We didn't have time to think, except for Saturday afternoon in Bonn when Robert and I took a short but delightful walk along the edge of the Rhine, to Hitler's favourite hotel, and we saw the life of Berlin going on, steamers putting out from piers, children bicycling with flying hair.

Sightseeing mornings were arranged for Robert and me: on Saturday to the marvellous baroque schloss of Brühl, round which we were conducted by its loving curator. Here was a privilege I greatly relished – to have it all to ourselves, no jostling crowds, only the eager brown eyes of a lover gazing at us through his spectacles, beseeching us to admire the outstanding beauties of the beloved. As indeed we did – it was all elegance and fantasy, white stucco on delicate colour. Thence to Cologne cathedral, a great dark gloomy Gothic pile which left me quite unmoved. I'm sorry we went there and had perforce to skip Beethoven's birthplace.

Travelling by plane to Berlin with the Ambassador, absurd though it might be in a Gilbertian way (and back to Bonn the following day), was highly enjoyable, partly *because* absurd. The Daimler driving right up to the aeroplane, bowing officials with crests on their caps (representing heaven knows what), ease and smoothness, all of which Robert and I noticed the absence of when left to fend for ourselves as ordinary mortals, and laughed about. Though there was a time I felt doubtful about tagging on to Robert's visit, I do now think it made it more fun for him to have someone to go sightseeing with (Nicko and Mary were always occupied) and to chop up and retaste experiences with afterwards.

Saturday evening was relaxed – the Berlin Embassy, with its eternal Morris wallpapers and a new unoccupied look and Miss Taylor (ex-air-hostess) seemingly greeting us, was a little hollow and unreal. Almost at once it was time to go to my comfortable bedroom, take a stiff whisky from the well-filled tray (as at Bonn) and drink it in a refreshing hot bath. Then off we glided to the grand new Philharmonic Hall where the Concertgebouw Orchestra was giving a concert. Mozart, Brückner, Bartók, Mahler, read the programme. They struck up – *this* was not Mozart! What had happened? It soon transpired that the first two items belonged to a previous concert and we were listening to Bartók.

On Sunday morning Robert and I were taken in a car driven by a wooden soldier to East Berlin to see the Pergamon Museum with its famous altar and the gates of Babylon. All more strange than beautiful. We saw the famous Wall so low and unimpressive I felt even I could get over it. Apparently people are fairly often smuggled from East to West in the boots of cars, but we have just set up a British Embassy in East Berlin, as have other nations. People looked perfectly prosperous, skyscrapers were shooting up – but it's still a long way behind the West.

September 25th: London
After a lazy morning in bed, Moynihan came and looked at my

leg, said it would be all right now and re-bandaged it. I rang up Faith, because I can't go on with this nonsensical secrecy about our visit, told her of my accident and she came to tea. I'm sure it was a good thing, and I was able to repeat nice things about Nicko and I think slant the whole visit truthfully and yet to her liking.

Then she suggested that I ought to write to Cynthia, or make some gesture to her, otherwise it's hard on her. She pressed this so much that I felt shaken, but thinking it over I know why I feel almost sure it's impossible. I don't take sides in the affair and I think all in all Cynthia may have suffered more than Robert, but though I like her, I love Robert and rate him among my special friends. I think he feels he can confide in me and I think he also has an absolutely violent and irrational fear of going anywhere or seeing anything connected with his old life. If I were to make any contact with Cynthia he's so clever he would be aware of it and it would stop him talking freely to me. He's the one I worry about and want to help at present. He came in for a drink last night – and said he was going home to write letters and deal with business. I couldn't persuade him to let me cook him 'a square meal'. I do feel anxious about him. He needs a new love.

September 28th

An appalling item in today's newspaper; in Florida a crowd of three hundred people cheered and egged on a would-be suicide who was climbing a water-tower. When firemen and police started up to rescue her they were furious and shouted 'Jump, jump!' and threw stones at the rescue squad. She was a girl of twenty-seven, and she was safely brought down, but the crowd 'wanted blood and were mad because she didn't jump', they surged forwards and smashed the windscreen of the police car. It's hardly credible.

September 30th

Sunday evening, sitting over my electric fire. Robert to a drink – he was debonair, utterly charming, and more kind and sympathetic than I have any cause to expect over my leg troubles, bringing me *pour comble* two little pots of flowers. He told me that Susan had rung Cynthia up while he was there, and how he had armoured himself against being upset by not looking at her, or only without his spectacles (when she might be anyone). But he stayed for about three-quarters of an hour so presumably they must have talked a bit. I was able to raise the question of writing to Cynthia myself, and he agreed he would mind if there was communication between us 'mainly because I know I should try and get things out of you about her'.

Yesterday after going to an old-fashioned Priestley play with Eardley, I dined with Joan, but oh dear, our communication is better on the telephone; much as I tried to make relaxed old-friend contact with her, it seemed impossible; she didn't hear, or didn't listen, made no attempt to show interest in my trip to Germany, never followed up any subject more than perfunctorily and by yawning a bit gave me the excuse to get up and go home and put an end to this rather pointless evening.

October 1st

Leg more painful than ever last night and on removing the crêpe bandage I found it had oozed through the dressing and stuck. I had a bad night, waking to fulminate in my thoughts and then calm myself with pills and reading *As You Like It*. This morning a kind telephone call from Joan and a visit (kinder still) bearing flowers. We both implicitly recognised the failure of our last meeting by saying we had each worried about the other, and thought her preoccupied. Oh how grumpy one is when beset by one's own troubles. All, however, is now smoothed over, I believe. Eardley too had thought me not quite myself and I don't think I am.

October 2nd

I believe I'm healing, though I still have a disgusting half tangerine on my skin which oozes, sticks and makes movement uncomfortable. I only hope I shall be able to enjoy *Tannhäuser* in the Royal Box tonight.

Jaime came for a drink yesterday, looking so young, smart

and dashing that I instinctively feared for Janetta's future. He was full of plans and eagerness for Mexico, and we are provisionally fixed for November 15th.

Poor little Joan rang me up and burst into tears saying that her son-in-law Bryan had told her he thoroughly disliked her, or some such phrase, 'because of her odious meanness to Elizabeth'. It is intolerably rude behaviour and I suppose he has a violent temper. Joan said he just 'hates her' and I know from experience that she can be irritating, and obstinate too. But I personally think horrible money *is* at the bottom of it. Cochemé inexplicably left everything to Joan, not a penny to Elizabeth. Joan thinks this quite natural, but it's not. Bryan and E. asked her to guarantee their first child's education and she consulted her lawyer and took his advice ('the time has not come'). Of course she should have made some settlement on Elizabeth; of course they should have done something for her on her marriage.

October 9th

Janetta has come and plans for Mexico go on apace. To a party at Claridge's for David's new book. I talked to a superior sneering young man who advised me to contact Mexican millionaires: 'They all have wonderful collections, unless of course, you're one of those people who hate the rich.' I longed to shout: *Yes, I am*. But of course I didn't, as we stood there in that ornate temple of wealth, being handed disgusting little soggy canapés of frozen titbits on rounds of bread, by Spanish waiters. Poor Mirabel Cecil has given birth to a son with a hare-lip. Rachel and Sebastian Walker were laughing it off in a way that I found distressing because I knew it covered agony of mind. Dermod[1] says it can be dealt with.

October 10th

My flat crises filled a lot of yesterday. My gambling instinct makes me feel I am safe. My psychological dislike of having 'one

---

1 MacCarthy, a children's specialist.

foot on sea and one on land' is also operative. Meanwhile I was entertaining 'The General'[1] to lunch and to look through my photo-albums and to have a cup of tea – a long session and one which raked the emotional subsoil. He left with profuse thanks, having been the first person to go through all the albums.

October 11th: Stowell

Drove down this morning with Mary and Philip and now lie peacefully on my bed for two whole lovely hours. Conversation non-aggressive, except for one moment when Mary said she had quarrelled with (and nearly been *hit* by) Koestler because she had wanted to bring back hanging. 'On what grounds?' I asked. 'Saving the taxpayers' pocket,' said Mary smugly, and I couldn't resist saying, 'So you would commit murder for money, would you?' I must say I have *never* heard such a cynical reason given in its defence, and Mary had no come-back, which was just as well, as Philip might have got involved.

Janetta persuaded me to put off Mexico till January and I think it's a good idea. My flat should be settled by then, for good or ill. Julian took her and me to *Katya Kabanova*, one of the nicest evenings I've had for ages. Supper at Wheeler's afterwards, and Janetta's highly original thoughts weaving gently, firmly and subtly into words. She told us about talking about God to her hairdresser, and how she had said she supposed people found it difficult to get on without him. 'You don't seem to like God much, madam,' said the hairdresser whose name was Hugh. 'No – I simply *hate* him.' The hairdresser showed no dismay, but explained how he sometimes got pleasure from 'going to church, madam'.

October 12th: Stowell

The iron of this house is eating into my soul, and an iron grey day doesn't help. All Mary's outgoing sweetness can't quite obliterate the fact that I arrived into a room that was totally unheated and with dead flowers in stinking water. I know that she and Philip have electric blankets and fires, but I have neither

<hr />

1 David Gadd.

and no one fills the hot-water bottle I thoughtfully brought. Mary has nothing in the world to do and the garden is ablaze with dahlias and many other luscious flowers – roses included. (I have just relieved my feelings by throwing away the dead petunias and michaelmas daisies and their smelly water.) My bathroom is ice cold and the water for my bath was barely warm enough. I am not offered a second whisky when Mary refills her own glass. There! I've blown off my sense of being uncared-for, turned on the radiator in my bedroom and propose to luxuriate in a few hours' solitude.

Joan's two portraits sit side by side on the sofa and no one refers to them. I made a move in their direction when alone with Mary, but she said not a word so I shan't. It's odd, in that case, that they are put out so prominently. I don't really care for them very much – they are good, conventional likenesses.

October 13th

A very jolly evening with the Baths, Henry, Virginia and Georgia. Henry arrived quite plastered, and Georgia and Virginia shaking in their shoes from the drive. They were all in their different ways, however, quite charming, and he would make an excellent music-hall turn. Towards the end of the evening he sat beside me on the sofa, lurched towards me, forgot what he was going to say, and was amused by his own ineptitude going off into endearing 'Hm-hm-hms'.

October 24th

A lot of time has passed, emotions seethed and spilt; yet another hideous war has broken out, between Israel and the Arab States. One of the things that deeply shocked me was that Robert honestly admitted that this new horror thrilled him, gave him a lift and a feeling of excitement. Andrew Murray-Thripland was the same – he said thoughtfully, 'Yes, racing pulses.' Of the young, Stanley is most disturbed, but this characteristic reaction (on a par with all the fainting, falling off chairs and collapsing into tears produced in him by aesthetic experiences – and I'm not for a moment doubting that something corresponding to this really happens) is that he has three times said, 'I'm going to give my blood – people are *dying*,' and I don't think he has or ever will.

Of course people are dying all the time for reasons that are inevitable or even noble or might be prevented by blood donors. But this senseless, irrational slaughter of man by man produces in me nothing but a sad sour feeling like seasickness. *Again*? Susan was full of self-importance because someone of her generation, the journalist Nicholas Tomalin, has been killed reporting the war. As if feeling herself the youngest present, she said, 'But it's the first war I've been *in*.' 'What do you mean? There's never been a moment when there wasn't a war *somewhere*, ever since 1945, and reporters reporting it. Even this isn't *our* war.' The old stereotyped, highly coloured magazine illustrations do duty for emotion.

Then the flat crisis came to a head. I began to lie awake at night, was rung by Haskins in what might have been Javanese, and given advice by all my kind friends: 'You *must* settle it.' 'Take another flat' (there is one next door but two floors up and no lift). 'I'll go and see your landlord' (Janetta of course). 'I don't trust Mungo' (Robin).

October 26th

Inveigled into an absurd interview about Friendship with an *Observer* reporter. I am now faced with one of the, to me, worst of all horrors, of having my photograph taken. They will come in half an hour. I felt in a ludicrous way that I *must* testify, or wave a flag in favour of this now main element in my life. When the photographer rang up he suggested taking me 'looking at letters from friends'. F: 'Oh I see – the Old Lady Shows her Medals?' Photographer: 'Come again?' Yesterday I felt hysterically appalled. Now I don't give a damn.

Janetta and I are going down to the Hills'. Janetta rang up saying she had told Heywood she liked going first class and I liked going second and 'it would be awful if we arrived having had a ghastly quarrel all the way down.' No question of that – of course she gets her own way. As I told her, it wasn't so much a question of economy as of principle.

October 29th

The photographer was kindness itself and almost sent me to sleep. But like the dentist with his drill he kept on and on for nearly half an hour.

Janetta and I took our crowded first-class carriage to Saxmundham. I'm interested in her increasingly upper-class stance – whence does it come? It makes a breach with Rose; it is very alien to the girl she once was. I mind it quite a lot. She had been irritated by Rose insisting on travelling second class when she went to the funeral of a Jackson relation, and said quickly, 'I'm afraid I think it's a good thing for there to be some people who can make decisions.' And who are treated as superior, and have undeserved privileges, and much more money than other people? She was annoyed at Bernard Levin for accusing Vita Sackville-West of being a snob. I said, 'What makes you think she wasn't one?' J: 'Oh was she?' F: '*Yes*, certainly.' I fear that the crack of class distinction and privilege widens between us. But how youthfully charming she was, how kind to me and Heywood, how ravishing when she dressed up in Trelawney's Albanian outfit – little red cap with long tassel, red velvet embroidered jacket, red cummerbund and white cotton trousers. It's marvellous that at fifty plus she can have such almost juvenile elegance. Heywood, she and I had two long lovely walks through still pearly autumn mornings. A short comfortable talk about death with Anne. She and Heywood often talk about which will die first and what the other would do. 'I'm sure Heywood wouldn't live here without me – but I sometimes think I might buy a dog and stick it out, haw! haw!'

Looking out of my window: the softly graded colours of trees and fields, changing every moment, ravished my eye and melted my heart.

In the evenings some incursions from the unwelcome Knapp-Fisher[1] who believes everyone loves him, and from John and Sheelah.[2] Scrabble, telly. On the telly *Jane Eyre* was like over-stewed meat from which every scrap of good had faded. But last

1 Ralph, one-time manager of Sidgwick & Jackson.
2 Hill.

night a programme about Casals moved me so that I couldn't sleep – for nearly an hour a great bubble of emotion swelled in my chest almost painfully and tears oozed to my eyes. What a marvellous artist and good, darling little man.

I'm deep in Byron's letters, preoccupied by him – he felt truly and deeply the death of friends but had no sentimental feelings about funerals or belief in immortality. An intelligent, ironical man, but he had heart as well as head, when young at least.

October 30th: London

Still they come. A letter from a man who wants to turn Carrington into a play and to talk about Bloomsbury *Ay de mi*. Julian last night told me that awful Jill Bennett is set on being Carrington on telly with her horrid quacking actressy voice. Julian made me feel terribly guilty, and I still do, by saying how 'fierce' I am, especially with those I love. I know it's true and am ashamed. Of course it's because I love Janetta so much that I mind her new snobbery, but by what right? Why not more tolerance, more gentleness? Oh, I shall really try for it. But the awful thing is I do try, and seemingly to no effect. My feeling that I was a bit of an ogress to Julian depressed me. I'm not aware of a desire to dominate and be a bully – what an awful thing if I am one. As bad as Julia?

October 31st

Jenny Rees came to lunch and we talked – tiringly and drainingly – about Bloomsbury. While consciously searching my mind for the truth I think sometimes what she said seemed to me miles from it – for instance, were 'They' not 'precious and affected'? It seemed to me she couldn't have begun to get a clue if that was what she thought, and I told her so. She's a bright girl and pleasant. I don't know that I understand much more about her. Stanley, on the telephone, tells me that these adjectives 'precious' and 'affected' are the standard current criticisms of Bloomsbury.

A call from Julian, saying he had enjoyed our evening, but showing he knew he had made me feel guilty about my 'fierceness'. I do, I do. I am *touchée*, although I think there is an element of his being on the defensive himself, and like a little burrowing creature throwing out sticks to cover his retreat.

My heart is heavy as lead, or rather I have no heart for anything. A very great pleasure was hearing Magouche's voice, arrived back in London – otherwise, tick-tock, time passes. I have a slightly dreaded visit to the doctor, and dinner with Joan which may not be stimulating but I *must* not be fierce. I turn my eyes into my soul; there I see such black and grained spots as will not leave their tinct.

My heavy-heartedness had its cause in certain physical symptoms. Moynihan said I must have an X-ray. It might be a polyp, easily dealt with but that could 'turn nasty'. In my desire to face a possible death sentence calmly, I didn't ask all the questions I wish I had. Is there a third possibility? But I feel this confirms a subterranean presentiment that has for some time been with me. And of course I'm appalled to think that I have no quick way out in case of need. I *know* I've had enough. Of course I can make do, with curiosity, friendship, books, travel, music, while health of a sort remains, but how long will that be? I can't face wriggling slowly towards extinction, yet I rack my brains in vain to think how to avoid that contingency.

I came back suffering from shock and turned on the wireless, but a feeling of preoccupation prevented my taking it in and I only longed for oblivion.

The world is full of horrors – the Israeli war, industrial unrest, no electricity probably, winter, old age, decrepitude. I only want to look whatever comes straight in the eye, *get out* decently.

All this is I feel squalid, and not material for diarising. But it must be set down if I'm to go on talking to this book, and in a curious way doing so has been cathartic.

Janet Stone has just rung up to say they have both got flu, so thank heavens I can spend the coming weekend quietly in my burrow.

November 2nd

A very nice lunch with Robert here cheered me yesterday. I

veer between my ordinary level of optimism and a feeling that I have been long subject to semi-conscious presentiments. Tunes whose words follow after have for some time been a method of my unconscious voicing its content. Last weekend (after the 'symptom') I was suddenly haunted by a tune, and couldn't place it. Then realised it was Violetta's *cri de coeur* in the last act of *Traviata*, but incomplete '—— *morir si giovane!*' '*Giovane*' is a bit of a joke, but one is – it must be admitted – always '*giovane*' to oneself.

To *Simon Boccanegra* last night with Dicky.

November 3rd

A dinner-party given by Robert at Brooks's Club last night, slightly dreaded, but in fact enjoyed. The Annans, and Griggses – met once before, but he turns out to be ex-Lord Altrincham, attacker of the Royal Family and Conservatives, historian of Liberals. Robert said to me as we drove away, 'It's much nicer being with people who *think*, isn't it?' Mrs Grigg was clearly agog about the marriage situation; I heard her talking to Robert about it at dinner, and she did a bit to me.

November 4th

Approaching my D-day (tomorrow) and how exactly has my mood changed? More accepting, less panicky, but with ups and downs. I have a desire to be rather quiet, seeing few people each day. Yesterday I spent the afternoon with Georgia, and we went to see the Mayan things in Burlington Gardens, and the Chinese exhibition. Our reaction was rather fortunately the same: disappointment (except that I hadn't expected to like the Chinese things much). Georgia said with a comic look of distaste that the famous jade-covered princess was 'just a Michelin man' and it didn't 'turn her on'. I searched in vain for 'beauty'. The Mayans' curiously bestial curlicue designs crammed into rectangular shapes reminded me of Bowyers chipolata sausages enclosed in round-cornered boxes. There were some profiles of strangely low-foreheaded long-nosed beings that did perhaps seem beautiful? And so did some of the Chinese wall-paintings, bronze horses and their simplest pottery. But how is it neither of these great civilisations deal with the three major human emotional situations – birth, sex, death? There were no lovers, no mothers and children, hardly any references to the vegetable world even. It was all animals, animal gods and hunting: while fear and cruelty were the prevailing emotions. No gaiety or joy of life.

Back to tea off a brown soda loaf I had made – with honey and lots of talk about the nature of the cosmos.

November 5th

Just back from my X-ray, which lasted from ten to eleven-thirty. During that time I was richly aware of not being a human being, but a specimen. So, on return, I boiled myself some warming coffee and tucked into my own bread and honey. Since when the reaction has begun to set in and I see the experience no longer as an ordeal but now the means to knowledge that may alter my future.

However, here is what it was like: I woke and ate my one dry biscuit, all I was allowed since midnight, took my ever tepid bath (all we ever get nowadays) and set out. A cold wind blowing and soppy dead leaves making the pavements of Sloane Street slippery. I turned in at Fordie House and was immediately aware of no longer being me but an integer. Was instructed to 'empty my bladder' in the lavatory and then enter the chamber of horrors where I was greeted by a sallow-faced youngish woman with a look of worried misery on her face, not a ghost of a smile, no humanity even. 'Take off all your clothes and put on this with the opening at the back.' 'This' was a white robe made of what seemed to be paper, and jolly chilly too. I then lay on my back under the huge mechanical monster for over an hour, while she shot slides under me and retired to a cubicle whence came her voice at intervals: 'Breathe in. Breathe out. Don't breathe, lie still. Breathe away.' Halfway through, a large male doctor with a mop of yellow-grey hair and a big face came in. 'Mrs Partridge? Do you come from the Bahamas?' 'No – why do you think so?' 'Oh, Dr Moynihan has a patient called Partridge from there.' It was then apparent that the slightly (very slightly) dreaded injection of one of my veins with dye was to begin. 'Are they easy?' he asked. 'No, very difficult,' I said, 'and the last time was over ten years ago.' 'Well it'll be harder now as we have to get a lot in.' 'Away he went' twice without success, and finally with a fairly acute pain he had obviously 'made it'. I felt the invasion of my whole body by some alien substance, a strange taste (surely not imagination) in my mouth, my head slightly bursting, but not unpleasantly. Then it was over and my arm was bent up while the pain persisted but gradually dwindled. 'Good. Very difficult, but good,' he said and went. It seems to me that after this my sallow young woman was slightly more friendly, and finally announced 'the last shot', and then that I could dress and go. But it seemed all wrong to me that she and the young man knew what was inside me and I do not. And I have a curious irritation of the skin, as if I had a rash. The dye?

November 6th

Brilliant blue sky and fresh cold exhilarating air. Dined with Raymond, Joan and Julian last night, very jolly indeed, and Raymond in very sparkling mood. Now this morning I await, but have not yet received the verdict of the X-ray – though I have (perhaps unfairly) gained a certain confidence from the news that I have been proved to have the same old infection I had before.

Lunch today with Mary; I tried to egg her on to rebel against Philip for refusing to have Magouche to stay for the weekend at the same time as Robert. He has some reservations about her being left-wing, though Lord knows I'm a sight lefter (and so is Frances Phipps) and he's kind to us.

Rather on the hop waiting to hear about my X-ray. It has come, but Moynihan hasn't rung up. I shall therefore stay in till lunch-time. I rang up the secretary, who has obviously seen it and thought 'I had nothing to worry about'.

November 8th

X-ray shows nothing abnormal, though Moynihan still says he 'wants to talk about it to the surgeon'. A storm in a pee-cup?

Rachel and David and Eardley to dinner, which was delightful. David said on leaving, 'I knew I should enjoy myself, but I enjoyed myself even more.' I've heard him say that three times, but how many has Rachel, who is much too loyal to mind. A lot of talk about Vita — and Eardley defended her, but her diary is hysterical cliché-ridden slush, and the character revealed therein an appalling egotist and snob. Back to Byron.

November 11th

I saw no one all yesterday, but didn't feel a trace of loneliness. To the London Library in the afternoon, where I found myself staring at a book in the rack of unwanted new purchases: *The Technique of Dying*, by Partridge. I took it out (another omen?) and found it was all about how to dye stuffs.

November 12th

Mary came to see me yesterday in mollifying mood — I think because of my indignation against the Magouche ban. Magouche came to lunch here on Sunday and Robert to dinner, and no two friends could have been more communicable.

November 15th

Janetta here again and has paid me a perfect visit. I expect her and Jaime tonight, when perhaps Mexico will consolidate — or as much as it can in view of the rocking state of the world, industry and the pound. Nothing seems very real except reading about the past — i.e. history.

November 17th: Crichel

Mexico does seem to have become real all at once — dates fixed, Jaime masterful. I think the decision has infused some new energy into me and that I had been gradually unwinding like a ball of wool. But the 'economy', whatever the bloody thing is, is in uproar, and if nothing comes of it all I shan't, God knows, complain.

Down here this afternoon with Dadie and Raymond — and feeling positively, actively happy. The beauty of the afternoon light striking across the ploughed fields as Dadie and I took the dogs for a walk was great, and we chattered away. Dadie clamours for us to be alone without visitors. Raymond rings up and invites Kitty, Cecil Beaton, and is (curiously) a little more schoolmasterly than usual, whereas Dadie is adorably kind to him.

November 18th: Crichel

I had been looking forward to reading the new Life of Aldous Huxley, but the book has disappeared. Everyone in turn searched their bedrooms – no luck. 'It must have been Andrew Thripland!' says Raymond. F: 'What, d'you mean he put it in his suitcase and went off with it, without asking?' R: 'He's quite capable of it.' On a walk with Dadie I said I didn't think he was; he was scatterbrained, but not unscrupulous. Later I made my own search and at once found the book by Dadie's bed. F. to R.: 'I said Andrew wasn't capable of such wickedness!' R: 'It's not proved that he isn't.' F: 'But you must admit there's not one iota of evidence that he *is*.' R. still looked reluctant and it will I'm sure add a smut or two to the black picture he has of Andrew though aware of his charm and intelligence. For so kind and good a man it's odd how unforgiving Raymond gets. How many times he has complained of Janetta's inability to deal with Cyril's sulks when staying here. He is desperate for somewhere to go in February and I half suggested Tramores, but he has never said *one* thing to me showing appreciation of Janetta, and I don't think I will propose it.

My lively walks with Dadie have set me up no end and I feel stronger and in an odd way more hopeful. Pat arrived, and Kitty for lunch.

Gluck on the wireless. I must emphasise that Raymond was at his most winning; he appeared one evening in trousers of massive red and green check.

November 21st

I took the Hills and Parladés to *Iphigenia* at Covent Garden. Jurinac charming and dignified but the voice not what it once was, and I think my guests, though too polite to say so, were a little bored. Back here to cold food. The greatest pleasure of the evening was in Janetta's delicious gaiety, and almost flirtatious manner with Jaime, so that all at once he seemed to be a new admirer, not a husband. He obviously enjoyed her amusing bravura. How can someone like Raymond not see it, and talk only of her 'low vitality'?

J. and J. seem determinedly set for Mexico. But – but – my mind is rather full of 'buts'. I went to my travel agent today and they said many flights were being cancelled at once, the American fuel crisis is worse even than ours, and TWA has been on strike 'for ages'. If this extraordinary world fuel crisis goes on, it would seem madness to go, and perhaps not get back. I think I'll book in case it is settled, but if it isn't I can withdraw. Why even engage in what is meant to be joy joylessly?

How very strange everything is. I have sad letters from Bunny, and one from Gerald saying that he is being made to cut his autobiog. including the bit about R.'s character. I was of course delighted; I think Janetta was a little shocked how much, but I do feel he wished to assault Ralph and has been prevented though no doubt he will put him in an unattractive light when he describes his own affair with Carrington.

November 25th: Stowell

In bed last night thinking of the past and the future, suffused with waves of pleasure and uneasiness alternately.

It was a pleasure to visit Frances Phipps, a gallant pirate with one lens of her spectacles blacked out after an operation for a cataract. Such too was the arrival of radiant Nell, with her clear skin and clear voice and brood of boys. Also her lover (more of him anon).

This afternoon Mary and I drove to Savernake Forest, for a clandestine meeting with Magouche, Janetta and Jaime, and a long swift walk through that carpet of rustling leaves. The poor old avenues now have a mangy look, the beech trees growing tall, thin and old; a squirrel leapt from waving twig to waving twig, high up in their tips while Tuggy bounced impudently below. We shuffled partners as we walked – Mary in her Russian fur hat, Magouche all in leather like an airman, Janetta huddled, hands in pockets like a purposeful schoolboy, only Jaime both elegant and normal. Talk of Mexico, rather unsatisfactory. Jaime and I had made so many decisions, but I got the feeling Janetta wanted to loosen them again and her last remark was 'Well, *we'll see.*' Before that she had said, 'Jaime seems to want to fly the Atlantic with Frances.' What does that mean – that they want to come to England yet again? Or have to for business reasons?

I wish I knew how much I even want to go. Am I afraid, feeble, unequal to the standard set by Duncan, Bunny, Frances Phipps? One of my troubles is a manic-depressive attitude towards the enterprise. 'Nothing to lose,' I tell myself, which is true.

Magouche is still smarting rather under Mary's acceptance of Philip's ban, and wanted to know if he knew we were meeting her and how I manage to get on with him. I don't know, is the answer to the latter, and I'm a little ashamed of it. He has lent me 1,100 dollars in signed traveller's cheques – I'm stupefied!

No electric fire in my room; I pinched one as usual. With another form of generosity Mary gave me her Mexican diary to read. Had Philip expected a honeymoon? Had she?[1] They didn't have it, and there were more reservations about Ernie than I expected. Nell's young man is a computer expert, large, not very young, gentle, knows the Garnetts and Christopher Strachey. It would be foolish for me to ignore that I'm a great success with him, I have no idea why, I've become such an old tortoise. I try to forget my shell, but it's hard in both senses.

Sunday evening

Nell and party have left. I stay till tomorrow. I'm tormented about this American journey – I should never have agreed to go with J. and J. without someone more my coeval. They will want to be more adventurous than I can, and as I hate to be a mill-stone and foresee myself pretending not to be tired, and going on and collapsing. I think of how Magouche and Janetta relentlessly took me pounding on through the icy night of Leningrad, looking for a restaurant the first night of our arrival. Or of the mad attempt to drive across country without a map this summer from the Cueva de la Pileta, and how nearly it ended in disaster.

---

1 They were divorced but now back together.

How can they fail to resent my clogging presence? Feelings must at best be mixed towards the dependent old, and nobody knows what it is like to be in one's seventies, only that one is 'marvellous' if one keeps up. Janetta's overpoweringly delicate solicitude is more likely to give way to 'irritation' than Jaime's. Oh what shall I do? Who can advise me? Magouche?

I'm reading a book on Mexico highly recommended by everyone including Pat and Paddy Leigh-Fermor – it emerges in terms of menace, ferocity, blood and corpses, machismo, smells and squalor and brutalised sex …

November 26th

I do feel an upsurge of life when I pull out of the clammy unreality of Stowell and at once I become a more viable human being. So 'we'll see' as Janetta says. A brilliant frosty morning, cold as Leningrad. I went out with Mary to pick a few chrysanthemums under the watchful eye of Stollery the gardener. 'Did you raid the greenhouse yesterday, Milady?' It's stuffed with plants in pots and I didn't envy Mary her inability to pick more than half a dozen. I asked her if she thought Magouche was getting attached to Robert; she said, 'Yes, I do think so – but of course it's a case of a very old friendship. In a sense we've all always been mad about Robert.'

I sit now in a hot train opposite two female faces, both perfectly blank, and chewing – what?

December 1st

Took Stanley to *Ballo in Maschera* at the Coliseum last night – the performance as well produced and conducted as *Don Giovanni* (in the pleasant company of Mary and Robert at C. Garden the other night) was vulgar, pretentious and downright bad. Robert and I agreed absolutely about this, *sotto voce*. Mary thought it 'Glorious – right?' Why must everyone tear about the stage, caper and flourish? Why must Don Giovanni prance and snap his fingers and carry on like an ageing queer as he doubtless is? Why must the scenery be composed of metal tubing – now a modish and outworn gimmick? Why must Donna Elvira wear a vast iridescent wig? (She and Margaret Price both sang extremely well, however.)

215

There's no one I like going to the opera with more than Stanley. He increases my own attention and excitement by his own — just as Julian makes me feel anxious by accusing me of fierceness. Perhaps I am critical, but I can truly say that at *Ballo* I felt like a jug that was being filled with the liquid of a pleasurable thrill which gradually reached high water mark and stayed there throughout the performance.

Now, Saturday morning, I'm sitting in a warm train on my way to the Cecils for one night only. Frost sparkled on the ground as my taxi whizzed past Buckingham Palace, and the water-fowl were waddling awkwardly on ice in St James's Park under a blue sky. I feel a curious *elation* — even the adventure of Mexico doesn't dismay me.

December 3rd

A ramshackley put together dinner-party tonight has been like a huge hump ahead, partly because of icy weather and dwindling electricity. I drove back from Cranborne in the car of a perfect stranger — Ogilvy by name, brother-in-law of Princess Alexandra, who had been shooting at the Manor. 'Very breezy!' said David while he disappeared into the lavatory, and he had rather tactlessly told him on the telephone that I was anxious about conversation. 'Tell her I'm rather deaf,' Ogilvy said. Actually of course we chattered at length, and I was interested in the way he dropped his upper-class 'shootin' breeziness and talked perfectly interestingly about his children's education, Spain, how much he hated flying and how this was because he had lost his nerve in a crash and never regained it and that his wife had conjunctivitis and a passion for opera.

Julian was a visitor at the weekend and I tried not to be 'fierce'. At the risk of being rude to our hosts I sat up talking to him about his new love affair with an Irish singer called Allan (no money, no job, but he sounds charming). Again he returned to the necessity of not asking people direct questions — and I still disagree with him.

The weather has become a trifle warmer. I have made my dinner as simple as possible — made bread last night — and I think it is more or less *en train*, so do not greatly care, though 'never again'.

December 9th

That dinner-party was I truly think a great success measured partly by the fact that I enjoyed it myself. Everyone was charming – I've never known Pat T.-R. so smoothed down and benign, and there was no pause in general talk.

Last night I had a drink and conversation with Sybille Bedford[1] whom I liked very much. Faintly reminiscent of Elizabeth Bowen, with good ex-pretty features, scant hair dyed a carroty colour, a quick staccato voice accompanied by staccato changes of expression, a quick engaging smile, a gap in her teeth, the whole building up an intensely nervous personality, someone with, as she said, 'a tendency to panic'. When she got on to Aldous we were at once involved in rapid conversation, fascinating to me. Her quickness of response reminded me of Iris Origo, and what a pleasure it is when people understand instantly what you mean. Her attitude to Aldous and Maria is idolatrous but never unintelligent. I tried very cautiously to get her on to their religious, political and philosophical beliefs. As to immortality she said Aldous must really be called 'agnostic', though he had several 'contacts' with Maria after she died. But he probably believed in a sort of individual co-consciousness to which we returned, and strongly in the wicked uselessness of war. She was amusing about Gerald Heard's[2] change from a 'blarneying, story-telling Irishman to a self-consciously ascetic guru who caused other people infinite trouble by refusing to eat, or drive a car', and couldn't think why Aldous took him so seriously. When her mother died and she was still quite young and very much upset, the Huxleys sent Heard to see her. In he came, sat down and 'spouted forth an oration about death, life and bereavement which had no bearing at all on anything I had been experiencing. Then he suddenly stopped, looked at his watch and said he was sorry but he must go and visit someone else "In Need"'.

Though I write little about it here, everyone I meet, the wireless, the newspapers are entirely preoccupied with our

---

1 Novelist and biographer of Aldous Huxley.
2 He was a guru who advised on religious matters and health cures.

'situation' as they endlessly call it. Are we, or not, heading for starvation, slump and a return to austerity, pony-traps and bicycles, shortages of food, clothes and everything else? Is it in fact the end of the world as we know it?

December 11th

Last night's dinner 'passed off'. I rate it no higher; melding was poor. Stanley much the best at it, but he was for him rather stern, and I felt this was partly disapproval of Julian. Julian, who came about nine having set off just as Allan was entering his flat with three boon companions, was as ever quicksilvery and intelligent, but showing little social sense. That is he talked in-talk to Rose about people not known to Stanley and Jenny. Rose was dressed in her most droopy style, sweet and soft-voiced, and taking everything back to 'the sufferings of the working classes'. Well, she's right there, many things (though not all) can and should go back to base, but I would define that base as the 'under-paid' or the 'poor' as against the rich and privileged. Stanley's Jenny is a bright girl with a pretty figure and pretty hair, stylishly dressed, but for my taste too given to clichés. I wish she wouldn't keep saying '*Right*' and 'you know?'

Yesterday Robert came to lunch and that was pure pleasure. How I enjoy his company. He's 'all right', I think, about Cynthia which is probably healthy, and had taken a little BBC girl known as 'the Mouse' to Paris, on a visit to Georgie. He said she was quite uneducated, and very unconfident and thought he was ashamed of her, as he probably was.

Just as I was building up my libido for the American project I hear from Mary, just back from Málaga and Tramores, that Janetta is still saying 'We'll see', and doesn't want to go to New York, though Jaime does. Shall I cut my losses and cancel the whole plan? When I said this to Stanley on the telephone he charged me with pessimism. He will be in New York himself when I should be there. But how could I struggle alone to Mexico with all the time a sneaking doubt whether I should find the J.'s there when I got there? Or ever get home again. No – it's too much of an adventure for me. Mary comes to lunch tomorrow and will tell me more.

Robert's view of world conditions is that we are all facing poverty and steady decline of the value not only of stocks and shares but objects. He hinted at unheard-of deprivations and austerity. We already have a ferocious petrol, electricity and train crisis, cooping us into our chilly nests.

Dinner at Magouche's last night; she's a splendidly lavish and a subtly attentive hostess. Eight little roast birds (four grouse and four partridges) melting and perfectly cooked – the eight guests were the Sylvesters, the Campbells, Peter Eyre (with a thick moustache which made him look Mephistophelian), a youngish man from Colnaghi's. The accent therefore on art. I sat between the latter, an easy pleasant fellow, and David Sylvester[1] who has become extraordinary looking, rather too fat and a face half covered in black bristles of varying length, and a gentle voice saying such things as 'I don't think it's a good idea to go to bed with one's daughters.' I liked him very much even when he turned and looked at me so strangely that I said 'Why are you looking at me so fiercely?' Then he smiled rather charmingly.

December 12th

Mary has been to lunch, and given me – honestly and sweetly – her account of the Parladés' attitude to Mexico. To begin with the Fonda is still not sold; on the very point of signing, it was once more abandoned. Janetta said that she wasn't keen on New York, but Jaime was; the attitude was still one of 'We'll see'. She said Janetta had been '*sweet* and welcoming', taking especial trouble with Ernie. She thought she felt 'protective' to me and she had jumped at Mary's suggestion of giving me a first-class ticket as a present. But how is it that she tells both Mary and Magouche she doesn't want to go to New York, but *not me*. I've sent her a telegram asking her to ring me up tomorrow before two, and propose to put before her several possibilities – such as our going somewhere quite different and much cheaper like Marrakesh or Lanzarote or Madeira.

---

1 Art critic.

December 15th

No telephone call from Janetta and meanwhile a national crisis of such increasing intensity that I have lost all desire to go to Mexico. What to do instead is a bit of a problem, but go there I will not.

Suddenly everyone is facing the fact that England 'is on the edge of a precipice', though exactly what lies beneath it – poverty or revolution – it's hard to say. So much has happened in the public sphere that attention is withdrawn from private things, if indeed they can be said to exist. But at times the two blend – for instance having tried twice to get petrol from 'my' garage yesterday, I got up early (eight) and with a fur coat thrown over my nightgown and no hot coffee inside me I drove there and to two other garages in vain. At the fourth I found a queue, in which after one hour and ten minutes' wait I got filled up. My electricity has not – yet – gone right off, but it dwindles at times to a thread. The central heating is at most chilly, and the water can only be raised to bath or washing-up level by adding three large saucepanfuls, boiled on my electric cooker.

I am beginning to hate pig-faced pig-headed Heath more and more, with his stubborn desire for confrontation with the unions. As Levin, and indeed Harold Wilson pointed out, he has done so far nothing at all that might narrow the 'widening gap between rich and poor', lower the cost of living nor do what he promised to do, take measures against the property speculators (Centrepoint etc.). A wretched Conservative MP on *Any Questions* last night had the nerve to say the latter were 'public benefactors', and I'm glad to say he roused audibly grumbling indignation.

My remarks on friendship and a little blurred photo appeared in the *Observer* last Sunday in such a garbled form that I was furious; I put it straight down my rubbish chute. Joan rang up at once (rather characteristically) to say the photo was 'awful' and so was the rest of it. I really agreed with her and was therefore surprised to get positive testimonials from unexpected quarters. Dicky wrote me a most touching letter – 'a love-letter' he called it, saying I had been the greatest influence in his life after Denis and that meeting Ralph, Burgo and me, our friends, way of life, etc. had entirely altered his outlook and that 'there had been times when our friendship literally kept him alive.' He went on, more touchingly still, 'we have always spoken openly about death and I don't mind telling you that the day you go will be one of the worst in my life.' The oddest consequence of this episode was that, listening to the wireless in the middle of the night, I heard someone say, 'In the *Observer* colour supplement in an article on friendship – can't remember who – said something marvellous' ... and quoted my words. Oh and best of all Julia rang up and said, 'I'm proud to be your – friend.' But all this only increases my annoyance at not having said what I wanted to say.

December 18th

I've gone into reverse utterly, capitulating to a call from Janetta and Jaime and a telegram from Jaime in which they suddenly seemed genuinely disappointed at my saying I couldn't make it. I have even got two strings to my bow (because they do want to go to New York) – either I'll join them at Málaga and fly direct with them, or if the Pan Am flight is still on I'll meet them in New York.

God grant that indecision doesn't persist to the last, as I find it soul-destroying.

Apart from cold water and central heating, lack of petrol and trains, my personal sufferings from our 'greatest crisis since the war' have not been great. But *if* the electricity is actually cut off, and *if* one cannot get away from it all by car, train or aeroplane, how is it possible not to feel trapped.

Dicky and Denis came to lunch on their way out to Spain – Denis as good as gold and off the wagon because Francis Bacon has cirrhosis of the liver as a result of drink. Mary's brother Hamish has died of it and poor Mary had to go and break the news to her mother today.

I spent a perfectly delightful afternoon with Magouche two days ago (Sunday). Lunch with her and Missy Harnden[1] (goodness what a chatterer), a lovely nap on the drawing-room sofa,

---

1 Friend of Magouche's.

tea with Robert and his two children, a drink and so home. Robert brought his 'Mouse' (the girl he has been telling me about) to tea. She is soft, pretty and shy; as he truly says uneducated and probably not very interesting. Does he really prefer them that way?

December 21st

Soaking wet and mild. Almost everyone I know, including vulnerable little Sophie, is flying off somewhere today — Magouche to Corfu, Stanley to San Francisco, Robert to Germany. Whether just to get us through the Crisis or not I don't know, but there seems a more optimistic note. Wild spending goes on, avid crowds throng Harrods; Centrepoint was seen with all its lights blazing though absolutely empty. I have a feeling Heath's star is setting. 'Flexible' is the political word of the moment and no one could call him that.

I've been to two parties and nothing could be more different — the first given by the Telephone Dolly,¹ smart, mean (I had one glass of the filthiest red plonk I ever drank). It was full of faces one had seen in the papers, Bob Boothby, Jeremy Thorpe; powerful, unsympathetic, self-satisfied faces. Among them all suddenly I caught sight of the Mad Hattery visage and long teeth and wildly unbrushed hair of Ben Nicholson. He was almost the only person I enjoyed talking to. Raymond and I left early but there was no transport, not a taxi in sight and I walked all the way home in a drizzle in my velvet slippers, down the endless dark tunnel of the Mall and Constitution Hill, which might have been enjoyable had I not been cursing the horrible rich I had been among.

Last night — a very different affair — at Robert's. Lots and lots of 'human beings', young and old, Jonny, Magouche, Spenders with Alexander and Sarah helping. Sarah's little mincepie face held horizontally peering hopefully over her plate of tapas. 'Mouse' was there, movingly lost, but sweet and friendly. Also Lindy Guinness. I asked her how Robert's portrait was going on. She stamped her feet. 'The trouble is I'm in love with him.' 'So are we all,' I said, and it's true.

---

1 Lady Cynthia Noble.

Dinner alone with Robert was perfect. We always talk at our ease, as I do with hardly anyone except sometimes Stanley.

Coming back from Robert's party I switched on a programme about the aristocracy – a sort of patchwork of remarks by 'aristocrats' as they still think of themselves, one of whom was the best of a really pathetic bunch. They still believe in class, that the world thinks them 'superior', and in a welter of 'sort of's, 'you know's' and 'something like that's', managed to convey their futile condescension towards the plebs. 'We have our privileges but after all we *do* work for them.' 'I didn't find him, you know, *objectionable*, just because he had inferior status', 'There was no one there (at university) that I could identify with', and so on. None of them, not a single one, questioned the rightness of class, nor that their privileges had been earned by their ancestors and they should be proud to inherit them. (What about the innumerable bought titles?)

Christmas Eve: The Slade

After a still pale morning of changing iridescent beauty down came the thick mist and in it we have remained plunged all day. As the house is very well heated and no windows seem to open, I stumped out for an hour before lunch, walking through the silence to Prior's Dean church. Such suffusion in dense white dampness I could never have endured all alone, and I doubt if Eardley can. He and I get on like one o'clock, talking and arguing, and reading and playing Scrabble. We have ranged over taboo subjects, like the miners and social and financial inequality without blood being drawn. At lunch today he launched an attack on 'feminine women', or really just 'women', instancing Alvilde,[1] Joan, Mary Hutchinson, to some extent Rosamund (and having first said that 'I wasn't at all feminine'). I fear many criticisms of 'Joanie' have been uttered, and I think my suspicion that the French holiday wasn't a success was true. I love the peace, and Eardley's kind affectionate company. I'm reading Dicky C's autobiography and correcting its many mistakes of English, spelling, etc. That goes for 'work'. Now I've just put

---

1 Lees-Milne.

the turkey in the oven and come up to my bedroom. E. goes to his studio. Tomorrow Joan comes. I for one feel her restless chatter makes it hard to read or talk – yet what a brute I feel writing that when she is always so flattering to me. Eardley thinks her 'very indiscreet; she repeats everything at once and usually incorrectly.' I must beware.

Boxing Day

We are still shut in completely in strangulating mist. More about women and men, I maintaining that their differences were due to their biological functions, and each had their drawbacks – men, aggressiveness and violence; women passivity and lack of invention. Drove through hideous militarised country, reminiscent of my childhood, to the house of the ffordes where Joan was staying. Three clever sisters, one a depressive (kept sane by pills but looking shut away), her ebullient husband and a son. Intelligence, interest in books and music, easy talk and a splendid Christmas lunch with champagne and back here with little Joan.

December 28th: Snape

It was easier and emptier than usual travelling by train here. A sympathetic, intelligent and articulate taxi-driver, discussing the 'Crisis', said to me: 'You know, it seems an awful thing to say, but I think it's time we had another war. It's greed, greed, the whole world over,' and went on to advocate capital punishment and discuss the psychology of murderers, though he himself couldn't understand the desire to kill.

Shopping earlier today, I exclaimed at shirts for £17. 'Do you really get people to pay these prices?' 'Oh *yes*, and much more.'

December 29th

All is gentleness and quiet here with the dear Hills. They read me a letter from Harriet who had arrived at the main Rome airport to meet the twins an hour or two after the ghastly massacre there by Arab terrorists; vividly describing her fears, the lack of news, and the equal terror on her behalf of the twins diverted to another airport, and of Tim seeing it on television.

This gave me a nightmare in which Heywood said to me in a quiet voice saturated with grief and love, 'Did you know Harriet had killed herself?' (We had also talked of Amaryllis).

Reading Magee on Wagner in bed. One essay on the important output of the Jews – the three greatest men of the century are Marx, Einstein and Freud. Seventy years after Marx's death one third of the world lives according to his beliefs. Magee, an adorer of Wagner but not uncritical, goes into his passion for myths – it was because of the Greeks, and also their 'Universal validity'. But this is what I find so tedious: the presentation of *naked* Universals. Far better, like Shakespeare, ingeniously to use Particulars, behind which Universals can be seen looming and glimmering (e.g. *Hamlet*).

December 30th

Calm happy life continues. Heywood and I took two walks in a marinade of mist. Anne toils too hard, won't let one help and doesn't like walks. She has bought a very small bicycle and wobbles about on it. I'm terrified she'll break a limb again – she's already fallen off once.

Winding my watch this morning and thinking about time, I pondered the extraordinary fact that my ego, individuality, mind, has been for seventy-three years locked inside the prison of my head. Even when I wake in the night (as I invariably do) I am thinking away, usually in words. No wonder one feels the need of relief by talking.

A constant thread of argument about the miners. I mind about them passionately; Anne also has passionate feelings and argues fiercely and somewhat reactionarily so it seems to me, because her children now have money.

We hear that all transatlantic flights will now be fuelled on a form of fuel disallowed ten years ago as too explosive and therefore unsafe. Jonny came to supper and for the night with his two children. Delightful talk.

III

1 JANUARY
TO
30 DECEMBER
1974

January 1st

I got back into a dead shut London, and though it opened up briefly yesterday I expect it is equally hermetic today. I continue to exist in chill silence, fuming inwardly at the insensate way we are governed.

January 2nd

Whoops – up and down I go. One hour before I set off to get smallpox and typhoid plugged into me for Mexico, Lep rang up to say that the flight between N.Y. and Mexico City had been cancelled. Would I like to go a roundabout way, changing, via Chicago? No, I said, with a sharp dip from the plateau of equable and detached calm on which I had been sailing; I half hope the whole thing is called off and I merely have a sunny breather in Spain. Because if we *do* get there, shall we get back again, who knows? No more checking in at the bus terminal. Pilots are uneasy about using the explosive fuel and want 'different procedures'. I put through a call to Jaime's office and found only his secretary. I doubt if she took in my name, perhaps my telephone number, or even tried to.

I feel out of key with almost everything that is happening.

January 3rd

My sense that Jaime's secretary wasn't trying to take down my telephone number was quite accurate. She never even mentioned to him that I had called. However, oddly enough he called me, and caught me in to boot. They too had been advised of the cancellation, but have booked for us all three via Dallas. His quiet optimistic voice was greatly reassuring. Dickie and Denis, as I guessed, had lingered on and only leave tomorrow.

January 6th

Madder and madder does this island's life become. Yesterday we were told that hundreds of police, soldiers and tanks were encircling Heathrow, to prevent some Arab gangsters who are loose in Europe with Russian rockets, blowing up airliners. Coming back from dinner with Anne and Heywood at Chapel Street I heard a bang as I entered my front door. 'A bomb' I thought and noted the time. It was, just off Sloane Street, I felt no emotion whatever.

January 8th

Thinking of the tanks, rockets, etc. as I drove to Heathrow with Mary I felt rather like *Maria Stuarda*, the last act of which I had found unmoving, because I simply can't imagine 'death on the scaffold'. Yesterday packing, fidgety and restless. A girl and a dog dashed up my stairs with my vaccination certificate. Eardley came for a drink; then an evening with Mary, Robert first.

My aeroplane to Málaga was not at all full. I sat next to two little Scotch girls of seven and nine travelling alone and talked quite a lot to them. Many babies and one airsick mother.

And here I am, in beautiful Tramores – in my familiar darling room with its wood fire. The symphonic scents; silence and clarity, the pink hills as we drove from the airport were soothing and lovely. Rainbow and Pusí[1] and a new little grovelling, rather obscene black and white puppy. Janetta angelic, I feeling *strong* and not a bit panicky as I did when setting off with Desmond. Perhaps I am, though older, stronger. (Certainly I'm vastly glad to be here and out of the gloom, chill and menace of dim-lit England.) My arrival was too stimulating to relax or snooze. Ed Gilbert has filled my room with charmingly arranged flowers.

January 9th

I've woken and am about to ring for breakfast. In the absence of poor Toni, whose children are very ill, a character with a dark fringe low on his forehead, known as 'the Youth', does almost everything. Jaime got back last night, we talked a little about

---

1 The Parladé pets.

plans, and went early to bed, but like a child I was almost 'too excited to sleep'. Jaime is charming, gay and affectionate, but I fear the Fonda sale is a hopeless frost yet again. An Irishman who has paid a deposit (dud cheque?) and gone away. J. and J. have gone to Marbella to get our tickets. We fly straight to New York — extraordinary words — and after a few days, on to Mexico City via Dallas (even more extraordinary). I think I shall return the same way.

Gerald, Lynda and her brother to lunch — Gerald looking rather monomaniacal, his mouth turned down in a thin line, with his hair in a long greasy bob and food-spotted clothes, and very thick glasses which made him look like some strange quest-ing beetle. I fear he can't see the food-spots and Lynda doesn't look after him. Lynda said she had flu; her brother Keith was stronger and healthier than anyone I've seen for a long while. It's rather cold windy, and grey, 'like England,' I said tactlessly to Janetta. However after a delicious lunch Gerald asked me 'to come and look at the garden'. This meant sitting down on the nearest seat, and his pouring out for the fiftieth time. He's 'schizophrenic', 'never looks at a picture or reads a book', nor speaks unless Lynda is present. F: 'Does Lars want to marry her?' G: 'Oh, *yes*.' He then said he was himself no longer 'in love with Lynda though she is with him'. His book is to be a bestseller. I begged him not to worry about what happened to Lynda after his death, said that 'when one is dead one is dead' (but that didn't in any way affect his desire to control her 'outre-tombe'). He dreads Lars coming to live in his house — though he had made it over to Lynda. 'She says it's a house for writers and he's a painter. And her work is the most important thing to her.' Meanwhile in the kitchen Lynda was giving the impression that she was driven almost out of her wits by Gerald. What was she to do? He is certainly taxing company and I longed for them to go, and when they did I went to my room and fell fast asleep.

Jaime came back with no news of his Irishman, but he will come with us all right and is as excited as we are.

January 10th
Really do we go tomorrow? I can hardly credit it — I'm alone in

the house with three animals. My ticket home is booked via New York.

January 11th

Brilliant morning, blue sky, hottest day yet. But off we go in thick clothes, fur hats, coats and boots as when we went to Russia. Our plane was not a Jumbo after all and only three-quarters full; we bagged two seats each. At first time went fast. Jaime wrote hundreds of letters as if at his desk, J. and I read. We waved aside lunch but accepted a sort of high tea later; we put our watches back five hours. I can't remember what I thought about, but certainly not the Atlantic Ocean spread beneath us. The aeroplane rolled slightly like a ship, people got more and more fidgety, finally we were told we should be an hour or so late, owing to having to circumvent a 'disturbance in mid-Atlantic'. Some Japanese children in front of me, who had been impeccably good, began screaming hysterically as we slowly descended, I think from the pain in their poor little ears, and their mother did nothing at all to comfort them, with Japanese phlegm. Boredom was the most unpleasant aspect, and Janetta and I relieved it by playing Scrabble. Dazed arrival. Was this really IT? And soon I was sitting beside a taxi-driver heading for Manhattan. It was dark and the sky was filled with a whole astronomy of lights. We're here. We're across what I never expected to cross in the whole of my life. Drove to a flat lent to Jaime by the friend of a friend. It was a very nice flat for two, but I should have had to occupy a folding bed in the cupboard of an unheated dressing-room, and I longed both for warmth (the air was icy, snow was thick on the ground) and privacy. So off I went to the San Carlos hotel where I'd booked for us all. It was a very sleazy place and when I came to after being left in my room by the 'bell-hop', an old fellow with white hair, I realised there was no heating of any description and only one thin blanket on the bed. Telephoned down and said I must have another room, whose heating was working, and three blankets. I got both and gave over to pills and oblivion. Messages from Stanley, Henrietta and Desmond.

January 12th

American way of life: Breakfast, telephoned for, was brought in a brown paper bag by a huge negro porter – a cup of aeroplane coffee and a sweet bun. J. and J. rang me to say there was a hotel exactly opposite them which could give me a room. I gratefully accepted, packed, checked out and moved over. I found them lively and optimistic although they had gone out and had a late dinner, getting in at 6 a.m. Spanish time. The atmosphere is very brisk, and the new hotel far more congenial than the last. Janetta had done some shopping and cooked us an egg and bacon lunch in their flat. After which we went to the nearest museum – the Frick. A lovely small gallery full of surprises – Rembrandt's *Polish Rider* the most famous, also Vermeers, Goyas, El Grecos. I'm astonished and bowled over by New York; its space, light and sparkling champagne air, the speed of its yellow taxis, combine with a curious ramshackleness. The streets are not as I had always imagined deep dark canyons between high cliffs but full of light and air. Street surfaces, however, are all bumps and pot-holes and my Venetian blind fell to the ground when I pulled it. A telephone call from Desmond[1] asking us all to a drink. His suite of rooms is delightful, and looks straight out on to Central Park. (I'm bewildered and excited to find such long heard-of names congealing into solid reality.) As I looked out of Des's window I had the sensation of falling in love with this huge town: with the snow-covered park and spindly black Lowry trees, little figures tobogganing among them and beyond it all the majestic skyscrapers decking themselves out in diamond lights. And I cannot see it as frightening. Even London is more so.

We took Desmond to a French restaurant where we had a decent but fantastically expensive meal. Janetta takes gentle care of me, is anxious to preserve my 'calm' and picks up what I drop. Early to bed. The time change is something that baffles me intellectually, but I *feel* it.

January 13th

The time disorientation, which I have always felt sceptical

---

1 Shawe-Taylor, who was temporarily acting as music critic.

about, is real, and so is one's consequent 'bad performance'. I doubt if I should be able to do the *Times* crossword, forget even more than usual, and am only just ceasing to be bewildered by the very simple structure of the town. Yesterday dawned marvellously crisp, bright and cold. I walked over to breakfast in Jaime and Janetta's flat – a great improvement on the brown paper bag. They were strolling around in their nightclothes.

We had arranged to meet Desmond on the corner of Central Park and see the town by way of a culture Bus Loop – one dollar, as many stops as you like. So it was that the impossible occurred – we got Janetta into a bus. Exciting glimpses of this extraordinary place and the river embracing Manhattan. Got off at the Empire State Building and shot up its more than a hundred storeys in several lifts. Before we started Janetta said, 'I'm absolutely petrified. My jaw's shaking,' and she wouldn't take the final ascent. At the top the sun was so warm one could go out on the balustrade and look down on a view of staggering beauty – no other word will do – but one I seem to have known all my life. After a rather plastic self-service lunch we went to the Pierpont Morgan Library, where there was a temporary show of Old Master drawings. It needs a blockbuster to get through one's stunned condition, and though the view of Manhattan springing up like a forest below me could do this, these Old Masters couldn't and I found them quite dull. Home for a rest.

Stanley Olson[1] this evening. I found it strange that there he was in his camel's hair coat, black hair and specs. There was only one tumbler and the room not done – the blind still on the floor. Feeling I was floundering in my new environment I telephoned and asked for another glass and a splendid portly negress appeared with *five* glasses, calling me 'sweetheart'. I was much aware of being in Stanley's native land and that this had an element of potential awkwardness for both of us. Stanley described his appalling flight to San Francisco: seventeen hours in a full aeroplane; the lavatories became blocked and urine

---

1 I think this was his first meeting with the Parladés. They later became great friends.

streamed down the aisles, someone had a heart attack and the stewardess did not know how to work the oxygen masks, someone (he thought) actually died. But he was over-excited, 'very happy' and had had several new jobs offered him.

January 14th

Awoke at six-thirty still bewildered. My mind will hardly focus on a detective story, and I feel a little depressed at my difficulty in dealing with this agitating town. Beneath the love impact a small surge of dislike is coming out like a bruise. But breakfast over in J. and J.'s flat raised the mercury in my thermometer. Janetta and I taxied to the Wall Street area and called at Mary's bank for the huge sum of money she has so generously given me. No inefficiency here in the realm of money, the temple of the American God, where floor upon floor of efficient secretaries tapped typewriters, and executives rose from big leather armchairs and said, 'You're welcome.' Walked to the Museum of Modern Art. A large room of Miros, Picassos, Cézannes, Rousseaus, a youthful self-portrait of Kokoschka. In the evening I went to Desmond's hotel and was taken by him to a concert. First he gave me a drink and a snack meal — a tin of black bean soup was heated very slowly on a minute ring after a fearful fuss with the tin opener. This was followed by small 'crackers' the size of a postage stamps and some dried-up pâté. D: 'I can't *imagine* what all the fuss over cooking is about. It's no trouble at all. I'm going to insist on a change when I get back to Crichel.' He talked of his work and got me to read an obituary he had written on Raymond to go into cold storage — very good. I read it appreciatively but made some comment about a ';' followed by an 'and'. Yes, the Editor had objected to that, but Desmond had won, in spite of his deep respect for his Editor from whom he had learned a great deal. Some talk about the miners' strike — naturally we didn't see eye to eye. But all of this was delightful, more so than the concert, which was a Dolmetschy affair of rather dull very early music on prehistoric instruments, played by a group of performers dressed in velvet and jewel colours, counter-tenors, etc.

Baddish sleep, in spite of too many pills, but I must survive somehow.

235

15th January

At last I think my 'performance' is improving though I must admit that though J., J. and I looked at an immense number of masterpieces at the Metropolitan and I knew they were beautiful I didn't always feel it to the quick of my being. Was it just that the meal was too big, the plate overloaded? We looked and looked, running into each other now and then, but each on our own, and I don't know that I absorbed any picture with the same intensity I felt for some of those we saw in Switzerland; my grappling irons only caught a few. Coming on a room full of Cézannes after an hour and a half I realised my muscle of awareness had given out, as one's leg muscles sometimes do when descending a mountain. We repaired to the basement for drinks and frankfurters, but I couldn't take in much more and went home to lie on my bed longing in vain for oblivion. *Tristan* in the evening, the J.s, Stanley and I were to meet Desmond there twenty minutes before the performance, but he only just dashed in, white and breathless just as the bell was ringing. Almost at once out came the white handkerchief and Stanley wept and wept, saying he 'was in torture – the music was so unbearably beautiful'. It's some sort of reflex action, and he's too clever to be so uncritical, for as Desmond said in the interval, 'The performance was *very* poor.' The production began well, and then became pretentious and tedious. The opera house is too large for any singer to fill it and among a large audience someone is almost bound to be coughing. Stanley dashed out and flailed wildly for a taxi and we all went home to a delicious supper Janetta had made in their flat. Stanley rather drunk and bumptious. Jaime was the nicest to and about him.

January 16th

Awake, after bed at two last night, keyed-up and frantic at 6 a.m. What to do? I got up resignedly and packed, and in due course we set off to the airport in a dream. I don't *dis*like flying at all, nor feel a need for many whiskies like Janetta. The pilot's voice announcing 'bad weather at Dallas' where we were to change, and the 'need to refuel at Nashville' might once have made my heart stand still. Now, 'nothing to lose'. Squatting on the ground refuelling, while the passengers crowded into the lavatories, was faintly disgusting, as if the aeroplane itself were shitting. Then we were at Dallas, in a brand new airport, sitting in a row gazing at the pink plains of Texas. Our last hop was passed curled up on three seats failing to sleep, and Viva Mexico! Before landing we circled round a boundless carpet of jewelled lights in geometrical patterns. Airport officials very stern. Jaime turned out to have had cholera but no smallpox injection – he was pushed into a booth and quickly 'done' by a woman doctor.

Our hotel has heavy antique furniture and pictures, in the hall a tiled basin of water sprinkled with gardenia flowers. Got into bed at once, read and took a lot of pills, determined to sleep, and so I did after a fashion.

January 17th

J. and J. went out last night exploring and eating in a restaurant, 'delicious food', they said. I woke feeling pretty strong, glad to be here, and liking hearing Spanish spoken again. It's hot and the sky is blue, like an English summer. Jaime was out early and reported that the famous 'smog' was terrible. It soon went, but what of the effects of altitude?

We walked out along the main artery, the garish lively Avenida de la Reforma. Lots of flowers prettily arranged, in markets and stalls. The 'Indians' – for the first time we saw them, in the shape of forlorn women sitting on the pavement surrounded by children, each with a few oranges and nuts in front of them for sale. We walked for a long time, stopping at bookshops and travel agents. Are the J.s, I wondered, going to forget my age? I left and returned, footsore, to brush up for lunch with Mary's friend Marita del Redo. I'd once met her; she has an elegant model's figure, good but too-long teeth and an enormous busby of blonde hair. With her was her aristocratic Spanish mother, black-clad, distinguished, with sad eyes set in El Greco sockets. Marita gave us a quite delicious cocktail called a margarita made of iced limes, tequila and cointreau, with a line of salt round the rim of the glass. They both spoke English. Marita's mother said: 'You see I had an English governess; she was adorable; I loved her very much, much more than my mother and father.' I preferred her dry style to Marita's almost fulsome friendliness. She drove us home and I slept for a good two hours, when Janetta knocked and we drank whiskies and walked out among the flickering lights to dinner. 'Tortillas' here are not omelettes, but greyish limp and peppery poppadums. So far no great lassitude nor shortness of breath, thanks to splendid Dr Moynihan's pills perhaps.

January 18th

We have a common purse and I have wanted to give it a booster from time to time from Mary's present, but I have only managed to give it a hundred dollars so far. J. and J. have grander ideas than mine. Though I think all our hearts are melted by the poor Indians, I feel guiltier than they do, which is quite useless. No good pouring coins into their laps – the System is wrong. Then Janetta mollifies my dawning indignation at her assumptions of priority and privilege, by sweetly bringing me flowers. So yesterday I riposted with a huge prima donna basket of carnations and roses from the flower market. They are, both J.s, adorable and adored by me, and I'm very happy to see them seem to get on so well, with natural communication and gestures of affection, as when Jaime stops to kiss her cheek as they walk down the street.

This adventure is a swansong for me, the final burst of the privileged era, which seemed to be on its last legs before I left England, and for the moment I have gulped down my usual preoccupation with social and financial inequalities. Yet they are there, as I know, when appreciating an aristocrat of the old school like Marita's mother. Off in the inevitable taxi (though buses and a sort of taxi-bus go there) to the great Museum of Anthropology – a fine modern building, with a colossal concrete mushroom or palm tree in the centre of its forecourt from which water falls. There's much too much of it and one could wish for selection. Hurrying past the prehistoric flints and reconstructions of Stone Age scenes, I went from room to room, until we all converged at the restaurant, Janetta saying she felt faint and the floor was 'coming up at her'. We looked wonderingly at each other and said, 'But nearly everything's absolutely *hideous!*' 'The best museum in the world' say certain parrots like Esme. But where can one find beauty? And there is too much of everything, well-arranged and explained though it may be. Nearest to beauty: the masks for the dead, of black obsidian, a lovely sensitive material, or turquoise. I disliked most of the Aztec things, coarse fierce strange statements in rough, grey volcanic stone. Some of the Mayan reliefs and heads were more moving, but on the whole there was a surfeit of bowls, platters, and childish little figurines, beads.

Undeterred we looked at a temporary show of Inca gold and then walked across the park and went up in a lift to Maximilian's Palace. This was a long, very full day's sightseeing. Out to a grand and expensive fish restaurant where I ate a chunk of white fish and a boiled potato, served up as if it were caviare and lobster thermidor, with attentiveness, amiability and tinned music. The Mexicans look very Asiatic, round-headed, their brown oriental faces dimpling with smiles. Making my judgements far too quickly as usual, I size them up as a pleasure-loving race, friendly unless roused, with a delight in flowers and the brightest of bright colours.

January 19th

Today nearly broke me. 'You must see the Zócalo (Plaza) and cathedral.' 'Yes indeed.' Some air tickets had been endorsed, then on and on and on we pounded along the pavements of the Reforma for at least six kilometres, I reckoned. Arrived there I felt too tired to enjoy the great arcaded square and jostling shouting crowds of street vendors. Feeling for the first time rather cross at being so driven, I said I must have a drink, and we went into a plushy art deco hotel and ordered Bloody Marys. Jaime's vitality is inexhaustible and he dashed off to see about five other buildings before rejoining us. Then we threaded miles of Mexican Tottenham Court Road at rush hour – garish and noisy – to find a last sight, a convent (unremarkable). Stinking hooting cars filled the street. I wilted; I began to hate the town. But at last we found a taxi and went to lunch in the attractive flowery patio of the Hotel Cortés. Afterwards I made my way homewards in a taxi-bus, bent on my rest (I wake at six every morning). Blissful sleep. Jaime, uncomprehending, I'm glad to say, of my whacked condition telephoned later to say would I care to come and look at a grand hotel he had to visit on business? But these have been two gruelling days, and after whisky and Scrabble with Janetta I dined in the hotel and let them go off alone, which was after all nice for them too.

January 20th

J. and J. had had an exciting evening listening to mariachis (native bands) in the Zócalo. I feel fresh and revived after my night off, and was ready for our outing with Marita to the Pyramids of the Sun and Moon. I sat behind her in the car studying her remarkable construction of yellow hair and wondering how it was made. She can do (so she told us) nothing with her hands. She was very kind to us, patient, got on like anything with Jaime. The pyramids were sensational – on too vast a scale to be spoiled by the tourists, who even peopled them like Aztecs, the steps appallingly high and steep. None of us got to the top. We had our first glimpse too of the landscape of the Mexican plateau under a burningly blue sky, with cacti and pepper trees, and mountains all round. Marita drove us over a bumpy road to the hacienda of her brother-in-law. Here was privilege, wealth, but beauty and taste too. The horse was the supreme deity: saddles, spurs, and huge hats ranged along the patio, pictures of horses and stirrups but hardly any books in the 'library'.

We lunched in a restaurant in a grotto. A fine Sunday had filled it with a motley crowd. All the chairs were painted different bright colours and paper chains were innocently swinging about our heads. Our waiter's face was pure Eskimo. There were other long-nosed Mayan ones or round-headed orientals. All with quite black straight silky hair, and women in bright pink, mauve, orange, yellow. Back, looking at two charming convent churches and in through the horrors of Mexico City's industrial suburbs and smog. Dined in a good Swiss restaurant full of Americans. One clawed my arm from behind: 'Is the red snapper good tonight?'

January 21st

We have hired a bright yellow Volkswagen and today we set off, independent and free, through the ugly outskirts of the town (a cross between a White City fun-fair and a collection of modern cathedrals). Out – into the beautiful country, for so it is. Janetta is the best map-reader I know, as good as I once was (but am too anxious to be); Jaime an excellent planner. However, the monastery church of Tepotzotlán, with an elegantly elaborate façade ('debased baroque' as our earliest guidebook says) was shut. On to Pashuco, where silver is mined and shows greyish in the sliced earth. Janetta a little princessy: 'I want this, and also that, but not this and that together.' Jaime makes a wry face but laughs and is patient. And it must be said that, more than anyone I know, she wants others to have what they want as well as herself. And *exactly*. She can't eat meat, doesn't like the look of Mexican poultry and there is little fish, so she is left with eggs and vegetables. She also sleeps very little and looks tired – Jaime is good at dropping off for a short nap and always takes a siesta. I still sleep badly from too much travel-stimulation.

Up a winding road we drove, over mountains, between prickly pears and palm trees brandishing fists of leaves, and stretches of blue water invaded by succulent green leaves. In some villages, tin roofs – everywhere appeared to be relics of the last great earthquake. Jaime had looked out two possible sleeping-places in full country, haciendas functioning as inns. We rejected the first, to my relief – it was too plushy – and bumped on over a cactus-sprinkled plateau (the Regla) very wild and beautiful, to where we are now, deep in tousled greenery, a real farm built round a spacious courtyard. A lot of strong square little girls ran out to take our suitcases, willingness in every movement, rushed to make up beds, or just pounded hither and thither as hard as they could. They talked in staccato soft voices in careful Spanish, and turned out to be Otomis Indians from the mountains, so the Hippo proprietress told us. She said she had had to teach them Spanish, as they only spoke Indian, but these were 'good girls', '*muy nobles*'. One characteristic of Mexican Spanish is to add 'ito' on to everything. I asked when dinner was. '*Aherito*' (a little now, nowish).

Our rooms are enormous – the J.s' has four beds and a sofa covered in huge flowers. I have two beds, and all around the room at a height only a giraffe could appreciate are tiny pictures. My palatial bathroom has a note begging me only to use the shower, with taps marked K and W. If only we strike as lucky elsewhere – this place is heavenly, and all round us hacienda-life goes on, with horses and farmyard animals being looked after. We ate quite alone in a long high *comedor*, and very well too, ending with hot chocolate and sweet buns.

Rather cold in the night – we are still high up.

January 22nd

Sad to leave the Hippowoman and running girls. There is also a smiling little crumpled grey husband in the background. Bumped off towards the monastery of Actopan, curiously painted inside in greys and browns.

To my surprise and pleasure J. and J. do not like long days driving and are eager to stop for a flowering tree or a view. At night we got to Tequisquiapan, a small pretty place, unfortunately recently painted all white, for the Mexican colour-sense is lovely. Stayed in a very nice holiday hotel with a garden and a spring of clear very warm – almost hot – water making a stream and pool in which Jaime and I bathed.

January 23rd

To Querétaro, Maximilian's town, with some fine houses but disappointing churches. Jewel shops, where Janetta pored over presents for her children – amethysts and turquoises – and I bought a crystal heart for Sophie. Fountain with dogs debouching water from their mouths, a courtyard of grotesques. Lunched at a smart hotel built like a castle for tin soldiers outside San Miguel de Allende. We all love margaritas and drink them more than wine, which is expensive and not particularly good. Janetta, and perhaps Jaime, are keener on grand hotels than I am, though I must say they enjoyed the hacienda quite as much as I did. San Miguel was rather touristy but had charm. Every town has its Zócalo, and they are usually pretty and full of trees and flowers. Here we settled for a hotel right on it – and noisy, though I slept better than usual. Janetta always beats me at Scrabble, at which my 'performance' is bad. A good many hippies and artists about. Coming here we crossed plains covered in every description of cactus – fists, balls, candelabra. The light is soft and brilliant, the colours incomparable.

January 24th

To see an orchid garden, shown over by a girl with a very soft gentle voice and movements, and dead straight jet black hair.

A tall stringy American wearing an absurd little hat came up to me as I sat reading in the hotel patio. 'I thought you were an apparition,' he said. 'No, I was reading a book you probably know' (Sybille Bedford's splendid *Sudden View*). 'Naw. I did read a few pages but it sent me to sleep. You Britishers' – Well, I've never been called *that* before.

Lunch at another grand restaurant full of rich Americans, with margaritas. Lovely drive to Morelia, past great lakes, flowers, cacti, churches richly lined with gilt. A magic moment: crossing a causeway across the middle of a lake by afternoon light, stopping the car and getting out to look at water birds and pick flowers.

January 25th

Morelia is a vine town built of pinkish stone dominated by its cathedral – handsome except in detail. We might almost be in Spain, which may be why some people prefer the exotic pyramids. Jaime loves the Spanish colonial architecture and snaps away at windows and mouldings. Decided to stay two nights and have washing done and go to Pascuaro today. This is a village 'protected' for its beauty, largely Indian-occupied, and standing on the edge of a lake in the middle of which is an island crowded with Indian dwellings and nothing else. I find this romantic and longed impotently to go there. It was most fortunately market day and they had come in with their wares and hundreds of charming dark-eyed lively-looking children and babies. Pored over baskets, *rebozos* (long woollen scarves) and so on. Janetta and Jaime bought recklessly, I less so. Then down to the edge of the lake where, as the market was now drawing to its close, we watched Indians setting out in primitive dugout canoes for their island, while the women stuffed themselves into covered motor boats, chattering in Indian and giggling, with babies at the breast, inside their shawls and their bodies. Such fecundity!

January 26th

Today we drove south, but encircling the city, in the direction of Tasco. It was too far and we stopped at Ixtapan, getting in in the dark and finding the only hotel in the guide quite full. It was very grand and full of Americans in evening dress and white dinner jackets. Instead we stopped at a simple family hotel, all-Mexican. I wish we could more often stay at such places, which hit me off absolutely.

On the way we climbed and descended through a forest road with not many – but exciting – flowers, often bright scarlet, and then dipped into a luscious tropical deep green valley for lunch – another simple family hotel with a swimming-pool, very much liked by us all. Agua Blanca was its name. Marita's mother told us Toluca had one of the best markets, but when with difficulty we found it, it was tawdry – Kentish Town in Mexican terms. Thought a lot about Mexico. Its pluses are largely landscape, people, flowers, Indians, colours. As to art – there seem to be no pictures, and we haven't really capitulated to the pre-Columbian. The great minus is poverty.

Vivid dreams about Cyril, and twins (one stabbing the other).

January 27th

Brilliant mornings are almost infallible but they sometimes deteriorate later. To add to yesterday's summing up, or further analysis: the Indians are a miniature race, interesting-looking but not beautiful. The Mexicans, who are I suppose generations back mestizos, charm by their desire to please, gaiety and soft voices, their taste for brilliant colours.

On to Tasco – generally known as the 'silver town' and full of shops where silver and turquoises and other jewellery are sold. I liked it more than Jaime did, who felt that it was a 'tourist trap'. As it is, car-loads of Americans kept driving up as

244

we sat sipping margaritas in a bar directly opposite the beautiful pink baroque cathedral, where a wedding was going on; festoons of pink flowers hung over the main door and we watched the bridesmaids and guests going in. The tourist herds have not yet spoiled the town, in the way Marbella has been totally spoiled; but the quacking voices of female Americans from Acapulco, who are always saying 'my darter tells me' or 'it only cost us six dollars a night', do grate on the ear.

Light lunch in a bar on the outskirts and on to Cuernavaca. This and Tasco are supposed to be centres of homosexuality, and when we at length found a rather plushy hotel with a big and peaceful garden, it was assumed that the double room was for Janetta and me. Not for the first time – the trouble being that Jaime looks fantastically younger than he is. So does Janetta with her elegant figure, springy walk and hair untouched by grey, and I admire her for not trying to enyouthify her face. The hotel is run by an elderly American and we sleep in an outside separate house. The lawns are clipped, exotic birds sing, and the garden chairs are very comfortable. Jaime had been looking in vain for a hotel belonging to someone he knew – a queer? – but we couldn't find it, and when he telephoned, they said they were almost sure it was full. He said he was 'whacked' (I sometimes fear he does this out of sensitivity because he thinks I am, but I wasn't) and suggested we dined in and stayed two nights. He is really an adorable character and is sweet to me as well as to Janetta, whom he teases very slightly when she is wilful, as she can be. Janetta – always herself, as I've so often remarked – wants what she wants intensely, and sees that if possible she gets it. Has Andrew[1] 'spoiled' her a little too much? But I remember how this used to upset Ralph on our travels, dearly as he loved her, and how at Brantôme once he lay awake fuming about it and I had to calm him. She thinks and talks a lot about her children and grandchildren, loves buying them presents and is hurt by Rose's disapproval. I admire Jaime's direct and dignified acceptance of his stepchildren and grandchildren. And a lot more about him, more than before we undertook this journey.

1 Devonshire.

245

January 28th

Janetta dreams every night that she has killed someone: once it was Freddie Ayer.

10 p.m. I have a horrid catarrhal cold and retired to bed after omelette supper, reading *The Ambassadors*. Cuernavaca all day. I breakfasted alone in the sun in a gallery opening off the garden, waited on by a deliciously pretty dark-eyed maid – a moment of peculiar sweetness. As for the sights of the town – Cortés's castle was shut, and the famous Borda Gardens were a disappointment, containing little but some dusty old poinsettias, and ducks floating on khaki-coloured water. There is a famous guru called Ivan Ilyitch, somewhere, but we saw no signs of him or his followers. The town itself is attractive and animated. When I sat in a café waiting for the others I was surrounded by small children trying to sell me beads, paper flowers and baskets. Seeing my camera they clamoured to have their photos taken. I told them the roll was finished and took it out to show them. 'But where are the pictures?' they said. Later a little boy of about six with almond eyes and a brilliant smile talked to Jaime, who always asks their names and who they live with. 'Andrès,' he replied and '*yo vivo solito.*' '*Solito?*' Jaime asked in amazement. '*Si. Vivo solito. Usted dele reconocer que hablé la verdad. Vivo todo solito-o-o,*'[1] smiling all the while.

Lunch at a frightfully grand restaurant fairly flattened me out, partly from waiting and drinking and eating tapas, while waiters elegantly dressed in the tight black trousers of a *cuadro flamenco* moved among the rich noisy Americans filling the wicker chairs in the gardens. Cranes stalked about and gaudy parrots perched here and there. There was too much of everything, and I began to revolt against the flat uninflected voices of the elderly Americans posting enormous quantities of food into the letter-boxes leading to their enormous stomachs – as wasteful as was the amount of food that was removed uneaten on loaded plates. I felt shocked – very much shocked in fact – by their greed and waste: shocked in the same sense as one is by an accident, and perhaps rashly said so to Janetta and Jaime as we drove away and

---

1 My name is Andrew and I live alone, or 'all alone'.

thought of the poor street vendors and little Andrès living '*solito*'.

We were all pretty well knocked out by the meal. Jaime slept. I wrote letters – then back to the town to fetch my watch from the menders and shop. I'm much attracted by the silver and turquoise things and J. and I bought quite a few.

January 29th
Off on our way south to Oaxaca – through lovely country without 'sights' except for the cactuses which began to dominate the landscape in all their splendour and a variety of forms – candelabras, large hands with fingers upraised like an advertisement in the underground, organ pipes, and – perhaps the strangest of all – tall phallic pencils, unbranched and each alone though sometimes covering a hillside like a silent advancing army; palms and palmettos and in the distance range upon range of blue and pink hills. Today was as simple as yesterday was luxurious. We ate eggs and *frijollas* (dark brown beans, delicious), drove without stopping through the town 'where the best modern pottery is made' (it looked hideous). Our only stopping place before Oaxaca was derelict, like an extinct mining town, but we were put up at a rather sleazy hotel with a stupid couldn't-care-less girl reading comics at the reception desk. On the whole Mexican hotels have been surprisingly good and our rooms have always had showers and lavatories and bedside telephones. While giving most of our tough chicken dinner to a black dog with a famished expression, a large unattractive elderly American approached us with complaints about the inordinate expense of the hotel and invited us to visit his New Zealand wife who was 'fixing dinner' in their caravan (whose name was 'Frolic'). They decided not to sleep in the hotel but 'do a deal' with them to 'use their toilet'. Ugh.

January 30th
In bed, having woken thankfully from a horribly painful long and vivid dream – based on the theme of one I've had before: Ralph doesn't die but deliberately leaves me – in this case to join someone else in Lisbon. Janetta showed her true sensitivity

and kindness and said 'I'll go with you there' and gave me whisky. We found Ralph, and knew it was him though he was in every way the opposite of himself, wearing smooth dark clothes, looking at me with hard unloving eyes, and making an impression of dishonesty. Still dreaming I cried and cried and cried, and then thought if that's what he's like I don't love him any more.

So here I am awake, looking out at a beautiful Mexican dawn – the lemon and orange sky, very dark men in white straw hats talking on the street below and a woman sitting wrapped in grey blankets on the pavement opposite some sacks waiting for Godot, with impassive black eyes. How very strange, I thought for the hundredth time, to be here.

Then at breakfast, awful news. Jaime came down to breakfast with the look of a little boy in disgrace. During the night (all through which they had been kept awake by thundering buses and lorries) thieves had caught sight of Janetta's handsome red suitcase which was in the back of the car, instead of the boot where it's generally stowed, and broke open the window and stole most of its contents. Not, marvellously enough, a briefcase of Jaime's with his tickets, passports etc. He blamed himself, and of course it was madness, but as Janetta said she was just as much to blame. It mainly contained a nice new corduroy suit of Jaime's and some shoes, also presents for Georgie's children – little dresses, *rebozos* for the servants. But the red suitcase is a beloved symbol for Janetta, dating from luxury days with Derek. The police came, the horrid people in the hotel tried to blame the night porter, saying such a thing had never happened before. 'Then they are lying,' said the police, 'several cars have been stolen outside that hotel.'

I told J. and J. my dream to distract them, not deliberately to point the moral, as I suppose it did, that there are worse losses than suitcases. By then my dream had lost its sting for me but I saw it upset them both.

We drove off under the shadow of this our first disaster. Janetta looked worn and sad, and Jaime showered her with loving caresses and attentions. Our road traversed spectacularly splendid country and then an almost too turgid mass of mountains, chaotic, reft by yawning crevasses showing red earth like bleeding flesh. Earthquake country surely.

Got to Oaxaca at lunch-time and stopped on the outskirts for two margaritas each, at a plushy garden hotel full of rich old American ladies quacking away. Says one to another: '*I* don't know why you *warry* about your hair, dear. No one but *me* will see it.' And then *da capoi* to the news of relations and the costs of hotels. Unseduced by the green garden pool and excellence of the margaritas we decided this was unbearable and drove on to the centre of the town. Put up at the once best hotel with spacious marble halls, now running down, its tablecloths filthy and an appalling smell of disinfectant in the bedrooms. Nevertheless, I rather liked it, and was happy in my room, looking on to the pale green cathedral.

Walked in the town and gradually as it grew dark and the lights came out, its charm (not instantly apparent) stole over us. Because of earthquakes the houses are mainly two storeys high and built of pale green stone in large blocks. Even the churches have unusually stumpy towers, many with cracks: in a square outside one, children were bouncing balls among the white-painted trunks of innumerable trees. The Zócalo is large and charming with an extra large bandstand. We chose an upstairs restaurant there for dinner. Poor Jaime, still broken by the 'disaster' and has not recovered his calm.

January 31st

To the church of Santo Domingo, peeped into last night. Inside it is an ebullient riot of gilt and rosy-cheeked cupids, with a distinct Indian flavour, bishops leaning out from the ceiling, a tree of Jesse. In the cloisters there's a marvellous museum, which I think we all enjoyed much more than that in Mexico City. Or is it that we begin to understand the idiom more? I still find the rough tormented fierce Aztec figures ugly. The most exciting room contained the treasures found in a tomb at Monte Alban – delicate gold and silver jewellery, a crystal chalice, turquoise death-masks and so on.

Very hot. Drove up to the Hotel Victoria, recommended on all sides, but very grand. On Mary's advice we had margaritas and sandwiches brought us by the large swimming-pool. Janetta never bathes, but is happy to sit and read. There is always masses of salad and fruit – melon, avocados, pawpaws.

Then in the afternoon to get the evening light, we drove up the winding road to Monte Alban, and found it deeply impressive and moving. A surprise was its height above the valley below and the extent of the smooth grassy plain between the temples with long shadows sweeping over it. Behind, the pleated mountains turned from pink to blue. Bogus *objets trouvés* from the site are hawked round by the Miztec Indians, poor, small and pathetic. We ladle out brown coins but avert our eyes. When we were leaving – and almost last to go – they crowded round the car and asked for a lift down the long descent. '*Una sola,*' said Jaime. A woman looking about sixty got in the back, carrying a baby she seemed much too old to be the mother of, which stared out of her shawl with eyes bulging so noticeably we suspected goitre.

Jaime is impeccably humane to Indians and children, and he questioned her about the child's name, age, and how many more she had and when she was going to stop having them and what language they spoke at home. 'Miztec,' but she knew a little Castilano. When we dropped her off he gave her two pesos and this and his kindness suddenly made her look about twenty-five, as she probably was, and almost pretty. She pressed one of her souvenirs on us as a '*regalito*'. They are a tiny race and dreadfully poor. When you ask the age of a child who looks about four they tell you it is seven. These souvenir-vendors were living in a shanty town of reed huts under Monte Alban. Impossible to believe their roofs would keep out the rain and harrowing to think of them toiling up that long hill every day and bringing back a few coppers from the tourists, many of whom are beastly to them and brush them aside like flies.

February 1st

Left Oaxaca with sadness, we've become fond of it. First, though, we went the rounds of markets and visited a new museum of pre-Columbian art, just opened; some things in it really *were* works of art. Regiments of children, minuscule in size, were marching in behind flags and teachers. They behaved remarkably well, seemed interested and scribbled heaven knows what in their notebooks.

Heading south-east, we stopped (in what order I don't remember) at the largest oldest tree in Mexico, a church whose decoration of embossed angels set off by mirrors was supposed to rival Santa Domingo and a fine unfinished Dominican monastery. Then on to the dusty little Indian village of Mitla close to the ruins. All the village bars had notices up proclaiming tequila or mescal to drink, and paintings (like inn signs) of the agave from which they come. The *posada* was also a museum, kept by the American widow of an archaeologist and her obviously queer Major-Domo. An attractive old house with a large flowery patio and cries of exotic birds filling the palm trees. One or two archaeological students were sitting at a long table covered with fragments of pottery. 'Are you hoping to put these all together?' Janetta asked one with a fair beard, like Rose's Robert. 'No, that would be impossible, Ma'am; we're just sorting them according to glaze and finish.' 'They' were very small fragments and I didn't envy them their futile job, happy though they looked doing it. At Mitla we had a really excellent lunch – black bean soup began it, and it ended black too – with some fruits whose name I forget. Our rooms were spacious and furnished in charming taste, though to have a bath you would have had to light a log fire under the boiler yourself. Our margaritas had been based on mescal, not tequila, but I noticed no delusions.

After lunch to see the ruins, described by Aldous Huxley accurately as 'fossilised weaving', curious but with none of Monte Alban's magic. Jaime and I crept into a tomb and saw the 'column of life' worn smooth by many generations of Indios wanting to know how long they would live. Early dinner and bed and to sleep after a short anxious spell of thinking about scorpions, tarantulas and circumambient Indians whose padding feet I seemed to hear.

February 2nd
Woke to royal blue sky; breakfast in the courtyard – fresh

orange juice, toast, butter and honey, coffee. Janetta arrived looking harassed. She had had an 'awful night, feeling she couldn't breathe'. Last night she said she 'couldn't bear to eat anything with a spoon'. Her inhibitions are multifarious. She eats no chicken now, but only eggs and vegetables and fruit. She passionately needs every room she occupies to have a charming view.

In this little hotel a photo of D. H. Lawrence by Brett was hanging. I said to the friendly queer Major-Domo who showed it to me, 'You must have had lots of very distinguished visitors.' 'Oh yes, and royals too!' Off again on a long hot drive to Tehuálacapan down near sea level on the narrow neck of Mexico. Janetta is excited by the nearness of the Pacific. Bumped over a dirt track to the Playa Ventosa, where we spent a blissful hour or two on a long sandy beach, with many fallen coconuts and few bathers. Hairy spotted pigs rootled among the reed huts where cracked loudspeakers played to people (mostly Indios) swinging in hammocks. After our bathe we did likewise in the Paraiso bar, and sucked milk from coconuts with a straw. This indeed was life in the tropics – I would have liked to swing in my hammock for hours, dreamy and sensuous. When we left, an Indian woman was swinging her sleeping grandchild high in the air in a hammock. It was fast asleep with hands crossed on its chest.

February 3rd

After breakfast, we started on the long drive to Tuxtla Gutierrez keeping as close as possible to the Pacific. Lunching there in a big cool hotel (Tuxtla is the ugliest town in Mexico) and then climbing up breathless lacets with the plain receding vertiginously below to San Cristóbal at 7,000 feet, passing the Indians of this strange area in their traditional dress: a pink-and-white-striped belted poncho, flat hats with a cascade of bright coloured ribbons behind. Here, the men are the peacocks, and wear their famously well-shaped legs bare. There was a fascinating Indian village of them occupying reed huts round the lake in the crater of an extinct volcano. Topping our vast climb, we found the town of San Cristóbal surprisingly large and civilised

with its Zócalo and bandstand, black-haired noisy crowds, fireworks exploding round its baroque churches. The 'best' hotel
was full. The next best unattractive, except for two parrots
swinging on a perch outside my fusty little room.

Occasional doubts assail me, based on the two plus versus one
relationship. Am I too much of a package, do I irritate J. and J.? I
try to accept their suggestions, and leave them to themselves for
a while every day. Talk at dinner about fuss and adaptation and
fastidiousness. Janetta defending the latter and inclined to accuse
Jaime of fuss. An analytical sort of conversation rare among us
and I enjoyed it.

February 4th

San Cristóbal market was the best yet. A high sea of pic-
turesquely dressed Indians among their wares. A girl of about
fourteen stands suckling her baby. I get the impression that the
Indians are apart but friendly. Jaime has transferred us from our
rather sordid lodgings to the 'Ranch of the Gringos', a long low
building standing under the hills some way from the town with a
lovely view. Here we have very nice rooms, log fires, and spent
a peaceful day. I was happily in my room with the fire lit when a
servant came to say cocktails were being served. Our host, a tall
horsy American with a roving blue eye, stood by the bar, super-
vising the making of margaritas. Then dinner was announced
and Jaime muttered 'My God' as we saw that we were part of a
dinner-party with *placements*. 'Are you from Britain?' our host
asked me. 'Well, you'll be interested to hear the miners have
voted 90% against going back.' 'Quite right,' I said, 'so would I
if I were a miner.' Silence. Beside me was an intelligent English-
speaking Dutch lady, who introduced herself by name. Jaime
said afterwards he was astonished to hear us discussing our royal
families and me saying, 'And what sort of character is *your*
queen?'

February 5th

Possibly the most exciting drive yet, over a jungle pass and
down to the tropical region bordering the Caribbean and the
Gulf of Mexico. But, first we climbed even higher I think than

San Cristóbal and then suddenly we were in thick white woolly clouds on the pass. As we slowly wound down the northern slope with our lights on we exclaimed with excitement. This was the jungle, Little Black Sambo, tiger-butter world. The rich lusciousness of the greenery, proliferating wildly, with creepers embracing trees, lianas over creepers, flowers spouting from palms, ferns and orchids in the boughs, dog eating dog, great fleas with little fleas. Some orchids and cacti already had red buds, creepers were a mass of butter-yellow flowers. The language of Mexican flowers defeats me – I merely gaze in wonder. But Jaime is very knowledgeable about tropical trees and he and Janetta keep leaping out and taking cuttings for their garden. We saw mangoes coming into flower, bananas, coconuts, sugarcane. White and grey cows with humps and velvety dewlaps lay or wandered in the lush bright green grass. By afternoon we had reached sea-level or nearly and great stretches of blue water made a stunning contrast with the vivid arsenical green; everywhere it was invaded by sheets of water-hyacinths, armies of beautiful lilac flowers picked out in a Persian design of navy blue and surrounded by succulent leaves. And among the water, tropical trees and verdure were the reed huts of the Indians. We were heading for Palenque, the only Mayan site we can include in our schedule.

Turning off the village of Palenque we groped our way to a motel practically buried in the jungle, echoing with the wild cries of heaven knows what birds. Decent supper and a little two-bedroomed house to ourselves.

February 6th

By morning light we found a miniature zoo beside us – with four wicked spider-monkeys, a sad plain little mountain pig and some species of racoon gazing at us large-eyed.

We set off early to see the ruins, for we are in tropical heat here, and found them almost deserted and embowered in forest trees. Steep grey steps led up to the temples, which were crowned by mysterious grey stone combs. I *am* gradually coming round to the pre-Columbian art – I suppose Monte Alban struck the first spark, and the Mayan sculpture is much more elegant, finished, 'fine', composed and therefore exciting than the coarser fiercer Aztec. I've been reading about the Mayans and their life with astonishment that so much remains: they still eat the thin flat aromatic poppadum-like *tortillas*, which one sees the Indians rolling in their hands still. Why did the Mayans vanish? Disease? Locusts? Conquest? No sign of earthquake cracks in these buildings. We wandered off and explored separately. The sweat poured off me, leaving salt on my lips. The heat was terrific. When it had reached its height, the terrible march of the '*grupos*' began, arriving in buses, stumping, striding, hobbling red-faced towards their objective, while guides marshalled them: '*Mesdames et Messieurs, venez ici s'il vous plait.*' Germans, French, and one group wearing tickets saying 'Senior Citizens of Cincinnati'. Some of these were monstrously fat and hardly any attempted the temple steps, preferring to sit under a shady tree and say, 'I know my own strength.'

February 7th

The outdoor museum at Villahermosa was a disappointment – only one huge stone Olmec head and some muddy pools containing a crocodile or two. On westwards and down to Coatzacoalcos where with difficulty we found a long fine sandy beach and bathed in the Caribbean. Ate in a fish restaurant built over the river, watched fishermen arriving, smelt their catch being cooked and ate it, while the ferry boat plied to and fro with a heavy load of Victorian-looking passengers under sunshades. Another long drive to Vera Cruz, arriving in the dark. Jaime in trouble with the police, who only wanted a bribe. Jaime has rather touching Spaniard's feelings about this town – Vera Cruz – as being the place where Cortés landed. So at least I diagnose, though he doesn't actually voice them. We put up at a large grand hotel outside the town with a view to a bathe next day, but in the night a howling wind got up.

February 8th

Gale still blowing, sky whitish-grey. I asked the waiter would it last long. 'Certainly all today – probably more.' Indeed it worsened steadily into a hurricane, whipping sand into eyes and mouth, till one seemed to be lined with it. We were nearly blown off the old fortress prison in the harbour, where Juarez and others had been confined, and made haste to turn inland to get away from the withering gale. We have been lucky in our weather, but I sadly missed the bright tropical green, the blue lakes covered with water hyacinths, from a world that was now drained of colour.

February 9th

I realise that this journey has long been for me a sort of full-stop – the end of the passage, and here I still am, having enjoyed it more liberally and unanxiously than I ever expected to, but still here all the same.

The England awaiting me probably will be, and I strongly believe should be, much less pleasant for people as privileged as I am.

I've got into bed therefore in a slight state of melancholy and am reading Octavio Paz's *Laberinto de Soledad* – it was impossible to concentrate in the cruise-ship atmosphere of the lounge full of chattering tourists.

Janetta and Jaime returned earlier than I had expected. No luck, poor things.[1] Day ended with a jolly session of Anglo-Spanish Scrabble.

February 10th

We climbed out of dank misty Fortín. Winding upwards into a blue sky and warmer air. Across a plateau to Puebla and stopped outside the town at the Lastia Hotel where – what a change! – people were basking and swimming in the pool and a delicious tempting *merienda* lunch was spread on a long table in the garden, like a wedding feast. A band of *mariachis* arrived to entertain us with folkloric tunes. 'Oh, *don't* hate them,' Janetta said to me – unnecessarily for I loved them. They wore dark suits embossed everywhere with silver buttons like coasters. Two trumpeters stood a little way behind, others had fiddles and guitars of different sizes. They threw back their heads of

---

1 They had gone on a forlorn drive after the stolen suitcase.

256

silky black hair, opened their dark faces and sang for all they were worth. A grey cat shot into the bushes in alarm.

Later, we reached the town of Pueblo, unlike any other we've seen – a town of tiles, some red and Moorish-looking sprinkled with small blue and white ones, others reminiscent of Seville. The great grey cathedral was surprisingly light and elegant inside – all white and gold. There are two streets of 'típico' stalls which sell enticing bowls and boxes, toys and jewellery. As dark fell the town blossomed into light, the massive cathedral was floodlit and the Zócalo came out in clustered moons like the inside of a London theatre.

Expensive dinner in the cold dining-room of our hotel. I had been hankering rather for general conversation and started one about myth and mysticism – could one accept the first and not the second and if so why? I think of myth as being a congealed symbolised form of deep human emotions and instincts, but mysticism as fuzzy thinking and feeling, based on lack of desire to face facts realistically. We had some good and eager discussion.

February 11th
Today week I should be setting out for England.

Café lunch and off along the autostrada to Mexico City and the hotel Marina Cristina, where two *complicadissimo* letters from Desmond awaited me.

February 13th
Sad, 'calm' homing feelings. Went to the hairdressers (I've been a golliwog too long) and felt more human. Jaime very sweetly drove me in our dear little yellow car round bits of the town he thought I hadn't seen enough before. Then we gave lunch to Marita and her mother at the Hotel Cortés – quite a social success though it is almost impossible to embrace Marita and Janetta in one *coup d'oeil*. Marita's mother said in her dry way, 'I do wish you had experienced an earthquake. It's really a most extraordinary sensation and *absolutely* terrifying.' Back then to the Museo again, where I found certain beauties not seen before. I still feel Palenque standing broken and overwhelmed in the jungle was worth most of it put together; but I shall

remember a Mayan death-mask which was comparable with Greek sculpture. When I think of our bewilderment after our first visit I realise we have come a long way. Janetta came away this time profoundly moved, her voice shaking with emotion; as for Jaime, one of his great charms on this adventure has been his passion for finding out, looking and experiencing, his interest in details of windows, mouldings and every sort of decoration.

Back to pack alas! Order myself to be wakened at 7 a.m. and out to dinner at the Swiss Restaurant. Janetta brought me flowers and I hope to get the carnations at least to New York. Their kindness and care of me makes me cry. I was even inordinately flattered because Jaime says my 'Spanish rings a very sound bell'.

February 14th

Although we had kissed a fond goodbye outside our bedroom doors, Janetta took the trouble to get up and come into my room, where I was gently pounding about at seven this morning, looking sweetly seductive in her dressing-gown of fine white wool, and incredibly young, with her hair round her shoulders. Another goodbye, and she melted me by saying that Jaime had said he felt very sad at our parting 'and I do wish I could be like Dicky and cry, but I can't'.

Well, it has been a marvellously rich and amazing and I hope unforgettable experience, but I must now fit it into the context of my days instead of looking at it standing like a wall at the end of them. These five weeks (and more) have been packed full of pleasures, and short on difficulties and irritations. Perhaps the strangest thing about my visit to the New World has been its lack of strangeness. This enormous continent, whose shape has been familiar since I was a small child, is now something known and made a part of my consciousness. Special moments will I feel sure start up from the groundwork in time perhaps from re-reading these scanty notes, whose main purpose is to prevent experiences disappearing down the waste pipe.

I have been so pampered and taken care of that I feel hesitant about making my getaway (ticket, passport, spectacles). But I did and the journey to New York passed in a dream. An unusually small plane would be used we were told, and would therefore be an hour late and have to refuel at New Orleans – presumably this is due to the fuel crisis – but where shall we refuel in mid-Atlantic on the way back to London? At the airport stood beaming Desmond holding three shining cards of different colours bearing the words I WELCOME YOU, which he was anxious I should understand must be given back to him. We got into one of what were now old friends – the grubby, shapeless, hard-to-get-in-and-out-of, but extremely speedy yellow New York taxis and whirled to the Mayflower Hotel. What an odd thing familiarity is. I had a nice quiet two-bedded room, with filthy windows, good bathroom and kitchenette (useless because unfitted) and I had time for a short rest and bath before going to Des's room for one of his strange little meals. 'This is tinned asparagus soup – French asparagus. Oh dear, it's rather lumpy!' There followed some Persian caviare on toast and a slice of apple pie. Then booted and fur-coated we walked arm in arm to one of the concert halls in the Lincoln Center to hear Mahler's 8th Symphony, Boulez conducting. Very cold here, with polished lumps of dirty snow lying about and the air as dry as in Mexico. I crave England's moistness but I regret the trees, flowers, Indians, bright colour of Mexico. Still I feel love for this great sensational ramshackle place. Didn't think much of Mahler. Des ineffably kind. Back to bed and a good sleep.

February 15th

But he has filled up my few days here much more than I expected, so that today promised to be my only 'free time', when he went to his editor's. I got up late, telephoned for a disgusting breakfast in a brown paper bag from the coffee-shop and got up slowly. Outside the sky was blue from pole to pole and a bright sun shining. I decided to walk across the friendly-looking Central Park (famous for its crimes of violence) to revisit the Frick. It seemed harmless enough – grey squirrels came up for crumbs, children romping, dogs being given their constitutionals. In fact I've seen no signs of violence in N.Y., nor of race feeling though there are a lot of blacks, far more than in London, mostly well-dressed and confident-looking. After the

Frick, I recrossed the park and had fish and chips in the hotel coffee-shop. This evening rejoined Des for our little meal (whisky, 'crackers' as big as postage stamps, pâté and apple pie) which I suspect he has every night of his life, and off to *Otello* at the Met. I had found two letters from faithful Stan, one saying the Met is 'the most beautiful opera house in the world', but I can't see it through his loving eyes; it's too big and vulgar. The opera gave us great pleasure because Vickers was so good, but Desdemona feeble and missish. She should convey a passionate nature. A letter too from Eardley, saying Joan 'is delighted because her pelvis is out of alignment'. I'm afraid she's becoming a *malade imaginaire*.

February 16th

Particularly full day. Touchingly, Des had remembered, like the unforgetful elephant he is, my mentioning that I wanted to see the Barnes Foundation and arranged it. It's quite a long way, outside Philadelphia (one and a half hours in a crowded train). People were standing down the middle and Des and I were separated. I anthropologised the American family character: they are I think remarkably kind, patient with their children and even other people, of whom there were many, it being Saturday. I noticed their honest directness, outgoing friendliness, humour and articulacy. What lacks? Subtlety, irony. They don't make an impression of being very interesting as a race. Arrived at the colossal town of Philadelphia, we missed the branch-line train (Desmond over-optimistic as usual) and took a taxi to Barnes. I never saw such a badly hung collection of masterpieces, crowded together in tiny rooms and many skied and almost invisible. A surfeit of pink Renoir nudes, some superb Cézannes, famous Seurats, Bonnards and here and there an El Greco, Tintoretto or Goya. It was defended like an armed camp by unhelpful military figures. We made desperate efforts to absorb too much in too little time as a super luxe train had to be caught in time for the first night of *Rosenkavalier*. (Desmondian frenzy because it was forty minutes late.) 'We might have stayed longer!' We sat in revolving chairs drinking whisky and Desmond fell instantly asleep.

(I'm writing in a Jumbo crossing the Atlantic, and have just seen the lights of London. We have bumped down.)

Rosenkavalier was pretty good, but an American audience chatters and coughs appallingly. The introductory love-making music was entirely spoiled by a couple talking steadily in the row behind us, and as they wouldn't respond to my glares I was amazed to see my programme shooting from my hand at them. So were they.

February 23rd

I am bumped again – into responsibilities, real life, piles of bills, a marvellously warm and flowery welcome from many kind friends who I couldn't help feeling never expected to see me again, and even the offer of a boring translation, which I have wormed my way out of. So ends one of my most exciting travel adventures.

I've seen Mary, Magouche (just going off to Spain), Margaret and Max, and last night Joan. Robert to dinner one night, up to his eyebrows in the election, about which we talked almost as much as his private life. I again noticed that some prestigious values have rubbed off on him, from his grander associations. Wasn't it rather nice, he said, to go to very expensive restaurants and have sumptuous meals. Of course it is for those who can, but it doesn't prevent one deploring that there are so few, but I find no one agreeing with me. We had a delightful evening as usual. I told him my dream about Ralph, and he was sympathetic and enlightening – he said the feeling behind it wasn't childish but the strongest I've ever experienced in my life, but my *reaction* was a child's. Like a child I kicked out and wanted to hurt Ralph as I had been hurt by his 'leaving me'. But it didn't quite hit the spot. And last night, my unconscious, wanting perhaps to circumvent his interpretation, produced another very vivid long dream in which R. and I lay in bed together in our room at Ham Spray and argued absolutely calmly and reasonably (but there was despair in my heart) as to why we had drifted so far apart and could no longer communicate.

February 25th

I spoke to Julian on the telephone yesterday and was delighted at the thought of seeing him again. I will soon discover, he says, how glum English life is after America but the poor fellow hasn't quite recovered from flu.

A weekend in London: Saturday was devoted to work on the proffered translation, a highly technical and learned and under-paid one, and the decision not to accept it. I then walked round in the darkness to see Faith,[1] who looked frail, and remarkably pretty for eighty-four. Sunday afternoon devoted to going to the Hayward Gallery with Stanley, and the evening to dining with Robert and his Mouse. Were I to boil down these contacts to make a sort of Knorr cube, what would I get? Though heaven forbid my making a habit of such a thing, I occasionally feel the need of taking stock of relationships.

Stanley – I *enjoy* conversation with him. He thinks; and, much as his dog Snuzz comes up with my gnawed darning-mushroom, he too comes up with results. The logical attitude for a pacifist in wartime was one of his subjects. They are tossed about a bit, and then left to simmer – that is they produce a sediment of what has *not* been said. I think in this case that there are several good grounds for being a pacifist: for instance respect for human life, feeling that war never does any good but always much harm and solves no problems; internationalism rather than pacifism.

I have just been rung up by the agency that sent me the sample to translate – almost crawlingly begging me to do more work for them. I have held firm and said I won't, but am feeling disturbed as a result.

February 27th

I took Magouche to *War and Peace*[2] on Monday night and thought it was splendid as before. She and the Hills have now set off for Spain and will not be back for some time, but from a letter I got from Bunny I rather fear he has already arrived, unannounced and unexpected, at Tramores.

Election eve and I've not decided to vote Liberal or Labour.

---

1 Henderson.
2 Prokofiev's opera.

What on earth does it matter? I rang up the Liberals, complaining of having received no literature. An extremely pretty and intelligent girl came to see me.

I'm gradually getting level with my tasks and think I may have been foolish to reject the translation I was offered. But no, I'm not up to the pressure involved.

March 2nd

Election over I was due to come down here to Stowell – the least favourable milieu in which to digest what I supposed would be a fairly easy Conservative victory. But it's not! After a very exciting evening's ding-dong listening, Labour is ahead by five seats, and no one (what with Liberals, Irish, Scotch and Welsh Nationalists) has a clear majority – the final proof of Heath's complete lack of imagination and being out of touch with facts. That was some satisfaction, but what was my amazement to read in this morning's paper that though he had asked for a mandate and got the reverse, he proposes to try and make a deal with Jeremy Thorpe and *stay on*. Here I am in true blue surroundings, so ridiculously blue that they don't annoy me. Even the graceful and attractive butler Page comes in and announces discreetly, 'We've held Aberdeen South, Sir Philip.' Good heavens, how Ralph would have laughed, I never stop thinking. Philip is in a frenzy and suspects Jeremy Thorpe, thinks he's ruined. The other guests are the Manager of the *Financial Times*, Allan Hare, and his jolly friendly wife, Jill. I was briefed by Robert about Allan whom he had been at Oxford with: 'He's extremely clever, and I like him very much.' The atmosphere is thick with class prejudice and the snobbery of wealth. I said Philippe de Rothschilde had been talking on the wireless. 'About his women?' 'No – about the pleasures of being rich.' Jilly: 'Oh I'm so *glad* – no one ever seems to speak up for it.' (F. thinks: no, nor realise that they are pleasures everyone might like a chance to enjoy. Or very nearly everyone.)

Allan Hare said he fancied Robert was moving to the Right politically. F: 'Well, he didn't vote Conservative' (he *told* me anyway he would vote Liberal). Much curiosity – I at first refused to say, but was teased into outing with the truth.

Surprise. Philip luckily out of the room – it would have shocked him deeply, for it's not a mere matter of politics; so many other horrid concepts like patriotism, loyalty, royalty, my country right or wrong, war service, Jack *isn't* as good as his master, float in this atmosphere also.

March 4th

As usual at Stowell, I begin to crave to get into a more sympathetic ambience, for all dear Mary's affectionate goodheartedness. Philip went to bed very tired at 9.20 last night, but came down this morning, says Mary, in a much more optimistic mood and even apologising to her, and thanking her for her patience in view of his sudden announcements that they were to move to the stables, or other vital changes of plans. One can't help feeling sorry for him, just as I do for Mr Heath, for getting everything so hopelessly wrong. In Heath's case he would have done better to have had no election and a moderately good majority to get on with his plans. As it is the idiotic wooden smile has been wiped off his face, and he has overnight lost the premiership (I can't but think), and the confidence of a lot of his own party.

I find it extremely interesting and speculate all the time about what will happen next.

Stowell had a sort of a wartime atmosphere, as if accepting that we were in for a tough time.

March 5th

Flatness and slight depression. My existence has become repetitious. I only really like being with friends for whom I don't have to put on a mask; and though Mary is certainly a good friend, some of her world is not. I'm a little worried that – Magouche away – she wants too much of my time to 'play with her' or worse still with her and Philip. I don't want to 'play with' anyone. Though friends die off like flies there are still plenty I can be my dreary old self with. Last night Raymond and Paul[1] to dinner on the spur of the moment – they are cookless. Paul is I

---

1 Mortimer and Hyslop.

think, oddly enough, more humane and left-wing than Raymond. Just before they came I had been listening to the absurd explosions of housewives on the wireless who quite obviously felt shocked by the *unpatriotism* of those who didn't vote Conservative!

Very nice evening last week with Julian by the way. Appalling Jumbo crash, the worst ever, killing over 300 people including the son of a friend of Joan's who rang me up in tears.

Eardley has been promised a show, but I'm 'not to tell Joan'; Mattei has an eccentric new friend – a bearded and shoeless, 'not *sortable*', Australian – but I'm 'not to tell Joan'. I forget sometimes that I'm supposed to be a model of discretion – it's not natural to me – Janet Stone is coming to dinner and doubtless will talk about her affair (if it is one) with Kenneth Clark, and I 'mustn't tell anyone'. Stanley comes to tea. His theme is still pacifism at the moment.

And Harold Wilson is Prime Minister again. How long will it last?

March 8th

I'm still low, submerged by anticlimactic pointlessness. Shops full of the 'upper classes' doing their own shopping and saying: 'It's just like the war.' I had some somewhat fruitless contacts with various people – even dear Stanley. Mary at lunch yesterday I found I had nothing to say to. Dicky[1] came to dinner and talked very enjoyably about himself and his book and his visit to Tramores, but surely it was a *little* odd that he never asked one single question about Mexico. Not one. Yet he's far from unfeeling.

March 11th

Driving back from Lambourn this morning (where thick damp snow fell on Sunday at dawn and melted – partially – into white mist). I tried keeping to the rule, or law, of not going faster than fifty. It produced a restful slightly melancholy trance, very

---

1 Chopping.

different from the tense agitation of going as fast as one possibly can, and much less taxing. The turning off the Baydon road signposted Rooksnest[1] brought a wave of nostalgia and memory of earliest days of loving Ralph, when the Japps lived there. Why is nostalgia thought of as a sweet form of self-indulgence often I wonder? Instead it can be a sharp sour aftertaste, a pang.

Margaret Penrose to lunch. I tried to get her to talk about her married life with Max Newman.[2] It doesn't sound very romantic, but much concerned with money. 'How does he spend his time?' I asked. 'Staring at unpaid bills.' She sometimes talks about him quite unsympathetically, as if he was almost mad, at other times proudly – for instance, that he's so musical that he can't bear any music but that of Bach, Mozart and Haydn. That irritates me – with him, not Margaret.

I see human individuals as tadpole-shaped, and I'm in the tapering tip of the tail.

Quiet evening, reading *The Ambassadors*. The time element is curiously different in painting and all the other arts. Only in painting can the whole work be grasped instantaneously, or in so far as it isn't, time is at the mercy of the viewer's exploration. In drama, literature and music it is an essential part of the creation of art.

Noel as usual talked on and on and on about Carrington. I listen as sympathetically as I can and I think it pleases him. Came back to a lovely bunch of letters – three from Tramores, Janetta, Heyward and Bunny.

March 15th

Like a mad rabbit I make for my burrow and plunge into it with relief, now at three-thirty on a Friday afternoon. How glad I am not to be going away for the weekend! To have an evening *alone* with books and wireless stretching ahead of me; yet, as I stumped along from fetching my mended spectacles I was violently conscious of isolation in a street where so many had

---

1 Former home of Darsie and Lucila Japp and their girls in reach of us at Ham Spray.

2 Cambridge don whom she married after Lionel's death.

companions, and remembered with a stab how unbearably I had envied such couples in the first months of being without R. at Menton. Should I ever get over it, I wondered? Well, no, in a way never. I can enjoy *real* solitude, indoors, but not the solitude of the streets.

Yesterday I had 'composed' a dinner-party: Mungo and Monica, Stanley, Eardley and Julia. All had been told whom they were going to meet which I think is important. At tea-time a call from Julia, in a quiet sober voice. (When I asked her a week ago she sounded drunk and wuzzy, and said she had been 'feeling so unutterably low that she couldn't get on with her writing'). This time: 'I'm afraid I have bad news. I've been in bed for two days – I'd love to see you – could you come here instead.' F: 'But my dear I can't. I've five other people coming to dinner. How horrible for you. Do you think it's gastric flu?' J: 'Well, I don't think it can be as I have had no temperature. The doctor sent me some pills but they aren't any use. He won't come and see me as he lives in St John's Wood. I ring him every day. It's an awful nuisance – I have to send my girl in a taxi for the prescription. But I mean to get to Leeds tomorrow by hook or crook. Lawrence will like to look after me I know, and it isn't far to carry trays upstairs. So I'll stay there till I'm quite well again.' I remembered when they were at Shalbourne in the war how maddened Lawrence and the landlady got when Julia stayed endlessly in bed taking her temperature and awaiting trays.

I have at long last finished reading that extraordinary book *The Ambassadors* and only for the second time in my life. It is an odd mixture of evanescence and obsession. But I feel humiliated to read the American editor's final note in which he had found a thread, a clue of time, watches and clocks, running through it, which I didn't explicitly take in, or 'make out' as H.J. would say. NB: 'You're magnificent!' the characters often say to one another, and the reader accepts it though I for one have never heard such a thing said – not once.

Two people from Jonathan Cape came to look at a thousand photos for Gerald's autobiography, and seemed excited and delighted by them. They were David Machin, a partner, who is noted for his charm, but I didn't respond to it, and a nice spectacled girl. I gave them drinks, and asked when the book was due. Gerald had agreed to certain omissions and I hoped he had kept to them, as he had for Joanna Carrington, 'otherwise I didn't really see why I should take all this trouble on his behalf'. I said this (or meant to) very lightly, but Machin looked a bit anxious and said that Joanna was most certainly 'in' the book. Pondering this afterwards, perhaps emphasised by the news that Peter Luke's bloody play is going on after all, I consulted Robert, who came to dinner last night – dear fellow, how I enjoy talking to him – and strongly advised my asking to see the text first. I wonder if this will make trouble with Gerald though, because I'm far from sure how to weigh in the balance friendship with the living against defending the image of the greatly beloved dead.

A lot of political speculation with Robert. Like me, he says he would vote Labour in the unlikely event of Pigling Heath[1] and Thorpe standing, dislodging Wilson. If they do, the news will be out tonight and Philip (who is coming to dinner along with the Pritchetts and Mary and Robert) will be cock-a-hoop.

March 20th

One more dinner-party over, and I hope the last for a long while, though I think the company enjoyed it and I did myself in a sort of way.

My state of mind remains on the whole that of a resigned sword-swallower – the sword, piercing and death-dealing, being life. Quickly, quickly down it goes. But resignation brings a sort of calm. I even sleep better. I nap often in the afternoon. I only hope my wits aren't getting too dulled.

I can't solve the question about Gerald's book and the photographs. I consulted Stanley, who 'invited himself' to lunch yesterday – he thought it 'an extremely difficult problem, but on the whole truth came before friendship'. Joanna comes tomorrow to see my album and talk about it. She says Gerald had told her he had cut the chapter about her but then wrote asking her to send a photo of the period in question to an address in

---

1 From the children's book *Pigling Bland*.

Oxford Street. She did, and heard no more. Then he wrote crossly, asking why she hadn't sent it. It was the only copy.

A lovely day with Sophie. Lovely photos of her enjoying the snow in Canada and a nice letter from Henrietta, who is coming back in time to take her to her test at Bedales – that is very soon.

When I was at Stowell I went as usual to see Frances Phipps, who wrung my heart on parting by saying that she couldn't decide whether to have her second cataract operated on, as the first eye is useless. I have been worrying at her saying, 'Oh it's so difficult to make up one's mind!' I talked later to Raymond about it. He rang up to say that he had mentioned it to Pat who said she certainly ought to have another opinion. So, greatly hesitant at my interference, I wrote her a letter yesterday saying that three of her loving friends, Eardley, Raymond and I, all wished she would take advice from Pat. She has rung up this morning saying that this was a ray of light in the darkness; she was beginning to descend into her old melancholy, and cry and cry and feel her courage ebbing. 'I almost *prayed* for something to happen – and then your letter came.' I hope to heaven some good will come of it. I've made an appointment for her for next week. But feel anxious at the result of what I've set in train.

March 23rd: Crichel

Here with perfect company – Dadie, Raymond, Des (who came later than the rest) and Pat. David and Rachel for a jolly drink.

First evening conversation ranged over real subjects: death, how much one thought of it. ('Not at all,' Raymond. Dadie and I: 'At least once a day.') Not fear of death but just preoccupation. Funerals. Wills. The horrible possibility that immortality might be true. I went to bed and dreamed of Julia, a younger Julia in a corridor with dark wallpaper. She said: 'I remarried last night and my husband has died. I want you to come to the funeral.' Then a glow of mysterious light spread over the wall and Rosamond, who was with 'us' (whoever 'we' were), said triumphantly, 'You *see?*'

This morning a fine long strong walk with Pat and Dadie. I

kept up well, which pleased me. At breakfast a slight reference to politics – nothing before or since, perhaps out of disagreement with me. Dadie has told me about Peter Luke's play and the actor who is to do Lytton is to come and see me. We agreed that if the play is to be done, and nothing can stop it, it's best it should be well done. Dadie, and more and more people I find, are dead against Holroyd and his book. I stick up for him. Pat, back from a holiday with Lindy Guinness in Peru and the Falkland Islands, is definitely changed – dreamy, bronzed, and rather far away. Could he have fallen for her? Raymond and I, briefly alone, discussed it. I said Des had pooh-poohed the idea of Pat having an affair with Freda Berkeley, and was amazed because Raymond was inclined to do so too and turn it into an elder sister relation. I think it's because he has, as Raymond admits, violent anti-female feelings. He's always nice to me.

This afternoon after lunch we were back on spelling, pronunciation and punctuation – alack!

March 29th

Something of a let-down from Dadie? – how easily I seem to believe what I would like to believe. He has written after seeing the producer and actor of Lytton in Luke's play and left me fuming by apparently going over entirely to their side. He had told them they must consult me and go into the question of my copyright (in the Carrington letter of which Luke wants to make a scene). Now he writes that they 'will talk to you about the double (treble) bed scene which he wants to treat very lightly ... I rather hope the Carrington letter can be put back.' He obviously hasn't even read the current form of the play. Meanwhile all my fume and fret has returned, and my desire to decamp from the country and life. 'I am sure you will find them both sympathetic,' says Dadie, but I hear nothing from them. I tried to ring Dadie at King's – he is away for ten days. I tried to ring H. M. Tennants. No reply. *Blast*.

March 30th: Comberton, near Cambridge

The house of Max Newman and Margaret. One couldn't be

anywhere else but in reach of Cambridge – the utter flatness, rows of new bungalows among older prettier houses. A blue sky and beginnings of spring do their best for it, but it all must look gloomy in winter. Indoors the house is meticulously neat – Max not Margaret. Everything has its place and the walls with their neat prints of the founder of St John's College exude the bachelordom of dons. Max mentions his college often and in a religious voice.

Before I left London, Tennants sent me a copy of their bloody silly play. I've been on the rack reading it. It is as bad as ever except that Carrington's letter to Lytton has been removed. I've given it to Margaret to read.

April 2nd

What a day yesterday – nothing but talks of other people's woes. Joan's continue, and when I ring her up I get a catalogue of them. Then Judy: symptom after symptom, and when her own had been listed I got Jill's, Jane's and Ambrose's.

While poor Julian was in the middle of a very sad conversation about his fortieth birthday and kindred sorrows, Isobel rang my doorbell. I propped the door open and went on talking to Julian with half an eye on whatever was happening in the kitchen – Isobel's voice like some insistent instrument boring a hole said, 'I'm sorry to interrupt but I'm bleeding.' Ran to get her cotton wool and back to make a plan with Julian who was I felt rather desperate, and then back to minister to Isobel. She had hit her shin on a bus. 'I think I'll put a little whisky on it.' She then put her glass of whisky on the floor and kicked it over. Ran to mop it up, and back to the cooking-stove.

The best moment of the day was the arrival of Janetta with a bunch of flowers smelling intoxicatingly of Spain.

Today too has been full of overlapping events of a stressful order. All spare moments – both yesterday and today I have devoted to the dreaded play. I'm now feeling the need of some support with it – and Robert, who has continually egged me on to resist, has failed me, after promising to come to see me yesterday and/or ring up yesterday or today. So at the moment I feel rather sore that I have to have other people's trouble unloaded on me and no one helps me with mine – a self-pitying sort of attitude I neither enjoy nor admire.

Well – the producer of the play has been here, a stammering, sympathetic man. I talked to him as one human being to another, said I hated it but supposed it was better to get it as nearly right as possible if it had to be put on. As it obviously must. I gave him *some* data to take away in the shape of R.'s conscientious tribunal statement. I agreed he should bring young Massey (who acts Lytton) next week. Was this sensible of me or not?

April 3rd

Just lunched with Robert who has carried off the play. As I expected he wants me to hold out on the producer until I get an agreement to alter certain things. I'm not at all sure he's right, but at present my object is to get as many opinions as possible about it, and in particular which of the fourteen things I object to they find most objectionable.

I've also been under pressure from Cape, who have failed to get in touch with Joanna and are getting frantic about Gerald's book. Hurrah! I speak mealy-mouthed to Mr Machin of Cape, but am aware of a deep-seated resentment against Gerald which makes me want – yes, *want* him to suffer for his 'betrayal of Ralph' as I see it.

Robert returned with the play under his arm. He thinks it quite futile and feeble, so much so that it is hardly likely to have a run; he has come round to my ideas of friendly co-operation. In the evening Julian cast an eye on it, and was full of dynamic suggestions, saying he would like to review it and pan it, and that I ought to write an article in the *Sunday Times* about my side of the 'situation'. But the truth is I don't quite know what 'my side' is, and feel sometimes that my friends must think me rather insane about it, and perhaps I am! Julian refused to talk about his own problems and troubles which are sufficiently serious to make him talk of wanting 'to get right away' somewhere for a year.

April 4th

Morning of concentrated and prolonged telephone calls, lasting without pause from nine till ten-thirty and thrice getting me dripping out of my bath. What a bizarre way to spend such a large chunk of each day. Talking to poor Joan, who is now told she has severe shingles, takes up a lot of my telephoning time. Early and urgent-sounding call from Stanley who had dreamed about me and my play! 'You had a brilliant red lipstick on, which you never wear,' and the result in some obscure way of the dream was that he felt I shouldn't try and impede the play, but help them get it right 'as I was doing', and this was obviously important though he wasn't very clear why. I got a clue from his going on directly to say that the Wylie family are putting up difficulties in the way of his writing Elinor Wylie's life.[1] I rather think he had also been seeing Michael Holroyd, who may stand to make something out of the play. I don't think it is mono-manic therefore to see that with my red lipstick (vampire), he saw me as draining the blood of would-be playwrights and biographers, and this interests me. I shall record all views of the play and get as many as I can, and I think I may explain or express more definitely to Cottrell and Massey how bad I think it is, perhaps even admit that I've shown it to a lot of friends who all think likewise. But I see that to show that I was egging them on to pan the play when it appears might be a great mistake.

Julian is the person who I feel is most likely to help me and I'm touched by his goodwill and interest. But Daniel Massey[2] is a friend from his Cambridge days.

Tomorrow I'm going to take the play to Crichel and drop it on Raymond, on my way to Kitty West.

Oh the intractable physical universe! Trying to return a bottle of sherry to Oakeshott (they having given me the wrong sort) I tripped on the step to Halkin passage, dropped and broke the bottle and fell on the broken glass cutting my knee quite badly, so that four stitches had to be put in. 'My dear girl, you *have* cut yourself!' said Moynihan's partner.

April 6th: At Kitty's in Dorset

One can't 'go on' about spring every year and yet one can't *not*

---

1 Stanley's first book.
2 The actor chosen to take Lytton's part.

go on. I glory in this garden blazing with daffodils, white and yellow, blue grape hyacinths, a wall covered in peach blossom, primroses and wood anemones tufting everywhere, birds singing.

After an easy relaxed glide from London I dropped the dreaded play in at Crichel for Raymond to read. We go over to lunch tomorrow and I shall hear what he thinks to add to my store. Des may look at it – he was inclined to say Luke was a good writer and 'full of fancy', perversely so I felt – so I shall not be surprised at lack of support from that quarter. Then perhaps Kitty can give her verdict. I think about it a great deal of the time, and wake in the night to it.

Yesterday morning I called in on Janetta at Chapel Street – she looked young and pretty and greatly pleased and soothed me as only she knows how. She told me that Cyril is now enraged with Gerald and his forthcoming book. He had got Gerald's permission to read the proofs and found in it some quite virulently disagreeable things about himself – his ugliness, his writing, his character. Janetta, who thought she had got Gerald to cut these remarks out, is herself furious with him, and wonders how much of what he *said* he had cut out about Ralph has actually gone in. Cyril was one of the first to praise Gerald's writing in print and has never ceased doing so. He says he won't dream of reviewing this book and never wants to see Gerald again. Gerald had written saying it was very important to 'get money for Lynda and her work' – 'What is her work?' says Cyril. 'And why can't she make some money by it if she works; and why should I care whether she does or not?'

I feel that in all this I'm giving way to monomania, and I'm doing so (I think) deliberately, as if by 'working through' my obsession I could somehow achieve catharsis. I only hope that the act I put on of being equally interested in other people's affairs (and I do try hard to do so) carried some sort of conviction. Not sure though. I wish, like some operation at a fixed date, it could all be finally over.

April 8th

The play's 'the thing' which occupies me day and night, and

Raymond's reaction has almost made me change my decision as to what my own shall be. He thinks it 'appallingly silly and vulgar, the portrait of Ralph grotesque'. He added that *he* wouldn't help the production in any way and implied that I should not either.

Stanley on the telephone told me I was 'worrying too much and should either help the producer to the best of my bent or wash my hands of the whole thing'. I rather think I shall do the latter, and even that it would be preferable to struggling to 'improve' the rubbishy thing.

April 9th

Joanna has had a letter from Gerald saying that what he had put in about her was a 'revised' version of what went before and 'Janetta liked it. As for Frances, she won't be pleased with what I've written, but I sent her a copy of it and Janetta liked that too.'

I have therefore, with Joanna's approval, rung up Cape and said I'm sorry but I can't lend any of my photos unless I see the script. Gerald may blow up if he likes – I do not greatly care at the moment. But I fear my blood is now thoroughly roused, and I know I'm capable of saying really silly things when I lose my wool. So now, sitting waiting for the two play monsters I say to myself I *must* keep calm.

April 12th: Snape

The two play-men came to see me, and the young actor, Daniel Massey, who is to do Lytton is quite charming. We talked for two hours, but I showed them no photographs. Deliberately starting on other subjects like Dadie, I then turned to Cottrell and said last time I had told him what I thought the main things the play had got wrong were and asked did he think any of them would be amended? He became amiably cagey and said it all depended on Luke, whom he was visiting in Spain after Easter. He had read and been impressed by the Ralph documents. So then I rather let fly and said it would be totally dishonest not to say that I thought it a hopelessly bad play, silly and piffling and that everyone I'd shown it to did too (naming no names, though

Raymond and Robert wouldn't have minded – but saying 'telly people', 'an eminent literary critic'). But we don't speak the same language and when I said they thought it 'vulgar tripe', Massey said, 'But Lytton was *gloriously* vulgar!' I had to explain that by vulgarity I didn't mean obscenity but bad taste. They didn't seem to know a thing about anyone. Massey had read what Dadie told him to and had fallen in love with 'all these people' but couldn't see that the play didn't represent them. After more talk, amiable but outspoken, I said: well, if no changes were made I was afraid I must wash my hands of the play and hope it would be a flop. All this was combined with jokes and laughter.

Janetta thinks Luke won't give an inch and I expect she's right, Heywood that the play is too piffling to bother about. I think it may be a success all the same. The two left me, giving me a definite impression that they felt I *would* be helping them. I warned them about the God Copyright, and asked them about the trashy Virginia monologues and the three-in-the-bed episode. 'Good theatre', was the reply.

So I shall set this beastly play aside and out of mind for the present. I don't think I can do more about it, and now Gerald's book has loomed large in its place. Noel, I truly believe out of friendship for me, went to see Cape and persuaded them to send me Xerox copies of some bits about Ralph. Gerald has improved them, but I am appalled and shocked by the way he has treated me.

All this makes me pretty unhappy and I fear a bore to my tolerant friends. I don't know *what* chance I have of affecting the text.

April 14th: Aldeburgh Festival

Janetta joined Heywood and Anne and me here yesterday, and we all went to a splendid concert of quartets at the Maltings last night – Haydn, the Mozart clarinet quintet, Britten's 1st. The Mozart was beautifully played and seemed to me the quintessence of ravishingly mellifluous sweetness. The day before at the Matthew Passion with Heywood, indifferently performed, I confess my mind wandered off now and again to my 'troubles'.

Anne and Heywood are happy and richly companionable. Good food at Tramores has made Anne very stout, and Janetta's presence produces in Heywood a rollicking swaggering flirtatiousness delightful to see. I think he is happier than he has been for a long time.

April 16th

Nipped by East Anglian cold winds we yet extract walks with corkscrews from the unsheltered lanes in bright fitful sunshine. On Easter Sunday, we lunched at the Oyster Bar in Orford, and then visited three gardens open to the public. Daffodils are still in flower and we strolled round among colonels, plebs and old gardening gals. Janetta showed no desire to see the Gerald extract, which Anne and Heywood had previously gone over point by point with me in the most practical, helpful and realistic way. This worried me a little and at last I pushed it under her nose. She read it and agreed on every point I had made. I think she dreaded it might be worse than it is. The decisions made, I tried to drive the subject from my head and conversation, and succeeded except in the watches of the night when it returned to plague me.

Now, Tuesday, I rang up Machin, suggested going to see him and said that if, as I firmly believed, all could be amicably settled I was most willing to let him have as many photos as he liked. It was an odd excursion into the past, for Cape's now live in Bedford Square and I have hardly been there since I left it at the age of eight. Arriving early I walked round, looked at the huge splendid houses and into the garden with its big black-trunked trees and round summer-house. Then boldly advanced on to No. 30. The splendour these publishers live in! No wonder books can't be produced except at a loss. When I told Machin I had been born two doors off in No. 28 he said that was theirs too and offered to take me there. We entered the enormous door where I had stood as a little girl looking at the ornamentations of fossilised white astrakhan which I identified with the fur collar of my father's coat, and the bearded classical head topping the arch. Then into the hall, unfamiliar except for the thick mahogany door into what I now remember was the dining-room. The huge drawing-room was occupied by a conference, but I saw the enormous bow-fronted arm of the L, now shut off by double doors, but still with its Adam ceiling and fireplaces. How strange and remote to look up from the outside at the balustrade protecting the window of the nursery top floor. The time gap was too large to be really moving, and it was mainly with curiosity that I looked at the noble house which that other little me had inhabited so many years ago.

Machin was friendly and I really think the whole business may have been fairly happily settled. Janetta – alas! alas! – returns to Spain tomorrow. I visited Joan, still lying poor creature on her bed of pain, and she showed me her poor swollen hand. Since I got back I have had alarmingly no contact of any sort with the outer world, but spent the evening like La Fontaine's *fourmi* storing away cases of wine in my cellar cupboard.

April 17th

Telephone call to Joan, entrapped in the obsessional and near-hysterical toils of her illness, now accentuated by total constipation. She can think and talk of nothing else, but rejects my proffered visits, and I'm left appalled by the thought of her imprisoned in her ailing body.

Last night I went to a dinner given by Vivien and Richard King[1] for Julian's fortieth birthday, where familiar faces and glamorous unfamiliar ones were congregated. Among the latter Germaine Greer, whose appearance disarmed the hostility her Women's Lib book had engendered in me. She presented Julian with a carefully tied-up parcel turning out to contain a teapot in the shape of a mauve sports-car – a quite repulsive object. Talked to beautiful Antonia Fraser, Patrick Kinross, who has become an elder statesman, Peter Eyre who dashed up to say a friend of his wanted to meet me as she was billed for Carrington in the bloody Luke play, and then dashed away; Andrew Thripland, sweet as he always is; Ed in his good boy mood, who made me laugh immoderately by describing the Hills in Spain. Anne had taken great trouble to mug up some Spanish, and one

---

1 Young couple from Cambridge.

day saw in the garden someone she took for the elderly washing lady, Carmen, so called out loudly and carefully: '*Buenas dias, Señora!*' The figure turned, and it was Heywood, wearing a hanky on his head against the sun! I enjoyed the party and could have stayed the course longer, but drove back with Robert about one. He had had Diana Cooper as a partner and was looking somewhat fagged. (Cross-purposes conversation between her and Patrick: P: 'Shall I get a taxi?' D: 'Getting sexy?' rocking slightly where she stood.) Sitting between Jonny and Julian at dinner, who reminisced about their Cambridge days. Jonny said he didn't get to know Julian for a year and then was 'very frightened of him'. Julian claimed to have been frightened of Jonny, who told him, 'You know you were in love with me'; but he didn't reveal whether he had been.

Nicko came for a drink. He declared he was profoundly worried about the international situation and the Labour Party's attitude to the Common Market; he also said he believed Heath had gone virtually mad at the end of last year, and Callaghan's rudeness alienated the Germans.

April 20th: Litton Cheney

The desire to write, to set words on paper grows on me, but for lack of imagination I'm left with only myself as subject. Janetta – did I say so? – made one of her most earnest and hard-to-resist pleas that I should write my own memoirs, even brought me a notebook, and I have promised to 'try', in spite of my conviction that there are too many bad books, and only very very good ones should be written, and anything else is pure self-indulgence.

So here I am, going to and from weekend after weekend like a policeman on the beat. Sitting at my writing table at the Stones' I look out through the treetops at the far downs, and survey also my changed attitude to life. It has become both more fatalistic (nothing to lose) and more relaxed; the two probably connected. My ideal of maintaining the greatest possible intensity of consciousness at any one moment is fading a little. But not my desire to keep contact with friends, growing more urgent as death removes them one by one.

I arrived to find John Sparrow here, a man I've never felt

drawn to, a dog-man always on the point of woofing or even barking. Last night Janet seemed anxious lest he and I wouldn't hit it off, this causing her to monologise frenetically and keep on suggesting bed before it struck ten. Sparrow sent a few cannon-balls rolling by in the shape of pleas for capital punishment or return of museum charges, but 'nobody marked them'.

April 22nd

The terrier dog has been wagging his tail and my resistance is lowered. A sharp attack of lumbago has given pathos to his stance. Yesterday with Janet I visited the magic camellia garden at Abbotsbury, the village shop (almost as magic), and walked up the Chesil Bank to look down upon and sniff the sea.

Reynolds' passion for trees is becoming quite unbridled. He admits he thinks them more important than people, and took me to show how all his frenzied plantings after the 'tree murder', which so punctured him a few years ago, had sprouted. Indeed they had, but so closely together that one could hardly see their trunks, a claustrophobic crowd round the house.

Dined at the Hubbards'. I talked to John H. about producing Shakespeare. The other evening, at a private view of Julian's excellent film on Isherwood, I talked to Jonathan Miller, who told me he was now going to produce opera – including at Glyndebourne. In today's paper Desmond quotes him as saying it is an outrageous old-fashioned notion that we need pay any attention to Mozart when producing his operas: 'we owe him absolutely nothing.' Monstrous, obscene vanity, as Hubbard and I agreed. I have even made a first tentative move at carrying out Janetta's behest: I don't absolutely rule it out.

April 23rd

Janetta rang up from Marbella, saying she had a frantic summons to lunch from Gerald who thinks I'm going to issue an injunction against him. Oh Lord! Wherever has he got that idea from? I fear rocks ahead in what I'd hoped was smooth water.

Paul Levy came to lunch, looking twice the man he was when rejected by Philippa Pullan, having lots of reviews to write (which he does competently) and a steady girlfriend. They have asked me down for a night.

April 26th

Trembling on the edge of a precipice of total chaos when the decoration of my flat starts next week. This may have been the cause of agonised dreams about Burgo.

I go down today to visit the Major-General, a prospect which rather alarms me – I don't know why it should, but being with people one doesn't know is always an effort.

I set about counting my blessings: Julian came to dinner delightfully, added his disapprobation of the play but was sure it would be put on though it might well fail. I put the question of the literary executorship to him and asked him to ponder and be sure he wants it. He says he does and I believe it is true, also that it isn't such an impossible task for him to deal with as I thought. I think he'll never get around to reading it all, but what does it matter?

Then a long call from Cyril, extremely friendly, to whom I had written a letter as a fellow-sufferer from Gerald. He told me what Gerald had written about him – real horrors. 'His ugly mug brooding over the lunch table, ready to talk but not listen.' C: 'How could I listen when he does nothing but boast boringly about his sexual experiences?' And according to Gerald, Cyril continues to write worse and worse reviews 'which nobody reads'.

Went to *Clemenza di Tito* last night, taking Max and Margaret and standing them dinner in the interval. It's a colossal extravagance but I think they enjoyed it and I certainly did. Cool and exquisite music, for the most part extremely well sung.

April 29th

My decorations have begun, and I have temporarily settled in my bedroom while Raymond Hall attacks the sitting-room, playing classical music on his transistor all day, which oddly enough is what I find most trying. To hear familiar strains in the margin of consciousness is strangely upsetting.

Well, the visit to the Major-General was very, very odd. We

drove through tame flowerless Somersetshire countryside and grey villages to arrive at last before a bungalow built I believe (but I hardly dare look) of synthetic stone. Around it virulent crazy paving planted with aubretias. At the door stood his Dutch *vrouw*, a stout red-faced party with snow-white hair and bright blue eyes. I learned later that she was just on seventy, but couldn't help thinking of her as older than me. Crippled by arthritis and perhaps by other ailments (the bungalow was for her, and the M.G. kept saying, 'I don't want Margaret to drive', 'I don't like Margaret to worry; 'Margaret couldn't manage the stairs'). It's the oddest marriage. She's not stupid, knows something of music but is a Dutch *bore* – neat, tidy, wholesome, relentlessly looking on the bright side. And her house! It was 'dinky'. Every object in it, furniture included, was outrageously hideous, yet in a cardboard way comfortable. My bathroom was papered with nesting snipe, and on the door two paper baby donkeys with huge heads and roses in their mouths had been plastered. On my bedroom wall was hung the metal outline of an old-fashioned car. Books: Galsworthy and Vachell mixed with R. Fry and Villon. Surely if David Gadd is able to appreciate 'and love' the Bloomsburies and be as intelligent as he seems to be he must be bored stiff by this deadly *hausvrouw*. But no, in every way they manifested that they were delighted with each other and their marriage. I gasp. My first night was haunted by consciousness of my strange surroundings. Could David's book be any good? After some demur he brought out the proofs, and I think it's all right – well written, if only a potted summary of other books: a Bloomsbury for beginners. No research, only selection and rather good judgement. I discovered a mistake which greatly upset him, and me – he had called Lady Strachey Julia instead of Jane. Another thing: he asked 'Where did you and Ralph live?' 'Didn't you realise we lived at Ham Spray?' 'But I mean after Lytton and Carrington's death?' 'Yes, indeed, we lived there for thirty years.' Well, that's not his period, but his amazement is typical of what the world thinks.

April 30th
My flat has become a junk-shop, and though I can still lurk in my

bedroom, I must pick my way carefully through the hall. On the whole this is the least worrying aspect of my days.

Yesterday I lunched with Magouche, when Sophie was left for me to take shopping while Henrietta went for a test to the doctor.

Then there is poor Frances Phipps, whose cataract is to be removed this afternoon, and Joan with her shingles. My visit to her wasn't a success. I was tired and not particularly pleased (even if it was what I want) to be told I 'should probably drop dead quite suddenly'. Also her lack of stoicism very slightly nauseates me. Over and over and over again one is told about her pain, and that shingles 'is known to be the worst agony there is'. I run out of remarks of sympathy, and wish she wouldn't just be there thinking about her pain and her body, but would force her mind to accept some other pabulum.

May 1st

My disconnected life has turned out quite different from my expectations. I pictured myself spending hours in the London Library – but I make short dashes and return to my painter and my flat. Yesterday lunch with Robert at my pub. In the afternoon Stanley and Snuzz came, both at their most winning, and we went out into my new square garden opposite the Carlton Towers, where Snuzz had an exciting time with innumerable other dogs (this part is reserved for their lavatory) while I corrected an article of Stanley's, whose writing still at times falls over its own toes. I don't know what my state of mind is – I hardly recognise myself. I rang up Joan again this morning and again received a screech of anguish to which I did my best to respond sympathetically. Frances' operation is said by Raymond to have been satisfactory and a weight off my mind. But tomorrow will be devoted to visiting the sick and this is hard work.

May 4th: Cranborne

Alone in the sitting-room, David, Rachel, Sebastian Walker and his boyfriend Donald having gone out for a drink, and I so glad to be here alone. The young men are almost too friendly –

Donald good-looking (and knows it) but charming: Sebastian rather too much of a gossip-hound and social climber but slightly pathetic thereby. Talking of the horrific revelations about the lethal diseases contracted by workers in asbestos and other industries and the fact that they weren't warned of it. David's response was terrifyingly characteristic. He cackled and said, 'I don't think *I'm* likely to contract that!'

Donald talked copiously to me last night and quite a lot of ideas flooded out rather naïvely among 'OKs' and 'you knows'. He is Australian and has worked among aboriginal children, is now trying to write a Ph.D. on the Indian Raj, loves opera, is drawn to the idea of death, calls everyone by their Christian names at once, but in a way that doesn't offend, as it does in Sebastian ('Aunt Mowcher!') who is probably a snob and certainly a name-dropper, though possibly not right-wing in politics, kind-hearted, but somehow a little absurd.

May 6th: London

Came up with the two boys. Something had happened between them – instead of talk of Donald going back to Australia, and Sebastian revolving a sad little round head on his phenomenally long neck, they sat lovingly holding hands all the way to the station and talked eagerly about what jobs Donald could get in England.

I'm now sitting in the top room at Robert's in Chapel Street where I shall spend tonight but only tonight. My own bedroom has become a delicious shiny grey-green. I'm delighted with it and with my painter – such an intelligent thoughtful man. But the shake-up has had an odd effect and made me cling with closer claws to my nest. I plan to clean my books and make all sorts of little improvements.

May 9th

Back 'home', for it is that in spite of all the confusion and the objects heaped in the wrong places.

All the same it's a non-life and I shall be glad when it's over – I hope by the end of next week.

To see Joan yesterday. Great groans, but her arm is appallingly swollen, worse than ever I think.

Stanley asked me to eat steak tartare with him last night, but coughed so incessantly and rackingly that I was quite worried about him, and left him soon after.

May 15th

Decoration still not finished – Raymond Hall (my painter) is taking the day off, but says he should be done at the weekend. Well, I'll be glad really. This disorganisation has spread like some liquid overflow into the rut of my life. Today I have a summons to attend the Rent Tribunal next week; also a letter from Henrietta about Dartington fees, and have made an appointment to see Mungo with a view to reorganising my will. I spoke to Stanley about it the other evening and have more or less decided to leave him my Bloomsbury books and let Julian keep the literary executorship.

Mary has asked me to stay in Majorca. She asked the Hills too, and they can't go. I don't really want to – nor do I feel I can be sure what I can afford till I have 'sorted myself out'. And this, at the moment, is my chief aim. Also the dreaded play should be going into rehearsal then. Also rehearsals for my next concert. So take it all in all, I'm backing out – or I rather hope so.

May 17th

What will it feel like when I come out into full normalcy on Monday? I've had three people to meals in my sitting-room – Robert after a glorious *Otello*; last night Julia and at lunch today Jaime. Julia has suddenly lurched into old age and it's a distressing spectacle. She stumped up my stairs groaning, 'It's my *knees* – old age, my dear.' She frequently alluded to her 'senility' and I fear not without reason – she was very often adrift in the conversation, didn't take in much that I said, and seemed to be in a world of her own. 'After all I am seventy-*two*!' she said as it were defiantly at one moment. I said: 'I know. And I'm seventy-four,' which seemed to surprise her. Really the saddest thing was that she *smelled* of old age, something so painful that I hardly like to write it down. I found myself quite longing for her to go, so that my nostrils should be relieved of the aroma of unclean flesh and clothes and of the sight of her brown teeth with gaps between them. Poor Julia – this time when she said her life wasn't worth living and she wished she had the courage to commit suicide I really believed her.

What has touched and flattered me more than anything is that my painter Raymond has invited me to dinner next week. I suppose with him and his 'friend', and perhaps also his 'Mum' of whom he often speaks.

May 20th – and like the best of days in June

I have just spent two days at Oxford, staying with Paul Levy and his girlfriend Penny Marcus in a Jacobean mansion of Cotswold stone set in lavish greenery, and lunched afterwards with Dick and Simonette[1] in their very pretty house in Parktown. I'm left feeling I don't know whom to trust, perhaps I don't trust anyone. How very few people one knows *greatly* respect and cling to the truth. Julia doesn't know what it is. Neither Paul nor Simonette seem to care about it at all. Paul is clever, physically repellent, bulging in front, genial, energetic, a marvellous cook, an eager gardener, an enjoyer, a social climber and snob. Yet in someways likeable and outgoing. His girlfriend a little nipped, 'like a man on a pier' as Virginia said of Henry Lamb, intelligent, quiet. I liked her. I got there for lunch of a miraculous and huge soufflé. Afterwards we walked in the gardens, among the various units of what seemed to be a research town – an anthropologist lived here, a researcher into Jewish history there; there an architect. Along bleached lime avenues that looked French beside the grey stone walls; through the wild garden, the sunken garden, the architect's arboretum, the knot garden. That night there was dinner for eleven – candles along a refectory table, Jacobean surroundings, a fish mousse, roast beef. And the company (Iris Murdoch and John Bayley) rather drunk; a cellist who was giving a concert the next day; her sister

---

1 Nephew of Lytton and his wife.

(a deadly earnest but rather beautiful Carrington-addict) and the sister's male attachment (middle-aged and even more serious – I never saw him smile once) were of the party. On Sunday morning the lawyer of the Strachey Trust arrived, and pounced on the Bloomsbury play, which Paul had also read. They both said it will be a roaring success, and seem to expect me to feel as happy about this as they do since they don't realise what one feels about people one loves being made laughing-stocks in so public a way.

Well, so much for the play. As to Gerald's book, both Jaime and a letter from Janetta to Heywood indicate that Cyril is Janetta's chief concern there. She hasn't written to me about it at all.

Then the Strachey Trust. Paul is busy living a social life and cultivating his garden. He has now added reviewing to his activities and has given me the start of his book on G. E. Moore to read. It is a detailed history of the Apostles, and Moore himself is consigned to two hundred pages.

May 24th

I have been visiting Frances Phipps at Moorfields as often as I can manage. She breaks, as one arrives, into unbridled pauseless talk and throws herself about in her chair, which is surely bad for her? I worry about her, but hope for the best. She is wonderfully charming. My other invalid friend, Joan, came to supper with Eardley on a brief visit to London. She really seemed better. There was, however, a moment of revelation of her least attractive self. Eardley, starry-eyed, was standing over her telling of the joys of painting which had occupied him all day and delayed him. Cutting his words in mid-sentence and shutting her mouth like a trap, Joan turned to me and said, 'Yes. I do think your new decorations are a great success.' It was cruel, but he didn't seem to notice.

Janetta writes saying, 'more trouble with Gerald,' but *only* going into what concerns Cyril, absolutely no reference to whether or not he is angry with me. She just may be coming to Nicky's wedding tomorrow however and I have written in case she doesn't.

There has been considerable silence on the telephone, and a Bank Holiday weekend stretching ahead will bring more, but I'm glad not to have to go away, and various new faces are expected: Magouche, Bunny, possibly Janetta.

Two nights ago I dined with my painter, Raymond, wondering what in the world I should find, though pretty sure he lived with 'my friend', a plain very 'camp' John who came to help with the books. This fellow, John, owns a whole house in Ebury Street and they occupy the basement. Furniture, china and pictures chosen with taste — Regency chairs, white china, several excellent Freuds, an Auerbach, good bird prints. Another guest — 'Doris' — had orange hair and confined her remarks to 'Ye-es!' or 'Oo-oh' on an upward note denoting surprise rather than inquiry. She mumbled (confidentially to me): 'They're such artistic boys — the most artistic boys in London.' Raymond *appeared* looking pretty smashing in a crimson shirt and smart black trousers.

May 27th: Bank Holiday

Janetta came over specially for Nicky's[1] wedding to her Patrick, and this gave enormous pleasure. Slight shrinking beforehand there was, at the prospect of all the elaborate paraphernalia — flags, flowers, etc. — but it was a triumphant success. There were flocks of children, including all their own, running hither and thither wearing pretty coronets of wild flowers. Patrick looked handsomer than I've ever seen him in a pale olive green velvet suit, and Nicky with her dark hair well cut and a charming floating dress, her face one beam of happiness. Among the children was my little Sophie, to whom I gave my Mexican crystal heart. To my great pleasure, several people (most important of course Janetta) came to tell me how 'ravishing' she was and how sweet her smile. Bunny stood by Angelica who, with formidable specs on and a scarf round her head, has suddenly turned into Vanessa. Julian came with me. There was Fanny Garnett, Robert MacGibbon, the Powells and a few other people I knew. The garden was full of flags and flowers and the

---

1 Nicolette Sinclair-Loutit, her eldest child.

ground-floor room, opening on to it, held a long and beautiful Turkish-looking repast, at which we sat on two rows of cushions. Fantasy, imagination, love and happiness infused the whole scene.

Glad not to *have* to go away because of decorations, I stayed in London for the wedding and was rewarded by Janetta coming to dinner on Friday, along with Robert and Julian. First-rate company – Robert, though, set his hair into a badger bristle and showed other signs of incipient desperation. Janetta thought Julian also rather desperate. If so, he was far more controlled, but he is making very great upheavals in his life, planning to give up his job for six months or a year and go to America. Are we going to lose him altogether? It is something he's been pondering for some time and given hints about but obviously not wanted to go into. Janetta entertained us at her most charming, with accounts of Tramores' household enlarged by an enormous Moorish woman whom they picked up in the street and who kisses Janetta whenever she sees her.

I threw one stone into the general pond in the form of my doubts, bred at Oxford, about how many people valued the truth. Robert looked rather sour and said, 'Let me tell you some home truths,' ironically. Julian – I can't remember – but he returned to the subject with Angelica and Bunny at Nicky's wedding.

Before disappearing to Paris Stanley rang up to say that the play is coming on on July 7th.

To see Frances again yesterday and be harrowed by what seemed her misery, near to tears. 'I can't see. This eye is quite blind. I shall never read, and I *live* in books.' Each sentence pierced me like a sword. Have I persuaded her to take part in this Greek tragedy? On the telephone she said to me, 'I can't tell you how much I love you.' But I don't know ... Going out I talked to the Sister and said Lady Phipps seemed very depressed. 'Oh it's because she's going out tomorrow. She has some blood in her eye, but it will go.' 'Will it really? She doesn't seem to believe it. Could she be reassured?' 'She asks the doctor every day and he tells her it will.'

I am so prone to believe what 'They' say but I can't help

wondering. I think Pat would explain, but she's leaving his aegis. The burden of human sorrows weighs on me and induced me to say I'll fetch Faith to tea this afternoon.

Entertaining Faith is literally the only thing I have done successfully this fine Bank Holiday Monday. Otherwise everything I've tried to do I've done badly – whether practise my violin, read philosophy or even write in this diary. Humility, depression, defeatism are the result – not diseases I probably succumb to as often as I should, so I must hope they have a stabilising effect. What is it about Freddie Ayer in particular that gives me a feeling of trying to pick up handfuls of dry sand, which run through my fingers leaving nothing. Or of striving to manipulate something inside my brain which is made of solid rubber and continually bounces back? I think I shall give up trying to read him, *after* forcing my way through this book in a disciplinarian way.

What oh what is there to look forward to? My confidence runs out and hope with it. It seems to me all of a sudden that I only want to be – but am not really – a person who enjoys reading philosophy. Or else think it good for me and do it out of a sort of masochism. Shall I give it all up and be a practising hedonist? No – because the fact that I have read it or thought about it has left its darts of morality in me.

May 29th

Divine summer weather, and general and individual despair. Does the state of the world contribute less to my gloom than the problems of individuals? – I really don't know. What a hollow merry-go-round it is; I don't like to think of Mark Gertler's picture but I do. Yesterday's one gleam in a defeatist and self-depreciatory day was the orchestra, to which Angelica came and played in fine style.

Stanley came to see me in the afternoon and temporarily cheered me by his youth and originality. We went together to look at an exhibition of Lambs and Anreps.

P.m. I've come out to my new square garden; and hearing the door clang behind me gave me a quiet influx of peace; here, sitting on a strong wooden seat in full sun, I have forgotten for an hour the spectres stalking the world, as well as being able to finish, polish off Freddie Ayer, even to enjoy his last chapter on God, Morality and Free Will, all subjects more congenial than the difference between analytical and synthetic propositions.

The shrill chirping of a little London bird, the sooty path, the gently waving trees quieten my restlessness, which I think may be largely a sort of guilt, because I feel I don't do enough for suffering friends.

May 31st

My guilt has concentrated like some horrible ulcer as a result of yet another talk on the telephone to Frances Phipps. Joan said to me that no one 'minded about other people' as much as I did, which – in the light of my feeling I hadn't done enough for *her* – amazed me. As to Frances, what I felt on my end of the telephone was unmitigated torture, and desire to blow my brains out. Her talk gets wilder and wilder, more compulsive, more desperate. 'I want to be *in now*' was something she kept repeating. Well, that isn't mad – it's her way of saying she wants to face the facts whatever they are, but I doubt if she is capable of it. I try to thread my way between her utterances to discover without asking *what* she sees, what she is told to expect. She went to see Pat, but he only had a few moments to spare. 'I love him for being so off-hand.' But she can't and doesn't. And the great question, 'Will she ever be able to read again?' is unaskable. I've come away shaken and shaking.

I turn my mind to last night's evening here with Bunny, Robin and Magouche. Conversation almost entirely *à quatre* until twelve-thirty – nothing could have been more enjoyable, and how Robin blossoms yet more.

June 4th

These fine days are still eaten up with trying to 'comfort the sick' – for that's what it amounts to. To Frances today and found her calmer and more philosophical. After letting her run off at innumerable tangents I faced her with blunt questions about her state. Another visit to Pat told her 'the haemorrhage had stopped.' Is it beginning actually to clear? I can't tell, but in the end she said, 'I shall never read again.' F: 'Have you been *told* that, or are you just thinking it?' 'I think it – but I daren't ask.' F: 'Don't you think it's just that it's going to be very slow?' 'To me slow is never. I'm impatient.' This leaves me with grounds for hope. But surely Pat should tell her what the chances are? He wants her to stay longer where she is. And today's visit was not anguish – we understood each other and I found her much calmer and was able to distract her by talk of Philip and Irish politics and she's ready to go off about the Irish at a touch. She's looked after by white-clad nuns.

Later, over an absurd Bogart spy film he burst out that 'these rotten American films had begun everything. No one thought of honour or patriotism any more. Democracy's a ludicrous farce. Why should it be worse to be a carpenter than anything else?' And so on. 'We shall have to get you a black shirt, Frances, you'll need it. We're in for terrible times – two million unemployed and fighting in the streets.' Luckily I diverted him by showing that I was in fact wearing a black jersey.

Talk to Robert at lunch today about Ireland and principle. We see eye to eye about Ireland but on principle I fear he's unsound: 'In a sort of a way Philip's right.' But he *isn't*, if you take principle to be a moral generalisation based on separate observations. Principle is what Ralph meant when he said, 'There are some things one simply would not do, to gain any end – torture for instance.' I often remember it.

Robert tried to egg me on to fight the 'Play'. But I'm not sure that it isn't only because of the fierce side in him. He thinks that about ten lines of my copyright have been used. Michael Holroyd thinks it will be a flop, disagreeing thereby with Paul Levy. Angelica, seen at the orchestra, doesn't care one way or the other, 'What does it all matter?' she says, and that Leonard always held that such things were of no significance whatever.

June 7th

A morning of incessant harassment by the troubles of friends. Julia first – an SOS delivered in a lost, miserable, drunken voice which couldn't be denied. She was ill (incessant diarrhoea), couldn't eat, confused – the old, old story. Could I come and see her and give her some advice? 'Yes,' I said, 'can I come this morning as I'm off to the country this afternoon.' 'The sooner the better. I don't know what to do and I must have food for the weekend.' I had got, dripping, out of my bath, with dripping (washed) hair, so I promised to ring her back. Meanwhile I rang up and consulted good kind Margaret, who had practical medical suggestions. Then I rang Julia again and suggested bringing her one of the excellent roast chickens from my charcuterie. 'I can't eat chicken.' 'Well, tell me what you'd like.' We boiled it down to ham and tongue, wholemeal bread and watercress, and I added (on spec) cheese, a comice pear and two bananas. Meanwhile the telephone rang again: 'Mowcher Devonshire here. I'm so worried about Frances Phipps.' I think she thought I'd been neglecting her but I think I succeeded in disabusing her. Next David[1] (I was out) to apologise for Mowcher, needlessly. Then I flew round on errands for Julia, Bunny and myself, and finally got into a taxi and sat for half an hour going to Julia. She didn't look too bad, poor unhappy creature, and accepted my offerings quite gratefully. What had happened was that she had 'had a row' with Jenny[2] – i.e. 'told both her and Lawrence that she, Jenny, was a foul bossy bully, and she *is* one too'. So as a result she hadn't been to Leeds for several weeks. Then we had her diarrhoea, the unhappiness 'of five years', the impossibility of coping. We had a practical and sensible talk about her health problems, but it was sad to see her coffined in that tiny attic room. A little conversation about other people and my life. 'What do you do, how do you get through the day, not having to work like most people?' she asked (rather sneeringly). I told her I had no shortage of things to do, but was aware she was prodding me and felt piqued after having been literally rushed off my feet and set back £2 on her behalf that very morning. Then her acidity emerged in mocking dove's laughter over my minding about the play. I said I was afraid I must be off

---

1 Cecil.

2 Lawrence's second wife.

and she came to the top of the stairs and said, 'That wasn't the main thing I wanted your advice about. It was to ask if you had any suggestions how I could get shopping done and food cooked.' I told her I was afraid I hadn't. The only way was to do it oneself. 'I can't make myself. I thought you might know some bureau or agency that would provide someone.' I said, 'No – I don't know a single one,' and bolted down the stairs feeling as though a puff adder had been making a cloud of poison round me.

Once in the train for Ipswich a certain calm settled and I elapsed into my researches into human credulity apropos of a book, *Supernature* by name, that has practically hooked Eardley into Rosamond's camp. What *is* Supernature anyway? The Cosmos = Nature, what is known, will be one day or perhaps never, all included. I kept a seat for Desmond who dashed in and retired to the first class. Anne and Heywood joined us, well and welcoming, glorious dears. The green peace of Suffolk under a grey sky. Asked Des if Pat had said anything about Frances, but he hadn't seen him. Damn. I had promised to ring her up on arrival and did, but she was confused and thought I was still in London and began talking Irish politics. Desmond kindly volunteered to ring up Pat and did, but came back saying he had 'done badly'. As for Julia, I realise what makes my heart sink when she sends for me – it's that I know that when things are unbearable she wants a whipping-boy, and I'm destined to be it. I knew it subconsciously as I headed towards her in the hideous traffic.

June 10th

Alas the weekend's over, and I truly feel wrenched by leaving. Desmond reduces Heywood and me to wild giggles and Anne to tremendous 'Haw! Haws!' We are infected by his gestures and little scurrying movements; he left all the tickets at home as usual, and went into endless reasons why it wasn't his fault and he hadn't really, or anyway never before. His interest in everything and everyone is boundless.

I had two fine walks with Heywood, good talk with him, and with Anne alone (which I don't always manage). On Saturday there was Gladwyn Jebb's lunch party, with lots and lots of familiar faces and cold rainy weather keeping us indoors. On Sunday my two musical events – *Manfred* in the afternoon, extremely exciting to Heywood and me, less so to Desmond who sat with Anne madly flapping about between Byron's text and the score. There was a fine reading of the verse by the Manfred, Dadie and others. I really loved it. Byron very much in the current of our weekend thought and talk, but again he is a bit outside Desmond's sphere of interests. A Haydn quartet produced in me that feeling of total magnetisation and satisfaction that is the summit of what music can give one. The Schubert quartet was a lovely work though it is less powerful.

Oh how important – it is borne in on me by seeing Julia – to be as *kind* as possible as much of the time, and also to keep one's mind as closely glued to reality as the leader of the Gabrieli Quartet (a fine player) kept his bow mated to his strings.

I forgot to mention lunching at Claridge's last week with Derek Jackson and his French wife, Mary, Philip, and Patrick Kinross, surrounded by a display of wealth, flunkeyism and snobbish consciousness of superiority.

The two millionaires talked aggressive fascism and Derek as usual boasted about his scientific eminence. I ordered salmon and was given sole.

Margaret to dinner last night. She had been to see Julia and found her 'fat and well'. She had said of my visit, 'I asked Frances for advice and she brought me ham.'

June 16th

Sunday of a weekend at Crichel – perfect June weather, hot with a light breeze: Raymond contented and benign, Dadie stimulating, Desmond excitable. Myself? Finding it impossible not to enjoy being spoiled and made much of by them all, feeling happily at ease and enjoying the dollops of rich sauces and equally rich flatteries ladled out to me. But one ghastly spectre haunted the background. On Friday night Pat arrived, obviously dead beat, and Raymond asked him about Frances' state. His reply was not only unsatisfactory, but surprisingly unfeeling. Raymond agreed when I asked him later; he had obviously assumed all was well before. 'She'll settle down in time,' he said, and I shut up, and shut away the cold horror I felt inside myself and shortly went up to bed, unfairly resenting Pat for causing this delightful old lady to lose even some months of reading through a magnifying-glass. There's occasionally something rather insensitive in him; one sees it in his roughly finished-off red features and clumsy movements. How can he have the delicacy necessary for these delicate operations? The extraordinary thing was that when, next day, he and I went for a walk alone together, he was perfectly charming and companionable – I couldn't help responding at the same time as feeling the echo of last night's horror, and the momentary determination that if I ever have a cataract I will never go to him, that I will never send another patient to him, nor to anyone.

June 18th

Weekend continued hot, delicious, with croquet, music, talk; only visitor Peter Heyworth. 'A crisis,' said Raymond on Sunday night. Desmond had signified his desire to stay on till Tuesday. Mrs Hughes had been near tears, said that her agreement had only been for weekends. Raymond shrank into himself and delegated Pat to tell Des it wouldn't do. Talks went on behind closed doors, and finally compromise was reached with smiles all round. Desmond came down to Monday breakfast beaming like a rising sun and saying he had heard on the wireless a bomb had gone off in the House of Commons. True enough – so it had, as we discovered by appalling traffic jams in the purlieus on arrival in London. Such strangeness, yet it doesn't give one a twinge. When I remember the malaise and anxiety of the war – and the present state of the world but so unlike it – I wonder at the casual fatalistic way it is accepted.

June 20th

How shall I come to terms with the various emotional volcanoes which send up their explosive flares as soon as I wake? First and foremost the worrying situation about Frances Phipps. Her own doctor and her daughter now seem to understand the outlook is bad. Then there's the approach of the horrid play, the increasing sense of political and economic doom, and my personal financial uncertainties. I visited my accountant at Mungo's yesterday hoping to find all in order and be able to clarify my position and know how much I possess. Far from it. I liked and respected him more than before, but am none the wiser about my richness or poorness.

Several talks with invalids. Frances – brave, and not (what I suppose I have secretly dreaded) seeming to hate me and feel I am the source of her troubles. Also she told me she had been aware of a patch of blue sky – through the operated eye I *think* – which sent my spirits rocketing in over-compensatory sympathy. But how people love to talk about their ailments. I do not mean Frances; I press her to, and she *is* so often evasive. Yesterday I had Kitty, today Jill's[1] husband Patrick. What eagerness bubbles in the voice that retails their symptoms. One must learn somehow to avoid that temptation whenever the time comes.

June 23rd

Weekend in London, a rarity. I had two invitations to leave but decided against on various counts, altruistic and egotistic.

Yesterday was anything but solitary. To see Frances in the morning. Found her flushed and excitable and raging against the hardness and obstinacy of the nuns. She is a mass of contradictions. A crucifix and a rosary lay beside her bed, as well as innumerable touching scrawls on bits of paper in separate plastic bags. She sees *something* – but what? One moment she tells you she has seen 'blue sky' through the 'golden eye' (Pat's), that she sees 'better through it each day'; the next that she sees 'worse every day'. I do understand his exasperation with her. Took her temperature and found it round about 101. Tried to telephone her GP. 'No line,' said the nuns down below in the office. In came a nice couple of grown-up grandchildren and went off with consoling words to telephone him. Later I left her in their hands and with doctor coming, after holding the fort for an hour.

---

1 My niece, née Rendel.

Exhausted.

Georgia to lunch, very different and very nice, but she stayed till nearly four. Her trouble is the usual indecision and 'putting off'. She wants to be married, but feels it is awful to confine yourself to one person, and shut out other possibilities – this at least is how I translate what she says. But she is now well over thirty and silver threads are appearing.

I have dedicated today to my financial problems and business (Sophie's school insurance), but (like Georgia) put off, and put off, and now it's twelve o'clock. I've done nothing but read the Sunday papers.

June 28th

Now a week later, grey windy weather and many doubts about everything.

Janetta has paid yet another visit here, delightful in her confidence, but making one wonder about her occasional restlessness. There was yet another seventieth birthday party at Patrick Kinross's, which depressed her 'by the general antiquity'. Something of Madame Tussaud about it perhaps. Betjeman had written a poem for the occasion but was in Oxford getting a degree, so Patrick and Tom Driberg stood like two South Sea idols in front of the fireplace while the latter read it aloud. 'Roy, this is Frances you're talking to,' Billa Harrod said to her somewhat gaga and sozzled spouse, who had alarmed me (as he is invariably wrong) by saying that 'Things' had never been better. Jock Murray spoke of a new possible translation (the second of late but do I want them? I'm reading a Carpentier for Gollancz at the moment). Henry Harrod looked haggard but attractive. Berkeleys newly knighted; Blakistons. All silver-haired and bulky and, yes I suppose so, out of the last volume of Proust.

I have had Dadie and Eardley to a jolly lunch to discuss a trip to Holland in September, and I spent a long time with Frances yesterday, reading aloud to her and listening to her vagaries ... She lay in a prison room with prison bars against burglars obscuring the light and comfort of an old-fashioned sort stifling her. (She is in the house of her sister Lady Vansittart, and burst out, 'Oh I *hate* it here, Frances'). The grim butler who led me

298

to her room with its rich antediluvian furniture would alone have finished me off.

I'm off to Kitty's for the weekend and then – next week – to Bunny.

July 5th

Off with Bunny, through driving rain down the repulsive road from London to Eastbourne. The endlessness of London in that direction, of its shops, huge WORDS everywhere, what ugliness! How unliveable-in it is. I'm keying myself up to take the strain of travel, which consists in trying to strike a balance between calm (lack of fuss) and alertness, and that isn't easy. We spent the night at Cobbe Place with Quentin and Olivier[1]; turned off the great road firing off its lorries like machine-gun bullets and were at once into a new world – an unkempt but flowery garden and then Olivier's warm welcome into the spacious house with beauty, books and pictures everywhere, rich colours. Life after anti-life. Cressida, aged fifteen, a tall girl of staggering pre-Raphaelite beauty with a heart-shaped face, long thick gold hair, a column neck and wide-set pool-like eyes, has the *confidence* of most Bloomsbury children and will certainly bowl over a lot of young men.

We talked and talked in the large sitting-room, settled in its four corners with drinks. Bunny descended with his silver hair brushed and shining, wearing a sky-blue linen jumper. He goes from strength to strength and almost makes one believe in immortality. Quentin and Olivier talked about the fascination of Virginia's diaries and made me want to survive the few years until they are published. We asked if anything would have to be suppressed. They hoped not though she 'could often be pretty savage'. Like what? 'Well, after lending her house to Sydney Waterlow she complained of the smell of stale semen.'

In bed the next morning; the weather is appalling: not a gleam of sun, obsessively tossing trees, rain. I dread the Channel crossing, but believe I haven't revealed that I do. And here and now I lie in a comfortable bed in fine linen sheets,

---

1 Bell.

surveying the horrors I leave behind – renewed trouble over my flat, colossal tax demands. My foundations rock under me. Then there's the Luke play. Janetta sensitively suggested going to the first preview and rang me up yesterday morning with a careful, detailed account. She went with Raymond and they both thought it awful, futile and vulgar, but the audience laughed quite a lot. She thought Virginia the worst, ranting and raving. Carrington hopeless, Ralph 'terribly unattractive', Lytton much the best. 'Did you ever feel you'd like to leave?' 'Oh *yes*, and Raymond and I talked and got ticked off. The dreaded author and his wife were there and I longed for them to have a curtain call so that we could shout *Boo*, but of course there wasn't.' I don't think I greatly care, and hope I shan't in future. Joan, less aware and less sensitive, rang up to say the Blakistons found it moving and touching. I said, 'That's exactly what *I don't want to hear.*'

Evening: To France with Bunny

At Jumièges in a humble but pretentious inn, ours being full. When it came to the point I didn't fear or mind the crossing though many paper bags were in use. I ate a snack on a tray, read and dozed and read again and looked at the grey-green sea and now we are in France.

Mine is a yonghy bonghy bò room, no curtains, a dim light over my feet. Bunny is good company though rather deaf in the car. The Bac over the Seine gives a loud bellow into the sweet French greenery and I am sleepy …

July 6th

I liked waking, and soon after six have removed my mackintosh from the window and lie in the faint grey morning light, considering. Considering what? All yesterday's themes: the Bells, Bloomsbury, the play.

We had a shocking dinner of frozen foods quickly hotted up and expensive. I'm determined to take my turn at driving.

July 7th

On my bed at Villeneuve-les-Périgord trying to get over my

deep sadness because I've lost my darling ring, the one that seemed part of me and of R. too, which was why instead of putting it in my bag when my finger swelled from a mosquito bite at Richelieu I put it on my little finger, unable to part with it, and it slipped off, perhaps when laying out things for a picnic and moving because of ants. I blame those ants. I loved it, I mourn for it, I don't think Bunny realises how much, nor do I want him to. I would almost rather have lost my finger.

The fatal night we spent in a delightful little inn at Richelieu, after a spell of driving when I hadn't been happy with Bunny's gears. My bedroom was lined with pink pears and green sparrows, among which lurked invisible biters. When next day I saw the ring had gone I couldn't believe it, I had a sense of nightmare. We searched and searched, in vain. And though I said to myself, 'Things are only things,' I felt too sick to eat. I drove to take my mind off it, and understand the gears now. I'm going to buy myself another ring such as R. would have liked to buy me, and it shall be his ring. We almost expected to get to Charry tonight, but settled here. Bunny thinks it expensive – it's frightfully cheap, £2 about, and we've had a good meal.

July 9th

Yesterday morning we left Villeneuve, a nice arcaded little town. It was very hot as we wound through the woods, to arrive at Charry mid-morning. Bunny has sensibly taken over what was the spare room with all his books and I have the studio, which now has a tiled floor, electric lights, curtains, a basin with hot and cold and bidet. So it was the familiar round of laying out thick pottery plates, old glasses, a splendid Wensleydale cheese and some cherries on the round table under the oak. Aired Henrietta's sheets on the line and remade the bed, unpacked everything and spread myself. After a little snoozing, in what I thought was the cool of the evening I walked up to the limestone plateau, where it was grilling hot and the low sun shone through white grasses and slim flowers like melilot and campanula and cupidone (yellow, purple and blue) and shone on a carpet of little scrambling ones. I thought I must at once ask to read Bunny's last story, *Puss in Boots*, and was enjoying it in its way, which is not mine at all (because it represents his love of the archaic, and of peasant processes and the technical names for them, and calls animals 'beasts') when I saw two figures pass the window and heard a voice say, 'It's Frances.' It was Rose Gathorne-Hardy on her honeymoon with her husband Ian, carrying in her hand her own ill-written p.c. announcing her visit, which had got no further than the letter basin at the château. We sat and drank under the tree. She prattled charmingly and disarmingly, but Bunny was anxious because his chanterelles were cooking and he had no dinner to offer them. He had really, as I discovered later, a Spanish ham hanging by the fireplace, but it was too soon for him to be his usual hospitable self. He asked them to sign the visitors' book and that pleased them. Rose said, 'I've never signed my new name before! Do you know what it is? Battye!'

10.30 a.m.

Sitting on a bank outside the Mairie of St Martin des Vers,[1] whither poor Bunny had been summoned as *témoin* in an absurd law case between Madame Blanc (who bought Angelica's cottage) and Monsieur Bru, a neighbour, over a tiny *parcelle* of land. It was a Jules Romains scene. Cars drove up and disgorged lawyers and experts, more *témoins*. The key of course was missing and had to be got. Bunny resented being called back to the scene of lost happiness for so trifling a cause and resolved to be 'frosty'. The Frogs all treated him respectfully and well, and took his evidence first. When he reappeared, looking large and distinguished, an old peasant couple greeted him with open arms and kisses. I didn't take to them much and thought they were enjoying the proceedings in the wrong way and determined to have a finger in the pie, while the old lady, who hadn't a tooth in her head, but the beady eyes of a hen who knows where all the best grains are to be found.

We had got up at six-thirty this morning and driven through Cahors and beyond in morning mists. As we started home and I tried to see if the pale flowers under the cliffs were small yellow

---

1 A small cottage which Bunny had lived in with Angelica.

foxgloves (as they in fact turned out to be), Bunny talked sadly about the way this visit to St Martin had revived his past life with Angelica. We discussed how to avoid the pain of dwelling on past sorrows: he thought one must live in the present and future, I that one must learn to enjoy remembering past happiness. One can – but then without warning a knife pierces the woof of memory and gives one a fierce stab. Bunny and I have plenty to say to each other, and I think we understand each other. Last night it was about values and morality, kindness and cruelty.

July 10th

I wake early, open the wide double doors of my studio and look out on the quiet valley. I am content in my studio – there's plenty of space, a large solid table to spread my flower books on,[1] a comfortable wide bed, opposite which hangs a striking portrait by Nerissa[2] of the old woman we saw at St Martin yesterday. Rugs and plates on the walls testify to journeys to Spain. The floor gets covered with bits from the roof, so yesterday I got a broom and swept it. The rough stone walls collect cobwebs, and there are typical Garnett collections of nameless objects – old musty tins, tubing, corncobs, the only cupboard is full of them.

After yesterday's *procès* we shopped in Cahors, then back to lunch off Spanish ham, salad and cheese. We both drink a lot of not very good red wine. I had an evening walk in the valley.

After dinner we sit on two upright armchairs and talk. Homosexuals and bisexuals was one of our topics. B. is hostile to homos and prefers 'real men'. Then he told me the subject of his new book – a true story about Constance Garnett's grandfather who was a fisherman on the bleak east coast of Scotland, was press-ganged in the early eighteen hundreds, carried off to sea and rose to be the captain of a sloop which fought at Trafalgar. Hearing that his ship was putting in at Plymouth his young wife walked all the way to see him and then walked back.

---

1 When abroad I always collected wild flowers.
2 Bunny and Angelica's daughter.

He was at sea ten years and that was the gap between their children. Then he trained as a naval architect, went to Russia, worked for Tsar Nicholas I and was buried at Kronstadt. I'm always interested in all Bunny has to tell about that remarkable woman, his mother. I'm reading one of her Turgenev stories now.

July 11th

A quiet, very hot day. Wrote to Henrietta, read Turgenev (with disappointment because like Henry James he deteriorates when he gets into the world of Supernature). After tea I went off with my basket and was drawn irresistibly to the limestone plateau, gazing at the small creeping plants growing between extinct orchids, and then on to where the lavender fields made a purple sea alarmingly abuzz with bees. In the evening Bunny and I tried in vain to listen to *Kaleidoscope* where, as I guessed, they were reviewing the first night of the play, but through so much fading out and throbbing as to be virtually inaudible. This led to talk of Bloomsbury and Bunny bringing out a book by Maynard with biographical studies of Frank Ramsey and old Willie Johnson,[1] a refreshing antidote, and as good at quelling distaste for Luke's play as our visit to Cobbe.

July 12th

Hotter still. Each morning in nightgown and dressing gown I wander up the grassy bank to the cottage, and find Bunny with bowls of delicious coffee, croissants, butter and honey. Then I bath and dress and read or study my collection of plants, soaking overnight in a stout brown jug. No use writing letters which won't get to England before me.

An outing today to fetch Bunny's cat Tiber from his friends the Ballards some twelve miles away: Bill Ballard is a tall raw American ex-architect and possibly ex-alcoholic. I liked him – over our excellent lunch he told me very simply how after the last war he felt an imperative need to get away and rest from his ghastly experiences, and had gone to Mexico and loved it. His

---

1 Professor of Logic at Cambridge.

wife Pam is a gentle soft creature, not pretty but loveable. As we left she said warm things in my ear about Bunny — 'he's got such *quality*'. They are rich and have made a converted farmhouse rather too grand, looking out over the plain and distant hills, with masses of brilliant flowers and a swimming-pool beside which sat a slim elegant lady called Lady Lovat, whose rather beautiful face fell into deep sadness in repose. We swam, ate lunch, drank pink wine and Bunny was reunited with Tiber. The poor cat mewed all the way home in his basket and looked round anxiously with heaving flanks on arrival, bewildered and frightened. He ran in and out of the house, but remained aloof till the evening when acceptance of reality dawned, he stopped panting and stretched himself in furry relaxation on the carpet. When later a thunderstorm broke he came to my studio and mewed to be let in, where he got on to my bed and made a great fuss of me.

Earlier I had been reading and talking about Maynard's beliefs, and feeling astonishment, by no means for the first time, at the very potent influence of Moore's puritanical views on such brilliant and pleasure-loving people as the Bloomsburies: also the religious attitude to Moore's views of people to whom religion was anathema. Pleasure, and especially Bentham, were *out*. They held indeed that 'good states of mind' were generally painful, and pleasant ones inclined to be suspect. Maynard wrote extremely amusingly about their views and exposed much that was ludicrous in them and much that was left out – all forms of activity for instance. The good consisted in contemplating the beloved person and beautiful works of art and nature. Physical beauty in the beloved was given slight precedence over mental qualities. Yet after criticising these flaws in the theory he concludes that it was the best available. And Bunny seemed to agree with him, though shrewdly divining that Moore's personal charm had much to do with the matter. Yet I feel that for all his charm Moore was a monk, a Puritan, spiritually speaking. I remember the constriction and immaturity of his handwriting in his letters to Desmond, in his way of expressing himself even. And his petty jealousies – of Bertie Russell in particular. To Bunny I deplored the Bloomsburies' religious acceptance of Moore's Bible; it was like James's of the Freudian bible. Bunny thought such an attitude beneficial or necessary to the young. I said they couldn't soon enough discover that their thoughts and beliefs were their own to take them whither they chose.

July 14th: In bed, 7.30 a.m.

After Friday night's thunderstorm yesterday was grey, cool and showery. I woke saddened by the sound of drops pattering on my skylight. I'm haunted too by thoughts of my return, with an accompaniment of indecision and lack of confidence. I meant to tackle my attempt at a memoir[1] here, and nowhere could be more suitable, but I make every excuse to look up flowers instead. I hate what I write when I look at it again. I recoil with a feeling of distaste though I know I can write decent English. What pleases me sometimes when I set it down horrifies me next moment. Yesterday we drove to lunch with the Elstobs – an old farm, rather 'Bedalian' in atmosphere. I hope Bunny doesn't realise that I don't take to them. Bysshe's head, now trimmed with a grizzled beard, is too big for his body, his voice too suave, he postures embarrassingly. Meg is a big coarse greedy good-natured woman who behaves like a small skittish one and expresses commonplace ideas in commonplace phrases. I know one can often get through the outer casing of anti-charm, but here I haven't succeeded, and have to force myself to look at her. This feeling of antipathy made me defend, too hotly perhaps, the view that though equality was unattainable in many things, it was desirable to aim at it in others. This at lunch, and against Bysshe and Bunny. I don't think they liked me any more than I did them.

Bunny has started writing his new book. Our regular evening talk began with his reading me a letter from Fanny[2] – an odd mixture of savagery and pathos, articulately expressed with a degree of communication unusual between parent and child. The savagery was aimed at poor Bunny's letters to her in which

---

1 For the Memoir Club.
2 Twin to Nerissa.

he had tried to convey his affection through accounts of Tiber's fights and other natural history *faits divers*. She suspected him of a desire for 'sugar-plums' – i.e. gratitude or gratifying remarks. I think this had wounded him deeply, and I felt wounded on his behalf but we both quickly assumed an armour of cotton wadding that I don't think grew of its own accord. There was however certain hurt pride in Fan's own self-analysis when Nerissa had her breakdown and swept the rest of the family into hectic mutual psychoanalysis, perhaps Bunny, with his feet solidly planted on the ground, his violent likes and dislikes, and sometimes his prejudices, may have seemed an alien. But Fan's letter was thoughtful as well as tortured; it took nothing for granted and plunged a fork into the subsoil. Our next subject – whence we got there I don't remember – was Blake, and Bunny read me some. Then Herodotus and the Scythians. How I enjoy his memory for what he has read.

July 15th

Yesterday the sky was washed clean, and it being much less hot I walked across and up to the other side of the valley, never seeing a soul, perhaps because it was Quatorze Juillet. After lunch I carried out my self-promise and tried to face my memoir, but in a moment I found myself getting into the course and development of my beliefs and ideas and I'm not sure if that's a good thing to indulge in. Later I discussed writing with Bunny and the problem of constantly wanting to rewrite, change and improve or delete. He said, 'Oh, of course if one gives way to *that* ...' and went on about 'bursts of inspiration' in which he wrote straight ahead. I think he is a little *too* uncritical. He is now writing his new book about his ancestors straight on to the typewriter.

Delicious dinner of veal in a tasty sauce, which tasted of the marsala advised by Elizabeth David and was I'm sure as good. Afterwards more talk, more taking down of books from the shelves and reading aloud.

July 16th

Gliding smoothly in the train towards Paris, my carriage filled with a too talkative Dutch family, reading in my *Figaro* about yesterday's frightening coup in Cyprus and the possible death of Makarios. Fine rain streaks the windows. Yesterday (hot) I had a last walk, through the château woods finding a red hellebore. Surfacing, I saw the lavender crop being cut and stacked, sending off an intoxicating scent but leaving shaven tufts where the purple spikes had been. I went to tea with Angela Derville[1] in the afternoon; we sat in a sixteenth-century summer-house drinking it from eggshell cups. She started with a rather hostessy manner which thawed amazingly as we talked over old times, friends and her relations. Then she confided that Alec had been 'a strange father', but she had got closer to him at the end of her life; Barbie[2] was more like a sister, she felt, than Sheelah.[3] Bunny cooked what he typically called a 'fowl' for my last dinner. He hasn't let me do any cooking, only washing up and preparations.

So that pleasant episode is over, and it's 'What's next?'

How much shall I mind that wretched play? I know now that I shan't go and see it.

July 19th

London again, and I'm bristling a little as a result of a conversation on the telephone with Angelica about Luke's play. She supports it more than any other friend of mine has, yet she knew nearly all the people in it. She kept remorselessly telling me the plot. F: 'Yes, yes, I've read the script lots of times, and I thought it quite awful.' A: 'Well, you can't always tell from reading a play what it'll be like on the stage, but *I* thought it funny; I laughed a lot, and it brought out Bloomsbury wit, and Lytton was very good indeed – exactly like him. What Virginia had to say was rather awful – Oh yes, of course you read it – but my friend Yvonne Mitchell was so absolutely *brilliant*, and in fact looked almost exactly like Virginia, so that it carried it through.' She told me afterwards that Harold Hobson's review

---

1 Née Penrose, wife of the lavender grower.

2 Her step-sister.

3 Her sister.

had such a bad effect on audiences that they nearly took it off at once, but now it's picked up again. When I said I wasn't going, had no desire to whatever, she was quite astonished. I told her I was interested in other people's reactions however. 'Yes, I thought of you while I was there,' she said, but didn't say what, and I credit her now with too little imagination. Or it may be that her vision of Bloomsbury, and of Virginia in particular, is so emotional and vivid that it veils what's before her eyes; because another actress Virginia (who came here – unspeakably prim and yet vulgar in pink silk pyjamas) also struck Angelica as 'remarkably like her'. I've heard from Stanley that rumours are afoot that 'the play is coming off'. God grant it may.

By contrast to Angelica, Julia last night was wildly critical of the play. I spent the best evening I've had with her for some time. Drunk at first, and reeling alarmingly about in her tiny flat, not remembering what one had said five minutes earlier, as the evening developed she sobered up and was interesting and funny about writing. She has at last gone to the dentist who looked into her mouth, started back in horror and said her teeth were all brown, rotten and hollow and must come out. She surprised me by the modest courage – I can think of no better words – with which she said this, adding: 'What *can* I expect when I've not been to the dentist *nor even brushed my teeth* for years.'

July 20th: Stowell
Robert gave a champagne cocktail party to a lively lot of friends, and (though I didn't find out till I'd gone home to give Julian dinner) to Cynthia also. I'm sorry not to have seen and talked to her. Robert is a magnificent host. Next day we lunched together and he told me he gave dinner to nearly thirty people at the Neal Street Restaurant afterwards. 'He must be mad,' said Allan Hare, thinking what it must have cost.

July 22nd: Stowell
Frances Phipps is really better, she sees almost as much as we do and why she doesn't read as much is a mystery. I paid her a visit and she came back to lunch. Mary has been really good to her.

Philip is abstracted and gloomy. The Graeco-Turkish crisis has manured his most militarist instincts. I felt I was out of favour, though Mary swears not. When someone wanted to know who it was who said, 'If it came to a choice between my friend and my country I hope I should have the courage to choose my friend.' 'E. M. Forster,' I told them. P: 'And what do you think about it, Frances?' I gave myself time for thought. F: 'Well. I rate friendship very highly, and as I would hate to say anything to upset you, Philip, but dislike not telling the truth, I think we'll leave it at that.' He roared with laughter. One never knows which way his cat will jump.

Mary is very sweet and kind to everyone and mellows every year. I was amused by the feline ballet movements accompanying Page the butler's goodnight to us both, while with a near-wink seeming to say, 'We all know Sir Philip's mad, don't we, my lady?'

July 23rd
Oh Julia, Julia, Julia, Julia. She has rung me up all today starting early about 8 a.m. in a voice of inspissated gloom. She's desperate, ill, suicidal, wants to be looked after, is coming out in bruises from within, will go out and buy aspirin and kill herself. I went round to see her (through crowds on a hot afternoon; Eros has filled up again with repellent hippies). Tried to talk her into some sense, but it's hard work. At one moment she says she's got no one to cook or work for her; then what a bore it is that she has a handsome young Hungarian student, doing more or less nothing for £3, then her 'secretary', then a Greek lady, etc. etc. She wants to go into a nursing home, or hire a nurse (nanny?) to look after her; had booked a room in a hotel at Shaftesbury for a week. It would cost her £70. She *must* see her doctor, rings him up and finds she has already got an appointment. In short, she's in a rare old muddle – but truly unhappy I fear.

July 25th
Two Bloomsbury hounds have been to see me. A young don of French literature, Fawcett by name, from Leicester, came to lunch yesterday and was perfectly charming, bright sparkling

black eyes, as intelligent as anything, lots of questions to ask. I really enjoyed his company, though in the middle of our lunch (and earlier this morning) worse calls from Julia came crashing through the ether. In a voice so disintegrated that I felt she was acting she said she 'couldn't go on living', was collapsing, 'feel like I'm dying somehow, think I'm having a nervous breakdown; what can I do? I can't go to Shaftesbury, I can't face the weekend in London. I've got my Greek lady coming this afternoon – I've given her your telephone number and address and told her to ring you any time. She's going to find a nursing home and take me to it this afternoon.' I felt a very heavy pistol was being held at my head: Why wasn't I, her oldest friend there, looking after her, putting off the professor who had come all the way from Leicester to see me? I said, 'But Julia, you told me you were going to the dentist this afternoon, and had an appointment with your doctor tomorrow' (i.e. today). 'Oh yes, but I'm much too ill to face the dentist and I can't possibly wait till tomorrow to see the doctor.'

So, full of remorse, as soon as Fawcett had left (and left me – though I enjoyed his visit – with that drained feeling given one by trying to get things right, to tell the truth), I rang up Margaret at Cambridge, asked her for Julia's doctor's name. Smith! It would be, but she knew his number. 'Tell him Julia was in a psychiatric ward for nine weeks three years ago,' were her parting words. I rang him, and got him, and told him. 'Tell her to ring me up,' was his reply.

First thing this morning I rang Julia to know how she was. Very perky she sounded, brisk as a bee. 'What *do* you think? My doctor sent a *nurse* round to see me at nine this morning. I sent her away, *of course*. I've got Miss Twemlow coming this afternoon to take me to the doctor in a taxi and cook me some food and she'll be much cheaper than a nurse.' Nothing at all about suicide or nursing homes. 'But will you be all right over the weekend?' 'Oh yes, Miss Twemlow will come on Saturday and leave something for Sunday.'

Well, what will it be next I wonder? 'Miss Twemlow hasn't come, so now I must start all over again *with no one to look after me*.' (?)

I won't respond to wolf wolf so violently next time. My heart really did go pit-a-pat over it all. I think I'll just tell her to take a taxi and come round here.

Today's Bloomsburian was a real horror. His rosebud features and egomania corresponded to the compulsive neatness of his writing. He bored me stiff as cardboard, and stayed two mortal hours, after which I sent him away. But I fear I was much too nice to him and he may want to come again. Most of the time he talked boastfully about himself, mispronouncing every name of all the people he pretended to know. Crikey!

August 2nd

Feeling set up by an extremely enjoyable evening with Georgia, Peter Eyre and Robert here last night. Lots of laughter and talk, and I think everyone liked everyone else. Peter arrived breathless to say, '*Bloomsbury* is coming off in five weeks.' I rather hoped it might be sooner – it's not going well from what Keith Prowse told me, and Stanley said there were parties of schoolchildren in a far from full house. Peter also said the cast couldn't understand why it should come off, and were too deeply involved in the play to realise how bad it was. Also that Massey thinks Raymond is to blame for killing the play by telling Harold Hobson to pan it, also that Eardley had written to him – Massey – about it, what I don't know.

A mad letter came to me yesterday from a female living in a castle in Wales who wants to write Carrington's life because 'a very disturbing young poet had told her she was like her', and because though 'up to now I have only been a dreadful but grateful bookworm nostalgically nibbling at the phosphorescent aura of the Bloomsbury group', she is convinced that 'the co-operation of Carrington's friends and contemporaries will rescue me and drag me out of my conventional rut'. She belongs she says to 'a young generation of cynical and iconoclastic wolves and yet because I fell in love with Carrington so madly and utterly I believe in her and know that I will be able to tiptoe gently back into the past since this is the only way to capture shadows.' She requests an interview, which request I have declined, with the suggestion that she abandons her project.

5 p.m.

Julia to lunch with me at my pub. She crawled up my stairs carrying a huge heavy handbag, which she contrived to drop twice however, so that all its contents were disgorged, on the way to the Turk's Head; also to fall on all fours on the stairs. She is really most dreadfully pathetic, and when she says, 'I really think I'm senile. I forget everything the next minute,' I'm inclined to think she's right. The knots she ties herself into beggar all description. She may go to Italy with Ian Angus and his female friend (Mrs Adrian Stokes). So, she thought, a passport must be got. 'But they want to know such extraordinary things, like the date and place of Olivier Strachey's birth.' Luckily she had brought her old passport with her – it was virgin, but only required to be renewed for five years, as I pointed out to her. She had gone so far as to get a copy of her divorce from her lawyers. Then she hunted for a bit of paper on which she had written the cost of the Italian hotel, but it was unintelligible. I turned it over and saw scrawled there, 'Go out and buy 2 bottles of aspirins and kill myself.' If death could strike her down in the street it would be the best thing for her as she gets no pleasure from life, and said that the last five weeks had been the most agonising ever: 'Lawrence away, all my friends on holiday (who?) and no help to be got.' (She has dozens.) We talked about the situation at Leeds – it's not only that she bursts out rudely to Jenny at mealtimes (the only time they meet) but she wrote Lawrence a letter telling him all his friends despised Jenny and thought her stupid and dull. As he said, 'that doesn't help', but the trouble is she thinks it humiliates *him*. She admits she says rude things to Jenny out of 'desire to cause pain'. I even ventured to suggest her biting them back unsaid. She doesn't consider the possibility of trying to control an impulse: 'some people can't.' Finally, almost as exhausted as she was, I got her into a taxi with, I must say, infinite relief.

Another day with Sophie, brought here by Fanny Garnett (voiceless and craving brandy, and curiously miles away yet at the same time attractive – attractive as a young man is attractive). After lunch Sophie read some Schumann correctly, carefully and slowly on the piano – her ear is good, she always knows if she's gone wrong. In the evening to *Sherlock Holmes* (theatre not cinema), not very good, and then I drove her back to Islington and myself back here and flopped into bed. She said to me, 'You've never *never* been unkind to me,' a testimonial I was mightily glad to hear and shall cherish, though I suppose I spoil her.

August 4th
Weekend at Pitts Deep, with its usual blend of magic beauty, hard physical toil, repose, and heavy weather from Susan.[1] This was really rather worse than usual – I couldn't see that providing supper of soup, cold meats and fried potatoes should have taken so long and so much yelling, especially as I was typing her article for the *Listener* while she did it. Robin came to dinner and drove me down through a marvellous night lit by a harvest moon.

I'm enjoying the outdoor work and it's a change from my London life: dead-heading and weeding a brick path and a flower-bed.

The great joy of the weekend, a joy whose savagery has quite surprised me, was seeing the words 'Last two weeks' in the advertisements for the Bloomsbury play. So Peter Eyre meant that the whole run was five weeks, not five weeks *more*. I wake up each morning thinking with vicious delight of Peter Luke's disappointment, the intensity of which is I suppose a measure of how much I have minded it. A letter from Dick Saunders[2] this morning asks for details about it, and hopes 'that poor Ralph whose nature combined so much courage and fire with sweetness and warm humanity is not taking another beating'.

August 12th
A sad wet Monday morning and I've woken very early. I think my weekend dashes among human beings are more important to me than I know, and that I could never stand Julia's hermit life.

---

1 Campbell.
2 American professor who wrote a Life of Lytton.

Even one day of total solitude, as this is likely to be, is almost too much. For Sophie's birthday I went to the little grey stone cottage Angelica had taken for the Purbeck Music School. How pretty these rough little quarryman's villages are, strung along the green ridge, with the milky blue sea lying below. Not one shop in ours, and you walk along a medieval footpath and over a stile to where great blocks of white Portland stone have been hewed out of the spine of the land and neatly stacked. Many thoughts about Angelica and her twins (Fanny met me at the station – Nerissa arrived next day with her lover Toby Saloman). Angelica's occasional likeness to Vanessa is astounding – she has the same half-amused *gravitas*, the bulk, the stately and slightly stooping carriage, the mellifluous voice. She quietly provides comfort and support, makes bread, and plays rather out of tune on her cello. She's adorable to Sophie, who really loves her, but what a loving little being *she* is; probably because of Henrietta's elusiveness she clings to all who belong to her. I'd been told she was very 'grown up' now – I find her on the contrary a shade over-childish. Yesterday Angelica and I sat talking in the sun against the cottage wall.

Most of my thoughts centred on Fanny. She can look really beautiful – like a Botticelli youth, with a little round cap on the springing curls, blazing blue eyes, a flashing quick, responsive smile. People are instantly attracted to her – in the concert we went to on Friday night she had her head close to the grey one of a female Dutch Buddhist long after the church had emptied. 'What were you talking about?' I asked. 'Buddhism. Emptying your mind.' F: 'I can't understand why you should want to. It always seems to me one wants to keep it as full as possible.' Later, in the pub, at once she was in contact with unlikely men, singing and thumping the table. She has a sort of physical magnetism, and fires off her remarks like a machine-gun, but I always want to say 'Why? Why?' to them all. Angelica says, 'she's immature in some ways.' In others, car-driving, cooking, carpentry, she's quietly efficient and full of goodwill. She's challenging and provocative, but a quick smile and 'Am I bullying?' takes away any possible sting and personally I feel her attraction strongly. Asking her about her work projects – theatrical, building etc., I got an extraordinary response. (She once wrote round begging letters for a theatre group she was mixed up in, and we all contributed. I asked about it, and it sounded as if she had drifted away from it.) 'My present idea is to produce *Macbeth*, with myself as Macbeth, covered all over in that woad I was asking you about, and Lady Macbeth as a man.' No further explanation – but a more alarming project was Opera. (She has quite a good voice and has sung in Bach choirs etc.) Again *she* was to be the centre. A huge snake was to be constructed in Trafalgar Square, and move with the crowd towards the Albert Hall where they would all stream in, and then *she* would *dance* the whole opera, in the centre of the arena. F: '*You*, quite alone?' Fanny: 'Yes. I expect it sounds impossible to you but I assure you it isn't.' Assuredly this is madness, or attempt to shock, put it at its most harmless, yet she talks most of the time alertly, responsively, gaily. And I was in fact too embarrassed to ask who would perform the music. Or would it be left out? By contrast Nerissa is gentle, quiet, speaks little and has long straight curtains of hair and a downcast face. She seems to have a close absorbed life with Toby Saloman.

What perhaps I felt most alien to was the way they all ganged up against Bunny. I had been questioned closely about my family, and tried to account for them and describe the Marshall inexpressiveness and undemonstrativeness I find so unsym-pathetic. (I've just had a p.c. from Judy merely ending 'The 16th is OK' – no sign that she would *like* me to go, no 'Judy', above all no 'Love'.) With one voice Angelica and Fanny (I'm not sure about Nerissa) declaimed against Bunny's *need* for emotional response and attempt to extract it from them. Well, it's no good of course doing that with a corkscrew. Fanny described her last drive in a taxi with Bunny before leaving Edinburgh recently. 'I sat on a tip-up seat because I don't want to sit beside Bunny, and he patted the seat next to him and said, "Come and sit here or I'll get out of the taxi."' Angelica: '*You* should have got out – that was the proper answer.' Fanny: 'No, because I called his bluff as it was.' I seethed with unuttered indignation. Do they quite fail to appreciate what Pam Ballard called Bunny's 'quality'? His courage, the value and splendidness of his love?

His sanity. His lack of self-pity? I did say that in the case of my family I felt refusal to express feelings as a sort of lack of generosity.

Yet I'm deeply interested in Fanny, touched by her and her raw, undigested but inarticulate ideas; would like to talk to her more. She accuses me, as it were, of being rational, as I indeed try to be, but I think she respects my views in a sort of way.

And I liked being there, especially with Sophie. It was a niche I could fit into. And there was a lot of 'doing' as well as talk – like decorating Sophie's chocolate cake with silver balls, and going down to bathe on Swanage beach in the cold grey sea – surprisingly enjoyable.

Angelica, Sophie and I all travelled up together in the train last night – and today S. goes on a visit to Italy until Henrietta returns. Fanny touched me for £5 on the station. 'I'll send you a cheque.' I doubt it – that too is in character. The political substratum of the three young was never broached – I would have liked to.

August 13th

Oh so grey and wet still – a heavy sight to open one's eyes to, and I open them early. Yesterday whizzed along, for all my solitude. I went to the Byron exhibition at the V & A, and fulminated – although curiously moved – at the lack of portraits etc. of Augusta. Asking at the entrance if there were one, I was directed to Lady Caroline Lamb. There is a tiny dim drawing in a corner. A sort of prudery? I am back on this period, with a new vol. of Byron's letters and a Life of Shelley to read. I seem to be, not by my own desire, in the fashion.

Several telephone conversations. Stanley, who has a way of suddenly popping out gobbets of news, now says that Luke constantly consulted Holroyd about the play – but never took his advice. Mary writes that new legislation makes it advantageous to marry Philip¹ – shall she? She doesn't really want to. I try to sort out in my mind the undoubted symbolical weight attached to the ceremony.

---

1 For the second time.

317

I rang Julia to remind her she was dining with me tonight, with Dig Yorke.[1] Of course she had forgotten. 'I'm hopeless, my dear. I'm quite mad,' she said in an extremely sane voice.

I walked across the park in melancholy drizzle to the public library today thinking (though that is hardly the right word) about the pathetic fragility of human beings and the anguish of ill-health. I can't quite dread the process of it. I feel I have nothing to lose. But poor little Sophie has so much, and so does Henrietta. And I can't but feel if I were Angelica, having lost Amaryllis as she did, I would feel I had a lot to lose too. But anxiety isn't relieved unless it takes useful practical form, and at times fear blinds one.

August 14th

My evening with Dig Yorke was perhaps more successful than I could wish. She's a nice creature but no soul mate. However she's sensitive enough to be aware of our regions of non-overlap. 'What do you think of the wealth tax?' she asked me. She's a product of her class, and class is as potent a force as ever in England, or almost more. So it is that the rich and privileged cannot understand that there are two separate things, which may co-exist: one may *enjoy* one's privileges, *and* one may feel one is not entitled to them. A simple enough matter I would have thought – Mary would call it 'a dichotomy'. Bryan Magee has put this extremely clearly in today's *Times* and I have on impulse written to congratulate him.

August 15th

Music again – Haydn trios at Margaret's. We played well enough for it to be highly enjoyable. Anne Ottaway asked if I had been to *Bloomsbury* and I said an emphatic 'No', whereupon Margaret repeated what she had said to me on the telephone, that 'she thought it terribly funny and had laughed a lot and so had everyone in the theatre. But I felt you disapproved when I said so on the telephone.' F: 'Yes; well, you know if someone wrote a play that was an absolute travesty of Lionel and

---

1 Wife of the novelist Henry Greene.

everyone roared with laughter, do you think you'd be extremely delighted to hear about it?' Margaret: 'No, of course not.'
This test of imagination is a sort of litmus paper by which I
observe people's sensitivity.

Last night with Desmond to a play by Stoppard called
Travesties. Only moderately good, the currants of wit were thick
in parts leaving stretches of blank dough between, and there
wasn't enough (only a few delightful moments) of sheer fun.
Dinner afterwards at Bianchi's – very sympathetic atmosphere
and ditto talk with Desmond about all kinds of things. He had a
row with Raymond (he called it the 'first in a lifetime' though it
certainly wasn't), about the servant problem at Crichel. I see
both sides as usual. I suppose Des must have got very excited
because Raymond said suddenly, 'I think you'd better go to
bed.' Desmond (getting scarlet in the face at the mere memory)
shouted: 'Raymond, you *can't* talk to me like that – you really
can't.'

August 16th

Evening of pathos with Julia, in which I tried to reassure her,
but should one? Will she ever make the journey to Italy? She
told me she had fallen 'in front of a bus' (bus later cancelled)
that afternoon and spilled the contents of her bag in Oxford
Street – all picked up by kind passers-by. She has such charm
and imagination 'when she is good'. 'When she is bad she is
horrid' and that takes the form of viperish beastliness to some
inoffensive waiter who is doing his best.

To me she was as nice as pie. This morning she has rung up.
She 'didn't sleep a single wink last night', and is wondering
whether she should go to Italy; 'suppose I got ill – and I am ill you
know – it would be terribly expensive and I don't want to die
abroad.' 'But Julia you're only going for two weeks and why on
earth should you die, in that time? I saw no signs last night.'
J: 'Well, I've got another of those bruises this morning.' F: 'But
since you fell full length in Oxford Street that's not surprising.
Has your doctor said you were dangerously ill?' J: 'No, but when
I said might these bruises come out in my head or heart, he just
looked at me owlishly and said nothing. And it seems to me

silence means consent.' From cross-questioning her I think all he said about her bruises is that as one gets old one bruises and tears one's veins more easily, as indeed I've been told. But she has convinced herself from some dreadful old book by Gayelord Hauser that she is suffering from vitamin C deficiency and that her doctor has confirmed this. 'And you see I ought to eat fresh salads and fruit and I can't eat.' Well, last night she cleaned up a plate of egg mayonnaise with plenty of good fresh salad, 'lettuce and cucumber', ate as much as I did of a plate of veg. and veal, and crème caramel. I reminded her of this – she had quite forgotten about the salad and murmured some Gayelord Hauserism about lettuces being 'grown under glass and so having no vitamins'.

I doubt very much if she'll go, and I perhaps shouldn't have encouraged her. She reels and staggers as she walks along the street (whisky mainly) so that people stop and stare.

August 20th

The tempo suddenly speeds up and the mood intensifies – I returned to London after a visit to Judy to find three bits of news: (1) My landlord has given me notice to quit (2) Angelica writes that I was right: 'Henrietta has not been eating properly', and (3) Gollancz writes that I'm to do Carpentier's book. I reel to left and right as if from a punchball raining blows in all directions.

Delightful lunch with Julian at his restaurant at Notting Hill Gate. I had been ringing him up hopefully from time to time, and so heard his voice with joy. Only in the third week of his three at Tramores did he feel really well (he looks it now, but how long will this last?) and this seems to have been partly the result of a wildly promiscuous sexual outburst.

Magouche blooming in her love affair with Xan Fielding. Janetta painting hard, going off with Jaime to Trujillo, not in the best of health. Jaime hardly visible he was 'working so hard' and an amazing falling off of the tourist population of the Costa.

I have felt mentally breathless all today, but am now more or less straightened out. I shall have to alter my way of life drastically if I do Carpentier's book.

As for the landlord – it may just be the first move in a game of chess. I have resolved to force myself to worry as little as possible about it.

August 22nd

Mungo on the telephone. Oh God – the landlord rang him up and said there was no question about it: I must vacate the flat. I'm a little afraid of Mungo's caution and defeatism. It now seems he's trying it on the other, so-called 'protected' tenants, the Smiths, Mrs Thom and the Lord Mayor. I have been in touch with the first two and written to Pirie. I mean to fight like a tiger to stay – but shall I succeed?

August 26th: Snape

Bank Hol. weekend. I live on two floors or layers. On the top one I enjoy being here as much as I always do. On the lower I am haunted by the threat to my life in the menace to my flat, the evil imagined face of my landlord, the horrid sense of the attack on me gives me something near persecution mania; yet a mania that is horribly rational. I wake in the night, or more often early in the morning and think about it. What's to be done? Two nights ago I thought suddenly: I'll jolly well stick it out until they take me to court, and if as Mungo thinks I'm issued with a court order to quit I'll *go to prison*. I so love my flat, all glistening with Raymond's pristine paint. Well, I try not to 'go on about it' too much but the final result is considerable sadness, depression, lack of appetite for life. When I return tomorrow will come the business of trying to settle the problems of Henrietta and Sophie.

Here there is a ludicrous sub-plot about Rosamond's attempts to get invited endlessly to the Hills and never once asking them back. Anne has become enraged by it, and even more by her attempts to winkle out visiting friends like Eddie and me. I am now the impotent object of this and I feel guilty because I tried to turn it into a visit by us all to see Ros's cottage, and instead she had the consummate nerve to suggest coming over to fetch me and dropping me back. I begin to think she must dislike Anne and wonder why and how. In the general

Bank Holiday turmoil the Hills are both staunch and sensitive – Heywood quite surprisingly the latter, while Anne toils away, and I feel ashamed of being so little help and the flat nightmare leaving me exhausted and inclined to drop into welcome oblivion in the afternoons. Walks with Heywood – one along by the sea at Thorpeness, a very pretty scene with grey diagonal waves far out, hard sand to walk on, seven kites flying and children seeming to thrive in the sun and warm wind. It has kept sunny and fine, and despite all the weather prophets' gloomy forecasts of rain not a drop has fallen.

I think a lot about Byron, and class, and exactly how good a composer Britten is (we went to *Herring* and it seemed a little silly, or 'arch' as Roger Butler said), and what must it be like to be stone blind like Roger Butler?

August 27th

Back in my flat I've been poleaxed by a crushing, feverish feeling of Angst. Oh God, to be quietly dismissed from this *beastly* schoolroom by the powers that be. Tormented by uncertainties and frustrations, I lay on my bed unable to listen to the wireless, read or sleep.

I try to think of the pleasures of Snape, how Anne and Eddie, both rather drunk, shouted louder and louder in the excitement of an argument until it was difficult to see where comedy became tragedy or love, anger, and poor Heywood put his head between his hands and groaned, 'Oh Anne! Anne!' And how, smoothly travelling home by train, I looked down on fields turned pale spring green by yesterday's sudden shower, and winding streams reflecting the sky, and fringed with rushes, loosestrife and willowherb.

But no oblivion sweeps me off in the afternoons now. I'm too fraught with frustration and worry. Henrietta has rung up, and she and Sophie arrive tomorrow.

September 4th: Amsterdam and in bed 7.30 a.m.

I don't much like to think about the intervening days. It seems to me I was on a sort of rack all the time, except for a weekend with the Cecils, when both of them (but Rachel in particular) supplied the marvellous unguent of their sympathy and understanding.

Well, here I am on another 'Spring Holiday' with Dadie and Eardley, and I fear it doesn't promise as well as the others. I've resolved to put my worries under hatches and not speak of them, nor – if that is possible – let them seep through to my companions. But this is not my natural form of life and it must be all too plain that I'm in a ghastly mood. The weather has turned horrifically cold and windy (we were delayed two hours at Southend by a gale which sank Mr Heath's yacht *Morning Cloud* and drowned two wretched young men).

Here we are in an old house on a canal on the outskirts of the old town, a humble hotel with simple rooms and little furniture, but a charming proprietor. E. and D. are on the fourth floor and I on the third, poor Dadie in a mere cupboard, and *what* floors. The stairs are winding and perpendicularly steep and there is no lift. A communal shower on my floor. While waiting at Southend I bought my chums a copy of *Playgirl* – a ludicrous colour mag full of fully frontal male nudes over which Eardley drooled lasciviously, while Dadie declared he 'hated sex without love'. It's bitterly cold and I've slept in a woolly vest and shall wear it today.

September 5th: evening

Two days spent in Amsterdam. A beautiful town but Oh God the rain! It never stops, ruffles the surfaces of the canals, produces lakes in the streets and lashes them with cold winds. No gleam of sun. Umbrellas sprout like mushrooms. So we simply gaze and gaze at pictures. Yesterday the Rijksmuseum and the new Van Gogh one, to which we returned today. Good dinner last night at a popular bistro, but I drank and ate too much, slept badly and woke to think miserably of *verboten* problems. What *am* I doing here? What place for me (literally) in this world? Better after an hour or two's sleep but the weather has been *far* worse today. Van Gogh again and the Modern Gallery next door, which has little beside one beautiful Cézannne. A brave excursion by tram to the Dam and Neue Kirke and then back to the Rijksmuseum again. I doubt if further looking would add much.

September 6th: 7 a.m.

Great difficulty in finding anywhere to eat last night. E. and D. have no notion how to master a town map, and would have taken us back to the Dam, were it not true that I luckily can, but this means a lot of hard homework. Ended in an Indian restaurant.

Today is cold and grey but not actually raining, Eardley is developing a strong interest in homosexual pornography; but they are both very kind to me.

September 7th

Yesterday was miraculously fine after the horrors of the days before. Drove up the west coast of the Zuider Zee to Broek in Waterland, a dear little village cosseted in flowers, Edam, Volendam, Marken, Hoorn (with a peasant museum) and Monnikendam where we lunched off eels on toast. Huge dramatic blue and white expanse of sky, flat fields meltingly green, millions of black and white cows and fat woolly sheep; everywhere water reflecting the sky, canals full of pretty fishing and pleasure boats.

Today we leave for our night with Julian and Robert's friends the Gatacres. E. drives all the time, I do nearly all the map-reading. I am astonished sometimes by the things Eardley is *in*curious about. He seems hardly to know the rudiments of geography, won't look at guidebooks and says, 'Shall we go near The Hague on the way to Zutphen?' when it's absolutely in the opposite direction.

September 8th: Chez Gatacre. Die Wierse, Vorden

We didn't get here till quite late last night because of stopping to look at a fair in Zutphen, and not daring to brave the forbidding notices on the gate.

Left Amsterdam in pale sun and the everlasting cold. Dropped in on several southern Zuider Zee ports, their outgoing river mouths choked with boats, great and small. A good many students or hippies, it being the weekend. Another village where very odd clothes were worn by women – tight little bathing caps and cylindrical epaulettes. To the Kröller Müller museum in its dripping wood. It is arranged like a sadistic mousetrap, with doors locked so that one must walk all round in the rain, lavatories concealed, guides unhelpful. Eardley in his element, very much the painter. After we had lunched (I off a delicious very thin crisp pancake with bacon and maple syrup), he would have liked to go back and look at them all again.

Apeldoorn is a handsome royal house, only visible from the outside; then Zutphen. The Dutch children are extremely attractive – tow-headed, with clear brownish skins and deep blue eyes, gay, bicycling wildly. In Zutphen fair some that looked about two were driving bumper cars.

The Gatacre children, four girls and one boy, are wonderfully well-behaved, sweet and friendly. So does tall slim Teresa their mother seem to be. The house a charming seventeenth-century Dutch manor surrounded by a moat. And Peter? I woke in the night after a splendid dinner spread with glasses and wines, to think: 'Perhaps he's a bit of a martinet.' Clever and well-informed, too much concerned for my taste with ancestors, war and tradition. He produced an illustrated diary kept by a forebear who had taken part in the retreat from Moscow under Napoleon.

Bedrooms 'tasteful' and a little demure. In my bookshelf, significantly, I find 'General E. Gatacre by B. Gatacre'.

I have woken in a bleak mood. 'Nothing to lose' right enough, but 'nothing to look forward to', either. Her elegant legs are the prettiest part of Teresa but her figure graceful, her face almost beautiful, and with good dark eyes.

September 9th

Perhaps I have misjudged Peter; but he *is* a trifle mysterious. He certainly suffers from family pride, but it may be justified, as his Dutch grandfather founded the Rijksmuseum and was a great collector. He and the two elder children left for England and we spent yesterday evening in the book-lined library with Teresa. Before that, sun emerging, we walked in the charming park with her and the two little ones. Dolly, at two, is immensely grown up and articulate. 'Have you got many friends?' she asked Dadie. 'Yes, quite a lot.' 'Are they alive or dead?' 'Some alive, some dead.' 'Are they *quite* dead?' Then to Teresa, 'What

325

has happened to the poppies I gave you?' 'I'm afraid they died.' 'Oh, poor Mummy.'

September 10th

How it poured yesterday, and how cold it was. We set off, however, bravely, not wanting to outstay our kindly and extended welcome. I see in memory our soaked figures in ineffective macs, doggedly going round Deventer and Zwolle, Eardley's face red and shiny with cold rain under his little beret. Lunch at Zwolle and on to Kampen, a fine town strung along a tidal river. A nice young man showed us round the town hall. Eardley thought him 'ravishing'.

Teresa had telephoned to book us rooms at Sneek (pronounced Snake), a jolly little town with lots of canals brim-full of yachts. The patron turned from very friendly to outrageously rude and said we must leave today. All in a few hours – I wonder why. Rain stopping. My companions are very British, and talk English loudly to everyone in a way I'm not used to. I expect them to talk about 'these damn foreigners'.

September 11th: Lemmer

We first tried a nice little place on the Zuider Zee recommended by Peter G. They only had one single, one double and we turned it down. Dadie to me: 'I don't know what's the matter with Eardley today – he's very unco-operative. We could easily share that double room. I often have, I shouldn't mind a bit.' Eardley may be irritated by Dadie's occasional outbursts of unassimilated information.

Anyway here we are, in three extremely comfortable rooms in a fine eighteenth-century building, each with a bath. The day was warm, sunny and still, and my desire to explore the Nord Oest Polder, reclaimed from the sea, was gratified by my kind companions. I loved it. For the moment I forgot my underlying conviction that there is nothing, nothing, nothing I now want of life. Urk (once an island) in brilliant sunshine and now linked to the mainland by ineffable green fields with black and white cows, its windows stuffed like Victorian glass cases with women in national dress looking out among potted plants. The only other island, suitably called Schokland, had been evacuated from terror of the encroaching sea and now holds a moving little museum of what was dredged up from the ocean bed, from horns of prehistoric animals to kitchen utensils.

Home and ate out at an Indo-Chinese restaurant and so to bed. I think I'm calming down a bit. But I don't *really* love this flat, unromantic smug little country.

September 12th, 3.45 a.m.
Awoken by a mosquito bite to gloom and Angst and wrestling with home problems such as poor little Sophie and her new school. At such hours of the night one can feel defeated and ready to give up altogether. Oh well. Plod on. As good be in this dull country as any other I expect.

Later
Yesterday was to be a 'lazy day' at Lemmer. Eardley was supposed to be painting but said afterwards he felt unstimulated. Dadie and I walked out towards the sea and lay with our backs to dunes of fine white sand, reading peacefully.

Delicious fresh plaice, fried while we waited, unlike anything tasted for years, for lunch, and afterwards we drove to a pretty little doll's-house village called Sloten.

I only wish I didn't feel so shut in with my lonely griefs that I am a poor companion for D. and E.

The best feature of Friesland, we all agree, is its children.

September 14th
Mist, wind and a few drops of rain didn't deter us from taking ship to the most accessible of the Friesian islands – Ameland. It was *deadly*, like Beckenham.

September 15th
Crossed the great dyke, eighteen miles or kilometres in a brilliant sun. It is a magnificent object. Thence down Western Friesland to Rotterdam. It is an agonising country to map-read in. The Boymans' Museum (never seen before) with a glorious Fabritius self-portrait; Rembrandt of course, the ever-unique;

Impressionists, and little surprises like a charming Le Nain of two composed little girls. Dadie is very thorough. Eardley makes rather futile sketches from masterpieces. Snack lunch and more pictures.

Getting into Leyden was a nightmare – one-ways, markets and roads up. We finally dossed down in an annexe. Trying to open my window, a glass ashtray I hadn't seen was hurtled into the street. Angry cries from two young men, who shortly after threw it against my window. It (the ashtray) broke in smithereens. This incident amused E. and D. and was a source of much teasing of me.

September 16th

Still based on Leyden, we made an awful journey to The Hague and found a large area cordoned off by police. The French Ambassador and ten others were being held hostage in his Embassy by Japanese gangsters. Great excitement in the Mauritshuis. 'They are hanging toilet paper out of the windows!' Why? Unless, as I read later, to signify that they were not being allowed to go to the lavatory. Glorious Rembrandts and Vermeers, *genre* pictures painted with Dutch humour – bottoms being wiped or teeth extracted. Then back along the motor-roads to Leyden – not my idea of fun at all. Eardley drives patiently and well but doesn't listen to (or perhaps hear) the map-reader's instructions.

September 17th: Delft

Left Leyden in soaking mist after going to the museum there to see a remarkable *Last Judgement* by Lucas van Leyden. This town is charming; the sun came out and we had perhaps the happiest and hottest day yet, and were able to sit out in the market square drinking our Jenevers (mild Dutch gin which we all like).

In the late afternoon we took a canal tour with two Dutch and two French. Excellent dinner and a good deal of jolly talk and laughter.

Home tomorrow and I think (in spite of all my grousing) this little hol. has been in its way a test and refresher as God knows I shall realise when the London pincers close.

September 24th

They have and I do. Agitations about my flat take up all my
time. I have been served with a County Court Summons.
Another flat has turned up in Eardley's house and maybe I shall
take it.

One happy item – Sophie has settled in well at Dartington.
Julia found Italy 'beastly' and hated her kind hostess – as one
could have confidently foretold.

October 7th: West Halkin Street

I haven't written because anything I wrote would have been
gloomy, except for the delight of Janetta's visit here, firm,
gentle, taking me in hand. Well, I had decided that I must go
quietly from this flat and there is the hope of getting the one
along the street under Eardley. But though he told me about it I
feel he is suffering from some sort of invasion of his privacy, and
would maybe rather I didn't.

It rains, rains, rains. Few friends are left in this wicked
world. Poor Cyril is very ill. Not that he is exactly a friend, but
I do feel for the poor fellow in the loneliness of decline. Janetta
and Joan Leigh-Fermor are truly sweet to him.

And Julia!! I have asked her to dinner I think three times since
she came back from Italy and she has eagerly accepted and then
after I have gone out to buy her meal, often after an extra call
about what she can eat or can't – she sent me haring through the
rain for fish when I know all she gets at home is meat – she will
ring up and say, 'I wondered perhaps – you know I've got this
diarrhoea still, I don't really like to go out,' and ask me to go
there. Or as yesterday, to go round and take her out to a restaurant. I compromised by making the watercress I had bought into
a soup for her and taking it round in a saucepan. She doesn't
remember a thing. She doesn't understand a word one says,
when she is as drunk as she was last night. My God it was awful
in her hot fuggy little room, trying to talk some sense into her.
She peered into my face with a rather eerie smile. She remem-
bers nothing about my troubles, and I'm bored with rehearsing
them, so one listens to the long litany of 'diarrhoea – doctor no
good – then he lives in St John's Wood you know – I can't work

– Italy's *beastly* – then I don't really like Lawrence's avuncular kisses – not what I'm used to.' I had to force myself to stay an hour and then clatter home through the rain. But how can she survive like that?

I don't think I look forward to anything any more. My 'pleasures' are merely working at my translation, or reading.

October 8th

I plod on through grey London and in grey but calmer spirits, feeling that this must be rather what it's like to 'do time'. Henrietta came to see me yesterday and was beautiful and sweet. She goes to see Sophie next weekend. I got her to talk more about Michel and his mysterious activities which are always going to – but never quite – get 'taken up' and make a fortune. As for the election: it is degrading the way they all abuse each other and I don't feel like voting either way.

October 12th

At Kitty West's. Out of my bedroom window a marbled blue and white sky, browning vegetation and utter silence. I got through my life in a sort of trance and can remember almost nothing of my journey yesterday in my rattling Mini. Of what did I think? The election is over and I realised I wanted Labour to get in and voted for them, and they did, with a small overall majority. Kitty is one of the few people who agrees about the desirability of this. On Friday I began to work up into a frenzy, and some of it against poor Mungo. Nothing, nothing to confirm that I can have the flat at No. 16. Doubts as to how dynamic he is being? I hate the law. I have got down so far, so close to the ground that there's no effort in trying to stay there – I just creep along like a worm.

November 7th

More than a month gone and pretty destructive it has been. But now it is over and I have signed the contract for the flat at No. 16, engaged Raymond Hall to decorate it for me and find me a mover, rung up a man from Sotheby's to come and see surplus furniture, nearly got through the basic draft of my French translation, and decided between the two on offer in the new year. Now that I've done all that and am not mad or absolutely done for (though I have been sleeping shockingly and having palpitations), I really do feel rather proud of myself.

November 11th

I've certainly moved into a new gear but am about to move into another. At present it is work all day: either translation or concerned with my move, and the only people I see are *real* friends. In London every other weekend, struggling to save about £5 a week and finding it surprisingly easy. I think I've moved away from the acidulation of last month – certainly Saturday night with the Kees and last night with Julian here, were uncritical and warmly affectionate.

Julian last night opened doors on to his new world and promiscuous life. *He* was as lovable as ever – I don't greatly take to the sound of *it*. Talk about Desmond. Julian says he is prouder than Lucifer and for that reason has not told me or allowed his housemates to say that he has had his driving licence taken away, and is due to be tried for driving dangerously when adversely breathalysed. I had no idea he was proud, am ashamed not to have realised it, but did know that he couldn't take the smallest guilt on his shoulders and always shovelled it on to someone else. This is why the dear lovable fellow is a strain to be with sometimes, since one's own guilt is enough in all conscience without having to be burdened with other people's. He dined with Julian before this trouble with the police, and Julian, seeing he was very tired as well as drunk, pressed him to stay the night. He wouldn't – but afterwards wanted to make Julian responsible: '*Why* didn't you make me stay?' Oddly enough he can't bear it that Raymond won't take responsibility for *his* misdeeds. Julian has overreached a little I think, even deciding that Desmond writes less well than he did. But as he (Julian) has five people in his flat (two black, three white) and never 'opens a book' I wonder if he's qualified to judge at the moment.

November 22nd

I seem to take my life – if it can be called life – in gulps. What I gulp isn't altogether distasteful, nor yet can I credit it with much flavour. I suppose what I'm most aware of is that the inexorable tide is washing me within a month to what I devoutly hope is my last abode. And as I go with that tide I snap at a few passing midges like a trout.

Another lovely visit from Janetta, mainly to see Cyril,[1] who is dying it's thought, and support those who are helping him to do it. He has no money, so a fund is being raised among his many rich friends to pay the medical bills. Mary told me that Philip was in the forefront of these, but apparently he hasn't paid a penny; all he has done is badger Janetta to get Andrew Devonshire to organise the Cyril Dying Fund. Reading in the papers that Covent Garden needed more subsidy he blew his top and said it was unfair that racing and hunting people had to support the opera. There were also occasional references during the weekend to Lord Kissing.

Contact with Pansy[2] at Stowell, and we travelled up together on Sunday night. I admire her looks, her upright carriage, her sweet smile, her enterprise in taking lessons in Ancient Greek – and really feel glad that there is someone like her in existence, though her logorrhoea stuns and anaesthetises one and I feel sure I should disagree with all her views if I knew them. She has amazing fortitude, based I fear on religion. She's one of those people, like David, who do seem to thrive on marriage to the Deity. Poor Frances had lost a front tooth, as I feel I'm going to any day. She was gloriously enjoyable to be with.

Dicky, to dinner last night, was also delightful company, and told me a lot about the Samaritans. I asked did being one give him a sadder view of humanity? 'Yes.' Then there was a dismaying picture of Denis and Francis Bacon. Bacon treats 'you boys' to lunch, spending £60. I can't find reckless spending glamorous. Many do though.

My evening (before) with Joan was less agreeable. Why is she so livid because her oldest friend Eardley has done so well with his exhibition? That shocked me, as did her pride at her own

1 Connolly.
2 Lamb.

unforgivingness towards her son-in-law. 'I'm *not* going to forgive him.' Yet she pretends she wants to 'get on terms again with the whole family'. What sort of 'terms' can that be? I'm also tired of her telling me, as she does every time we meet, that I'm sure to die before her because I'm three years older. Her husband Cochemé's death should have cured her of that, one would have supposed.

December 4th

I lead a rather solitary and hard-working life, hurtling towards my waterfall. Doom-laden feelings are not only connected with that, however.

A gap in the clouds was Robert inviting himself to lunch yesterday. For it is nice to talk to him as an individual, not one of a pair of carriage-horses. Asked how 'everything' was going, he replied 'All *right*' in a pretty unenthusiastic voice. He had been to Cyril's funeral (yes, he did die and seems to be enormously missed — even, in a strange way, as I saw little of him, by me) the day before, so we talked a lot about death and grief and mourning. And when I asked him what he felt about the desperate state of the world or England ... he said quickly, 'I'm enjoying it,' and I realised at once: 'so am I.' 'It's so *interesting*,' he went on, 'and then I think it's good for us.' I felt of course exactly the same. In the train to the funeral some rich girl had said she couldn't keep her horses any more as there 'was no hay'. This struck me as funny. Is the earth on strike? The bakers are, and we are told there will be no bread for ten days. In Harrods yesterday there was a long bread queue winding through many departments, businessmen in dark blue overcoats with rolled umbrellas, and women with blue-dyed hair. We OAPs have been issued with cheap meat coupons! I can't decide whether to use mine or not.

Few people are left in London. Nicko and Alexandra[1] turned up rather late to see me one evening. Another night Henrietta came and stayed till after 1 a.m., and was communicative and lovely. She described her feelings about not eating and said she thought she had been starving herself ever since Burgo died.

---

1 Nicko and Mary Henderson's daughter.

December 6th

Going round to the other flat, taking in its problems and possibilities has only put a fork into my subsoil and resolved nothing. I feel as unearthly as ever, and all I can do is plunge into my Spanish translation and read Michelet in between whiles. I feel that no one else is aware I exist — for no one telephones me.

I think what obsesses me is the gloomy bedroom, with its pinched outlook, and the consciousness that in it I am preparing my coffin and that it looks all too like one. I must try and cheer it up somehow. The slim roots with which I am fastened to my earth are getting almost too tenuous to hold me.

December 9th

A bad weekend. How glad I shall be to get my move over. Joan this time was a real standby, and makes me guilty for any criticisms. She came yesterday to look at No. 16 and gave her outright, if conventional opinions, which really helped. Then came a rising frenzy, because of the disappearance of one set of keys into thin air, leading to one conclusion only — that I'm incapable and crazy, nearly as bad as Julia! (This morning I've found them — they had dropped right down into the heart of my Mini's brake, so I feel better.) Migraine. A call from Julia. 'I wonder if you'd have a moment. I've been feeling suicidal. The doctor doesn't send my pills and my sink's full of dirty washing-up and I have no food in the house.' F (silently): *No. No. No.* J: 'Good old Anne Talbot will come — she said she'd come even at three in the morning. As I had no pills I got drunk and fell down and cut my nose.' Horrible heartlessness. I told her I needed support myself, was in as bad a case as she was. At the time I felt I was. Now I have these keys, I'm not.

December 14th

The start of painting at No. 16 has made all the difference — a flow of energy instead of a drain. But now at six-fifteen on Saturday, which may be the last Saturday I spend in this flat, I have got into bed, feeling bed is where I want to be. Sophie and Henrietta to lunch and buy Christmas presents. Sophie looked lovely and grinned broadly in a well-cut coat of nylon 'fur', soft and warm. They go to Canada next week and Henrietta said: 'I'm dreading it, really; hate the cold,¹ don't like anything about it except seeing Michel of course,' and it flashed through my mind that perhaps her remarkably curative sessions with Hévesi had affected her feelings for him – or maybe some other relationships which she can hardly do without for these long months, had cropped up.

While she and Sophie were here, Raymond rushed in, with his friend Richard and a nice little boy and removed my Boris fireplace in the twinkling of an eye.

December 15th

Before I got into bed I had a visit from the sadly unattractive John Favell and Raymond's² nice mum. After that – oh mercy, oh relief – I got into my nightdress, and went to bed, eating my supper there and slept uneasily (with an intervening migraine) till nine this morning.

What I dislike about this stage I am in is its lack of practicality. I can only be practical by an *immense intellectual* effort, and there are many lapses into forgetfulness. I want, oh so badly, to be back thinking again, not in terms of 36 x 39 but of ideas, and the most I can do is listen to the wireless, or – as I did in the watches of the night – follow the characters in *The Nigger of the 'Narcissus'* through the horrific jerky cold, wet, terrifying vicissitudes of their storm at sea.

I miss Stanley and wonder if he'll be home before Christmas, with his extraordinary directness and bright-wittedness, but very likely he's vanished for good.

Well, I think I shall quietly sit down to my Spanish translation and then maybe walk out on this cold bright blue day and buy some food.

Christmas Day: 16 !!! West Halkin Street

I have slept here three nights, and Raymond (marvellous fellow) has made it lovely and like home. Tomorrow I leave for Spain.

---

1 Henrietta's boyfriend lived in the extreme north.
2 Hall, the decorator.

335

But I have never – or not since I shingled mangel-wurzels in the First World War, or scrubbed the floor of the nursery in the Second – done such unremitting, really hard physical labour. My own fault – I couldn't stop. Also when houses are close at hand you *have* to go to and fro between. My 'best friends' in terms of help were angelic Heywood, who did two hard afternoons, and Georgia who helped me hang pictures. Eardley's basic selfishness came out (as it did when he wouldn't make a move to see poor blind Frances Phipps). Not *one* thing did he do for me, but as he 'dropped in' on his way up one day I invited myself up for a five o'clock whisky.

The day before yesterday exhaustion set in, but a lovely appreciative visit from Robert. Migraine. Yesterday I simply felt so tired I thought I might be dying. Better today. The one and only Stanley came back a week ago and asked me to lunch today – a nice young couple shared it. I am as pleased to see him as I thought I would be.

December 26th

At Heathrow, sitting in that limbo which tries not to watch or hear the ticking over of names: 'Oslo', 'Lisbon' and – mysteriously – 'K-K-K – KI'. Shall I really be in Spain with those dears in a few hours? I can't believe it.

Slight horror on leaving, because having as I thought organised everything, there wasn't a taxi in sight or on the rank. Went back to my flat and telephoned two special numbers in vain – no reply. Decided to drive my Mini and bugger all. Found that a Christmas reveller had backed into it and bust my headlamp to blazes. *But*, the only taxi adrift in London now floated into sight, and here I am, much too early of course, but whisky-bright, and Málaga has now appeared on the list, which I find curiously reassuring.

What do I feel about my new life at No. 16? Certain problems remain about heating and round plugs in square holes. But on the whole that it will be solider, kinder, more restricted maybe, but I shall get the hang of it I think, and be as happy as it's in my power to be therein.

Later

In the air. I do love flying, and I'm sorry for those who don't. It's so marvellously soothing and restful. An apparently grown up young man next to me is reading comics, all he is obviously capable of. I see now they are a family of rich smooth stupid Arabs, two wives, seven children, able miraculously both to whistle tunelessly and chew at the same time, *just* able to play beggar my neighbour.

December 27th

Halfway there it grew *hot*. Too hot. Cloudless skies and here we are and there is Janetta, and as so often before catching up – she tells me Xan has come out to Magouche, and the break with Daphne is made.

A puncture halfway home and there we were and no one in sight.

Now I'm in bed in my lovely corner room – the ashes of the fire crackling. Too excited to find myself here to sleep well. And last night, a very animated dinner. Xan looks radiant (silver hair, blue shirt and velvet jacket). Joan[1] elegant and austere, very thin with her black specs and enormously high-necked collar and trousers. Why do I harp on about clothes? – because I think they seemed significant. I've come pared to the bone, nothing remotely dressy, no books, no camera. I don't want to be social and hope I shall be let off. I want to work, and sit and read and think and talk. Last night's talk was stimulating, exciting, highly coloured, full of laughter. I feel rather guilty at faintly discouraging Julian from coming – but did I? After I'd said Robin wanted to come and was still trying for a ticket – but told me he couldn't get one or afford it.

The sun at nearly ten is just coming on to the terrace, where some dead leaves lie in a thin carpet, water trickles, they have had no rain for months, so soon will. I shall – or shan't I? – get up.

December 28th

This morning after better sleep and later breakfast, the sun is striking the cobbled terrace diagonally and it's after ten o'clock.

---

1 Leigh-Fermor.

337

Yesterday morning a long satisfying talk with Magouche. She and Xan seem radiant, like young lovers; she says Janetta is very happy, and loves having us all here. Joan came out with her head in rollers: 'I'm a gorgon! Don't look!' and Janetta went off to the town. She does work hard. Paddy[1] came in and out.

Thought I'd see if I could strike a pick into my translation; so collected dictionaries and spread myself on the upper terrace, and did, and found my mind was working slowly but fairly steadily – a sure sign that my crushing fatigue of Christmas Eve is wearing off. Thank heaven. Paddy is writing a book – I thought Xan had a translation but it seems not, which is rather embarrassing. He talks of writing a non-book about Monte Carlo.

Xan and Magouche went off for a monster walk, and Joan, Paddy and I settled to lunch on the kitchen terrace in lovely hot sun. Much talk about Gerald's book and Bunny; they seemed interested, but it's my territory and I must drop it, bad dog. Also not talk *too* much. The contrast between the ebullient Paddy with the (forgotten) large gap between his front teeth, this machine-gun Oxford voice – though he was never there – and uproarious spirits tinged with coarseness, with the almost too thin, distinguished, languid Joan, is very striking. Yet they seem a perfect match.

Last night Jaime appeared early and I gloriously enjoyed his company (the night before was too late, I too tired, and he hazy from a 'cocktail party'). The staff here consist of two only – a large pale plump Arab lady called Zorah, radiant with goodwill, and the 'youth' of last year, a willing homosexual. Miguel works the garden and there is a paradisal sense of harmony.

The ethical problem about Magouche and Xan seems to me as clear as day – it's love, no question. Xan is a different person from the man he was with Daphne. As for poor Daphne she is the sufferer, and everything must be done to make it as little painful for her as possible.

December 29th

Why do I get patches of desperation during the night hours, wake to see all black, and pressure too great to be borne, and

---

1 Leigh-Fermor.

the exacting demands of conversation intolerable? Now with my morning tray everything looks differently. But I had determined to lead my own rather quiet working and contemplative life and not be social at all, and contract out of things, and sleep and return to normality. I can't somehow – I don't sleep and can't relax, and though in a sense I'm quite a success with Paddy and like Joan and Xan more and more and love Magouche, the pace is too hot for me.

Yesterday was an outing which I'm delighted I didn't back out of – it was marvellous and unique. In a village some miles from Málaga, a *venta* and a few cottages towered over by a collection of small round hills with deep valleys between, a crowd like a swarm of active bees was buzzing (nearly all locals, hardly a tourist among them) to watch an age-old competition between bands of musicians with lined leather faces, wearing hats composed of tightly packed artificial flowers fringed with beads and mirrors, which swing as they violently, intensely, and with dedication sang *malagueñas* or played them with expertly thrumming fingers on guitars and drums, or squeaking on shiny violins, while one figure in a black Andalusian hat danced alone with a flag, furled and whirled and raised aloft, a downcast gloomy face, a sort of bullfighting dance – one in each hand.

We left while the buzzing was still on and a few totally drunk men were being propped off the scenes, drove to the beach fish restaurant I've once been to with Janetta and ate from great plates of *boqueróns*, *chanquetes*, octopi, *coquillas* by a still silver sea (which if not inspected too closely looked quite clean). Drove back, Xan driving expertly, the Leigh-Fermors fast asleep behind, stopping to look at Málaga Cathedral and its charming little square. They all responded enthusiastically to the carvings, and indeed *response* is, one could almost say, the trouble with Paddy. He keeps it up endlessly and expects it of one, and re-response, and 'What?' if you don't at once respond to *his* response. Yet I like him enormously, admire, am amused and delighted by him. But one turns with relief to Joan's die-away tones and smile that is half-sadness. Xan is much more articulate, interesting and intelligent than I realised.

December 30th

A source of agitation in the night watches had been that after leaving us, the other carload had gone up to visit the Brenans and some odd plan had been hatched, which I didn't like the sound of – a sort of set-to-partners: Magouche and the Leigh-Fermors and Xan going to the Brenans while Bunny came here with Janetta and me. 'He's so longing to see you,' I was told, but this is an exaggeration, and there was also the rather too overt scheme of keeping him away from Xan, of whom he's naturally jealous, and me away from Gerald. I don't know which was the more important issue. But though I'm deficient in desire to see Gerald, I don't want to avoid him, and feel a little 'manipulated'. All this is to happen today and I don't know how it has settled. On my talking to Janetta, she transferred the plan to 'everyone coming here'.

Yesterday was perfect, except for wind. A glorious day, a wonderful lunch of couscous brought by Zorah from Morocco, with turkey, a long afternoon's nap, some work, and the 'dictionary game', which they play with rather childish competitiveness, in the evenings, keeping us up till between one and two. A great invading tide of circumambient gentleness, beauty and the sense that everyone likes everyone else, is restoring me gradually.

INDEX

FP = Frances Partridge
Footnotes are selectively indexed.

Powell, Anthony and Virginia 36, 149

Powell, Tristram 36, 139, 149, 153

Price, Lynda 5, 64–5, 68, 169–71, 184; relationship with Lars 166–7, 192, 231

Price, Margaret 215

Pritchett, V.S. 65, 179

Prokofiev, Sergey: *War and Peace* 91, 94, 262

Pullan, Philippa 24, 280

Quennell, Mrs Peter 187

Radev, Mattei 103–4, 162, 193, 265

Ramsey, Frank 304

Redo, Marita del 237, 240, 257

Rees, Jenny 206

Rendel, Judy (FP's sister) 56, 96, 150

Reynolds, John 141

Rooksnest (house) 266 *1n*

Rothenstein, Johnny 163 *1n*

Rubinstein, Artur 177

Rüdiger (friend of Stanley Olson) 99–100, 101, 134

Runciman, Steven 87

Russell, Bertrand 60, 305

Russell, Ken 153–4

Russell, Maude 35

Rylands, Dr George ('Dadie') 4 *1n*, 136; with FP in Skye 26, 39–44; seventieth birthday 87; Swiss journey with FP 134, 154–7; in Holland with FP 298, 322–8

Sackville-West, Vita 205, 211

Salisbury, Elizabeth ('Betty'; wife of 5th Marquess), Marchioness of 108 *1n*

Salisbury, Marjorie ('Mollie'; wife of 6th Marquess), Marchioness of 108 *1n*

Saloman, Toby 315, 316

Sand, George 67–8, 69, 72–3

Sargant Florence, Philip 146

Saumerez-Smith, John 141

Saunders, Dick 314 *2n*

Schumann, Robert: *Manfred* 295

Seven Voices (anthology; translation by FP) 94

Shawe-Taylor, Desmond 6, 10, 29, 45–7, 49, 72, 106, 331; with FP in France 53, 58–9, 68–83; at Wexford Festival 88–9; with FP at Crichel 119, 132; and in NY 233–6, 259

Shelley, Percy Bysshe: 'Julian and Maddalo' 78

Sheppard, Sydney and Clare 9 *5n*, 10 *3n*, 130

Shirley-Quirk, John 142

Shone, Richard 115

Sippe, Richard 27, 29

Slade, near Alton, Hampshire 103 *2n*, 223

Smallwood, Norah 131 *1n*

Snape, Suffolk 48, 94, 141

Sparrow, John 39, 87, 279–80

Spender, Liz 9 *3n*

Spender, Matthew and Maro (née Gorky) 157 *2n*, 158, 159, 160

Spender, Saskia and Cosima 158 *1n*, 159

Spender, Stephen and Natasha 9, 222

Spinoza, Benedict 60

Stendhal (Henri Beyle): *Le Rouge et le Noir* 82, 83; *La Chartreuse de Palme* 83

Stephen, Adrian 30

Stern, James ('Jimmy') and Tanya 7 *1n*, 97–8, 135